The Fallen Colossus

The Fallen Colossus

ROBERT SOBEL

BeardBooks
Washington, D.C.

Library of Congress Cataloging-in-Publication Data

Sobel, Robert, 1931 Feb. 19-
　The fallen colossus / Robert Sobel.
　　　p. cm.
　Includes bibliographical references and index.
　ISBN 1-893122-88-3 (paper)
　1. Penn Central Transportation Company--Management--History. 2. Bankruptcy--United States--History. 3. United States--Politics and government--1969-1974 I. Title

HE2791 .P4326 S64 2000
385'.06'574--dc21　　　　　　　　　　　　　　00-037903

Copyright © 1977 by Robert Sobel
First Published by Weybright and Talley
Reprinted 2000 by Beard Books, Washington, D.C.

All rights reserved. No part of this publication may be reproduced, stored in a retrieval system, or transmitted in any form, by any means, without the prior written consent of the publisher.

Printed in the United States of America

for Sam and Rose

Contents

INTRODUCTION ix

I. *Origins* 1
II. *The Pennsylvania and the Central* 23
III. *The Eastern Destiny* 49
IV. *A Yearning for Security* 71
V. *The Last Hoorah* 93
VI. *Indian Summer* 117
VII. *Decay* 141

INTERMISSION 163

VIII. *The Coming of the Barbarian* 173
IX. *Under New Management* 197
X. *The Mood to Merge* 221
XI. *A Recipe for Disaster* 243
XII. *The Dead Phoenix* 265
XIII. *The Fallen Colossus* 291
XIV. *Metamorphosis* 311

CODA 333

Bibliographical Essay 347
Index 357

Introduction

On June 23, 1970, the board of directors of the Penn Central Transportation Company entered into reorganization proceedings under the terms of the federal bankruptcy law. Insiders had been expecting this to happen for months and had unloaded their holdings. Up to the last minute it seemed a federal bailout would save the company. How could the nation's foremost transportation company, an entity resulting from the largest merger in history, be allowed to fail? But it did, in the most famous bankruptcy in an age of failure.

The news appeared on the front pages of newspapers throughout the nation for a week or so. There was talk of scandals and discussions of government intervention. There was no major crash on Wall Street, however, no crisis of confidence in Washington, and hardly more than a ripple throughout the business community. The Penn Central's passenger trains continued to run—off schedule—while the freight operations were barely affected.

The court selected trustees to direct the line, and for the next six years the matter was debated in congressional committees and investigated by the Department of Transportation and the Association of American Railroads. Little of this was done in the public eye. It was not because of cover-ups or a penchant for secrecy but rather a general lack of interest on the part of the public. The railroad malaise had to compete with the Vietnam War, the energy crisis, and Watergate for public attention, and so it was relegated to the inside pages of only the larger newspapers. The Penn Central was followed into bankruptcy by most of the other northeastern railroads. A large part of a vital industry was crumbling; the rot was spreading rapidly. Even this could not capture public attention. Transportation policy played no significant part in the Presidential elections of 1972 and 1976. By the latter date Amtrak and Conrail had become key entities in the industry. Few outsiders knew what they were.

Three years after the collapse Congress produced a new transportation bill, which was signed into law. It was a patchwork solution to a nagging problem. Even then, it was not final, for implementation had to await additional legislation in 1976. These measures, together with actions taken by public agencies, will guide transportation policy for the rest of this century. More important, the policies pertaining to railroads contain implications for the rest of American business as well, which if carried to their logical ends may prove at least as significant for the nation's future as any of the more spectacular events of the early 1970s.

This is a familiar phenomenon in American history. Often the most important events of a period are not perceived as such until generations later. A century ago, while most newspapers featured stories concerning political scandals and corrupt elections, Andrew Carnegie was organizing the modern steel industry and John D. Rockefeller was doing the same for petroleum. Today we realize the scandals of the 1870s were of minor consequence when compared with the activities of the great tycoons. The alterations in the fabric of national life caused by the rise of the trusts were of paramount significance, though they were not recognized as such by the general public for two decades.

A major change is in the making today. The Penn Central collapse was its catalyst, and the reactions to the failure offer an indication of what may be expected in the future.

This book is about that bankruptcy, an attempt to place it in a proper historical perspective and draw from it implications regarding the next stage in American business development. It is concerned with the nature of change within the business community; the way decisions are arrived at, and their impacts.

The flaws which eventually precipitated the collapse of the Penn Central could be discerned when the two roads that made it up were organized. Were it not for the political climate of the time, the Pennsylvania and the Central would have been created by their states, or have resulted from a partnership between the public and private sectors. This had been the pattern in the past—the turnpikes and canals had set the stage—and left alone, natural inertia would have produced a public railroad system. The open partnership might easily have been extended to other large-scale enterprises as well, for finances could have been handled with greater ease in this fashion than in any other.

Wholly private enterprise would have been confined to a relatively narrow area in this scenario, and the United States might have created a form of capitalism quite different from the one that existed a century or so ago.

As it was, the Pennsylvania and the Central expanded rapidly, became powerful, and then clashed with one another as well as with other roads that made up the eastern rail network. Next began the long debate regarding the proper balance between private enterprise and perceived public interest; this question has never been satisfactorily resolved.

The situation was complicated by a shift in the nature of American capitalism. In the early twentieth century the principles of private enterprise gave way to those in which state intervention was not only welcomed but demanded. Governments on all levels gave assistance to the automobile industry in the form of roads, and to aviation by providing airports, services, and subsidies. The railroads had to compete against rival forms of transportation that were aided by governments. Unable to meet this and other challenges, the industry declined.

The Penn Central bankruptcy was the end product of this chain of events. Just as the origins of the railroad industry were the results of opportunism and improvisation, so the developments of the past six years have reflected compromises on the parts of legislators not certain of what they are creating, special interest groups that sometimes cancel one another out, and an Executive branch preoccupied with other problems. Whatever else they was and are, the railroad and transportation policies are not rational. But out of them may develop the signal that a new approach is being fashioned to direct American capitalism in the next stage of its metamorphosis.

The Fallen Colossus

I

Origins

It did not originate with an inspired moment of truth, a stroke of genius, or a grand design. Great undertakings and key technological and economic transformations rarely do. Instead there was a problem—or, to be more precise, a complex of interrelated problems—that demanded attention. Talk, dreams, and empty resolutions no longer satisfied. Action was demanded, and, given the circumstances, those in positions to make decisions and carry them out did the best they could. As is the practice in such matters, they explored solutions to old issues for answers to apply to the new ones. In the process they set in motion a chain reaction they could not have anticipated.

It began in 1792, with the incorporation of the Western Inland Lock Navigation Company. Land speculators in the area south of Lake Ontario in New York State realized their holdings would never amount to much unless a means of transporting people to the region and their goods to market was created. The farmers agreed, while merchants in Albany, Troy, and New York City appreciated the need for better transportation in the state. Western Inland Lock was to dig a ditch running from Lake Ontario to the Hudson, a distance of over three hundred miles. Work was to begin as soon as shares had been sold, a management organized, and a construction supervisor selected. The company hoped to sell 1,000 shares of stock, each with a face value of $100, of which $25 would be called initially, the rest to be subscribed as construction proceeded. The state agreed to grant the company an additional $12,500 after the seed capital had been committed.

The project was a disaster. Not only was the sum hopelessly inadequate, but the farmers and speculators along the proposed route were not interested in committing their limited capital to such a chancy project, and only 722 shares were taken in the first three months. An engineering survey of the area between Albany and Fort Stanwix indicated that almost a half million dollars would be needed for this short line alone. Furthermore, available technology might prove incapable of resolving several major problems, such as overcoming grades. Finally, there was some doubt that farmers along the way would be willing to pay the fees necessary to support a canal once it was completed, while the state's resources to do so were limited.

Still, the organizers proceeded with construction, and the first stage was opened in 1796. It was a financial and technological failure. The short ditch was in constant need of dredging and repairs, and many farmers refused to use it. Toll revenues in 1803 were $10,000; that year, close to $400,000 was spent on construction and maintenance, the money coming from an increasingly disillusioned state government as well as a small handful of private capitalists and several foreign speculators.

Why did governments and individuals invest in the canal? Of course, they hoped for profits, and the promoters had assured them the ditch would pay its own way and return handsome dividends. They referred to the turnpikes of the time for examples of what might be expected. The sixty-two-mile Philadelphia and Lancaster, which cost $465,000 and was completed in 1794, was a success, and had sparked a turnpike boom along the eastern seaboard and into the interior while at the same time helping Philadelphia assert domination among American cities. The Western Inland's promoters swore canals cost the same per mile of construction as did turnpikes, that upkeep was similar, and transfers as simple. In addition, the turnpikes had to contend with "shunpikes," roads paralleling the pikes that were used by carriers wishing to avoid tolls. Canal boats would face no such competition.

It sounded good, especially to those unfamiliar with canal technology. But even had revenues not been anticipated, the project might have been attempted. Without such a waterway, western New York would remain undeveloped while extensions of the Philadelphia and Lancaster would slice into the West, leaving New York City in the backwater.

And there were other considerations at the time. Even a deficit operation would stir activity in western New York. The price of land there would rise from pennies an acre to dollars, and the farmers of Onondaga county and neighboring areas would be able to market their grain in Manhattan at a reasonable cost.

News of this would attract settlers to purchase land, organize new farms, and use the canal. In other words, the capital created by having the waterway would far exceed any losses suffered in construction and operation, and in time some profits might be realized.

Many politicians and businessmen understood this. Often the two professions were united in the same individual: A state legislator might be the owner of a western tract as well as an investor. Thus, his interests in one area would dictate actions in the other. So they proceeded. Work on the Western Inland Lock did not halt because of losses on operations, then, but rather because of a scarcity of private capital in a developing nation and an inadequate technology. For the time being, improvements in transportation would center around the turnpike, the ancestors of which had been perfected by the Romans and the form known to generations of Europeans. During the first decade of the new century, they appeared to be the best solution to the problems of internal improvements.

New York quickly pioneered in roads, so that by 1812 the state held the lead in the nation in total mileage and planned to retain it. On the eve of the second war against Great Britain the Albany legislators sketched a series of interconnected turnpikes. To the east would be a wide road from the Massachusetts boundary to Albany and Troy, which hopefully would divert trade from Boston. Then the road would proceed westward to Buffalo, with feeders on either side, draining the trade of upper New York. Albany, then the nation's tenth largest city, with a population of 9,500, would become the focal point of the transportation system, uniting the products and markets of the area with New York City by means of the Hudson as well as its turnpike interconnections.

The war interrupted the project, but it was resumed soon after the peace. By 1821, the rough outline of a state highway system could be perceived. The turnpike boom was in full swing; New York alone had some 4,000 miles in service.* Hopes for profits led private investors to bid against one another for shares; subscriptions for new turnpikes were quickly filled, so government aid was no longer required for short lines. All the symptoms of overbuilding were present as turnpikes were hacked into the wilderness, in the belief that trade—and profits —would soon follow.

*Joseph Durrenberger, *Turnpikes: A Study of the Toll Road Movement in the Middle Atlantic States and Maryland* (Valdosta, Ga., 1931), pp. 156-58.

In 1808, Secretary of the Treasury Albert Gallatin, in his *Report on Roads and Canals*, urged the federal government to take the lead in financing national roads and canals. He spoke of a "tide water inland navigation" running from Massachusetts to Georgia as well as a national road across the Cumberland Ridge in the Appalachians, all of which would be sponsored by Washington. Gallatin knew that most of the projects would have to run at a loss, but their utility to the economy would be such as to make them worthwhile. President James Madison favored the development of internal improvements, especially transportation, believing them necessary in order to create a nation and a truly American sentiment. In 1815 he wrote of "the great importance of establishing throughout our country the roads and canals which can best be executed under national authority." But Madison held back from complete agreement with the Gallatin *Report*; he felt the federal government lacked the right to finance such systems.

Representatives Henry Clay and John C. Calhoun had no such doubts, and in 1817 they sponsored a measure to finance a road and canal project, which passed after prolonged debate. Under its terms, $1.5 million was to have gone to New York, for a canal in midstate. While the measure was being debated, Albany planned such a canal, anticipating a limited line to Oswego or some other Lake Ontario port. A few legislators wanted a more ambitious line to Buffalo, which could tie the Midwest to New York and so make Albany a key inland center, diverting trade from Baltimore and Philadelphia.

Madison opposed the measure on constitutional grounds, and his veto of it was sustained. The New York legislature did not abandon its plans, however, and spurred on by Governor DeWitt Clinton, it adopted a canal appropriation in the spring of 1817. The line was to run from Albany to Lake Erie, and so tie the entire Midwest to New York City, diverting traffic from New Orleans and St. Louis as well as Philadelphia and Baltimore. The waterway's supporters thought it would cost some $7 million. As had been the experience with turnpikes, they would try to sell shares to farmers and speculators along the route, people who would benefit by having the ditch, even though the shares might never pay a dividend. As for the rest, the state would provide funds in the name of the general good.

Sales went slowly at first, but interest mounted as new sections opened and showed profits. By October 1819, when the connection between the Mohawk and Seneca rivers was opened, the stocks and bonds sold at premium prices. The waterway was completed in 1825, at which time Governor Clinton poured a keg of Lake Erie water into the Atlantic at New York City. "They have built the longest canal in the world in the least time, with the least experience, for the least money, and to the greatest public good," wrote one of the celebrants at the ceremony. The total cost was slightly more than the $7 million budgeted, and even before completion, toll revenues exceeded interest charges. The state's Canal Fund, which helped finance the waterway and acted as its bank, had a continual surplus, which was used to finance other New York canals at low cost. During the next few years the Erie was improved and tolls were lowered, and all the while revenues increased, the value of western New York land skyrocketed, and New York port and Albany grew rapidly. By any and all standards, the Erie was the economic wonder of the nation, the pride of New York, and a major source of concern to its competitors—Philadelphia and Baltimore in particular.

The Pennsylvania turnpikes were doing a good business in the early 1820s. River traffic from the Allegheny and Ohio came together at Pittsburgh, was loaded onto wagons, and taken by turnpike to Philadelphia, where it was unloaded once more for transshipment by sea to Europe. By then, however, it was obvious that the all-water route from the western reaches of Lake Erie to New York would be cheaper, perhaps faster as well, and that Pennsylvania would lose the western trade. Clearly the state's transportation system would have to be revamped; the turnpikes would no longer do. But there would be problems. The Erie Canal went through fairly flat land in upper New York, and even then, there were seventy-one locks between Albany and Buffalo. A canal from Philadelphia to the West would cut through mountainous territory, and so require far more locks and higher costs per mile than the Erie.

While agreeing that the New York challenge would have to be met, some Pennsylvanians rejected the idea of a canal from Philadelphia westward, and instead wanted to construct a railroad in the region—the first in the nation. Unwilling to chance their fortunes on experiments, the state's western farmers and land speculators pressed for a canal, and in 1824 the legislature passed and Governor John Schulze signed into law a measure providing for a survey. Prodded by news of the Erie's success, the legislature passed another law in 1826 "to provide for the commencement of a Canal, to be constructed at the expense of the State, and to be styled, 'The Pennsylvania Canal.'" Work was begun soon after, and by 1835 a canal system was completed. This ditch—or, to be more precise, series of ditches, since there were some breaks—was 359 miles long and cost over $12 million. In the same period another $7 million had been spent on other Pennsylvania canals—projects that all but exhausted the state's funds.

Few were successful. Due to high construction costs and unexpected technological difficulties, tolls were high, so that western farmers kept to the roads or diverted traffic to New York. The state was unable to operate the canals as public services; even though its leaders understood it might be necessary, they lacked the capital to put such a plan into operation. A later experiment combining sections of canal with railroads also failed to show profits. As Job Tyson, a Pennsylvania writer, put it in 1852, "the chain that was to bind Philadelphia with the west was ... severed, disjointed, fragmentary. It was an amphibious connection of land and water, consisting of two railways separated by a canal, and of two canals separated by a railway—happily elucidating the defects peculiar to both methods of transit, with the advantages of neither." The failure of the "Main Line," as it was called, was one reason for Philadelphia's continual decline in relation to New York.

With a population of 62,700 in 1820, Baltimore was the nation's third largest city, with hopes of becoming America's leading export port and terminal of the western trade. New Orleans had the Mississippi, Philadelphia and New York their turnpikes and talk of canals, but Baltimore had the National Road, to be built at public expense, toll free in sections, which began in Cumberland, Maryland, where it connected with Baltimore's Frederick Pike. Wheeling was reached in 1818, and within a decade the National Road would extend to the Ohio border. It benefited farmers and land speculators—and aided Baltimore at no cost to the city.

In the early 1820s, however, Baltimore contracted canal fever, even though, as was the case with Philadelphia, the state's terrain was not suited to artificial waterways. Again as in the case of Pennsylvania, Maryland had its railroad advocates, who competed with the canal forces for private and public funds. The Chesapeake and Ohio Canal was hastily chartered and construction begun in 1828, even while the railroad forces initiated the Baltimore and Ohio. The canal began life with $3.6 million, of which $2 million came from the federal government and the city of Washington. This fund was spent in little more than a year, with only a few miles of waterway in operation. Plagued by technological problems, insufficient capital, and competition from the B&O and businessmen in other cities, the Chesapeake and Ohio Canal never went beyond Cumberland and wasn't completed until 1850, by which time the canal era was over, and the C&O redundant. Baltimore lacked the capital and transportation facilities to mount a challenge to Philadelphia, much less New York. The city continued to grow, but its period of national aspirations faded in the 1830s and 1840s.

DeWitt Clinton's grand gamble paid off; of all the American canals constructed in this period, only the Erie was a major success, both in terms of economic development and financial rewards. New York received an added bonus in luring other states to canals, when railroads were more suited to their terrains. Still, a dimension was lacking in the victory; given the growing nationalism of the period, a political cachet was required, and this came not through the conscious efforts of DeWitt Clinton but the indirect and often unwitting help of President Andrew Jackson.

No American President before Jackson had traveled so extensively through the nation. Others had recognized the need for good transportation; Jackson, as a military chief, lawyer, governor, legislator, and businessman, had actually used the waterways and turnpikes. Also a land speculator, he was aware of the impact of good transportation upon prices and sales. Jackson traveled widely when he ran for the Presidency in 1824, seeking to influence electors along the way. He actually set out for Washington in December, believing he had won, only to turn back in Virginia when news of John Quincy Adams's election reached him there.

For the next four years Jackson organized his coalition, one important part of which was the Van Buren group in upper New York. With its help he won the 1828 election, but was unable to go immediately to the capital due to the illness of his wife. She died in late December, and on January 18, the aged and shaken President-elect embarked on the trip. He did not head east, for there was no direct land route to the coast. Instead, Jackson took a river boat to Cincinnati and then another to Pittsburgh, each going a few miles an hour. From there he went on to Virginia by turnpike, staying at inns along the way. In all, the trip took more than three weeks, fair time for the period.

While Jackson organized his government and met with political leaders, his supporters from all parts of the nation also took boats and carriages to Washington, so as to be present at the March 4 inauguration. Some came by a combination of turnpike, shunpike, river boat, and canal. Newly elected legislators from coastal states went to an ocean port to catch a packet ship; in 1829 these were the fastest and often the most economical means of travel. Meanwhile, the losers sold most of their household goods at auctions, often to dealers who would soon offer them at higher prices to the Jacksonians. This too was the practice of the time. The costs of transporting bulky items to inland locations were so high as to make this the wisest course of action.

Jackson would be President for eight years. In this period he transformed the face of American politics and gave his name to the era. Yet Jacksonian Democracy lacked a clear rationale, a coherent philosophy, an inner consistency. At times the President reacted to individuals rather than consulting his beliefs, and his supporters noted these inconsistencies, even while they praised the man. Still, Jackson did undertake three separate actions that affected transportation during the next generation, and their impacts are still felt today. The net result was to seal New York's dominance of its rivals, and to determine the ways by which the American railroad industry would develop. What to later Americans would appear the unraveling of a natural order was in fact determined by the prejudices and instincts of Andrew Jackson and those who helped fashion his ideas.

The President alluded to transportation in his inaugural address. "Internal improvement and the diffusion of knowledge, so far as they can be promoted by the constitutional acts of the Federal Government, are of high importance." That was all he said on the matter, and the meaning was unclear. Did Jackson favor federal aid to road and canal companies? His supporters and opponents were interested in the answer. Martin Van Buren, the new Secretary of State and spokesman for the New York Bucktail faction, had a deep concern in the matter. Van Buren had opposed construction of the Erie Canal on the grounds that it would serve only a small portion of the population, whereas all would have to pay for it, and that the canal would increase the powers of banks, which would finance operations. He had been supported by landholders whose properties were far from the waterway—and so would not benefit from it—and by workers who saw no direct connection between their well-being and internal improvements. The canal's success led Van Buren to change his mind, but he remained opposed to public support of transportation. As a United States senator in 1825, he had worked against federal financing schemes, noting that New York in particular would oppose any program to construct local projects which would be paid for by taxes on all. "There is no state in the Union that has so much interest in it as ours," he said of one such measure, "growing out of our past expenditures and liability to future contributions for like works in other states." Jackson had always distrusted federal economic power, and Van Buren's ideas both supported and refined his earlier sentiments.

In May 1830 Congress passed legislation authorizing government purchase of stock in a proposed road that would run between Maysville and Lexington, Kentucky—a measure that not only would commit federal funds to a state road but one for a particular state, the home of Jackson's chief rival, Henry Clay. Jackson vetoed the bill. The states, he said, should "manage their own concerns in their own way." As for the road, Jackson described it as bearing "no relation to any general system of improvement," while the bill conferred "partial instead of general advantages." On the other hand, the President indicated that he might be willing to accept truly national projects.

But he could find none of these in the next seven years, during which time Van Buren became the architect of the Jackson stand on internal improvements. Even the National Road suffered; appropriations continued, but completed sections were given to the states through which they ran. John Quincy Adams had committed the federal government to the Chesapeake and Ohio Canal Company; Jackson withdrew the commitment. He pocket vetoed an appropriation bill to aid the Louisville and Portland Canal, and made it known that similar measures would receive the same treatment.

The message was clear enough. The federal government would not take the lead or become directly involved in the financing and operation of major transportation projects. New turnpikes and canals—and future railroads—would either receive state and local support or be privately financed, controlled, and operated, perhaps under the supervision of state legislatures. The Erie Canal experience might be expanded upon so that a hybrid form could emerge, a corporation in which the common stock was held by private individuals and bond issues by government agencies. But whatever would take place, the federal government rejected responsibility and leadership in the Jackson years. New York was heartened; the business class had its canal-river connection in place. New York City and Albany were growing rapidly, Buffalo had dreams of inland empire, and towns along the canal became cities. As for the Bucktails, they would not be taxed to pay for internal improvements emanating from Washington. And all the while, Philadelphia and Baltimore, which needed federal assistance for their projects, would fall further behind in the race for continental domination.

In the 1829 inaugural address, Jackson spoke of the management of the public revenue—"that searching operation in all governments"—which he considered "among the most delicate and important trusts in ours, and it will, of course, demand no inconsiderable share of my official solicitude." Although a speculator who had not shirked personal debt, the President had always had a deep dislike for public debt and a distrust of banks which financed it. The national debt had declined regularly during the Adams administration, falling from $83.8 million in 1825 to $58.4 million in 1829. By the end of Jackson's first term, it stood at only $7 million, and it was clear that within a short time it would no longer exist.

But the opposition to the Bank of the United States, implicit in the inaugural, was still more striking. This bank, headed by Philadelphia grandee Nicholas Biddle and located on Chestnut Street in that city, was the most powerful financial engine in the nation, its branches located in all sections. The bank's supporters claimed it was a vital part of the credit structure; Jackson thought it had too much power. So did Van Buren and his New York allies, and they had another reason to oppose Biddle's bank. The New York financial community could not claim national leadership so long as the B.U.S. was in existence—and in Philadelphia.

In 1828 Van Buren ran for the governorship and won, serving only a few weeks before stepping down in order to accept the State Department portfolio. But in this period he obtained enactment of the Safety Fund Law, under which the liabilities of New York's banks were insured. This measure, designed to increase confidence in the state's banks, indicated that New York would press Jackson to assist it in the struggle against Philadelphia. The President was more than willing to oblige Van Buren, and during the next four years intensified his attacks against "the monster." Among other things, the 1832 campaign was a plebiscite on the bank's future. Jackson, Van Buren, and New York won; Henry Clay, Nicholas Biddle, and Philadelphia lost. As had been the result in the Maysville veto, the elimination of the bank confirmed New York's leadership in the nation. Wall Street in Manhattan, not Chestnut Street in Philadelphia, would become the leading financial pump in America. The latter city would lack the financial muscle to put together complex financial deals, to engineer combines, and act as a conduit for foreign funds wishing investment in American projects.

The final Jacksonian action that affected the long-term future of American transportation emerged from the second. In the place of the B.U.S.—which remained in operation at its old location but as a Pennsylvania corporation—was a group of old and new state banks, which acted as federal depositories as well as financiers for economic development. Expansionary credit policies resulted in both inflation and an economic boom, the leading edge of which were transportation companies. States and localities had little difficulty in marketing stocks and bonds. Foreign investors and speculators, especially the British and Dutch, rushed to purchase American paper. Rhode Island's Blackstone Canal, capitalized at $500,000, received more than $1.5 million in bids, much of it from Europeans. The Morris Canal and Banking Company, a well-publicized venture, went to the capital markets to raise $1 million, and received $20 million in bids.

This fast and free situation encouraged the formation of private companies. Why petition the state or lobby among municipal leaders when foreigners were eager to invest? Private canal and railroad companies would be formed in a matter of days, with little capital or knowledge. They would print stock certificates and bonds, the latter in pound sterling denominations for easier marketability, and entrust them to an agent who would board a Europe-bound ship. Upon landing he would head for London and make his presence known. Often he could dispose of a million dollars in stock and bonds in less than a week. Or a London banker might take on an American partner—in the 1830s it would be a Philadelphia firm, perhaps Thomas Biddle and Company or, after its recharter in 1836, Nicholas Biddle's Bank of the United States of Pennsylvania—and entrust him with the task of accumulating a portfolio. In this way, foreigners sparked the transportation-investment boom of the mid-1830s.

In 1833, when the B.U.S. charter ran out, America's aggregate foreign indebtedness was slightly over $100 million, and at the time it appeared canals and railroads would be largely financed through the support of local, municipal, and state governments. In early 1837, foreign indebtedness was close to a quarter of a billion dollars, most of which was invested in transportation projects in all parts of the nation. Although Philadelphia retained its lead as a marketer of bonds overseas, the New York financial community was growing more rapidly. The Canal

Fund and foreign investors made it possible for the state to keep its public debt low. By then, New York's borrowings for canals, railroads, and banks totaled only $2 million. In contrast, Philadelphia's bankers, while able to sell securities for projects in other parts of the nation, did not do so well with their own state's notes, with the result that they had to be financed by public agencies of various kinds. That same year, the Pennsylvania canal, railroad, and bank debt was over $20 million.*

The New York Stock and Exchange Board boomed in this period. Railroad and canal issues—the Mohawk and Hudson; Saratoga, Boston and Providence; Delaware and Hudson; Morris Canal; Utica, Paterson, and New Jersey—were features on Wall Street, and all were headed upward. A combination of Jacksonian events—the rejection of the public transportation network, the creation of a speculative boom following the disestablishment of the B.U.S., and the rapid payment of the public debt—seemed to assure that the railroads, then an infant industry, would be constructed through private, not public, enterprise.

There was a great fire in New York in 1835, in the course of which much of the city was burned to the ground. Yet the prices of railroad and canal stocks continued to rise. Europe was struck by a series of financial stringencies, and foreign purchases of American securities slowed down. Even this could not halt speculation in stocks and bonds. English visitor Harriet Martineau marveled at it all. "The commercial credit of New York could stand any shock short of an earthquake," she wrote.

But the financial equivalent of an earthquake appeared two years later. As a result of overexpansion, chancy banking policies, and sudden attempts to halt speculation that were misapplied, the nation underwent its worst securities crash to that time. Then followed an eight-year depression. In this period the Jacksonian coalition came apart, the Presidential career of Martin Van Buren was shortened, and the nation turned to other interests. But some things did not change. New York continued to dominate the banking scene; Philadelphia would never recover from the Jacksonian interlude. Even though the federal government would later help the railroads in many ways, there was no chance of a federal line along the model of the National Road. So there would be no integrated railroad network, but instead a patchwork quilt of roads, each developing according to local needs at first, and then coming together due to changes in

---

*New York Herald, February 14, 1837.

markets, technology, personnel, politics, and vision. The government would provide services in such areas as surveying and geological data. It would manipulate the tariff so as to lower the prices for rail equipment of various kinds. Some states and municipalities experimented with direct ownership, but eventually abandoned the efforts. The states stood prepared to purchase bonds from important lines; in 1843, some $43 million in state debts were connected in one way or another with aid to railroads, and in the next twenty years they contributed another $90 million to various bond funds. Diverse agencies on all levels of government would regulate the lines, and since these were politically based, they were susceptible to pressures from several constituencies—including the railroads themselves.

All of this was discernible in 1840, in the midst of the depression, when for the first time the nation had more miles of railroad than of canals. It was also evident that the next stage in the development of American transportation was well entrenched. And even then, at the beginning, the seeds for the failure of the railroad systems in the twentieth century had been planted, along with the factors which ultimately led to the downfall of the Pennsylvania Central.

Americans hailed the western advance of the National Road, and they cheered the opening of the last link of the Erie Canal in 1825. The turnpike was a wide, man-made road, well constructed and maintained, but not unlike earlier European and American paths. As for the canal, it was an artificial waterway designed to improve upon nature—to extend the Hudson to Lake Erie. Given sufficient money and time and a more advanced technology, its engineers would have constructed a new river, without locks, so that the linkage between the Hudson and the Erie could not have been discerned. Canal boats were not much different from river craft, except for their shallow draft and connections for ropes that were attached to animals which pulled them through the countryside. Similarly, wagons did not operate differently on the National Road from the way they did on other paths.

The technologies of roads and canals seemed natural to Americans in the early nineteenth century, as they had to ancient Romans. Their sights and sounds, their methods of operation, were in no way exotic or amazing. Constant improvement and perfection of the old, not a foray into the new, was deemed desirable and was anticipated. But should improvements not be possible, or should a new technology appear that was clearly superior to the old, drastic change might take place.

The locomotive and the "rail-road" were two such technologies. Few Americans knew of them in this period, and of these, only a handful thought of the locomotive as more than a toy or experiment. It was in effect a steam engine mounted upon a wagon, its pistons connected to the wheels, which they were supposed to propel along a conventional road. The idea was not new; the Alexandrians had dreamed of steam cars in the fourth century B.C. and Leonardo Da Vinci had sketched one in the sixteenth century. The locomotive of the early nineteenth century was more an ancestor of the steam automobile than anything else; in the beginning it was not associated with rail-roads. These—literally roads with rails—were an outgrowth of the turnpike. Rails would enable beasts to pull larger loads, perhaps at faster speeds, since they would reduce friction. They could be used to transport bulky materials, such as coal and stone, from mines to depots. The Granite Railroad, the first of these, was designed for that purpose.

Oliver Evans, an American pioneer in the development of industrial machinery, tinkered with locomotives and believed they could be wedded to rail-roads. Shortly before his death in 1819, Evans wrote: "I do verily believe that carriages propelled by steam will come into general use, and travel at the rate of 300 miles a day. But one step in a generation is all we can hope for. If the present generation shall adopt canals, the next may try the railway with horses, and the third generation use the steam carriage."

The evolution was more rapid than Evans had anticipated, due in large part to the rivalries of eastern cities for western trade. Events were telescoped in Maryland, for example, where in 1826 a group of businessmen, backed by promises of strong state support and financing, organized the Baltimore and Ohio Rail Road, designed for horse-drawn vehicles. Work began the following year, and the first part of the road was operational in 1828. Locomotives soon made their appearance, but a decade later the engines were accompanied by horses, to be used in case of breakdowns and to assist on sharp grades. In 1823 Pennsylvania granted inventor John Stevens a charter for a railroad from Philadelphia to the Susquehanna River, but the inventor lacked the skills and capital for the job. Five years later the state sponsored the Philadelphia and Columbia Rail Road, which was opened in 1834, and the following year took delivery of its first locomotive. Boston also had a state-sponsored line, and scarcely an eastern city lacked for committees on railroad construction.

But not New York. Perhaps because they were convinced that the Hudson-Erie could not be challenged by the new technology, or due to a lack of state support, few in the city gave railroads more than a passing thought. It was different upstate, however. In Auburn, for example, a group of citizens petitioned the state legislature in 1827 for a study to determine the feasibility of railroads in that part of the country. They would be "of minor consideration to canals, yet as tributaries to them, they will become of vital importance." What Auburn really wanted was a short spur line that would run between that town and the Erie. Nothing came of it for several years. Some turnpike companies applied for charter revisions to enable them to place rails on their roads, if and when the demand became pressing. There was no such demand, and the turnpikes did not become railroads. The Erie Canal was fresh and new and—more to the point—profitable. Over time it would be improved. Railroads would not be required so long as the Erie performed as promised.

Still, there were problems. Oliver Evans had believed railroad cars would travel at fifteen miles an hour. There were some who thought this impossible, yet a man on horseback could go faster than that. But this was not an age of speed; nor was it one in which most Americans expected to travel more than a few miles from their homes except when relocating. Travel time on turnpikes and canals was measured in days and weeks, not hours and minutes. Merchants in Buffalo who sent their goods to New York didn't expect to learn of safe arrivals for two months or more. If they had to go to New York, they would estimate the trip to take several weeks, and would inform friends that they would arrive "toward the end of June or the early part of July."

Still, for most of its route, the Erie was predictable. Given good weather and no breakdowns, a barge would travel at a speed of around four miles an hour. Passengers would sit on the decks of flat boats and watch the countryside go by, knowing they were making decent progress, and that a coach, which would stop for meals and rarely travel at night, could do no better. But passengers on the Erie headed eastbound often would disembark at Schenectady. There the canal merged with the Mohawk River and traveled a winding route, stopping at several locks, often for hours at a time. By water the route from Schenectady to Albany was forty miles, and the trip often took more than a day. This presented no great difficulty for cargo, but it was otherwise for passengers, who were charged by the mile. The land route, by a decent wagon road, was seventeen miles, and could be covered in less than a quarter of the time and at half the expense. Generally speaking, passengers would disembark at Schenectady and board one of several coaches for the trip to Albany. In this way, Schenectady became an important town which, like Auburn, realized the need for improved transportation as part of the canal structure and system, and which considered railroads a possible response.

On December 28, 1825, George Featherstonhaugh of Duanesburgh, a gentleman farmer who lived on the outskirts of Schenectady, ran a notice in a local newspaper announcing the formation of the Mohawk and Hudson Rail Road Company, which would apply for a charter, and planned "for the construction of a Rail Road betwixt the Mohawk and Hudson rivers, with a capital of three hundred thousand dollars, to be increased to five hundred thousand dollars, if necessary; and to receive such certain tolls on the same, as may seem fit for the legislature to grant." Featherstonhaugh had no idea of how the project would be received, or whether the money could be raised. He had read all he could find on railroads, and knew the land between Schenectady and Albany. Could an engine pull a car up the grades, and what might happen on the way down? Experience could offer no guide, for there were no American lines in operation. (The first true railroad, the Stockton and Darlington, in Britain, went into operation only three months before the advertisement was placed.) Still, he had little to lose, not even the printing costs, for the publisher wrote to Featherstonhaugh, "If the application succeeds, my bill for advertising will be $1.56; if it does not succeed—nothing."*

It was to be a modest line, with equally modest expectations. Featherstonhaugh believed that there were sufficient Albany and Schenectady merchants willing to invest in a railroad, and no "outside" capital would be required. The market to be served was well defined, the need for an improvement evident, and the transportation mania intact. A few years earlier John Stevens had spoken with Erie Canal officials about a railroad paralleling the ditch, and had been rebuffed. The Featherstonhaugh proposal was not as ambitious, and clearly was realizable. Indeed, as soon as it was made investors appeared, as did a rival. The

---

*Frank Walker Stevens, *The Beginnings of the New York Central Railroad* (New York, 1926), p. 1.

Albany and Schenectady Turnpike Company, which had been chartered in 1802, constructed a rather poor road, and was doing badly, challenged Featherstonhaugh, opposed his application, and tried to have its own plan for a railroad approved. The contest was not serious, but it did hold up matters for a few months. The Erie Canal interests were also concerned about the proposed line, and blocked the charter until it was amended so as to limit the Mohawk and Hudson to passenger traffic, and to rebate funds to the Canal equal to the losses it would suffer. Not until then would the assembly vote upon the charter, and it did so favorably in March 1826, with the measure being signed into law the following month.

The charter in hand, Featherstonhaugh set about seeking subscriptions for stock. As was the practice at the time, each share would carry a par value of $100, but not all of this sum had to be paid immediately. Instead, Featherstonhaugh expected to "call" $30 initially and more as construction costs mounted. If the line came in as projected in 1826, it would have cost less than $350,000, and required perhaps half the par in subscriptions. Dividends would be paid as a percentage of par, and even though the nation had no experience with railroads, profits were expected to be both generous and immediate, as had been the case with the Erie Canal. Just as early canal promotors referred to the turnpike experience, so Featherstonhaugh hearkened back to the canal.

Such were the expectations and the prospects set forth to potential subscribers. Still, Featherstonhaugh had difficulties in finding customers. It was not because the area's merchants failed to understand the need for better transportation. Albany's leaders in particular feared a challenge from Troy, a few miles to the north on the other side of the Hudson, which was taking Erie Canal traffic. A Schenectady-Albany railroad could help thwart Trojan ambitions. Stephen Van Rensselaer of Albany, a leader of the upstate aristocracy and a well-known politician, did subscribe for 100 shares and paid $3 on each, and a few other Albanians indicated a willingness to consider purchases. That was all. Whether due to an ignorance of railroads, a belief the Canal could not be bested, a realization that the Erie charter would limit railroads, or a mistrust of Featherstonhaugh—who was deemed a newcomer—the upstate line foundered.

Several New York City merchants and speculators were interested in the Mohawk and Hudson and contacted Featherstonhaugh, spoke with him, and in the end purchased shares. Nicholas Fish, James Duane, John Jacob Astor, and others took shares on subscription, and in the summer of 1828, Featherstonhaugh and Van Rensselaer boarded a river boat and traveled to Manhattan to meet with them and organize the company. Van Rensselaer was elected president and Featherstonhaugh vice-president, with New Yorkers taking the other offices as well as a majority of seats on the Board. Within months they had united against Featherstonhaugh, who had family difficulties in this period that occupied his time and in any case rarely could get to Manhattan for meetings. Van Rensselaer lost interest in the railroad and began selling his shares. In late 1829, isolated from the others, Featherstonhaugh resigned, as did Van Rensselaer. Now Churchill C. Cambreling—a Van Buren intimate—took the presidency, and it was then that construction began. Thus the creators were replaced by the speculators.

Mohawk and Hudson stock was traded at the Stock and Exchange Board in early October 1830—two months after the work commenced. At the time the security sold for 110. Then it rose, declined, and shot up to 174 in the autumn of 1831, shortly before the first horse-drawn cars were put into service. As Featherstonhaugh had predicted and promised, the line made money immediately, even though the sum was small; from August 10 to September 30, receipts were $6,610 and expenses, $2,442. Later on the charter was amended to allow the line to carry freight, with the understanding that the Erie Canal would receive proper rebates. Once again, Mohawk and Hudson stock rose on the Stock and Exchange Board. And the initial backers began to sell, making sizable profits. Astor disposed of 320 shares and Nicholas Fish, 50, while Peter Jay, who had taken 100 shares and had never paid more than $3 a share on them, owned only 30 in September 1831, having sold close to the high.*

From the first, then, the New York railroads were dominated by speculators and manipulators who, while providing a needed and desirable service, considered railroads little more than a vehicle for profits. For all of his failings, Featherstonhaugh hoped to become a builder. This was not the case with Astor and Fish, who soon after pocketed all of their profits and looked for other promising speculations. This, too, was the beginning of a pattern that would come to full fruition almost a century and a half later with the collapse of the Penn Central.

"It is almost impossible to open a paper without finding an account of some railroad meeting. An epidemic on this subject

*Ibid. pp. 24-25.

seems to be as prevalent as influenza." With this, the editor of the Goshen *Independent Republican* reported on the birth of a railroad mania in late 1831. By then it appeared that the Mohawk and Hudson, though still unproven, would assist Albany in meeting Troy's challenge, and at the same time help Schenectady become a major upstate city. Other Erie towns planned railroads. Then a small village, Utica wanted a link to Schenectady, seventy-eight miles away, with an eye to a possible merger with the Mohawk and Hudson. Cambreling was interested, and helped organize the Utica and Schenectady, agreeing to serve on its board as well as purchase stock. The new line, chartered in 1833 and capitalized at $2 million, had no trouble obtaining subscriptions; indeed, the shares had to be allocated, with Utica, Schenectady, and Albany receiving most of them. Erastus Corning became president and Gideon Hawley treasurer; both were Albanians, indicating the growing interest there in railroads. The line was completed in 1836, and almost immediately showed a profit and paid dividends. That same year saw the organization of the Syracuse and Utica, capitalized at $800,000—again, oversubscribed. Work on the line was begun the following year and completed in 1839. Meanwhile, Rochester, with ambitions toward becoming the leading railroad town in western New York, planned several railroads. The Tonawanda, which extended southwest to Batavia, was chartered in 1832 and completed five years later. The Auburn and Rochester, which was organized in 1836 and finished in 1841, went eastward, passing through Canandaigua and Geneva. There it joined with the Auburn and Syracuse, completed in 1839. The Schenectady and Troy was opened in 1842. This was a municipal line organized to combat Albany's domination of central New York, and although it was a financial failure, the Trojans were determined to keep it in operation. The Rochester and Syracuse and the Rochester, Lockport and Niagara Falls received their charters in 1820, and the latter line was in operation by 1852. Finally, there were three small lines in the West—the Buffalo and Rochester, the Attica and Buffalo, and the Buffalo and Lockport.

In a generation, without a master plan and with each railroad setting off others like a row of dominos, the rail equivalent of the Erie Canal had been constructed. In varying degrees the lines cooperated with one another, and several individuals served on the boards of two or more. There were regular conventions of presidents who united to lobby in Albany and share information.

In other words, there had been created a community of interests among the upper New York railroads.

In addition, some consolidation had taken place. The Tonawanda had merged into the Attica and Buffalo, and the Auburn and Rochester united with the Auburn and Syracuse. From 1842 on the Mohawk and Hudson and the Utica and Schenectady had flirted with one another. A unification of all the lines in upper New York was in the works. As early as 1841 the state legislature considered proposals on the subject, and they were discussed regularly in subsequent sessions. Some of the legislators who owned railroad stock and served on boards had an interest in keeping the idea alive. They were opposed by the Canal nexus, which in turn was backed by reformers and antimonopoly forces, who were wary of a major line that would dominate the central part of the state. United, these two factions had sufficient votes to prevent action. The deadlock would not be broken until the railroads felt obliged to act and had the power to do so, and a new argument could be added to the equation.

The power and the argument presented themselves in the early 1850s. In February 1851, as the Rochester, Lockport and Niagara Falls neared completion, the logic of unification appeared compelling. In that month representatives of ten New York lines gathered in Albany to consider a new plan of consolidation. After several brief sessions they adopted a resolution "that a Committee consisting of the Presidents of each Company on the main line between Albany and Buffalo, be appointed to make application at the present session of the Legislature for a law authorizing any two or more Companies on this Line to consolidate their stock and become one Company. . . ." Similar resolutions had been made in the past, and always they had been defeated by reformers and the Canal nexus. But the situation had changed by 1853. In embryo, New York possessed the makings of the largest railroad in the nation, one that ran from Albany to Buffalo. Furthermore, the Hudson River Railroad, a line going from East Albany to Manhattan, was completed that very year. If united with the upstate line, it could afford continuous passage from Lake Erie to New York City.

The state legislature came to believe such a line was needed, not in order to provide the Erie with competition, or even because members understood the technological and economic issues involved. Rather, it was due to the arrival of competition both from within and without the state. That same year the

Baltimore and Ohio completed construction to Wheeling, and planned to drive farther west. Soon after, the Grand Trunk of Canada opened a service between Montreal and Portland, Maine, and was hoping for further links with Toronto, after which it might cross again into the United States around Buffalo. The Erie Railroad had already reached Dunkirk and was driving through central New York toward Lake Erie, thus opening a rival route to the lower Hudson, one that could turn Albany and Troy into backwater towns if proved successful, while Rochester, Utica, and other growing communities in the central part of the state would suffer irreparable damage. Most important, in 1852—months before the legislature met—the Pennsylvania completed its Harrisburg to Pittsburgh line, while through an already existing road Harrisburg was connected to Philadelphia, a city with memories of a glorious past and a population intent on recovering it through the railroad.

The last was the most serious challenge of all. Six years earlier a group of Philadelphia businessmen had gathered to plan this new railroad. Unlike the Main Line, it would be unbroken by canals. Their intention was clear, and broadcast throughout the state: The Pennsylvania would capture for Philadelphia the commerce of the West. The line, which was originally called the Pennsylvania Central, was incorporated soon after, and construction initiated. The Albany legislators knew of this in 1853; by then the success of the Pennsylvania was no longer in doubt. Thus, a response was necessary. Perhaps it would have been most sensible to give state grants to the Erie Railroad, for its route westward was more direct than any other, the line was already in operation, and its leadership eager for the contest. The upstate lines had been erected as feeders to the Erie Canal, without a thought of extention westward beyond Buffalo. The Hudson River Railroad went north from Manhattan, and if connected with the upstate lines, would provide a most indirect route to Chicago and St. Louis—assuming railroad links to those cities were possible. Still, the power of the Albany leadership was such that this would have to be the main New York response to the Pennsylvania and B&O challenges. The state would bless a union of the ten small carriers and hope that in some way the leadership of the consolidated line would be able to carry the day.

Negotiations for mergers were difficult and protracted and were not completed until 1853. Even then, details remained to be ironed out, connections created, and managements coordinated and consolidated. But it was in that year that the two "centrals"—the New York and the Pennsylvania—began their century-long rivalry. Given the circumstances at the time, it appeared the Pennsylvania would regain national leadership for its state, and that Philadelphia would win the next round in the continuing battle with New York.

II

The Pennsylvania and the Central

Charles Dickens embarked upon an American lecture tour in 1842. He visited most of the major cities in all parts of the nation, traveling by boat, coach, and railroad. Afterward he wrote of the experience and, as had other European visitors, concentrated upon the new kind of western human that was emerging in the United States. Dickens was disturbed by poverty and slavery, of two minds regarding the nation's middle-class ethic, and intrigued by the way Americans so readily adapted themselves to new technologies. The English still considered railroads a major novelty; by 1842, some Americans at least were taking them for granted. "In the ladies' car there are a great many gentlemen who have ladies with them. There are also a great many ladies who have nobody with them: for any lady may travel alone, from one end of the United States to the other, and be certain of the most courteous and considerate treatment everywhere." Dickens took a train from Boston to Lowell. "There is a great deal of jolting, a great deal of noise, a great deal of wall, not much window, a locomotive engine, a shriek and a bell. The cars are like shabby omnibuses, but larger: holding 30, 40, 50 people...." The passengers took all of this in as a matter of course. The conductor performed his tasks in a casual manner; some passengers read newspapers but most chatted with friends, even engaging strangers in conversation. Few peered out the windows to marvel at the speed and wonder about their safety, as would have been the case in England, even among seasoned passengers.

The road between Boston and Lowell was relatively flat, the

landscape not particularly interesting; perhaps that could explain this blasé attitude. But the terrain was fairly rugged around Harrisburg, Pennsylvania, where Dickens traveled the Main Line to Pittsburgh a few months later. The Americans took the train trip in stride; Dickens was horrified.

> On Sunday morning we arrived at the foot of the mountain, which is crossed by railroad. There are ten inclined planes; five ascending, and five descending; the carriages are dragged up the former, and let slowly down the latter, by means of stationary engines; the comparatively level spaces between being traversed, sometimes by horse and sometimes by engine power, as the case demands. Occasionally the rails are laid upon the extreme verge of a giddy precipice; and looking from the carriage window, the traveller gazes sheer down, without a stone or scrap of fence between, into the mountain depths below.

The train moved erratically, swaying in the wind as it went, and this added to Dickens's fears of imminent death. There must have been moments on the upward leg when he thought the line might slip, the train plunge to destruction at the bottom of the hill. The trip downward was still more frightening:

> We . . . rattled down a steep pass, having no other moving power than the weight of the carriages themselves and saw the engine released long after us shining in the sun, that if it had spread a pair of wings and soared away, no one would have had occasion, as I fancied, for the least surprise. But it stopped short of us in a very business-like manner when we reached the canal; and before we left the wharf went panting up the hill again, with the passengers who had waited our arrival for the means of traversing the road by which we had come.*

Dickens then boarded a canal packet for Pittsburgh. The entire trip from Philadelphia, transfers included, took slightly more than four days. This was a vast improvement over turnpike travel; a coach running at top speed during daylight hours and discharging its passengers at prearranged stops along the way in the evening would have taken the better part of a month, and the trip would not have been nearly as comfortable—the inclines

---

*Charles Dickens, *American Notes* (Boston, 1885 ed.), pp. 61-62; 153.

excluded. Of course, the passengers were somewhat inconvenienced by the transfers between boat and railroad, but Dickens didn't have to worry about most of his baggage. By 1842, some canal boats were specially constructed so as to be loaded on the trains and carried from portage to portage. Thus cargo would be carried without transfers; only the passengers would have had to make the switches.*

An inability to overcome geography with the limited technology of the day—not Pennsylvania's lack of capital or commitment—prevented the Main Line from achieving financial and economic success. The state had invested over $33 million in canals and railroads in the decade and a half ending in 1843, and of this amount, $14.3 had gone to the various components of the Main Line. Had the route been as flat as that from Buffalo to Albany, this experiment in state-owned and -operated rail-canal transportation might have flourished, or at the very least offered meaningful competition to rival systems in New York and Maryland. Were it not for Philadelphia's defeats on the issues of the B.U.S. and federal aid to internal improvements, Pennsylvania might have continued its support for a while longer. As it was, disillusionment set in during the last days of the Jackson administration, when it was clear that his successor, Martin Van Buren, would not only continue the old programs but favor his home state more than before. The panic of 1837 was the last blow; now it was evident that state aid could no longer be expected. Old obligations would be honored, but no new ones were to be made.

Supporters of private all-rail transportation won their first important victory over those who favored public hybrid lines the following year. They organized a mass rally in Philadelphia in March, and as a result obtained state approval for a survey of an all-rail passage from Philadelphia to Pittsburgh. The work went slowly and wasn't completed until 1845, when Pennsylvania's transportation future appeared bleak. By then farmers in the northern part of the state had grown accustomed to shipping their goods via the Erie Canal. Meanwhile the Erie Railroad was driving its way through central New York, thrusting feeders into Main Line territory. A link from the Hudson to Goshen was in operation in 1841, and though construction was stalled tem-

---

*A century later the same differentiation existed on transcontinental railroads. Most cargo could go coast to coast without being unloaded and reloaded; passengers would have to switch in Chicago. And soon after the end of World War II, the "piggy-back train" was reinvented, though in quite a different form and for different reasons than those that existed on the Main Line in the 1840s.

porarily due to a shortage of funds, the line was certain to be completed, after which it would draw additional commerce from Philadelphia.

To the south were the National Road, a powerful rival, and the B&O, which reached Cumberland—only a few miles from the Pennsylvania border—in 1842. The Maryland railroad had received permission to construct a link to Pittsburgh, but it hadn't been built due to political troubles and a capital shortage. By the time construction resumed, the permit had run out, but the B&O remained interested in a series of branches that led to Pennsylvania's western counties.

Pennsylvania seemed a foundering giant. In 1840 it had led the nation in railroad mileage, with almost twice that of New York, its nearest rival. And with all of this expenditure, it had not managed to construct a single line that might be considered a railroad counterpart to the Erie Canal.

Mass meetings in favor of a railroad were conducted throughout western Pennsylvania in the autumn of 1845. Some concluded by passing resolutions demanding a link with the B&O, but most urged their own state to begin construction. "If the merchants and other capitalists of Philadelphia who are deeply interested in this measure would subscribe with proportionate liberality compared with their donations for political purposes, there would be not the slightest difficulty in immediately commencing and rapidly progressing with the work. . . ." wrote the *Philadelphia Pennsylvanian*, while the *Indiana* [Pa.] *Republican* stated that "Philadelphians must open their purses as the Bostonians and New Yorkers are now doing." If action were not taken, Philadelphia would become a third-rate city, not only losing whatever remained of the Ohio trade but control over the Pennsylvania west as well.

Thus prodded, some Philadelphians acted. A group of the city's leaders organized a meeting for December 10, at which resolutions in favor of a Pennsylvania line and opposing the B&O alternative were passed. When the state legislature met in Harrisburg in early January several railroad enabling bills were in readiness. One of these, "An Act to incorporate the Pennsylvania Central Railroad Company," was introduced by William Haley of Philadelphia, known as a representative of the city's Whig bankers who had opposed Jackson throughout the 1830s. Almost immediately it became the focus of attention and debate. Canal advocates opposed the measure. Western farmers still wanted a B&O connection; one could be constructed in little more than a year, they said, while an all-Pennsylvania line would take much longer to complete. Others noted that the Main Line would be destroyed by the new railroad, the state's investment wiped out. Some Jacksonians feared the railroad would be a financial failure, and they insisted that no state funds be granted any private line. Others, convinced it would be a success, did not want private capitalists to make fortunes out of what they felt should be a state project. A much-amended measure, supported by Philadelphia Whigs and anti-Jacksonians elsewhere, passed the legislature by slim margins in late March. A second bill, which provided for the B&O connection, backed by Democrats, failed by a single vote. The governor signed the first charter into law on April 10, 1846, and three days later the new line—now called the Pennsylvania Railroad Company—received its papers.

Under the terms of the charter, the railroad was to be constructed from Harrisburg to Pittsburgh, with feeders to be added later on. But it would be denied entry into Philadelphia; the Philadelphia and Columbia, a part of the Main Line and state-owned, would retain control of the Philadelphia-Harrisburg route. As a concession to the B&O forces, the charter contained a provision granting that line a right of way into Pittsburgh if the Pennsylvania was unable to sell $3 million worth of stock and construct at least thirty miles of track along the Pittsburgh-Harrisburg line within little more than a year. The state was to receive five mills per ton-mile carried—those who believed the new road would draw business from the Main Line insisted upon this, and they modeled the provision after the New York experience with the Mohawk and Hudson Railroad. The Pennsylvania was to be capitalized at $7.5 million, but that figure would soon be raised to $10 million. The stock was to be sold privately; the state would not purchase shares. Should the company fail, the taxpayers would have lost nothing, and the general assumption was that the B&O would then take over, draining western Pennsylvania's commerce to Baltimore. But if the Pennsylvania Railroad was a success, the state would have the right to purchase the line after twenty years, at the initial construction costs plus 8 percent, but minus profits. Furthermore, if the option were not taken up in 1866, it could be renewed for another twenty years, and so on in perpetuity.

The Philadelphia Whig politicians and businessmen who had labored so hard for the charter were determined to control the new line. The stakes were too high for it to be otherwise. One or more slips and the B&O would obtain a right of way into Pittsburgh, in which case Philadelphia would suffer a damaging blow. Their attitude was understandable, but at the same time caused serious difficulties. None of the organizers had direct experience with railroads; of the thirteen original directors, six were merchants, four manufacturers, two bankers, and one a man whose time was divided between trade and manufacture.* Each had a business that would benefit from the new line, but none of them was willing to leave it to give the Pennsylvania his full attention; to this group, transportation was a means, not an end. Even Thomas Cope, a Quaker shipowner who led the effort in Harrisburg, was unwilling to do so, and he didn't join the board during its first year.

If the directors knew little about railroads, they did understand the ways by which money could be raised, and had the positions and power to accomplish that task. The charter had specified that Pennsylvania would not take stock in the line, but it said nothing about municipal support. Even before the charter had been signed, the organizers had obtained a commitment from Philadelphia for a purchase of 30,000 shares at $50 each, and indications were that more would be taken later on. The directors made purchases for their own accounts, and encouraged friends to follow suit. This they did; to hold back would indicate a lack of confidence and civic pride, and perhaps have adverse business and social consequences. Still, there were few large subscriptions—only twenty-two were for more than a hundred shares. By early February, individual subscriptions had accounted for 30,570 shares by 2,634 individuals, or an average of 11.6 shares per person.** Most were Philadelphians. This was to be a city project.

In late February 1847 the railroad obtained its letters patent from Harrisburg, based upon the letting out of contracts for the first thirty miles of track. In effect, this meant that should the lines be set down as planned, that part of the charter granting the B&O a right of way would be nullified.

All of this had been done without a formal stockholders' meeting. The original directors had been state-appointed, in effect operating without a formal mandate. This was corrected on March 30, when the first official meeting was held at the Board of Trade in the Philadelphia Stock Exchange. As expected, the temporary directors were in command. Those who wanted to remain on the board did so. Some did drop out of their own volition, to be replaced by others of the organizing

---

*James A. Ward, "Power and Accountability on the Pennsylvania Railroad, 1846-1878," *Business History Review*, Vol. XLIX, No. 1 (Spring, 1975), p. 41.

**George H. Burgess and Miles C. Kennedy, *Centennial History of the Pennsylvania Railroad Company, 1846-1946* (Philadelphia, 1949), pp. 42-43.

group. All were Philadelphians, of course, and with the proper credentials. "Outsiders" would join soon after—the first Pittsburghers arrived the following year—but never had a major say in operations or strategy. This pattern would not be broken. What was to become the largest corporation in America, one of the world's great enterprises, was from beginning to end dominated by the Philadelphia aristocrats, men of talent and at times vision, but for the most part narrow and inbred.

The next day the board met to select one of their own as president. Samuel Vaughan Merrick, then forty-six, accepted the post. Though born in Maine, his uncle, John Vaughan, had been a Philadelphia merchant, who had sent for his nephew in 1816. For a while Merrick worked in a manufacturing establishment. Then he established a company that turned out fire engines for volunteer companies. Merrick helped organize an iron foundry, constructed the Philadelphia Gas Works, and produced heavy machinery for marine uses. He also established the proper social relationships, being one of the founders of the Franklin Institute and serving as its president. In other words, though not a native Philadelphian, Merrick was no outsider. And he had something else in common with his fellow directors. He would not be able to give the railroad his full attention, and he knew nothing about the business and its problems before 1846.

Merrick served as president for three years. From all indications and accounts, he was an intelligent and scrupulous man, who gave freely of his time with little in the way of financial reward. Merrick did a creditable job of selling stocks and floating bonds, and in keeping political fences in repair. More than anything else, he hoped to retain control for his group, and this was his most difficult task. Lacking the time and interest to make technical and engineering decisions, he had to hire a chief engineer to do the job.

J. Edgar Thomson, who assumed the post in April, was thirty-nine years old at the time, and already had two decades of engineering experience. He had helped survey the right of way for the Camden and Amboy Railroad and was chief engineer of the Georgia Railroad when he accepted the Pennsylvania position. In addition, he had traveled extensively in England, absorbing the latest techniques in the field. In 1847, Thomson was considered one of the nation's leading railroad experts. He was also aggressive and ambitious, unable to accept criticism from those he considered his intellectual inferiors.

Merrick and others on the board understood they would need

a man of Thomson's skills and knowledge to lay the thirty miles of track by July, and so fulfill the pledges made to the legislature. Also, he was one of the few men who understood the problems involved in pushing a railroad across the Alleghenies, and had the knowledge to accomplish the task. But could they control him? They were in no position to challenge his expertise, and from the first the board realized the dangers of having such a man in their employ. For in time, he could control them, obliging his nominal superiors to support plans they little understood. Thomson could and did claim that unless his advice were accepted the railroad would commit serious blunders. He was located in Harrisburg, at the site of the initial construction, while the board met regularly in Philadelphia. In those early years Thomson often acted on his own, making decisions and later justifying them on the grounds that he lacked time for consultations. On occasion he would attend board meetings—even though not a member—and such an action was highly irregular. Also, as time went on and construction proceeded smoothly, the board met less frequently, the members more concerned with their primary occupations, and this too enabled Thomson to assume more powers. Finally, Thomson had the ultimate weapon. He was the only person at the railroad who understood all aspects of the business and was capable of making plans for future developments. Were he to leave, the line would have been severely damaged.

Merrick understood this, and tried unsuccessfully to curb Thomson's powers. On such occasions, Thomson would threaten resignation, and thereupon Merrick would back down, the result being additional transfers of power to the chief engineer. After one such squabble in late 1847, Thomson agreed to remain only after his salary was raised from $1,000 to $5,000 a year plus expenses, a clear example of his value to the Pennsylvania.

The clashes between Merrick and Thomson increased during the next two years, with the engineer winning most of them. Tired, weary, and frustrated, Merrick resigned as president in September 1849, although remaining on the board. He was succeeded by William Patterson, a banker who also had varied interests in real estate and who was one of Merrick's closest associates. By then it was becoming obvious that Thomson had a small group of allies on the board, even though the Merrick-Patterson group controlled a majority, and in addition the engineer had the confidence of many stockholders. One sign of this came at the first stockholders' meeting after Patterson's election, at which time a resolution limiting the president's salary to $2,500 was introduced, "unless he possess the qualifications of an Engineer, and act as President and General Agent, Manager, or Superintendent of the Company."* Nothing came of this resolution, but the meaning was clear: either Patterson would have to acquire engineering skills and work at the job full-time, or accept a diminished salary—less than half that of Thomson—and power. There was a third possibility: Patterson could step down and make way for a person who possessed these qualities, and Thomson was the only man at the company who did.

Thomson's powers increased during the early Patterson years. He, not the board, hired station agents and technical personnel, first making certain they would be loyal in a showdown. One of these, Chief Assistant Engineer Herman Haupt, was selected by Thomson for the post of superintendent of transportation, and given responsibility for drawing up an organizational structure for the Pennsylvania. Patterson and the board majority opposed the Haupt appointment, and a contest of wills developed, which ended with a complete Thomson victory. But in late 1851 the Merrick-Patterson group reopened the issue and tried to fire Haupt once more. The battle raged for several months, with the board almost evenly split on the issue. Then in January 1852 Thomson headed a slate of candidates determined to oust the leadership. It was a bitter and dirty campaign, one which Thomson won. Merrick and Patterson left the board and were replaced by insurgents. And on February 3 Thomson was elected chairman and president.

Merrick and Patterson had never been more than figureheads, symbols of the power of the Philadelphia aristocrats. In terms of actual planning and building, they had been obliged to follow Thomson's wishes, even when initially opposing some of his plans. Thomson added the symbols to the reality in 1852. For the next twenty-two years the Pennsylvania Railroad would be dominated by the greatest builder of his generation, an engineer-businessman whose innovations and ideas were studied and imitated by others. Yet even at the height of his power and prestige, during the Civil War, Thomson was not accepted socially by most old-line Philadelphians. He had his victory, but it did not mean they had lost. After all, Thomson could not have achieved the presidency had most of the aristocrats opposed him, for in 1852 they still controlled a large majority of the stock. Rather, the Philadelphia elite understood

*Ibid. p. 55.

that none of their members possessed the abilities and interests required for the leadership of so great an enterprise, and that they needed Thomson's talents just as a man of his ambitions required the arena only they could supply. It was not really a marriage of convenience, but rather, a long-term liaison, which over the years took on the appearance of a marriage. In time Philadelphians would take great pride in Thomson, especially when he was contrasted favorably with some of the buccaneers of American railroading in the 1850s and 1860s. To the aristocrats, however, Thomson was "their man," and not much more. He was celebrated throughout the nation, and enjoyed the confidences of Presidents and Cabinet members. Many major lines collapsed during the panic of 1857; the Pennsylvania not only remained intact, but actually expanded. The railroad was a key factor in the Union victory in the Civil War; President Lincoln and others acknowledged this and proclaimed Thomson a hero and genius. But he rarely was invited to the large balls organized by the Philadelphia elite, and never to their intimate parties, where majority stockholders sipped tea, ate little cakes, and discussed the arts. Thomson was agreeable to this arrangement, and so were they.

The aristocrats made three demands of their president; so long as he complied with them, he would have a free hand. The first was that no scandal or even rumors of one should touch their line. For the Pennsylvania was not only an economic entity but a certified product of individuals who guarded their reputations. This meant prudent financing, no wheeling and dealing, and cooperation with the state's political leaders. This suited Thomson, who was more interested in the technology and efficiency of railroading than in the manipulation of paper. Too, the majority stockholders insisted their railroad be an innovative leader, offering excellent service at low prices. The Pennsylvania was not to seek maximization of profits but rather minimization of complaints—especially from influential shippers and travelers. Thomson thought along similar lines, and was able to comply without difficulty. Finally, the stockholders wanted a good and reliable return on their investment. This was vital, for increasingly the aristocrats had come to depend upon their investments for income. Philadelphia continued to decline in comparison to New York; the railroad was to become their major source of income and pride as well as the life line between Philadelphia and the West.

It was here that Thomson excelled. The price of Pennsylvania Railroad stock was unusually steady; it declined on occasion—as during the 1857 panic—but always came back. It was not subjected to manipulations as were most other leading railroad issues, in part because the Philadelphians refused to sell, passing their certificates down to their children as though they were heirlooms. So careful were they in guarding against outsiders that they refused to allow the common stock to be listed on the New York Stock Exchange until 1901—from 1876 to 1900 it was officially listed on only the Philadelphia Exchange.* The stock always paid a good dividend, and a continuous one from 1847 on. The initial rate was 6 percent and it held until 1856, when Thomson raised it to 8. In the panic year the dividend was lowered to 4 percent, and then raised to 6 in 1858. The Pennsylvania showed excellent profits during the Civil War, and the distribution rose sharply, reaching 10 percent in 1864 and 1865. In addition, there were stock dividends: 30 percent in 1864, 5 percent in 1867 and 1868. During Thomson's last four years, 1869 to 1872, the dividend was 10 percent, and Pennsylvania common stock the bluest chip of all. It was little wonder, then, that the aristocrats praised the man, even while not completely accepting him, questioning some of his actions, and refusing to allow him entry into the inner circle of Philadelphia blue bloods.

Unlike Merrick and Patterson, whose visions were limited to the line between Philadelphia and Pittsburgh, Thomson had continental ambitions. He expected the Pennsylvania to dominate commerce within the state, to be sure, and to stave off challenges from the rival lines in New York and Maryland. But at the same time he had plans to invade Pennsylvania's neighbors, and in addition take from them the midwestern trade. What the Erie Canal had done for New York in the late 1820s, Thomson believed the Pennsylvania Railroad would accomplish for Philadelphia in the 1850s and 1860s. He realized that the New Yorkers would continue to exert leadership in banking and finance, but Thomson thought that, given a successful railroad, Philadelphia would undergo a commercial revival.

The first step, of course, was completion of the passage from Pittsburgh to Philadelphia. The Pennsylvania's track from Pittsburgh to Harrisburg was ready in late 1852, and then connected with the Philadelphia and Columbia. Complete through service to Philadelphia was not ready for another year and a half. At that time, it became possible to travel from Philadelphia to Pittsburgh

---

*Pennsylvania common was traded over the counter in New York, however, much to the dismay of the Philadelphia aristocrats, who feared New Yorkers would accumulate shares and perhaps seek representation on the board.

in less than seventeen hours—almost a third of the time it took to go from Manhattan to Buffalo by boat and railroad.

Thomson had no intention of stopping there. Soon after he took office the railroad's lobbyists advocated a measure that would permit the Pennsylvania to purchase stocks and bonds in other railroads, to the extent of 15 percent of its own paid-in capital. A bill embodying this passed the legislature and was signed into law in March 1853. In the interim, Thomson opened negotiations with several small railroads, all in shaky condition and requiring financial aid, and all west of Pittsburgh. When the act was signed he took interests in four such lines, and then announced that the Pennsylvania would soon invade Ohio and Indiana. Three of the lines failed, but the Ohio and Pennsylvania was a success, and through it the Pennsylvania entered Crestline, Ohio, in April. Then he financed the Ohio and Indiana, which laid track between Crestline and Fort Wayne, Indiana. This railroad merged with another to form the Pittsburgh, Fort Wayne and Chicago, a major line which took the Pennsylvania into Chicago—over 450 miles from Pittsburgh —on the eve of the Civil War. The Marietta and Cincinnati, in which the Pennsylvania had a $750,000 interest, formed a link with Cincinnati. The Springfield, Mt. Vernon, and Pittsburgh went into Columbus. Other lines were projected to additional cities, and Thomson had his eye on all of them. By 1861 there was scarcely an important part of southern Ohio, Indiana, or Illinois that was a significant distance from a line in which the Pennsylvania had an interest or was in the process of obtaining one.

Thomson financed these purchases through exchanges of stock and outright cash advances. In order to continue his program, he had to increase the net worth of the Pennsylvania and consolidate its position in its home state. Furthermore, he had to come to terms with the railroad's old enemies, those in Harrisburg who had supported the B&O connection and the defenders of the Main Line. He set out to do so in 1853 by proposing that the Pennsylvania purchase all assets and rights of the Main Line and incorporate them into the railroad. Serious negotiations were opened in 1854, which were not completed until 1857. Under the terms agreed upon, Thomson paid $7.5 million for the Main Line's canals, railroads, and other properties and rights, almost all of the sum in bonds, the last of which would mature in 1894. In return for this the Pennsylvania received assets which had originally cost some $14.3 million, but in 1857 were either run-down or bypassed. Thomson would sell off some of the canals and abandon others. As for the railroads, they had to be resurveyed and in large measure reconstructed. Even the Philadelphia and Columbia, which had taken over $4 million of the state's money and was a financial success thanks to its link to the Pennsylvania, required funds for better rails and modern equipment. Thus ended the state's attempt at railroad and canal building, ownership, and operation. The Pennsylvania Railroad now dominated the state's transportation.

The 1857 act also nullified the state's right to purchase the Pennsylvania. Furthermore, since the Main Line was now part of his railroad, Thomson claimed that the tonnage tax—which had been passed ostensibly to protect the Main Line from the Pennsylvania—was automatically void. The state disagreed, and after lengthy litigation, won its point. But in 1861 the law was repealed, and the tax no longer collected.

When Thomson assumed the presidency in 1852 the Pennsylvania operated less than 350 miles of track and its gross revenues were close to $2 million. Ten years later, in the first full year of the Civil War, the Pennsylvania's mileage was 438, and the revenues almost $11 million. In 1871 the Pennsylvania owned over 1,000 miles of track, and its gross revenues that year were well over $22 million. It was the premier success and growth company in the largest and fastest-growing American industry.

In addition to its own lines, the Pennsylvania had a dominant voice in the management of many other railroads, most of them west of Pittsburgh, where they operated an additional 3,000 miles of track. In effect if not in law, these were part of the Pennsylvania system, and Thomson had to manage them as well as take care of his own operations. Consolidation and coordination were clearly required, and in order to achieve them, Thomson organized the Pennsylvania Company, which received its charter in 1870 and became an operating entity the following year. The Railroad gave the Company its common and preferred stock in the western lines, and in return received the entire issue of preferred stock in the Company—$8 million worth. Two years later the Railroad exchanged its ownership of the Union Railroad and Transportation Company, a fast-freight operation, for $3 million worth of common stock in the Company.

Thomson completed organization of the holding company in 1872. It was to be his last major accomplishment for the railroad. When he became president twenty years before, the United States was about to enter a period of rapid industrialization, and there were fears Pennsylvania would not play a major role in the new era. In 1872, shortly before the high noon of the industrial age, Pennsylvania was the nation's leading coal producer and possessed most of the known petroleum reserves and wells. Pittsburgh was a foremost iron and steel center. Pennsylvania's geographic location gave it an edge over New York in the matter of western development and colonization. The state did not have as many miles of railroad as Ohio or Indiana, but many important lines in those states were affiliated in one way or another with the Pennsylvania. Several lines entered Cincinnati, Chicago, St. Louis, and Cleveland, and in all the Pennsylvania was deemed the foremost railroad, the one that led in most fields, had the most consistent safety and delivery record, and the most competent management. The Pennsylvania was the first American railroad to use steel rails produced by the Bessemer process; the first to utilize steel fire boxes under boilers; it pioneered in the use of air brakes and signal systems; it innovated in the use of loading and unloading procedures. The others followed. So for the moment, as Thomson completed his work, it appeared that Philadelphia might undergo a considerable economic revival. Of course, New York still held a large lead in finance and banking, while Boston was making a bid for a new national role. But the power of the railroad might negate the advantages these cities held.

This situation was only dimly perceived by the Philadelphia aristocrats. They cheered Thomson from the sidelines, and appeared content so long as their dividends were intact. The president had not consulted them regarding organization of the Pennsylvania Company and in general ignored their representatives on the board. The Pennsylvania Railroad, originated as a vehicle for the aristocrats to regain power after the Jackson interlude, was by the early 1870s a power unto itself. If anything, Thomson showed more regard for and interest in the emerging Pittsburgh steel tycoons, who had a continental viewpoint, than for the narrower and somewhat provincial Philadelphians.

The New Yorkers could understand this. A less distinguished and more aggressive lot than the Philadelphians, they had taken steps to meet the Pennsylvania Railroad's challenge by backing two lines to Lake Erie. One of these, the Erie, quickly became a speculative favorite on Wall Street, a line that was raped by her leaders and whose potential was never realized. The second, the New York Central, had an indirect route to the West and lacked a clearly defined long-range strategy. It was strikingly different from the Pennsylvania in organization and philosophy, and for a while seemed to lack both, substituting for them the occasional insights and part-time management of a businessman for whom railroads were a peripheral interest, and the Central one of several in his bag of companies. And while the Central searched for a proper role, the Pennsylvania established itself west of Pittsburgh and consolidated its position as the principal line in that part of the country.

John V.L. Pruyn, secretary of the Utica and Schenectady Railroad, sent identical letters to the presidents of each of the other nine upstate lines on April 5, 1853. In them he asked for a meeting the following week, in Syracuse, to discuss the new state law permitting railroad mergers. The meeting was held; all were present.* There it was decided to form a committee to plan for consolidation. From the first there was no doubt that a single line would be formed. The only questions to be answered were the terms—what would each line receive for its stock?—and who would become president of the new railroad, even then referred to as the New York Central.

The upstate leaders agreed to accept the Central's stock and bonds in exchange for their own. The only problem was determination of exchange ratios. For different reasons, most lines demanded premiums above their book values. Some of the railroads paid large and regular dividends, while others had never paid a cent. There was no assurance the Central would be a money-maker, or when dividends would be declared, so those lines that paid dividends felt they should be compensated accordingly. Several lines were badly in need of repair, but insisted upon premiums for good will and intangible items. Those in good shape wanted compensation for past expenditures.

In the end, nine of the railroads received premiums, ranging from 17 percent for the Albany and Schenectady to 55 percent for the Utica and Schenectady and the Mohawk Valley. The tenth railroad—the Schenectady and Troy—was a money-loser and in poor shape. Instead of a premium, the sole stockholder—the city of Troy—was penalized 25 percent, while its leader, Russell Sage, was relegated to a secondary position in the new organization. Still, the line had been losing over $100,000 a year, and at least this burden would be lifted from the city.

*These ten railroads—some descendents of the original lines—were: the Albany and Schenectady; the Utica and Schenectady; the Mohawk Valley; the Syracuse and Utica; the Syracuse and Utica Direct; the Rochester and Syracuse; the Buffalo and Rochester; the Rochester, Lockport and Niagara Falls; the Buffalo and Lockport; and the Schenectady and Troy.

In the end, the New York Central was capitalized at over $23 million, a huge sum at the time—almost half the 1853 federal budget. But according to some estimates, close to a quarter of this was water. The Central had 650 miles of track, much of which had to be coordinated and some replaced. A good deal of the line was single track; parallel lines had to be constructed. Its station houses were in bad shape. Ten years earlier the state had abolished the tax the railroads had to pay to the Erie Canal, and now new freight areas were needed.

In other words, the giant line was bloated and had many problems. But it also possessed great potentials. The Central went through an established, rich area, with several fast-growing cities, all of which required carriers. The line would not have to engage in colonization; that task had been completed. Rather, it would gather the fruits, and if it did the job well, could hope for a profitable future.

But was that all? What of the West, the Great Lakes trade cultivated by the Erie Canal? Would the railroad equivalent of that waterway be continued? To do so would require additional lines to Cleveland, Detroit, and eventually Chicago. In 1853 J. Edgar Thomson was planning his western invasion. The New York Central's leadership had no such ambitions for the time being. So it ran the danger of falling behind before the race was properly begun.

That leadership was centered around Erastus Corning of Albany, who had been president of the Utica and Schenectady—the line which, together with the Mohawk Valley, had received the largest premium for its stockholders, of which Corning was the biggest. In addition he served on the boards of the Mohawk and Hudson, the Hudson River, and the Michigan Central. Corning was fifty-nine years old in 1853, at the height of his influence and in the prime of life. He had been mayor of Albany in the 1830s and a power in the state's Democratic party, one of Van Buren's close allies. Corning had gone on to the state senate in the 1850s, and later in the decade served two terms in the federal House of Representatives. All of these were part-time positions, which he took when pressured to do so, and he always stepped down voluntarily; to oppose Corning politically would be to invite oblivion.

For the most part, he took care of his varied business interests. Corning was Albany's leading merchant, the head of Erastus Corning and Company. He owned the Albany Nail Factory and the Albany Iron Works, which sold their wares through Corning and Company. Later on, the Iron Works produced wheels and the Nail Factory spikes, which Corning and Company sold thoughout the region, the prime customers being the Utica and Schenectady and other Corning-controlled roads, which also used rails he imported from Europe. The guiding force behind the Albany City Bank, Corning made certain it financed his mercantile business as well as provided services and received fees from the railroads. He had supported Andrew Jackson's campaign against the Bank of the United States as well as Van Buren's legislation to assist the New York financial community. He had interests in other banks too—in Binghamton, Batavia, Buffalo, and Cazenovia—so that in 1853 Corning was the dominant force in upstate banking. He also was a landlord, owning large tracts in western New York. That year the town of Corning was third among inland state shipping points, due in large part to his efforts. In addition, Corning owned potentially valuable acreage in Michigan, which explains his interest in the Michigan Central.

More than a century before the term originated, Corning was a conglomerate. Financial historians have another term for such individuals: sedentary merchants. But Corning was not sedentary. He traveled through upper New York, went to Manhattan by river boat, and even to Europe, seeking new outlets for his money and energy.

Each part of the Corning empire fed upon and in turn nourished the others. Clearly the New York Central had a role to play. It would tie upper New York into one neat bundle, using Corning banking services and Corning iron products, and also make his land more valuable, while at the same time enhancing his political power. But that was all. The railroad would be part of the empire, and not necessarily its prize. In fact, there would be no centerpiece but Corning himself, always coordinating and manipulating, accumulating wealth and influence and then seeking more.

He presented a striking contrast to Thomson, that professional railroad man and builder, a Whig and later Republican who cared little about politics, however. Thomson was the leader of the Pennsylvania, nothing else, and he subordinated himself to it—or, to be more precise, identified his ego with the line's fortunes. Corning was a merchant-financier-manufacturer who had interests in railroads. He was an organizer, not a builder, a Democrat in what had become a one-party state, intimately concerned with the political process but always viewing it as ancillary to business. As for the Central, it would be subordinated to the man. This did not mean he would use the line badly, but that it would flourish along with the rest of the body should all go well. When the requirements of the empire clashed with those of the railroad—or when both required Corning's attention at the same time—the empire would take precedence.

The New York Central Railroad came into being on July 6, 1853. It had thirteen directors, all of whom lived along the line in upper New York. Pruyn, who was one of them, noted that "Mr. Corning held a large majority of the proxies." Many had been gathered in by Pruyn and Dean Richmond, a prominent Buffalo merchant. Pruyn was selected as secretary and treasurer of the New York Central. Richmond became vice-president. Corning, of course, was to be the railroad's first president, being elected with no opposition.

Like the others, he exchanged his stocks and bonds for New York Central paper. His total profit from this transaction was in the neighborhood of $100,000. Then he announced a major renovation program, which would cost in excess of $1 million over the next two years. The Albany bank was to act as agent in raising the money. Almost $750,000 of the sum was to be spent for new rails, imported from Britain by Corning and Company, which received a commission of 2.5 percent. The bill for spikes was $84,000, and in addition the railroad required $71,000 worth of axles and wheels. Both were provided by the Albany Iron Works. Corning decided the railroad needed more land in the western part of the state, and it was purchased—from his companies. How much was all of this worth? By some estimates, the Corning interests profited to the extent of $250,000 a year from New York Central business in one form or another. Corning saw nothing wrong with this. He charged fair prices, and on occasion permitted other merchants and manufacturers a share of the business.

Some New York newspapers learned of these transactions and published rumors of large profits. A stockholders' group was organized in early 1855 to look into the matter. It concluded that while there was no reason to doubt Corning's essential honesty, "still the principle of buying articles required for the use of the Railroad Company from its own officers might in time come to lead to abuses of great magnitude, and in that view of the case, the Committee are of opinion that the system of purchases now conducted should be . . . placed under such regulations and restrictions by the Directors as they may deem best calculated to protect the interests of the Company. . . ."

Corning was hurt and angered. He announced that in the future other firms would be allowed to sell rails to the Central, and at the same time refunded $10,000 to the company, which he claimed represented his total profits and those of Corning and Company. Defenders appeared to protest Corning's innocence of wrongdoing, his high-minded idealism.* His actions were no different from those of other railroad presidents, and in no way were the interests of the New York Central compromised by its president, who, in addition to his essential disinterest, had demonstrated his loyalty to the stockholders by refusing to accept a salary for his work.

This was certainly so. Corning conformed to the business and political ethics of his day. The concept of the soulless corporation owned by faceless stockholders, financed by huge impersonal banks, and served by anonymous directors and managements did not exist in the 1850s. Instead, the corporation was viewed as a variety of the partnership, even though of a more limited form. It was a period in which proprietors gave their names to their companies, as though a bond to potential customers—the "Generals," "Amalgamateds," and "Nationals" would not appear in force until the twentieth century. Erastus Corning viewed the Central as his railroad, no different in this respect than Corning and Company and the Albany Iron Works. He had a sizable financial interest in the railroad, as did most of the other officers and directors. The small stockholder—there were some of these—was considered a minor partner, whose interests were to be respected, but whose views were fairly unimportant. These interests consisted, primarily, of obtaining a good return on investment. Corning understood this, as did others at the company. Dean Richmond, the blunt vice-president who had no formal education and was known for his directness, put it to Corning in mid-1854. "It is not necessary for me to say to you that the important thing for the Central Co. is to arrange to pay Dividend." There were rumors of stockholder and director "deviltry." "I have no fear of them if we can carry along our money matters."** So they did.

The Central had a deficit in 1854, its first full year of operation, but still paid a 9 percent dividend. Business improved in the boom years of 1855 and 1856, when the dividends of 8 percent were well covered. Then came the 1857 panic, and the Central suffered two years of losses. Still, the dividend held, the only concession being a reduction to 7 percent in 1859. Some of this money came from borrowing; Corning was anxious to establish

---

*Alvin F. Harlow, *The Road of the Century* (New York, 1947), pp. 81-83.
**Thomas Cochran, *Railroad Leaders, 1845-1890* (Cambridge, 1953), p. 453.

the railroad as a regular dividend payer—this would enhance both its reputation and the value of the common stock—and so was willing to borrow money at premium prices. "Where can such financing lead?" asked *Harper's Weekly* in early 1858, after the railroad announced its "regular" dividend. Doubtless the railroad had a bright future. "But how can any business, however promising, be profitably conducted if money is perpetually borrowed at ten percent discount and seven percent interest, to be distributed in the guise of profits?"

This was the price Corning felt he had to pay to maintain a free hand. He was in the practice of sending blank ballots to stockholders, asking their signatures and nothing else; he would fill in the rest. And for the most part he received them. Thus an unspoken bargain had been struck. Management would maintain dividends at all costs, and in return stockholders would permit it a wide degree of latitude. This was the situation in the 1850s. It would remain the case in the 1960s, and is another explanation of the way by which the Pennsylvania Central collapsed.

Freed from restraints of business ethics and stockholder opposition, Corning set about fitting the Central into his empire. This involved a rationalization of the system and consolidation of Albany's position as the Queen City of central New York. There would be no important connection to Troy; that city's dreams of glory ended, and within a few years its representative on the board, Russell Sage, was carefully shoved aside.

At the same time, Corning pushed the Central westward, utilizing three vehicles for the operation. The Great Western of Canada was one of these. This line began at the American border, directly across the river from Buffalo, and projected a line to Detroit, all on Canadian territory. Several of the small upper New York railroads had subscribed to Great Western stock on the promise that a bridge would be thrown across the Niagara and that it would open the Canadian and American west to the goods and services of New York. When these lines joined to form the New York Central, they surrendered their Great Western stock to the new company, which in 1854 had $500,000 of it.

Corning was interested in the road; in 1851 he had backed a law permitting the state's railroads to subscribe to Great Western stock, and he had shares of his own. That year he joined the Great Western board, and he served the line until formation of the New York Central. Still, he retained his stock, and the Albany Iron Works provided the line with wheels and spikes, even after several Canadian firms protested that they were being discriminated against. Thus the Great Western was a member in good standing of the "Corning group," and so fit in well with the New York Central.

So did a second, smaller railroad, the Buffalo and State Line (later known as the Lake Shore), whose sixty-eight miles of track skirted the southern rim of Lake Erie from Buffalo to the Pennsylvania border. This railroad had been organized by two groups, one representing the Erie, the other the small central New York lines. Dean Richmond was its vice-president, and Daniel Drew, head of the Erie, was on the board. Immediately they clashed over the matter of gauge. The central New York lines used a standard gauge, the Erie a broad one. Thus the rolling stock and locomotives of one line could not be used on the other. Under Richmond's leadership and with Corning's support, the Buffalo and State Line adopted the standard gauge. In 1853, the central New York lines owned close to $400,000 worth of the small line's stock, and all of this went into the New York Central's portfolio.

The Buffalo and State Line opened some of Corning's land holdings to colonization, and so he benefited doubly by having the road come under his control. In this period Corning worked well with Richmond, but the two strong-willed men did have their differences. Corning wanted the Buffalo and State Line to pass through the new town of Irving, which, like Corning, was a company property. Richmond refused, seeking to assist his own holdings, and he had his way. Corning was unforgiving, but he never let a grudge get in the way of business. Besides, he had bigger plans afoot.

In 1846 Corning obtained his initial interest in the Michigan Central, and at the same time began selling it spikes, wheels, and rails. In addition, he purchased large tracts of Michigan land in areas to be served by the new line when it was completed. It was a familiar pattern; in the mid-1850s, Corning hoped to add Michigan to his empire via the railroads. This was accomplished through a working arrangement between the Great Western and the Michigan Central, both of which went into Detroit. Then the Michigan Central obtained interests in several minor Illinois railroads—the Aurora, the Central Military Tract, the Peoria and Oquawka, and the Northern Cross. These were merged to form the Chicago, Burlington and Quincy, which was designed to open Chicago to the Corning interests and unite with the Buffalo and State Line in the east.

It was a grand design and project. The Corning railroads

encircled Lake Erie, just as the Pennsylvania was capturing southern and central Ohio, Indiana, and Illinois.

Meanwhile a third vehicle controlled the lake itself. Among his other interests, Richmond was the owner and operator of several Lake Erie freight carriers—and Corning had shares in these, too. Thus the empire stretched from Chicago on the west to Buffalo on the east. It was not harmonized under a single umbrella, as would be the Pennsylvania Company, but rather juggled in Corning's brain; this was the style of the man. He fitted this western project into the New York Central at Buffalo, again, like a piece in a puzzle.

But what of the East? Corning's next step might have been to take the railroad into New York, and so have an eastern terminus greater than that of the Pennsylvania. He did not make the move, however, and appeared content to rely upon the river boats that docked in Albany and made the Manhattan trip—they were cheaper and the river did not require constant rebuilding. But he did work out arrangements with the Boston and Worcester and the western railroads, which provided him with access to Boston. As he saw it, this meant his railroad had two ports into which to feed—Boston and New York. Actually, this was a diversion of resources, perhaps the biggest miscalculation of Corning's railroad career. The Boston link did not work out as well as had been anticipated. And until the New York Central reached into New York City, it could not be considered a true equal of the Pennsylvania.

Corning, who was sixty-five years old when the Civil War began, could not fully comprehend this. It was not that he lacked vision or ability. Instead, his ways had been fixed during the era of mercantile capitalism, and he was so powerful and secure that he did not feel obliged to adjust his actions to the new demands of the period of industrial capitalism. To a sedentary merchant, the New York Central existed to serve the requirements of the whole; to an industrial capitalist, it could be the focal point of all interests, an enterprise to which individual interests had to be subordinated. And this Corning could never have done.

Corning viewed other important businessmen as rivals, each with his own empire. At times there would be differences of opinion and conflicting claims, but these could be mediated. After all, in such a large and still undeveloped country, there was plenty for all. He was particularly interested in avoiding railroad rivalries. In Corning's view it was expected that businessmen would contest one another for railroads, but once the battle was decided, harmony should rule.

What might be done if the contest ended in a stalemate? In such a situation, compromise and conciliation were required. He had united the central New York lines in the hope that in this way differences would be ended and greater efficiency and profits made possible. In the autumn of 1854, before the New York Central was a year old, he called a railroad convention in New York, at the St. Nicholas Hotel. Representatives of the Baltimore and Ohio and the Pennsylvania were there; it was as though the barons had gathered to listen to proposals made by a new, somewhat brash noble, who conceivably could become larger and more powerful than any of them. Did Corning mean to declare war or offer peace? The latter was the case. He suggested the companies cooperate rather than compete, that they charge the same rates per mile and refrain from seeking new business at the expense of other lines. No railroad would invade the territory of another; each empire would be respected. In other words, Corning wanted a community of interests.

The railroads accepted "the St. Nicholas Agreement." But it did not last for long. As soon as the newspapers learned of it they railed against the "conspiracy" and attempts at stifling competition. Reformers warned that unless it was ended, federal legislation would be demanded. This was not necessary. The railroads themselves didn't want cooperation, but rather were intent on gathering as much traffic as they could in order to obtain revenues to cover fixed charges and pay off bondholders. The Erie withdrew from the agreement in March 1855, and the others followed soon after. In this way, the first significant attempt at national railroad cooperation came to an end.

The ideology and economics of railroading at that stage of development would not permit such arrangements, and Thomson understood this, even while Corning did not. Thomson had a solitary interest, the Pennsylvania Railroad. Just as one line alone could dominate the Philadelphia-Pittsburgh line, so the commerce of the Midwest would not be shared. The Pennsylvania had started to incorporate territories upon which it placed a stamp. The New York Central, the Erie, and the B&O wanted some of these areas, and Thomson would do all in his power to halt their advances. There would be no community of interests at that time in regard to the Chicago trade, for example, simply because there wasn't enough of it to provide handsome profits for one railroad, much less several. Cooperation would become necessary afterward, but only because the rivals came to understand that the strong lines were there to stay, and that competition would create more problems than rewards for the victors.

These were some of the fruits of the Jacksonian victories. The Gallatin *Report on Roads and Canals* conceived of a coordinated transportation network, planned by the government and carried out by businessmen with a national vision. John Quincy Adams accepted this concept and had hopes of putting it into operation. Jackson's victory and subsequent transportation policies put an end to such plans and insured that, in the beginning at least, railroading would have some of the benefits and disadvantages of a competitive environment. Democrat entrepreneur Erastus Corning supported Jackson, but also brought to railroading the outlook of the sedentary merchant. He helped nourish an atmosphere of cooperation among the railroaders of his state, and then brought them together to form the New York Central. But he did not understand the potential of the railroad—just as the canal managers thought of their waterways as extensions of rivers, so Corning conceived of railroads as replacements for canals—or appreciate the tactics and strategies required by this new technology. For that matter, neither did the Philadelphians who had put together the Pennsylvania Railroad and operated it initially. Thomson, the professional railroader, was of a new breed. His enterprise already possessed definite advantages in terms of location and territory. After divorcing his management from the owners, he set about exploiting his assets, and in the process created the best-managed major enterprise in the nation. So long as the New York Central lacked this kind of leadership it would lag in the race for the midwestern markets.

For all of his excellent qualities, Corning was not up to the task. Neither were Pruyn, Richmond, and others of his group, who brought the attitudes and outlooks of the age of mercantile capitalism to the prime vehicle of the era of industrial capitalism. Thomson divided the Pennsylvania into geographic divisions, placed subordinates in charge of each, and held them strictly accountable for results. Along with the managers of several other lines, he helped create management teams, pioneered in accounting procedures, and adjusted techniques to developing circumstances. Although he was vitally interested in the fortunes of the Michigan Central, Corning never inspected the line, and made his decisions on chance information and incomplete reports. He ran his affairs out of his hat. Corning would leave the office for extended periods, either to look after other businesses or go on European vacations, and at such times Pruyn was left in charge of operations. Richmond resented this, and clashes resulted. In the end there were confusions, overlaps, and ultimate demoralization. The New York Central was operated by men who had come up through the ranks at the small constituent roads, and they were unable to operate the large carrier successfully. What was more, they did not recognize their problems in the 1850s, and so were unable to make necessary adjustments.* Not until their power was broken would the modern history of the New York Central begin, or would that line be able to compete on an equal basis with the Pennsylvania. This happened in 1867, when Cornelius Vanderbilt assumed the presidency.

*Daniel McCallum, the general superintendent of the New York and Erie and a pioneer in railroad management, wrote the following in a memorandum to the line's president, Homer Ramsdell: "A Superintendent of a road fifty miles in length can give its business his personal attention, and may be almost constantly upon the line engaged in the direction of its details; each employee is familiarly known to him, and all questions in relation to its business are at once presented and acted upon; and any system, however imperfect, may under such circumstances prove comparatively successful. In the government of a road five hundred miles in length a very different state of things exists. Any system which might be applicable to the business and extent of a short road, would be found entirely inadequate to the wants of a long one; and I am fully convinced, that in the want of a system perfect in its details, properly adapted and vigilantly enforced, lies the true secret of their failure; and that this disparity of cost per mile in operating long and short roads, is not produced by a *difference in length,* but is in proportion to the perfection of the system adopted." Alfred D. Chandler, Jr., ed. *The Railroads: The Nation's First Big Business* (New York, 1965), p. 101.

III

The Eastern Destiny

Shortly after New Year's Day, 1867, Erastus Corning met with Cornelius Vanderbilt to discuss relationships and possible cooperation between the Central and the Hudson River Railroad, which the Commodore had controlled for the past few years. Although no longer the Central's president, Corning was still its dominant force, and speaking for the board he rejected Vanderbilt's proposals for closer relations. Still, the two men were not enemies, and they continued their conversation while headed uptown in Vanderbilt's carriage.

"Mr. Corning, I am very sorry we cannot get together in this matter," said the Commodore.

"I am too. If it was left to you and me we could fix it up in a little while."

"I believe we could."*

Vanderbilt fixed it up in his own way. Within little more than a week he would begin an assault against the large upstate line. Before the year had ended, Vanderbilt was president of the New York Central.

The two men did understand one another, in part because they were of the same generation and occupation. Corning was six months younger than Vanderbilt, and his Connecticut childhood was not too different from the one Vanderbilt had experienced in Staten Island. Both men were involved in land speculation, banking, and transportation. To these Corning added the iron and mercantile businesses as well as politics. Vanderbilt had little interest in such matters; but he was a master of securities manipulation, was a leading figure in oceanic transportation,

---

*Irene Neu, *Erastus Corning*, (Ithaca, 1960), pp. 185-86.

had helped foment a revolution in Central America, and preferred purchasing the votes and services of politicians to spending his own time and energies in state and federal offices.

The men bore a striking physical resemblance to one another; both were tall, handsome, and vigorous. But Corning had a cautious cast to his eye, while Vanderbilt had more than a touch of arrogance. Corning was a prudent man and, despite his widespread interests, had a rather limited view of his empire. He aspired to domination within it, but was prepared to concede other territories to rival chiefs. For example, he wanted to take northern Ohio and leave the southern part of the state to the Pennsylvania, if Thomson would only agree—which he would not. Vanderbilt was a bolder man, more imaginative, and he could be ruthless where Corning was subtle. He was capable of abandoning years of successful efforts because projects no longer interested him, or when more challenging and rewarding opportunities presented themselves. Corning had a solid core of belief and philosophy; Vanderbilt was ever ready to adapt to the times. He lacked a sense of limitations, and this was always present in Corning. Typically, Vanderbilt considered his sometime rival a gentleman, whereas Corning believed the Commodore played fast and loose with the Central once he took command. "I think Comdr Vanderbilt has watered the New York Central Rail Road stock a little more than it would bear in my judgement," he told one of his brokers, and he did not change this view, holding it until his death in 1872.*

Vanderbilt had purchased shares in the Hudson River in the early summer of 1863. At the time he was perhaps the wealthiest man in the nation, the most respected speculator on Wall Street. Although known as a ruthless man who had no mercy for those who opposed him, Vanderbilt generally played by the rules, entering the gutter only after his opponents did so first. When two of his associates in a steamship venture betrayed his confidence, Vanderbilt sent them a short note. "You have undertaken to cheat me. I won't sue you, for the law is too slow. I'll ruin you." So he did, in a matter of weeks.

Vanderbilt's most spectacular activities took place on Wall Street, where he made and lost several fortunes, often while matching wits and purchased politicians with such scoundrels as Jim Fisk, Daniel Drew, and Jay Gould. Drew controlled the Erie, but was more interested in manipulating its securities than in making it run; in 1865 the Erie was known as "two streaks of

---

Ibid. p. 186.

rust." Gould's railroad career had not yet begun, and Fisk was never more than a gaudy speculator. But Vanderbilt was—in addition to his speculative activities—a constructive businessman. Starting with a single boat, he became one of the masters of the Hudson River, often clashing with Drew, who ran his own fleet. Then he purchased sailing vessels for the transoceanic trade, and when steamships were perfected he sold his clippers and within a few years owned the largest fleet of paddlewheelers.

During the 1849 gold rush Vanderbilt moved more men to the California fields than any other individual or company, and he nearly succeeded in organizing a company to dig a canal across the Isthmus of Panama. By the 1850s he was considered one of the half-dozen or so most important businessmen, and certainly the most enterprising. Had Vanderbilt retired around 1859, when he was sixty-five, he would be remembered today as a master of water transportation, for most of his business activities had been connected in one way or another with rivers and oceans. But at that point he began to dispose of his previous interests and turn to railroads, with hardly more of a thought given than when he sold the clippers and went to steamships.

The New York and Harlem, a 131-mile-long operation that went from Manhattan to Chatham Four Corners, was the first of the "Vanderbilt railroads." It was not a particularly promising line, for there was little business in its territory, which was several miles to the east of the Hudson. Chatham Four Corners was a railroad town; there the Harlem joined with the Albany and West Stockbridge, which entered East Albany, some forty miles to the north. The farmers along the route preferred to use the river to take themselves and their goods to market, just as others avoided turnpikes to use shunpikes. Like Corning and his colleagues at the New York Central, they did not believe a railroad could compete with the river. Still, the line seemed an interesting speculative vehicle, and Vanderbilt purchased some shares in the early 1850s. Then he took command, bribed members of the New York Common Council to grant the Harlem a franchise within the city, and saw the stock rise sharply. Vanderbilt sold and bought, and then repeated the operation, making small fortunes each time. The New York and Harlem was his plaything, but it also enabled him to learn the ways of Wall Street and the nature of railroading. Vanderbilt became vice-president of the line—leaving the day-to-day operations to subordinates—and soon after began dealing in other railroads and their securities.

There was nothing extraordinary about his methods of operation, except that they were bolder and larger in scope than pre-war practices. Vanderbilt would begin with a few purchases, then take a leadership role at the railroad, and next use his position to manipulate the securities. Most of the money he made from railroads came through stock speculation, not operations. But while engaged in this, Vanderbilt would also revamp the system, improve rolling stock, and in general bring to bear upon the corporation the powers of a fine business intellect. Then and later, the public saw and concentrated upon the speculator; railroaders appreciated the businessman, but their view hardly became the accepted one.

Although he took interests in many railroads after the New York and Harlem, he was occupied with three other New York lines for the rest of his life. Vanderbilt's work at the Erie was perhaps his most famous—or notorious—speculation. Daniel Drew had approached him for loans as early as 1854, and these were granted, at high rates and with iron-clad assurances. He knew Drew from the days when they ran ships, and didn't trust him as a partner. Twelve years later, Vanderbilt purchased some Erie shares, and for a while seemed intent on taking control of the railroad and using it as a major part of an eastern transportation complex. But Drew foiled him, and in the process Vanderbilt lost several million dollars. This was the first round in what came to be known as the "Erie Wars." On the one side were Vanderbilt and his lieutenants; on the other were Drew, Fisk, and Gould. Each bribed judges and politicians, and won rounds and points. In the end Drew wearied of the struggle and signed a separate peace with the Commodore, but control of the railroad went to Gould and Fisk.

While speculating in Erie, Vanderbilt obtained control of a second, smaller enterprise, the Hudson River Railroad. This 144-mile-long road was organized by New York City merchants in 1846 who hoped to challenge the river boats with a fast rail line that ran along the east shore. It was a financial failure, in large part due to inexperienced, part-time management and the high costs of construction. Still, the Hudson did have potential. Its track ran into East Albany, and might easily be joined with the New York Central by means of a bridge. If this were done, there would be a unitary railroad line from Manhattan to Buffalo, and, through connections with other railroads, to Chicago and beyond. Vanderbilt saw this, and in 1864 purchased control of the Hudson and began working toward this kind of connection, in which case his stock would be worth many times its original price. So he improved the tracks and rolling stock of the Hudson and the New York and Harlem, and began to woo the Central.

Vanderbilt had purchased a few shares of Central stock in 1863, and had tried, unsuccessfully, to obtain a board seat. Corning understood what was about to happen, and did all he could to block the Commodore. Despite his railroad operations, he had always preferred waterways to land transport, and could not understand why Vanderbilt had made his switch.* The Central was better than the Erie Canal, said Corning, because it was more economical. But by the same token, the Hudson River was a better passageway than either of the Vanderbilt lines. During Corning's regime, cargo would be unloaded at the Albany docks, put on boats, and taken downstream at low cost. In deep winter, when the river was ice clogged, Corning relented and shipped via the Hudson and the New York and Harlem. Thus, the Vanderbilt lines might be busy and prosperous for three months a year, while during the rest of the time their facilities were underutilized.

For several years Thomas Olcutt, an Albany merchant, had attempted to oust Corning from the presidency. Olcutt had cooperated with Richmond on other ventures, and he tried to enlist his support at the Central. The alliance was rejected, but at the same time Richmond chafed under Corning's cautious leadership and came to think the old man had selected Pruyn over him as a successor. Although a Lake Erie shipowner, Richmond believed in an all-rail enterprise from Buffalo to New York, and had urged Corning to make his peace with Vanderbilt.

Olcutt challenged Corning once again in 1864, and this time it appeared he had Vanderbilt's tacit support. Troubled, weary, and eager to avoid a conflict, Corning met with the Commodore and worked out a compromise. He would step down but remain on the board, and Richmond would become the new president. Working with Vanderbilt, Richmond would obtain board approval for a trans-Hudson bridge at Albany, a direct connection between the Central and the Hudson. As though to seal the agreement, Richmond purchased shares in the Hudson and was given a seat on its board.

He did all that was expected. The bridge was erected and the

---

*In 1883 Vanderbilt had taken a ride on the Camden and Amboy. An accident occurred, and his ribs were fractured, his knees torn, and one of his lungs pierced. Vanderbilt vowed never again to ride a railroad, and for many years did keep the pledge. Corning and others knew of this, and so the interest in railroads, which appeared so late in life, was a surprise. W.A. Croffut, *The Vanderbilts* (New York, 1886), p. 5.

Central's track improved in anticipation of the heavier traffic once the linkage was made. Then Daniel Drew entered the picture. He controlled the People's Line, a major river carrier, which would lose business once the railroads were united. Drew bribed several Albany legislators to vote against a cooperative arrangement, and in other ways hold it up for as long as possible—or until Drew could figure out what to do next. At the same time, Richmond was caught up in the machinations of national politics and had to be away from his office a good deal of the time. Still, his lieutenants met regularly with Vanderbilt's men, and together they worked out a merger agreement somewhat favorable to the Hudson, which, if it went through, would make the Commodore another fortune and give him a major say in the Central's future. It appeared certain the union would go through sometime in the summer of 1866. Even Drew was baffled, unable to find ways to prevent it.

But Richmond died in office, and acting president Richard Blachford lacked the authority to complete the transaction. For a while there was confusion. William H. Vanderbilt, the Commodore's son, did all he could to bring the parties together, but the weakness on the Central's side made action impossible. It was then that a new force entered the arena. William Fargo, a former Central officer and now a leader in freight forwarding—one of the founders of Wells, Fargo—had been purchasing Central shares. So had LeGrand Lockwood and Henry Keep, two prominent Wall Street operators. Keep—known as Henry the Silent—was one of the most adept pool managers in the history of the financial district, skilled at running stocks up and down and doing so secretly. Wall Streeters claimed he and the others had plans to manipulate Central's stock and ignore the railroad itself. Keep knew little about transportation, and Fargo wasn't interested in taking a personal role in the line's affairs. Within a few years, so it appeared, the company would replace the Erie as "the Scarlet Lady of Wall Street." Had their plans transpired, New York might have fallen behind in the drive for western markets. Other carriers would have divided the traffic between them, and given their relative positions, the Pennsylvania would have had the largest share of the business. In this way, Philadelphia would have undergone a renaissance, and once more would have challenged New York for commercial supremacy.

For once, Henry the Silent couldn't keep from gloating. Years before, Vanderbilt had prevented the Central from leasing a railroad in which he had an interest, and this had cost him several hundreds of thousands of dollars. Now he would have his revenge. He ran into Vanderbilt in late December and told him as much. "We can live without the Hudson River Railroad; we don't want the Hudson River Railroad."

Central's stock was close to its high that month, as the Keep group planned its first move. The new leadership would sell the stock short and then announce termination of the Vanderbilt deal; there would be no merger between the Central and the Hudson. Then Central's stock would decline, and they would have made their first killing.

Vanderbilt had anticipated this. Shortly before the election he had sold 60,000 Central shares, telling reporters he didn't want an interest in property "owned by such men." Then he prepared his *coup*, to take place before the newly elected managers had fully organized their own.

The weather was cold that December, and worse in January. The Hudson was frozen from mid-Manhattan to Albany. As had been the practice in the past, the Central prepared to transfer operations along the Albany-New York line from steamships to railroads. This was Vanderbilt's moment. On January 15 he announced that the Hudson River Railroad would no longer carry transfer passengers and freight. As though to underline the situation, a newspaper advertisement concluded: "By the above notice passengers will observe that the ERIE RAILWAY is the only route by which they can reach NEW YORK from Buffalo and without CHANGE of coaches or RECHECKING of baggage." At the same time, the New York and Harlem put out a similar announcement. In effect, Vanderbilt had strangled the Central; it no longer offered entrance to New York. Keep tried to construct an alternate route by using the Boston and Albany, the Stockbridge, the Housatonic, and the New Haven, but it was a roundabout passage and didn't work. Central's stock collapsed, and before Fargo and Keep had completed their selling operation; they lost heavily. On his part, Vanderbilt sold short, and so did quite well. There was talk of a legislative investigation and state action to open the line, for passengers and cargo were piling up in Albany, with no relief in sight—even the weather turned colder, and the ice took on the appearance of permanence.

This intolerable situation lasted less than three days, during which time Vanderbilt was a heavy purchaser of the depressed stock. Dissident stockholders pressured management to bow to his will, and so it did. When a new, favorable agreement was concluded and traffic once more rolled via the Albany connection, the stock shot up; Vanderbilt had a second bonanza. In addition, he had the satisfaction of seeing his old antagonist, Daniel Drew, close to despair, for it was clear that the days of river traffic were coming to an end.

This time, Vanderbilt held his shares, and even purchased additional bundles. Clearly the Keep-Fargo group had been discredited and would shortly be ousted. Their performance had been poor. There was a rate war that summer between the Central, the Erie, and the Pennsylvania, which was won by the Pennsylvania, primarily because it had better and more efficient management and rolling stock. The Central was declining; its dividend was endangered; and the stockholders knew it.

They took action in early November 1867. Forming a committee whose members owned some $13 million in stock (out of the $28 million of capitalization), they petitioned Vanderbilt to accept the presidency, which would be offered him at the December stockholders' meeting. He agreed to do so, and was elected with ease. Almost all of the old group was deposed, to be replaced by Vanderbilt men, many of whom were relatives. William became the new vice-president, and Horace Clark, who had married his sister Marie, was named to the board. Brother-in-law William Kissam was another member, along with several Vanderbilt brokers. Finally, executives from other lines took places in the organization. One of these was James Joy, president of the Michigan Central. In January 1877 there was talk that William planned a merger between the two lines. As for the Commodore, he was an old man, and it seemed he wanted to erect a major railroad within New York with feeders to the north and west as his final accomplishment.

The Vanderbilt strategy was simple enough; in some ways it appeared a combination of the management techniques perfected by Thomson, the coordination of interests as practiced by Corning, and the stock speculation of Drew and Gould. Of course, there were differences, special Vanderbilt twists. Under his leadership the Central would become a family corporation, with William responsible for most of the day-to-day business. William had had differences with his father in the past, but by 1867 the two men had come to respect one another's abilities and opinions. The Commodore thought in terms of a three-way merger between the Central, the Hudson River, and the New York and Harlem; soon after, he hoped to bring in the Erie too, but he failed there. He was willing to spend money on the railroads and took an interest in their operations, but his real arena was Wall Street, and he knew it.

William was the true railroader—the Central's answer to J. Edgar Thomson. Together with Clark and another brother-in-law, Daniel Torrance (the husband of Sophia Vanderbilt), William had hopes of achieving a New York-Chicago network, one that could challenge the Pennsylvania and win. Feeder lines would be obtained through stock purchases, outright ownership, or the development of a community of interests. The Commodore would take care of the bold strokes—the stock raids, the wars—while William would harmonize the lines and make certain they could match or better anything done by the Pennsylvania. The father would manipulate the stock, water it, and take care of those legislators who wished to investigate the business or pass legislation to curb the railroads. William, Torrance, and Clark were charged with keeping the railroad profitable so as to support a generous dividend policy, and creating the good news the elder Vanderbilt required for his manipulations. The team worked together smoothly, but while he was alive, the Commodore held center stage, and non-railroaders wondered what might occur when he died. Was such a man replaceable? Were his heirs up to the tasks of managing his varied interests? Within the industry, however, there was no doubt that William was a key member of the family, at least insofar as railroad operations were concerned, and that he was the true master of the Central from the time of the Keep-Fargo ouster until his death.

The Commodore engineered the railroad's first important merger, with the Hudson River. Under the terms of the 1869 agreement, shareholders in each line were to turn in their old certificates and receive new ones, on a one-to-one basis. In addition, they would get a bonus. The Central's shareholders were paid a 27 percent dividend, and the Hudson River's 75 percent, in scrip exchangeable for stock. As a result of this gigantic watering operation, the New York Central and Hudson River Railroad was capitalized at $45 million, while the 8 percent dividend received by the old Central shareholders was to be maintained. Then, as though to signify to New Yorkers that their line would be the greatest in the nation, Vanderbilt planned and soon after constructed a magnificent new terminal at Fourth Avenue and Forty-second Street, which he called the Grand Central Depot.

The new depot was a symbol; William was more interested in

the reality of railroad power, and this meant a unified line from New York to Chicago. The community of interests Erastus Corning had arranged with the Lake Shore and the Michigan Central had broken down, and William meant to renew it. The Commodore rejected the notion. "If we take hold of roads running all the way to Chicago," he told William in early 1869, "we might as well go on to San Francisco, or even to China." Yet the first transcontinental was almost completed, and William saw no reason why the Vanderbilt interests could not eventually reach to the West Coast. The Commodore relented and offered to come to terms with the Michigan Central—its president, James Joy, was still on the New York Central's board and might be interested in some kind of merger. William wasn't satisfied. What good was having the Michigan Central without the newly created Lake Shore and Michigan Southern, the link between the two lines?

But there was a problem. President E.B. Phillips was a figurehead; the power at the Lake Shore and Michigan Southern was to be found on Wall Street; the line was controlled by LeGrand Lockwood, while Henry Keep was an important stockholder. Neither man was in a mood to cooperate with the Vanderbilts after their defeat only two years earlier, and besides, both were more interested in manipulating its stock than in making a one-shot profit. Still, the Commodore did purchase a few shares—perhaps to please William, or more likely in order to deal his old foes another blow. He did not have long to wait. In September Wall Street was shaken by the gold corner panic, and Lockwood was almost wiped out. Forced to the wall, he offered the railroad at a bargain price. Borrowing $10 million from the British banking house of Baring Brothers, Vanderbilt purchased the Lake Shore and Michigan Southern, placed son-in-law Horace Clark in the presidency, and so gave William what he had wanted.

William next urged a merger with the Michigan Central, and Joy and his backers were willing to make the deal, but at a price the Commodore thought excessive. Once again the Vanderbilts entered the market and began accumulating shares. Then, in 1873, Wall Street was hit by yet another panic, and the price of railroad issues fell sharply. The old man stepped in and purchased additional shares, not enough to take control, but sufficient to give him a major voice in the road's management. Five years later, in 1878, the Michigan Central was added to the Vanderbilt fold. The Chicago connection was completed.

The Commodore didn't live to see this; he died the previous

year, and William completed the task. The Vanderbilt estate was approximately $105 million—the largest in the nation to that time. Each of the Vanderbilt children received a half million in securities while the Commodore's second wife was taken care of with an annuity and the family home. William got the bulk of the estate, and with it leadership of the family.

William was fifty-two years old at the time. Until the age of thirty-six, he had managed the family farm in Staten Island, but for the next sixteen years was immersed in railroad management. Every bit as bold as his father but without the older man's flare for speculation and the dramatic, William considered himself a professional railroader. He would dedicate the remainder of his business career to the Central and related enterprises; William would not speculate on Wall Street. But even then, he lacked the time and energy to take personal charge of all the constituent lines. Increasingly, William Vanderbilt turned to professional managers for assistance, either promoting them from the ranks or hiring them away from other lines.

The Vanderbilt managers had less autonomy than those who worked for the Pennsylvania. This was to be expected, for the Vanderbilts united ownership and management in the same person, while the functions were separated on most lines. Still, the age of the tycoon-speculator had ended insofar as the eastern railroads were concerned, even though it would continue beyond the Mississippi until the end of the century and after. Revolutions are made by romantic and daring rebels who, if successful, are succeeded by bureaucrats. With the Commodore's passing, the Central's bureaucratic age began.

The Commodore had been accused of running the Central as though it were his private line. This was so, but he might have been forgiven this, since he did own 87 percent of the common. All of it went to William, who, despite his reputation for insensitivity, was concerned about such criticism and, in addition, wanted to diversify the family's holdings in case something happened to harm the Central.* In 1879 he called at the offices of

---

*In 1882 William Vanderbilt was supposed to have uttered that famous sentence, "The public be damned." He later denied it, but in any case the statement has often been misunderstood. The following, also from that period, is more indicative of his sentiments. "What does the public care for the railroads except to get as much out of them for as small a consideration as possible? I don't take stock in this working for anybody's good but our own, because we are not. When we make a move, we do it because it is in our interest to do so, not because we expect to do somebody else good. Of course, we like to do everything possible for the benefit of humanity in general, but when we do, we first see that we are benefiting ourselves. Railroads are not run on sentiment, but on business principles. . . ." Wayne Andrews, *The Vanderbilt Legend* (New York, 1941), p. 194.

Drexel, Morgan and Company, and asked its assistance in selling a block of 250,000 of his 400,000 shares on the open market in such a way as not to spark a panic or depress the stock. Vanderbilt negotiated with J.P. Morgan, then forty-two years old and still considered a junior at the firm. Morgan agreed to take the stock, which he would sell to Europeans, but he insisted upon conditions in addition to a commission in excess of $1 million. Vanderbilt would have to guarantee that the Central's dividend would remain at 8 percent for at least five years, and that Morgan or one of his men would be granted a seat on the board. Vanderbilt accepted, and the following year Morgan sold the stock as promised. From that point on he was one of the key figures in American railroading, and not only at the Central. But the pattern set forth in 1879 would be followed afterward, and was another sign that a new order had come into being in American business—the age of the industrial capitalist was being superseded, slowly, by that of the finance capitalist. Increasingly the Central would become a Morgan line, not one of Vanderbilt's jewels.

William spent his first years as head of the family and empire in completing this diversification program, revamping operations, and restructuring his holdings. Then, with Morgan's help and support, he embarked upon a dramatic and rapid expansion effort. It was motivated by business considerations, not those of speculation, as might have been the case had the Commodore been alive. In part it was due to Vanderbilt's desire to round out his system, and Morgan's to create a new form of community of interests. In addition, Vanderbilt sought markets; he recognized that steel and petroleum firms would require transportation, and he thrust his lines deep into their territories. In the past, railroads had helped create industries and carry their goods; now they existed to serve big manufacturing. Vanderbilt did not shrink from combat with rivals when the need arose, but he was willing to cooperate with them if this suited his ends. This need to cooperate clashed with the natural tendency to compete, and bedeviled him and other railroaders of the time.

The expansion began in early 1882, when William leased the bankrupt Canada Southern, which he merged into the Michigan Central. Then he thrust southward and, invading the Pennsylvania's territory, took the Pittsburgh and Lake Erie. Several minor takeovers followed, and to cap the year Vanderbilt acquired the New York, Chicago and St. Louis—the Nickel Plate. At the time the move was hailed as a stroke of genius, for this gave the Central access to St. Louis. But in the East the

Nickel Plate's lines ran parallel to those of the Lake Shore and Michigan Southern. Was there enough business for two Vanderbilt lines in the same area? Obviously Vanderbilt thought so at the time, but later on it was clear that the eastern lines were beginning to feel the impact of overbuilding, and this merger was one of the first signs of it. Furthermore, the challenge to the Pennsylvania would have repercussions as that company responded by launching a counterinvasion of Central territory. The railroad wars were on, even as William completed the last of his great 1882 mergers and acquisitions.

As for the area to the west of Chicago, Vanderbilt was on the Union Pacific's board, but that line was too large for him to court, and in any case there were other suitors. Still, he did flirt with the idea, but did not go beyond that. For a while Vanderbilt considered a role at the Chicago, Burlington and Quincy, but did not press the point there. On other occasions he had the opportunity to purchase shares and even acquire smaller western lines, but he always held back. The East was enough trouble without adding the West to the mix. By the early 1880s, Vanderbilt was not only involved in price competition with other railroaders but was striving to obtain new eastern territories while fighting off those who had invaded Central preserves. He negotiated with men of the stripe of Andrew Carnegie and John D. Rockefeller, who demanded special treatment in return for using Vanderbilt's railroad. Otherwise, they would shift their business to his rivals, and if that didn't work, go so far as to construct their own lines. The field was becoming crowded—five major lines ran into Chicago, for example—and such jostling was inevitable.

An Erastus Corning in his time might dominate a section of the state, or several states. Commodore Vanderbilt strode through Wall Street like a lion, and wagered millions on a turn of the market. It was different in the 1880s, however, when big business was entering its adolescence, not still in its infancy. The tasks presented to management were more complex, more subtle, and required a new kind of leadership.

William Vanderbilt recognized this, and, a prudent man, he knew his limitations. In 1883, at the age of sixty-two, he announced his resignation from the Central's presidency, as well as those of other lines in the system; he retained directorships, however, and would remain involved in long-term planning. Thus, the son became the father. And like the Commodore, William had an heir, Cornelius II, who took the chairmanship of the New York and Michigan Centrals. Another son, William K., was to be in charge of the Lake Shore and Michigan Southern. Both were amiable men, as were most of the other Vanderbilt heirs, but none had the Commodore's flair or their father's intelligence and abilities. William knew this, and so he selected James Rutter, who had been general traffic manager at the New York Central since 1877, as its new president and chief operating officer. In this way, the development of bureaucratic management progressed.

William Vanderbilt spent much of his time in the next two years dabbling in the arts, taking care of his horses, and making charitable donations. He suffered a stroke in 1885 which left him partially paralyzed—the doctors claimed it had been caused by overwork and great exertions while at the Central—and he retired completely from business. Then Rutter died suddenly, and William was obliged to seek another leader, for Cornelius II was still not up to the job. The next president would be Chauncey M. Depew, a Central lawyer who lacked practical experience in railroad management, but who had a reputation as a master lobbyist, one who knew his way around Washington. The railroads needed friends in Washington, and Depew's task would be to make certain the Central's interests were safeguarded. Meanwhile, technical experts would take care that the great complex begun by the Commodore and expanded upon by his son would run smoothly.

William Vanderbilt also made certain he would be the last in the line of great unitary family figures. He died in December, and in his will bequeathed a good deal of money to charities, and took care of his children handsomely. The Commodore had left an estate worth in the neighborhood of $105 million, most of it going to William. The son's estate was over $200 million—in eight years he had more than doubled his inheritance. Cornelius II would receive $67 million and William K., $65 million. But neither would inherit the crown; that was divided among the technicians, lawyers, and bureaucrats who now ran the Central and its empire.

In the late 1860s, as the Vanderbilts took command at the Central and attempted to organize a major national road. J. Edgar Thomson was putting his finishing touches on the Pennsylvania, by far the nation's leading corporation. Over the years he had constructed and managed the longest, most modern, and most efficient system in the nation. Corning, Drew, and others of the pre-Civil War era had been no match for him in any area of railroading. When it suited his purposes, Thomson might cooperate with them and even accept arrangements whereby the Pennsylvania would share ownership and operation of small feeder lines. He had accepted the concept of a community of interests—Corning's pet idea, and his hope for a quiet regime at the Central—and had submitted to the St. Nicholas Agreement. But Thomson insisted that the Pennsylvania be permitted a free hand, that its power not be checked. He had no intention of erecting a price umbrella to protect less efficient lines. Thomson did not shrink from rate wars, and when these erupted in the late 1850s the Pennsylvania usually triumphed due to its superior finances and efficient operations.*

Nor would Thomson respect the territorial interests of others. Even while completing his western organization, he struck out in the direction of New York and Baltimore. In the late 1860s the Pennsylvania acquired several small New Jersey railroads, which Thomson organized into the United New Jersey. This system contained one line that ran from Philadelphia to Jersey City—across the river from Manhattan. Thomson then investigated the means of acquiring a base in New York, and in 1871 was considering means of entering Manhattan and seeking a proper site for a depot there. While so doing, Thomson also completed a leg of his drive southward. Ever since 1861 the Pennsylvania had controlled the Northern Central, a short line between Philadelphia and Baltimore. It was used heavily during the Civil War, and in light of the emergency, the B&O did not retaliate. But a contest between the two lines did break out after Appomattox, which Thomson won. He organized the Baltimore and Potomac in 1871, and the following year it entered Washington, a clear invasion of B&O territory, yet another sign of Thomson's ambitions and abilities.

What was his ultimate goal?—or better still, did he have one?

*In the 1858 annual report, the board said: "It has been the policy of your Board to seek an increase of traffic for the road by securing freights destined to every part of the world, in all cases where they believed they could add to the profits of the shareholders, while they have with equal care sought to protect the manufacturing and commercial interests of Philadelphia, whose means have been so liberally embarked in the enterprise, by such differences in her favor in the rates of freight, as are due to the shorter distance it is to be transported to and from the West. More than this could scarcely be asked of this company, and more, if demanded, would not be permitted by the competing lines of transportation between the East and West. During the past year the New York Central Railroad, in an unreasonable (if sincere) effort to bring the rates to and from New York to the same level with those of Philadelphia and Baltimore, sacrificed hundreds of thousands of dollars to herself and rivals, without attaining her object, beyond temporarily destroying the uniformity of these differences in rates." Thus, the Pennsylvania insisted upon the rate differential, and won its point. Burgess and Kennedy, *Pennsylvania Railroad*, p. 234.

Thomson rarely spoke of such matters, but instead went about adding to his properties every year, always consolidating, restructuring, and expanding. By 1872 the Pennsylvania system ran along the east coast from Jersey City to Washington, as far west as St. Louis, into New York State at Canandaigua, while a line reached Mackinaw City in Michigan's upper peninsula. While William Vanderbilt was busily convincing his father to purchase the Michigan Central and enter Chicago in style, Thomson was eying the Far West and the South. A transcontinental alone would not slake his ambitions. Thomson wanted the Pennsylvania to reach into every corner of the nation, to dominate the rail transportation of more than half a continent. Not even at the height of his power in the early 1880s would William Vanderbilt conceive of such an idea as Thomson appeared to entertain in 1872.

Nothing came of it. For several years a major group of stockholders, centered in Philadelphia, had chafed at what they considered Thomson's arbitrary rule. They had wanted a line from Pittsburgh to Philadelphia, with appropriate feeders; Thomson had erected a huge trans-Pittsburgh empire—twice as large as the original Pennsylvania—and had done so without consulting them. Nor had they been considered when Thomson opened his lines to New York and Washington. By 1872, it appeared Thomson had taken over every aspect of the railroad, and that they had surrendered all in return for generous and regular dividends.

This situation might have continued for several decades were it not for the panic of 1873, the worst financial and economic crash the nation had undergone up to that time. Dozens of railroads went under, and the strongest were battered on Wall Street and suffered financial losses. But the Pennsylvania held firm, and even showed a profit increase that year. Still, Thomson was concerned regarding the future, and even before the panic struck declared the semiannual dividend of 5 percent in scrip rather than cash. It was not an unusual step; Thomson had done the same in 1857, and the scrip did carry an interest rate of 6 percent and was redeemable in cash within fifteen months. Although most stockholders appeared fairly content with the arrangement, others were angered, and they blamed Thomson for their distress. Joining with the dissidents, they demanded an investigation of the system and a full accounting of its administration. Their resolutions passed at the December meeting, and in March 1874 a stockholders' investigating committee was created, which issued a full report in mid-September.

The report indicated what all had known—the Pennsylvania was a giant. It was almost 6,000 miles long, with 7.8 percent of the total railroad mileage in the nation, while its capital, close to $400 million, represented some 13 percent of the entire sum invested in railroads. At a time when most lines watered their stock, Thomson had done the opposite; the Pennsylvania common stock was, if anything, underpriced. Nor did the report contain criticisms of past expansionary efforts, which had made all of this possible. However, the committee did oppose a continuation of these policies. "The trade centers in the West reached by your systems of railway are surely enough, and the responsibilities assumed sufficiently great, to satisfy the most ambitious. You can now stop with safety. . . ."

Although the report did not say as much, the committee appeared to have opposed the proposed entry into New York, as well as the expansion south of Washington and west of St. Louis. The Pennsylvania should refrain from interests in western and southern lines—recalling the recent bankruptcies, the committee feared these were not sufficiently conservative. Rather, management should concentrate upon a liberal dividend policy; a demand was made for quarterly rather than semiannual dividends, and in cash, not scrip. Thomson was not mentioned by name, but the report indicated that the job was too big for a single man, and that the president would have to consult more frequently with the board in the future. The committee resolved that "the stockholders, as the source of all authority, reserve to themselves the whole legislative power of the corporation. . . ."

Much of this had little real meaning. The size and nature of the Pennsylvania was such that strong presidential leadership was required. The boards consisted of part-time administrators, most of whom lacked the interest and often the intelligence to comprehend what was happening, or, if they had both, could not unite on a single program. Whether they wanted to or not, railroad presidents would have to act on their own; there was no real alternative. Nor could the stockholders really act as a legislative body, for most didn't bother to attend annual meetings, where in any case they would have been outvoted by larger owners of securities. (In 1871, there were 669,000 shares outstanding, and 7,284 stockholders; ten years later there were 1,561,000 shares and over 10,000 stockholders, more than one in five of whom lived overseas.) The committee was probably sincere in its suggestions, but the most important insofar as their immediate interests were concerned regarded dividends, not political control. The stockholders decided that in order to obtain a safe, regular, high return on their investments, the railroad should retrench and forego risks. Given the economic and financial atmosphere of the time, this was to have been expected.

Thomson watched the formation of the committee with misgivings. He knew that his position had been weakened, but at the same time was reasonably certain he could overcome the opposition. But Thomson was a sick man, and on May 27, at the age of sixty-six, he died.

The board had to select a new president while understanding that Thomson's passing had strengthened the hand of the committee. The new man would have to conciliate, to smooth over differences, and be as much a politician as a railroader. Even then the board knew what the committee's recommendations would contain, and understood that the next president would have to be willing to consider them and carry many of them out. Thomson had been an expansionist builder; his successor would have to be a man of retrenchment and an administrator.

Several candidates were considered—all within the company—but from the first there was little doubt that Senior Vice-President Thomas Scott would get the job. Fifty years old at the time, Scott was hired by the Pennsylvania in 1850, and for a while served as station agent. Within two years he was assistant superintendent of the western division, and in 1858 general superintendent of the entire line and one of the president's closest allies.

Unlike Thomson, Scott was a gregarious man, tall and handsome, with a fine instinct for the values of the Philadelphia aristocrats and an ability to soothe their fears and anxieties. Whenever Thomson had to approach the group for approval, he would send Scott, who performed the tasks required admirably. Scott was welcomed in society, something Thomson never attained.

Scott entered the army early in the war, as a colonel in charge of the entire national transportation system. There he made invaluable political contacts, and for a while considered leaving railroads for politics. He also provided advice to the managers of the new transcontinentals—always reporting back to Thomson, who wanted the Pennsylvania to have an interest in the new lines. Scott returned to the Pennsylvania after the war, while at the same time dabbling in other railroads. Among other things, he served as leader of the Union Pacific, and was involved in the Texas and Pacific, a line that collapsed and left several ruined fortunes.* Even though he was not responsible for this failure, some Philadelphians considered Scott a trifle racy, but he was able to charm the aristocrats, and was forgiven these "indiscretions."

An able railroader, Scott was an even better politician. He saw how the situation was developing and was prepared to move with the drift. In the past he had agreed with Thomson's view that the Pennsylvania had a continental destiny, perhaps through a merger with the Union Pacific. The committee knew this. Because of it, some members mentioned other candidates for the top post. But Scott was able to reassure enough of them that he could be trusted to carry out their will. He would cut back on previous commitments, sell off some operations and consolidate others, contract the railroad's debt, and convince the stockholders their wishes would be respected. Initially the committee had insisted upon a transfer of power from the president to the board. Scott delayed action, charmed the leaders, and persuaded them that this was not necessary—that despite his early relationship with Thomson he was now one of them. Then, in December, he announced that the dividend that year would total 10 percent, double that of 1873. In the annual report he wrote, ". . . your Board have concluded to adopt as a general policy that no further extension of lines should be made or obligations be assumed by your Company, either by lease or otherwise, except to complete the several small branches and extensions now in progress in Pennsylvania and New Jersey. The best energies of your Board and its officers will hereafter be devoted to the development of the resources of the lines now controlled."

With this, attempts at reform ended, and Scott ruled supreme. The old ways as practiced by Thomson would continue; the president would have a free hand. But the depression lasted longer than most had anticipated, and the dividend had to be cut—to 8 percent in 1875 and 1876, then to 3.5 percent the following year, and 2 in 1878, the bottom of the depression, when Pennsylvania common stock fell to below $30 a share. Yet even then Scott had little trouble with the shareholders, or, to be more precise, they made no serious objection to his policies. Other lines had declared no dividend that year, and Scott had so charmed the shareholders that even this would be accepted. He

---

*For a survey of the potential Pennsylvania-Union Pacific connection, which could have created a true transcontinental in the early 1870s, see Julius Grodinsky, *Transcontinental Railway Strategy, 1869-1893* (Philadelphia, 1962), pp. 15-25ff.

had most of the powers practiced by Thomson, with only one proviso: the Pennsylvania's destiny would be circumscribed; it would not extend west of the Mississippi. And Scott acceded to this, tacitly, as the price of power.

Thus vanished the last great opportunity in almost a century for a true transcontinental, a national railroad system that was rational, well managed, and efficient. In its place would be a conglomeration of lines, some of them huge, many small, each scrapping with the others, making deals with shippers, fighting reformers, working with and against governments, and attempting to win limited victories in an industry and under circumstances where complete success was no longer possible or permissible. Such was the situation in the late 1870s, the age of Thomas Scott and William Vanderbilt. The Pennsylvania chief was prevented from seeking a continental destiny under the terms by which he had assumed power. The Central had tarried too long in completing its eastern system; the Commodore had wanted bargains and he had obtained them, but at a cost of time lost and opportunities that passed him by. William Vanderbilt's flurry of acquisitions in the early 1880s was his last drive to the West. Both lines would stop at Chicago and St. Louis; they would not go on to San Francisco.

At one time or another in the 1870s, either the Pennsylvania or the Central might have made a bid for the Union Pacific, and perhaps it could have been obtained. The antibusiness crusade had not yet begun; there was no Interstate Commerce Commission; probusiness forces ruled in Washington. The capital requirements for such a merger would have been large, but it could have been managed, at least up to 1873, perhaps afterward as well.

By the 1880s, however, the times and the men were no longer in harmony for such an effort to succeed. It might have been otherwise. Had Thomson lived another decade, and had Commodore Vanderbilt lasted a few more years as a vigorous and daring rather than an aging and cautious man, both the Pennsylvania and the Central might have crossed the Mississippi, and then the nation would have seen a struggle for the West, in which the lines would vie with one another to conquer new territories.*

---

*Great railroaders would appear in the West, and by the turn of the century it seemed that two of them, James Hill and E.H. Harriman, might succeed in developing a coast-to-coast line—perhaps a transportation system that encircled the globe. They failed. Because of this, Chicago and St. Louis became major switching points, where passengers and freight had to change cars and systems—just as had been the case in the 1830s, when switches were made at Schenectady between the Erie Canal and the Mohawk and Hudson Railroad.

But it didn't happen in the 1870s, and couldn't in the 1880s. Rather than continuing the drive west, the Pennsylvania and the Central embarked upon a struggle for the East, attempting to win old markets from rivals instead of developing new ones. This was another sign that the age of daring had been succeeded by one of consolidation and organization. For the next two decades the major eastern lines would compete to obtain business from the same source, and in the process would enter into rate wars which made those of the 1850s appear minor scuffles. These destructive contests, which were wasteful and often simply foolish, resulted in new demands for a harmony of interests, though along different lines than those conceived by Erastus Corning, and of a different scope and nature. The efforts engaged the talents of some of the most powerful and capable lawyers, managers, and bankers of the period, while the leading politicians chimed in from the sidelines. They strove to fashion a compromise that would satisfy all interests, and then, as before, two of the leading powers were the Central and the Pennsylvania. A union of these two giants could have resulted in a new harmony in big industry and drastically altered the shape and direction of the nation's economy and politics. And had it occurred then, there would have been no Penn Central collapse in 1970, and the crisis of American capitalism might have been averted.

IV

A Yearning for Security

Thomas Scott was thirty years old in 1853, and already the Pennsylvania Railroad's general superintendent, recognized as a man with excellent prospects. That year he selected a young telegrapher, Andrew Carnegie, to be his private secretary. The two men had developed a strong personal relationship and a mutual respect; Carnegie later said that Scott's encouragement helped him begin his business career, and the two men were always more like brothers than business associates. As Scott rose at the railroad, so did Carnegie, who, in 1860, was named superintendent of the Pittsburgh Division. The following year Scott entered the army to take charge of the nation's wartime transportation. Carnegie also entered federal service and became superintendent of the telegraph system.

But Carnegie had interests other than telegraphs and railroads, as well as a desire to become the master of his own enterprise, make a fortune, and then settle down to a life of contemplation. He helped reorganize a company that made iron bridges, took over a railroad-car axle manufacturer, and then a small foundry, which he brought together in 1864 to form the Union Iron Mills. After the war Carnegie was invited to return to the Pennsylvania, and Scott urged him to do so. He refused, and instead decided to join forces with George Pullman, who was attempting to create a monopoly in the field of railroad sleeping cars. Two years later, with Scott's sponsorship, Carnegie was named to the board of the Union Pacific. In between he took a turn as salesman for his iron firm, and even sold railroad securities to European investors.

These activities dovetailed, and for a while it appeared Carnegie might become a latter-day Erastus Corning. But such generalized activity was difficult in the post-Civil War period, and in the end he decided to concentrate on steel, even while continuing an interest in related areas.

Throughout all of this, Scott and Thomson supported Carnegie, both with their influence and through stock purchases. They were with him in 1873, when, at the bottom of the financial panic that year, Carnegie purchased several small iron firms, united them with those already under his control, and formed Carnegie, McCandless and Company. This was to be his first instrument for national power. Thomson and Scott used their positions to assist him, primarily by giving the new firm contracts for part of the Pennsylvania's business. Carnegie was grateful, and showed it by naming his major new facility the Edgar Thomson Works, and utilizing the Pennsylvania to carry his goods to market.

Thomson and Scott both were dead by 1880. The new Pennsylvania president, George Roberts, knew Carnegie, but the two men were never close. In any case, for several years Carnegie had thought that the Pennsylvania's rates were too high, and he demanded special treatment in the form of large rebates. Others in the Pennsylvania's territory felt the same way, and they joined with him to form and begin work on the Pittsburgh and Erie, which would carry their goods to the lake steamers, and finally use the Erie or the Central to get to the coast. Then Vanderbilt obtained control of the Pittsburgh and Erie as part of his 1882 drive into the Pennsylvania's preserve. He met with Carnegie the following year, and together they planned a new line, which would start at Reading and go on to Pittsburgh, often paralleling the Pennsylvania's tracks. The company, the South Pennsylvania Railroad, was organized soon after, with the Central taking $5 million of its stock and Carnegie and his group subscribing for a like amount. Other western Pennsylvania shippers interested in squeezing the Pennsylvania joined it, the most significant of whom was John D. Rockefeller, who invested $400,000 in the line. And as they organized and planned the invasion, Roberts brought together his managers to plan a retaliatory move.

Ever since the late 1860s railroaders had been aware that the Central's New York operations had little in the way of substantial competition. The Erie was there, to be sure, but it was a decrepit line and clearly on the way down. So several groups of independent capitalists planned rival operations. Those organized during and immediately after the Civil War were either underfinanced, poorly led, or mere speculative vehicles that never amounted to much. The West Shore Hudson, which in 1868 absorbed the Hudson River West Shore, showed some promise, as did the New York, West Shore and Chicago, an ambitious operation that was put together two years later. Several New Jersey companies were formed in the 1870s, but these either didn't get past the surveying stage, or merely constructed a few miles of track before going into receivership. Then, in 1880, a New York investment bank organized the North River Railroad, while another new firm, the New York, West Shore and Buffalo, took over the rights and assets of the New York, West Shore and Chicago. The two lines were really closely interrelated, with the West Shore the operating arm. Furthermore, they were strongly financed by a group of New York bankers and George Pullman, who was angered when Vanderbilt refused to use his cars and purchased those of a competitor instead, and in this way hoped to obtain revenge. The West Shore did construct a line between Jersey City and Newburgh, then went on to Albany and to Syracuse. But there was a financial stringency in 1883, the prelude to a panic the following year, while the Central put on the pressure by cutting rates all along the line. By early January, the West Shore was in serious difficulty, with rumors of imminent collapse spreading through Wall Street. The West Shore entered Albany in early 1884, but by then its bonds were selling for fifty cents on the dollar.

Then they held, as did the quotations for the common stock. Clearly some force had entered the field to accumulate shares. The West Shore declared bankruptcy that spring, but the purchases continued. By June the Street learned who was behind them—the Pennsylvania announced that it controlled the West Shore and would take steps to bring it back to life. Thus Roberts indicated that his response to the South Pennsylvania would be a counterinvasion of the New York Central heartland. At the bottom of a depression, the two lines initiated a rate war. Both were powerful, but the Pennsylvania had greater resources. Had the struggle gone on for a year or so, the Central would have been defeated, but the Pennsylvania would have been so badly crippled that it couldn't have recovered for several years. The Central was forced to cut its dividend in half in early 1884, while the Pennsylvania's had been erratic since the 1873 crisis, and in 1883 was only 4.5 percent. Roberts wanted to avoid a further cut at almost any cost. Both lines had reason to end their contest, but they lacked the means to do so.

Vanderbilt was in Europe at the time, not only on vacation but formally retired from Central management. Chauncey Depew was president, but it was well known that he wouldn't take an important step without first consulting William and obtaining his support. J.P. Morgan, still the firm's banker, was troubled, since the British investors had purchased Central's securities on his word that they were good. Furthermore, he saw no sensible reason to continue a struggle that no one could win. So he went to Europe—ostensibly on a vacation—and there met with Vanderbilt. The two men came home by the same ship that June. On board, Morgan had convinced Vanderbilt of the need for a peace treaty of some sort, as well as an indication that his family still supported the Central and had confidence in its future.

Shortly after arriving home Vanderbilt began purchasing Central common stock—which had fallen below par—as though to signal the nation that he thought it was a good buy—and that some bullish news regarding the company would soon break. Meanwhile, Morgan contacted Roberts and set about organizing peace negotiations. Depew joined him, and while Morgan talked with bankers—usually Philadelphians—the Central's president went to Roberts to convince him of the necessity of an end to their contest. Roberts held fast for a month, but finally the knowledge that a further dividend cut would result from prolonged fighting led him to accept Morgan's intercessions.

In early July 1885 the Pennsylvania president came to New York to conclude an arrangement. At his side was Frank Thomson, J. Edgar's nephew, a vice-president, and the man who in 1897 would succeed Roberts. Together they boarded the Morgan yacht, *Corsair* (Morgan had insisted the final talks be held on ship, perhaps because then Roberts could not leave in a huff). Chauncey Depew was there already, as was Morgan, and shortly thereafter the four men settled down in deck chairs as the yacht sailed up the Hudson.

Morgan opened the discussion by assuring Roberts he was there as a mediator, not as a representative of the New York Central. Roberts understood this, for although all knew of Morgan's interests in the Vanderbilt lines, his ambition to become the national arbiter of railroads was also understood. If he could fashion a satisfactory settlement, the Pennsylvania would be in his debt, and although the line's financing scarcely would move from Philadelphia to New York, Morgan might extract a *quid pro quo* sometime in the future. In addition—although Morgan would not say as much until after the talks were completed—neither he nor the House of Drexel, Morgan would accept a commission for its assistance in effecting the settlement.

The final settlement was both simple and obvious, and contained few surprises. For its part, the Pennsylvania would sell off its interests in the West Shore, and shortly thereafter a separate group, which included Morgan and Depew, would purchase the shares on the open market and then lease the line to the New York Central. Vanderbilt agreed to relinquish his South Pennsylvania shares to the Pennsylvania, which would do with the line what it wanted.* In addition, he promised to withdraw support from the Reading Railroad, which was then competing with the Pennsylvania for the coal-hauling trade.

The *Corsair* Agreement climaxed a decade of conflict and controversy in the East. After the Civil War the major lines cut rates sharply, each hoping to win the business of others at a time when federal shipments had declined and the private sector had not yet picked up the difference. In 1874, Vanderbilt had led in the creation of a pooling agreement which included all of the major northeastern lines except the B&O. The members reasoned that through cooperation they could maintain charges and so survive the depression.

The B&O alone disagreed, and hoped to prosper by increasing the volume of its trade by using its facilities to the fullest. It was a difference in strategy that was well established at the time, and one that would continue into the next century. On this occasion, the B&O challenged the Pennsylvania, a rate war began, and in six months the pool was broken. Another was arranged in early 1877, at a time when it seemed widespread strikes might begin to further complicate an already profitless situation. This time the pool was violated by the Grand Trunk. The Great Strike erupted in June and July—its name indicated the scope—and closed down all the major roads in the East. The National Guard was called out to preserve order, while the railroad executives wondered how best to achieve harmony within the industry. The result was another pool, this one formed in February 1878. Albert Fink, the vice-president of the Louisville and Nashville who had organized a successful southern pool in 1873, was called in to harmonize differences. Following his suggestion, the members agreed to end rebates and retaliate against those who broke the united front. But the temp-

---

*Ironically, the Pennsylvania allowed the South Pennsylvania to fall into ruin, but more than a half century later its road bed was acquired by the state, which used it as the path of the Pennsylvania Turnpike—the road which did so much to destroy the Pennsylvania's passenger traffic. Although its victory was long delayed, the South Penn did carry the day in the end.

tation to cut prices to obtain business was too great—especially since economic conditions were still poor—and this pool collapsed in less than a year.

Other attempts followed, and all failed. In 1881 the Pennsylvania, the B&O, and the Central engaged in a ruinous rate war, which almost destroyed all three, while a similar outburst took place among the leading New England lines. There were cases of sharp price cutting in the Midwest, and a gigantic conflict was brewing in the West. Thus the New York Central-Pennsylvania clash was only one part of a continuing war involving all of the major railroads.

Roberts and Depew understood the situation. It occupied a good deal of their attention and time, in part because it seemed incapable of solution. Men spoke often about the virtues of free enterprise, but in the 1880s they were faced with a condition in which application of the theory might destroy the system, leaving even the victors in no condition to prosper. The heavy investment in equipment demanded continued expansion; not to compete for incremental business seemed foolish, since idle rails and cars were an invitation to bankruptcy. But competition would force prices below the break-even point, and then the struggle would be based upon financial stamina, not efficiency. Men like Carnegie and Rockefeller were in an excellent position to play one line against the other, and obtain favorable treatment from all. For even if the railroad carried Carnegie's steel at half the published rates, the business would still show a profit, since without it the rails and cars would not have been used. Could the lines get together to cooperate in the face of this situation? Perhaps, but the major shippers were wagering they wouldn't. Even if they could, men of the stature, power, and boldness of a Carnegie or a Rockefeller could always threaten to erect their own railroads or pipelines, and they had the resources for the task. In this way, they could cow the established eastern carriers into submission.

The Pennsylvania and the New York Central were among the largest corporations in the nation, and railroading was by far America's greatest industry. But the manufacturers and other major shippers had discovered their weak spot. In the process of constructing lines, equipping them, operating both long and short hauls, passengers and freight, the railroads had acquired large fixed charges, which would have to be serviced before anything was left for the stockholders and capital additions. More than any other industry, railroading was noted for this kind of financial "leverage." Given good times and stable rates, profits could soar. But recessions and rate wars could lead to severe stringencies. On such occasions the lines might have to borrow money for ongoing expenses—even to pay dividends, for without them there would have been serious stockholder rebellions. Sudden rises and falls in the economy could also hinder long-term planning, making it difficult if not impossible for the railroads to project new lines, finance old debts, and prepare for technological improvements. Logic dictated rate increases to cover the costs, the creation of well-stocked sinking funds, and the development of strong lines of communication to well-established banking houses. Competition demanded rate cuts in order to acquire additional business or protect territories that were threatened. The major lines, then, were trapped in a no-win situation, something Adam Smith had barely considered when he wrote *Wealth of Nations* a century before, in a world which knew little of big industry and nothing of giant, highly leveraged enterprises like the Central and the Pennsylvania.

The *Corsair* Agreement was Vanderbilt's last major action in railroading, and marked J.P. Morgan's assumption of center stage. This was a period of transition, in this case with the industrial capitalists in railroading losing power and influence to the finance capitalists. Morgan could offer the lines a steady stream of funds and so bring some order to his clients, and his price would be a say in their affairs. More important, however, was the promise of order his presence implied. Morgan saw little to be gained by the kind of competition that had marked the post-war period, and he meant to end it.

Roberts and Depew, as well as other, lesser leaders of giant corporations, welcomed his intercession, and in the years that followed came to look upon Morgan and his allies as their arbiters. Morgan's services were used by the Chesapeake and Ohio, the Big Four, the Erie, the Reading, and the Southern, among others, where he arranged for refinancings, reorganizations, and mergers. What Morgan attempted to accomplish from outside of the industry, Fink worked to do from within. Although lacking the banker's power, Fink was, after all, a railroader himself, and he empathized with the individual managers. During the next two decades he would demonstrate the benefits of quasi-monopolies and pools before conventions and at smaller private meetings and conferences. Fink hoped the leading managers would overcome their instincts for seeking additional business at the expense of their fellows, and unite to protect the interests of their industry and create a harmonious business atmosphere.

It was a period of organization, of increasing class consciousness, when Marxism still had the virtues of novelty and freshness. Fink warned against communism; in the Great Strike of 1877, the railroaders saw the specter of radicalism arising among the workers, and they called for strong measures to prevent this. But without realizing it, perhaps, Morgan and Fink were advocating their own versions of class organization; they were better illustrations for Marxist dogmas than any of the trade unions of the period. The bankers and group managers continued to preach the old theology of free-enterprise capitalism, complete with open access and competition, but they practiced communities of interests and accords that would eliminate competition.

On Independence Day, 1885, as Morgan, Roberts, Thomson, and Depew ironed out the *Corsair* Agreement, the *Commercial and Financial Chronicle* printed a communication from a retired Erie Railroad executive. "It has always been the fashion in this country to argue that the less government we have the better, and that this constitutes the main advantage of this country over Europe. But there are some things that the Government must do if society is to hold together." It was not an unusual expression; for the past eight years—ever since the Great Strike of 1877—leading businessmen had called for protection against what they deemed the anarchical tendencies of the masses. In the aftermath of the strike another businessman wrote that the government "will wither and die like a girdled tree if the thousands who pay taxes get no protection from the millions who govern," while Scott of the Pennsylvania thought Congress had to "take all necessary measures to secure protection to life and property." Depew, who for most of his life had opposed governmental interference in business affairs, now changed his mind, and later wrote that this had been caused by the Great Strike and the destructive competition that followed. In the late 1870s he called for the creation of a federal commission to help regulate the railroad industry; he was "convinced of their necessity . . . for the protection of both the public and the railroads."* The struggles between the Pennsylvania and the Central reinforced these views, which by the mid-1880s had become a majority sentiment in the industry.

---

*Gabriel Kolko, *Railroads and Regulation, 1877-1916* (Princeton, 1965), pp. 12-15 *passim*.

Others saw the need for federal intervention. Small manufacturers and shippers whose interest had been harmed by rebates and rate discriminations called for strong laws banning the practices, to enable them to compete with the Carnegies and Rockefellers. Antibusiness reformers, who by then had singled out the railroads as their prime targets, thought a federal commission could curb their powers. It was one of those occasions when conflicting interest groups could unite to support a similar solution to differently perceived problems.

Ever since 1877, Albert Fink had headed a body known as the Joint Executive Committee, which consisted of representatives of leading eastern railroads, and whose task it was to bring order to the industry. The committee had little real power to enforce decisions, or even to make them. It was moribund in 1881, and although Fink remained on the job, he knew it could not perform the task. Federal assistance in various forms would be required, said Fink, and he was willing to consider several of the proposals offered by railroad opponents. "I have little faith that any law prohibiting the payment of rebates will be of any use," he told the Committee on Commerce of the House of Representatives in 1882. "Still a law of this kind could do no harm; it would aid me in performing the duties imposed upon me by the associated roads of the Joint Executive Committee." Fink knew, as did others in the industry, that enlightened self-interest, not federal law, was required. Still, the discussions dragged on, and then, in 1877, Congress finally passed the Interstate Commerce Act, which was signed by President Rutherford Hayes—a man nominated by railroad Republicans, supported by the industry, and who had been elected by means of a compromise with Democrats in which the railroads were included. This kind of sponsorship indicated what was expected from the measure.

The new bill forbade rebates, mandated equal charges for equal hauls, and provided for the establishment of the Interstate Commerce Commission, which had the power to enforce decisions. The measure also prohibited pools and in other ways sought to promote competition. But this was only window dressing, which the reformers took seriously, but the railroaders meant to ignore. President Hayes selected conservative men for the commission—some of them railroaders themselves—and the sections of the law pertaining to competition were so vague as to be unworkable. Even the reformers did not believe they would be enforced. The clearest sign of this came shortly after the measure became law, when it was hailed as a step forward by the managements of both the Pennsylvania and the Central. They also applauded the selection of University of Michigan Professor Thomas Cooley as its first chairman. In the past Cooley had defended the roads, denouncing reformers who represented "hostility to railroad management which tends, also, in some degree, to strengthen a troublesome, if not dangerous, feeling of antagonism to acquired wealth." The other members were scarcely less probusiness.

But Morgan, Fink, and Cooley could not bring an end to rebates and rate cutting. At the same time many lines strove to improve facilities and even add to them. Profit margins declined, so that some major companies were close to insolvency, borrowing heavily to cover costs and dividends. Relatively minor economic declines could bring distress; larger ones could bring down parts of the system. And in 1893 the nation underwent a major crash followed by a severe depression.

Immediately several important lines declared insolvency. In 1893 alone, companies with more than 27,000 miles of track and an aggregate capitalization of close to $2 billion went under, and another 40,000 miles followed in the next five years. Among them were some of the principal railroads—the Baltimore and Ohio, the Erie, the Northern Pacific, and the Acheson, Topeka and Santa Fe. The Southern, the Union Pacific, and the Rock Island were in disarray, and as the nation's major enterprises fell, one after the other, it appeared the United States itself was tottering. Writing in January 1895, the coldly realistic editor of the *Railroad Age*, H.P. Robinson, stated: "It is probably safe to say that in no civilized country in this century, not actually in the throes of war or open insurrection, had society been so disorganized as it was in the United States during the first half of 1894; never was human life held so cheap; never did the constituted authorities appear so incompetent to enforce respect for law."

The crisis gave Morgan his opportunity; he was at the peak of power and form. Not only did he salvage the Cleveland administration's credit by selling United States bonds overseas but he managed to reorganize most of the collapsed lines, refinance them, and bring a semblance of order to a sector of the economy noted for internal strife. He took command of the Erie, the Reading, the Jersey Central, the Lehigh Valley, the Delaware and Hudson, the Northern Pacific, the Southern, and the New Haven, as well as lesser lines. Morgan had a major voice at the Norfolk and Western and the Chesapeake and Ohio, and through his allies dominated others. Before the depression had ended, Morgan would have an important influence, in one way or another, in railroads with 48,000 miles of track—one of every three in the nation—and capital of close to $4.5 billion.

In this period it seemed that Morgan and other investment bankers would be able to effect rational mergers between uneconomical lines, eliminate wasteful competition, and finally provide the nation with a unified, efficient, main-line system. Whether or not political and social democracy would have been well served by such a concentration of power is questionable, and doubtless there were benefits derived from competition. But nationalization was the driving force in western industrial life during the late nineteenth century. Throughout Europe, governments were taking over private lines and creating national networks for both passengers and freight. Opponents and defenders of the American railroads agreed on the need for unification, the former arguing for nationalization, the latter for action by the private sector. In the 1890s, it appeared Morgan might accomplish the task.

The New York Central and the Pennsylvania were interested in the idea, and were prepared to develop communities of interests and pools, but their leaders were not willing to enter into mergers through which they would lose their power. Both railroads had been strong in the early 1890s and, despite several difficulties, survived the panic and depression in good shape. They would cooperate with Morgan, who had great influence in their financial affairs, but could well afford their independence.

In 1893 the Central owned or controlled some 15,500 miles of track. It was a well-managed company, with fine rolling stock and excellent road beds. Given Morgan's guidance, the Central's finances were in good shape. In the year ending that June, the company showed record sales and profits, and after declaring the usual 5 percent dividend had a surplus for reserves.

As they did with every important railroad, the Central's earnings declined during the depression, but this was bearable. The dividend was cut to 4.5 percent in 1895 and was down another half of a percent the following year, but the price of the common stock remained firm, and in May 1895 Morgan was able to sell $5 million worth of stock in London without a ripple. Management was confident of the future and, as though to indicate this, purchased several small, distressed lines at the bottom of the depression, while toward the end of the century it acquired the Big Four—the Cleveland, Cincinnati, Chicago, and St. Louis—an important western carrier.

The Pennsylvania also survived the depression in fine form. The 6 percent dividend of 1892 was cut to 5 in 1893, and it remained at that level for the rest of the decade. But as with the Central, the price of the common stock held firm; from a pre-panic high of 57 in 1892 it fell to 48 in 1894, only to be back to 57 the following year. The Pennsylvania continued to expand through acquisition, concentrating on the territory between Pittsburgh and the Mississippi, but not venturing west of the river; in 1894-1896, when most lines contracted, the Pennsylvania added roads with almost 650 miles of track, while ruthlessly abandoning spurs that were no longer needed and even selling off complete subsidiary lines as part of a drastic cost-cutting operation. Continually the Pennsylvania pruned its operation, but also was prepared to expand when the time seemed right. Toward the end of the century President Thomson planned such a move, a tunnel under the Hudson which would provide the Pennsylvania with a Manhattan base, and he also initiated negotiations for a major terminal site on the West Side.

Thomson died in 1899, and was succeeded by Alexander J. Cassatt, an engineer who had risen through the ranks. Cassatt had a mandate to build. He was to revamp the Pennsylvania's major terminals and reconstruct outdated lines. As for the road's finances, that would be handled by several vice-presidents, but more importantly, by the road's investment banker. With Morgan's blessing, the Pennsylvania engaged Kuhn, Loeb for that task. Jacob Schiff, the firm's head, was able to float bonds overseas at low interest rates, just as Morgan had done for the Central. In addition, he marketed Pennsylvania Railroad stock in London, which was then undergoing a boom in American equities. This new money fueled a massive spending program. Within a ten-year span beginning in 1899, the company spent approximately half a billion dollars on improvements, additions, and new terminals, including the giant one in New York.*

The price was high. In 1870, less than 8 percent of Pennsylvania stock was held by foreigners. At the turn of the century almost half the shares were overseas, mostly in the United Kingdom. The Philadelphia aristocrats still dominated the railroad —some families had owned shares purchased by their

---

*E.G. Campbell, *The Reorganization of the American Railroad System, 1893-1900* (New York, 1938), pp. 270-71.

grandfathers in the late 1840s. They lived along the Main Line in splendid mansions and received regular dividends. They viewed the Pennsylvania as their creation, the symbol and reality of their power. But this was no longer completely the case. By then, the company's finances were handled from New York, while through equity ownership it had become a subject of international interest.

Like the Central, the Pennsylvania operated under the Morgan umbrella, even while Schiff remained its banker. The great financier dominated the eastern lines, and he would use both companies in his quest for industrial harmony. But Morgan spoke differently to and with the Central's Depew and his successor, Samuel Callaway, and Thomson and Cassatt of the Pennsylvania. Presidents of other railroads did what they were told; the managements of the Pennsylvania and the Central were consulted and advised. Morgan was particularly fond of Cassatt, an excellent engineer whose social vision matched his own, and who was willing to leave the financial work to others while he handled the construction and management details.

On April 27, 1894, with Morgan's blessings and guidance and while the ICC remained moribund, representatives of the Pennsylvania and the Central met to ratify a traffic agreement that brought to an end their long rivalry. They pledged to consult each other from that time on in setting rates and expanding into territories whose control was in question. To make certain the government would not place obstacles in their paths, the railroads dispatched lobbyists to Washington to petition for amendments to the Interstate Commerce Act. But this was not necessary; in the midst of dealing with serious threats to internal order, the Cleveland administration had no intention of further disrupting the economy by opposing the agreement. Encouraged by this and the smooth operation of their accord, the lines moved to broaden their community of interests. The following year they met with executives from other important eastern lines, and from this emerged the Joint Traffic Association, intended to become the nucleus of an organization that would end competition, maintain rates and profits, and harmonize expansion. It was, in embryo, a method by which a confederation of railroads could have been organized and maintained. But the ICC protested the creation of such a permanent organization, and when the railroads persisted, suits were brought against it in federal court. Three years later the Supreme Court declared the Joint Traffic Association illegal, and it was dissolved; but the spirit behind it remained intact, and cooperation continued for a while longer. Still, the decision resulted in the development of another plan for railroad harmony.

In the summer of 1899, Morgan and Cassatt came forth with a suggestion which, in effect, would create a Central-Pennsylvania community of interests, which in time would engulf all the other major eastern lines. Those railroads not willing to cooperate either would be purchased or crushed, and then obtained. It was about this time that Morgan began seriously to consider the elimination of Andrew Carnegie as a force in steel, through the creation of the United States Steel Corporation, which would dominate the industry. He could not do the same for eastern railroads, due to the law and opposition from reform elements, but through the community of interests, Morgan hoped to come as close to it as possible. There would be no monopoly; given the status of both parties, this would not be possible, for neither would bow to the other or accept leadership from a third force. Rather, in place of various competing elements, Morgan wanted to erect a "triopoly," consisting of those roads already under his domination, the Pennsylvania, and the New York Central. Each of the three would act independently within its empire, and would cooperate with the others in various ways.

Morgan already was the Central's banker, and it was expected he would work closely with its managers to coordinate activities. Cassatt would continue to use the services of Kuhn, Loeb and, in addition, would give some business to Speyer and Company and would undertake no major alteration of policy without prior consultation. In effect, Morgan would concentrate upon New York and New England, while Cassatt and Kuhn, Loeb held sway in Pennsylvania and Maryland. New Jersey would be shared, as would be the region between the western Pennsylvania border and the Mississippi. The system would be interlocked: The Central would enter the Pennsylvania territory with Cassatt's permission, while the Pennsylvania was given leave to exploit parts of New York. Morgan would referee the operations, and in matters under contention his decision would be final.

The compact was sealed in a spectacular fashion. Drexel, Morgan had recently completed the reorganization of the Chesapeake and Ohio, one of the most important eastern coal carriers that on occasion had clashed with the Pennsylvania. In late 1899, the Central and the Pennsylvania each purchased 25 percent of its stock from Morgan, and their representatives took places on the board. Given its special interests, the Pennsylvania was permitted to dictate C&O policy, and a little while later it purchased additional shares to make it the most important force at the road.

More important, however, was the conquest of the Baltimore and Ohio, which had gone into bankruptcy during the depression. Cassatt started to purchase its shares at the same time he was concluding the C&O takeover, and by 1902 the Pennsylvania owned $65 million worth of the shares and working control. When informing the Pennsylvania stockholders of the arrangement, Cassatt could be a master of understatement. "For the purpose of enabling closer relations with other trunk lines, it had seemed wise to acquire an interest in some of the railways reaching the seaboard and unite them with the other shareholders who control these properties, in supporting a conservative policy of management." The B&O had long competed with the Pennsylvania. It had a Philadelphia terminal and routes to all the major western cities. Rate wars between the two had been common, and often destructive. Now this would end. As Cassatt put it, "It was hoped in this way to secure reasonable and stable rates and prevent the unjust discrimination which inevitably resulted from conflicts between the railways and between rival communities, and that aside from the indirect benefits thus sought to be gained it was believed that these holdings would, as investments, be directly profitable."

With the Pennsylvania's encouragement, the B&O embarked upon its own acquisition program. Through its control of the Lake Shore, the Central had an important interest in the Reading. Its direct ownership had ended in 1885, with the *Corsair Agreement*, but it was still a major element at the line. Now, with the Central's permission, the B&O purchased Reading stock. This firm, which also controlled the Philadelphia and Reading and the Reading Coal and Iron Company, thus provided another link between the Pennsylvania and the Central. In addition, it owned shares in the Central of New Jersey, whose lines gave the B&O access to Manhattan. Under the circumstances, the New York Central did not oppose what prior to 1899 would have been considered a declaration of war. Nor did it retaliate when Cassatt dug his tunnel beneath the Hudson, purchased Manhattan real estate, and planned his triumphal entry into the city. Construction on the tunnel began in 1904. Six years later the Pennsylvania Station was opened with a grand ceremony. James McCrea, who had succeeded Cassatt in 1906, officiated.

Among the honored guests were representatives of the House of Morgan and the New York Central—the two Pennsylvania allies.*

Together with the C&O, the Pennsylvania controlled the largest portion of the bituminous coal trade. A third road, the Norfolk and Western, was one of its major competitors. So in 1901 Cassatt instructed his bankers to make purchases of its stock. Morgan cooperated, and by the end of the year the Pennsylvania was in control of the Norfolk and Western, at a cost of close to $18 million. In a period of three years, the Pennsylvania had assumed power at the C&O, the B&O, the Reading, and now the Norfolk and Western at a total cost of $110 million. At the same time, Cassatt acquired the Long Island Railroad in eastern New York and the New York and Pennsylvania, which gave him entry into Buffalo. Like the other acquisitions, these were made with the permission of the New York Central.

This extraordinary effort rounded out the Pennsylvania system; for all intents and purposes, it was completed by the time McCrea opened the New York terminal. Some small feeders were added afterward, and of course inefficient and unnecessary operations either were sold off or discontinued. The Pennsylvania continued to adapt rapidly to changing technology, such as the introduction of diesels and electrification. But never again would it attempt to expand its theater of operations, or even to oust an established rival from within its borders.

With Morgan's cooperation and the Central's good will, Cassatt had transformed the Pennsylvania from a leading eastern line to a force that dominated its territory. He made it part of the trio that controlled transportation in territories in which lived half the nation's population, and which produced most of its industrial goods.** There had been a price, to be sure. During the Cassatt administration the equity outstanding was doubled, the debt quadrupled, and a good deal of the new paper was

---

*The New York Central was constructing its own edifice. In 1903 it obtained approval for a new terminal, and Grand Central Station was demolished soon after. In 1913, the Grand Central Terminal was opened, even though construction work continued for another fourteen years. These two huge edifices not only provided for more efficient operations, they were symbols of the imperial railroad age (even the architecture was Roman) and a sign that the great era of competition had ended.

**In 1901 George Gould attempted to create an eastern railroad network in the Pennsylvania-New York Central Territory. This son of Commodore Vanderbilt's nemesis was already in control of several valuable southwestern properties, and had Andrew Carnegie's strong support. Yet he was blocked by the Morgan-Pennsylvania-Central combine. Later on, Morgan was able to prevent E.H. Harriman, perhaps the most powerful western railroader, from obtaining control of the B&O, which together with his Union Pacific might have created a transcontinental.

owned by non-Philadelphians. If this troubled Cassatt and the aristocrats, they gave no sign of discomfort or concern. Cassatt was hailed as a genius, the greatest Pennsylvania president since J. Edgar Thomson. Indeed, he had done his work so well that there seemed little for his successors to do but polish and adjust what they had inherited.*

Yet Cassatt had bequeathed them at least as many problems as possibilities. True, the Pennsylvania had a fine terminal system, rationalized rail networks, and far-reaching subsidiaries. But had Cassatt been too ambitious? Some of the new lines would do well enough in a good economic climate, but what might occur in a new depression? Despite its reorganization, the B&O was shaky, the C&O of dubious worth, and some of the other lines under the Pennsylvania umbrella of at least questionable value. Then there was the matter of capitalization and debt, both at record highs. Could interest and dividend payments be maintained in poor years? This was the unspoken question that bothered some railroaders, who recalled that Thomson had been followed by Scott, who had been obliged to cut back on expansion in order to insure stability.

Finally, there was government. Cassatt welcomed federal regulation, and believed that the ICC should be strengthened so that the Pennsylvania and other well-run roads could obtain approval for reasonable rate adjustments, while at the same time silencing reformist critics. But given the election of a radical president and Congress—and this appeared at least possible in the early twentieth century—the ICC could become the vehicle by which the bloated railroads could be destroyed.

The New York Central also grew during this period, though not as spectacularly as did the Pennsylvania. In part this was due to the fact that it was so much bigger to begin with—the Central had almost twice the trackage of the Pennsylvania at the turn of the century. In addition it serviced a richer territory and did not feel the need for the kind of rounding-out operation Cassatt performed for the Pennsylvania. Too, it had no major rival in the state; Morgan controlled the Erie and would not permit that line to intrude upon Central's territories. The line already dominated the nation's principal city, and so did not have to seek the kind of position and prestige there that interested Cassatt. The Pennsylvania had long felt the need for a Manhattan terminal;

---

*In the age of railroads, Cassatt was a prominent American. But that period has passed, and railroaders who lacked a dramatic flair are forgotten except by historians and families. Today, Alexander Cassatt is better know as the brother of the great American painter Mary Cassatt than for his work at the Pennsylvania.

the Central viewed a Philadelphia outlet as an interesting possibility, but hardly of great moment. A half century earlier, there seemed a chance that Philadelphia would contest New York for national leadership. In the late 1890s, Cassatt conceded New York the number one position, while the Main Line aristocrats contented themselves with assurances that although New York was bigger and more powerful, it lacked social status and tradition.

In other words, the Central had no quarrel with the status quo, but was willing to adapt to changing conditions in order to preserve its essentials. It had been so since the passing of William Vanderbilt, for his son, Cornelius, was an indifferent executive who spent a good deal of time away from the Central, and allowed others to exercise his powers. The Vanderbilts welcomed Morgan's interest in and caretakership of their property, and like the Philadelphia aristocrats, they became more interested in the collection of dividends and stability than in financial power. Depew served as their ambassador to the House of Morgan. He resigned from the presidency in 1899 in order to replace Cornelius as chairman of the board. That same year he entered the United States Senate, and he served in Washington until 1911, at the same time remaining involved in Central affairs. Depew continued on at the railroad until his death in 1928, at the age of ninety-four. An amiable Victorian who in the mid-1920s spoke over radio about conversations with Abraham Lincoln, Depew was out of place in the railroad world of the twentieth century and was wise enough to know it. For all practical matters and decisions, he followed the lead of others, especially his bankers, and while Morgan was alive, he was the true power at the line.

Unlike Cassatt, Depew had no great ambitions. Under his leadership the Central acquired the Boston and Albany, which meshed well with the Morgan interests in New England. Samuel Callaway was shifted from the Central's presidency to that of the B&A, and was replaced in New York by William Newman, the head of the Lake Shore. Both men followed Depew's directives, and he in turn worked in harmony with his bankers.

At the time, Morgan was most interested in securing domination over the coal fields. With the B&O and the Norfolk and Western, the Pennsylvania had become the leader in bituminous. Now Morgan and the Central would perform the same task for anthracite, with Cassatt's blessing. Quickly, Morgan took command of such lines as the Delaware and Hudson, the Lackawanna, and the Reading, the last being the most important anthracite carrier in America not yet under his banner. Then the Central purchased a major interest in the Lehigh Valley, the next largest factor, as well as securities in other lines. By the end of 1903, the Central and Morgan controlled almost every important carrier in the region, and those not directly under their umbrellas followed their leadership. Morgan had not been able to unite the eastern trunk lines, but that had never been necessary. Through the community of interests he had managed to do away with most of the evils of rebating, had eliminated competition between the three strongest elements in the region, strengthened each of them at the expense of outsiders, and brought them together through the medium of their banks. With Cassatt and Depew, Morgan had become the dominant force in railroading in that part of the country.

All that remained was to obtain a federal imprimatur for their actions, one that would supersede any attack on the part of national reformers or local legislatures. The ICC continued to smile at their efforts. In 1902 President Roosevelt had brought an action against the Northern Securities Company, and two years later that giant organization was declared illegal and dissolved. But Northern Securities was a holding company, and the decision would not affect Morgan's community of interests. The banker had his differences with Roosevelt, but he supported the President in the 1904 election, even though he ran against a conservative Democrat, and for the most part, the two men saw economic matters the same way. In 1903 Congress passed and the President signed the Elkins Act, which contained a strong antirebate clause. Senator Depew voted for the measure, Cassatt praised it, and Morgan gave the bill his blessings, but the shippers and reformers were bitter and vocal in their opposition, citing the Elkins Act as another example of railroad domination of the national government. Their feelings were understandable; the bill reflected the view that the community of interests concept was central to the age of mature capitalism, and that the railroads occupied a special niche in American business. In some of its effect, the measure exempted the great railroads from provisions of the antitrust act.

Reformers and shippers demanded stronger legislation. In particular, they wanted an expanded Interstate Commerce Commission, one that showed more vigor than the moribund agency. Some asked for the power to fix rates; others wanted the railroads to open their books for public inspection, with the federal government taking an active role in settling labor disputes through a policy of complete access to all records. In a deliberate attack on the Morgan empire, the reformers wanted the agency to prohibit those railroads that controlled coal mines and also carried the product to market from discriminating in favor of their own properties.

President Roosevelt supported many of these ideas, in part because he hoped to trade off a stronger railroad control bill for a high tariff. As for the railroaders, they were of two minds on the subject. On the one hand, they wanted to retain the right to set their own prices for services, deal with labor without outside intervention, and keep their books private. On the other, some railroaders—Cassatt was one—welcomed additional federal enforcement of antirebate regulations. "I have for several years believed that the national Government, through the Interstate Commerce Commission, ought to be in a position to fix railroad rates whenever the rates established by the railroads themselves are found, after complaint and hearing, to be unreasonable; provided, of course, that there shall be the right to appeal to the courts." Cassatt did not equivocate. "Let the Government regulate us," he told a reporter. "For my part and for my associates in the Pennsylvania Railroad Company, I am generally heartily in accord with the position taken by President Roosevelt, and we have been all along. . . ." Senator Depew of New York and the New York Central agreed. Like Roosevelt, he considered the issuance of railroad travel passes to those legislators the lines hoped to influence, as well as to favored businessmen, to be a scandal, one that should be stopped by federal law. In effect, this meant that the Central could refuse to issue passes, citing the law as its excuse.

Given such support, the Hepburn Act of 1906 passed with no real difficulty. Under its provisions, the ICC was empowered to fix rates, hear complaints from shippers and act upon them, and regulate terminals and express companies as well as the railroads themselves. Furthermore, the commission was granted the right to look into the railroads' books and prescribe bookkeeping procedures and methods. The act was a compromise. The reformers received a stronger policeman at the corner, while men like Cassatt and Depew were reasonably certain he would be in their employ.

By mid-1906, then, it appeared the Pennsylvania-Central alliance had been blessed by Wall Street and would not be challenged by Washington. But there were problems. Some were outgrowths of old rivalries which had never completely disappeared, but they were minor when compared with those involving the industry's economic aspects. This was a boom period, in which interest rates advanced rapidly and inflationary pressures were being felt. Railroad profits were high, but costs were rising. "The whole movement against the railroads is predicated... on the idea that they are extremely prosperous and that some of their profits might as well be taken from them and appropriated for the benefit of shippers and the general public," wrote the *Commercial and Financial Chronicle* shortly after passage of the Hepburn Act. But this was not necessarily so.

Given their large debt burdens as well as the need to maintain dividends on their increased capitalizations, the railroads could no longer afford some of the unprofitable aspects of the community of interests. For example, the Chesapeake and Ohio never fully recovered from the depression of the 1890s, and, given the other acquisitions, had become redundant. Both the Pennsylvania and the Central wanted to withdraw from it, each by selling out to the other. But neither desired majority ownership, and so they sold part of their shares on the open market. In need of cash, the Pennsylvania also marketed parts of its interests in the B&O and the Norfolk and Western, while the Central turned over stock in several subsidiaries to Morgan, who took it rather than see the shares fall into the hands of outsiders. Both railroads retrenched in the 1907 panic, when the community of interests had shown signs of major difficulties. Cassatt, the strongest defender of cooperation, had died the previous year, and McCrea lacked his force and personality. The Pennsylvania was now in the hands of men more interested in the line than in the future of the Morgan-inspired system.

Morgan understood this and knew the community was dissolving. Perhaps it was for the best, he thought, since the reformers had attacked railroad cooperation and were demanding a truly effective antibusiness policy. Dissolution would be an important sop to throw in their direction. Besides, the banker was an old man—Morgan was sixty-nine when the Hepburn Act was signed—and his period of great power was close to its end. He lacked the vigor for the tasks. And there were none on Wall Street with his stature to mend the shaky community of interests.

This did not mean a return to competition, rate cutting, rebates, and outright raids. Self-preservation and railroad economics militated against this. Both the Pennsylvania and the Central were mature roads, and each had a major stake in stability. Although they drew apart, they would not challenge each other for domination but instead would remain content within their territories. And these were sizable. The Pennsylvania owned or controlled more than 13,000 miles of track at the time of Cassatt's death, and the Central, 23,000. Together, they had one-sixth of the nation's mileage, and with the Morgan roads, one quarter. But they were also large and unwieldy, and, most important, with major financial obligations that required constant attention. The two roads would contest one another in areas of service and speed, not costs, for neither could afford such struggles. For that matter, there was some question as to whether they could finance any large scale operations other than those already owned and conducted. Cassatt had so exhausted the Pennsylvania's treasury that for the next decade it was unable to afford anything but improvements of already existing facilities. The Central was in somewhat better shape financially, and so could afford to undertake more ambitious ventures. In the twilight of his career, Morgan embraced several chancy operations, and almost as a matter of habit Depew went along with them. One was an ill-fated attempt to acquire control of the New York, Ontario and Western from the New Haven. Another was a foray into New England commuter lines—Morgan was convinced they would do well in the future, and had no confidence in the automobile. In addition, the Central erected several major terminals and embellished the Grand Central. As a result, the company's debt doubled in the ten years preceding World War I.

Both the Central and the Pennsylvania were giants. Morgan had made them so, although they had been major companies prior to the community of interests. But they had dangerous financial flaws. In retrospect, one can see that these should have been corrected—if possible—in this period, and that misspent funds of the pre-World War I era would haunt the companies in the 1960s. Still, given a calm social atmosphere, reasonable prosperity, and a stable technology, the firms might have recovered, the wound could have been healed. But there have been few such periods in American history. At the time of Cassatt's death, the two major railroads appeared indestructible, in some respects more powerful than the national government. This would change, and rapidly, in the next two decades.

V

The Last Hoorah

In early 1902, New York Central President William Newman announced that his company would soon offer a new, direct passenger service between Manhattan and Chicago. Regularly scheduled trains would make the 980-mile trip in twenty hours, at an average speed of over fifty miles per hour. The new Atlantic locomotives then being tested would have fewer watering stops than most models, but they would have to take them at regular intervals. In addition, there would be periods, such as around curves, during which the train would proceed slowly. Even though the tracks would be cleared in advance of the supertrain, it would have to sustain an eighty-mile-per-hour rate for prolonged distances so as to arrive on schedule. Furthermore, the service would be available on a year-round basis. Newman pledged the new train would not be slowed by bad weather.*

Reporters were skeptical. "Can so high a rate of speed as will be necessary to accomplish this feat be maintained daily without injury to the engine, the rails, and the coaches? The operators will soon find that they are wasting fortunes in keeping their property in condition, and then, loving money better than notoriety, the twenty-hour project will be abandoned." So wrote an English newspaperman. "Surely it is only an experiment," he thought. Other observers unfamiliar with the American railroad scene agreed, but those who had studied the Central's operations over the past decade knew that too much had been invested in the new service for it to be a mere showpiece. In addition,

---

*Later on, the Central would refund each passenger one dollar for each hour of late arrival.

there was no doubt that Newman was being cautious, for the train might make the trip in less than twenty hours.

Visitors to the Chicago Columbian Exposition of 1893 knew of the project. The Transportation Exhibit there held the Empire State Express, powered by the well-publicized No. 999 locomotive, which that spring had traveled well over one hundred miles per hour on Central tracks. The Exposition Flyer, an experimental model, took tourists from Manhattan to Chicago in twenty hours that year, though not on a scheduled basis. Two years later the Central demonstrated a test train that made the Buffalo to Chicago run at an average speed of sixty-five miles per hour, and it was no secret that this was the forerunner of a larger, permanent service.

The project was designed and organized by George Daniels, the Central's general passenger agent, who was certain the market for such a convenience existed and would expand rapidly in the new century. Passengers requiring such a train would be wealthy and important. They would demand comfort, promptness, and special treatment, and would be willing to pay for them. For many years the world's passenger liners had catered to their needs by offering first-class accommodations. The nation's leading railroad—as Daniels always called the Central—would do no less on a train that was wholly first class.

Daniels spoke to reporters of his plans. Wealthy Chicagoans would board it by 12:30 in the afternoon, walking upon the red carpet that would be unrolled at every stop, being greeted by porters carefully selected from among the line's best. There would be lunch soon after the train cleared the city. Master chefs would prepare the food, and although there could be no wine cellar, the selection would match that of most first-class restaurants. Dinner would begin as the train neared Buffalo, in view of Lake Erie, with the setting sun at the caboose. As the train traveled along the old Erie Canal route, the passengers could sleep in modern roomettes, play cards in one of several club cars, or remain in conversation at the bar. Breakfast would be served as the train moved south along the Hudson River. The trip would come to an end in midtown Manhattan at 9:30, allowing businessmen close to a full day for appointments. Vacationers would have no trouble obtaining taxis for a quick transfer to the docks, where they could catch a Cunarder for Europe. Daniels was certain no ship could match his project for comfort, dependability, and service. His train would offer full valet and maid services. It would have completely equipped barber shops and beauty salons. Secretarial services would be available, together with long-distance telephones and a telegraph. It would be, in effect, a rolling yacht.

For the next seven years, Daniels helped supervise a program of track upgrading, and he even had a say in the design of the Atlantics and the Pullman cars they would haul. The Central meant to purchase several completely equipped trains, and had the first call on new equipment produced by its suppliers. Daniels even gave the train its name, the Twentieth Century, which was meant to be an indication of the Central's progressive viewpoint. The new train made its first trip on June 15, amid great hoopla. Five days later, so as to stress the fact that it would make few stops between Chicago and New York, the name was altered to the Twentieth Century Limited.

Knowing of the Central's plan, the Pennsylvania rushed its own luxury carrier to completion. It offered everything that might be obtained on the Twentieth Century, although partisans of one or the other would claim theirs was the best. The Pennsylvania entry, which began service at the same time, was first called the Pennsylvania Special, and later on, the Broadway Limited. It took a more rugged route than the Central, but it had the advantage of being more direct. The Pennsylvania Special would leave New York and head in a northwesterly direction, while the Twentieth Century went due north. But by dawn the next day their tracks came within sight of one another, and at this point—in the early days, at least—the trip took on the appearance of a race, even though all knew that this was not the case. In fact, it was a friendly rivalry, indicating the détente that existed between the lines since the time of J.P. Morgan. There would be no cutthroat competition in the area of price and speed. A half century later, the Twentieth Century would make the trip in little more than fifteen hours—and so would the Broadway Limited.

But in a sense there was a competition. The two trains vied with one another in the area of prestige. These were the nation's showpiece trains, and they were as much status symbols in the early part of the century as space satellites would become in the 1960s. Their names evoked illusions of glamour and excitement, and the Central and the Pennsylvania managements naturally wanted their entries to be first in this respect. Trips on them became the subject of motion pictures and, in the case of the Twentieth Century, there was a successful play that took its title from the train's name. The majesty of the Grand Central and Pennsylvania stations added to the effect. The excitement just before boarding could be overwhelming. Those who recollect traveling on one or both of the trains in the pre-World War II days swear that their tenth trip was more thrilling than their first on a Europe- or Asia-bound jet plane taking off from Kennedy or O'Hare airports. The railroad stations were dark, shadowy places, the high marble cool, the smells musty and exotic, while the trains themselves were at the same time comprehensive in their technology and stately in appearance. In contrast, the airports and their planes seemed antiseptic and—after the third or fourth trip—ordinary and even boring.*

Like the Grand Central and Pennsylvania stations, the Chicago-bound trains were symbols of the power of the railroad age, and also—at least in retrospect—their last spectacular achievement. In the years that followed, the railroads and their suppliers would develop new technologies, but the Broadway Limited and the Twentieth Century possessed the stuff of glamour.

The Wall Street crowd considered the Pennsylvania and the Central to be the principal American corporations in early 1907, as well as the most secure of common-stock holdings. The Central owned, operated, or controlled more miles of main track than the Pennsylvania, but the latter held the lead in average train loads—529 tons against 403—due to its concentration upon coal hauling. Because of this, the Pennsylvania was able to earn $37,661 per track mile against the Central's $24,336. Net earnings on net capital, a key indicator of profitability, showed the Pennsylvania with 8.1 percent and the Central far behind, with 5.8 percent. The percentage of net income required for fixed charges was another important indicator—the higher the figure, the less secure the dividend. Fixed charges consumed 64 percent of the Central's income, and only 38 percent that of the Pennsylvania. Furthermore, the Central's earnings growth lagged behind that of its major rival. From 1900 to 1906, generally good years for the industry, the Central's net went from $20.5 million to $25.8 million, an increase of 20 percent. In the same period the Pennsylvania's earnings rose from $30.4 million

---

*These reactions, elicited from individuals who took both planes and trains, were almost uniform in sentiment and preference. In each case the person denied that his emotions were colored by the passage of time, or that the fact that he or she was young when taking the supertrains and much older when traveling by jet was an important consideration. The closest anyone under the age of fifty can come to the emotions of the great railroad age is a viewing of the early scenes of the motion picture *Murder on the Orient Express*, which was set in Turkey, of course, but in the 1920s. For a sensitive and lively account of this age, see Lucius Beebe, *20th Century* (Berkeley, 1962).

to $46.4 million, an increase of more than 50 percent. The Pennsylvania even paid a higher dividend, $6.25 per share against the Central's $5.25. Despite all of this, and the Pennsylvania's record of prudent management, the two stocks sold for around the same price. In 1906 the Central's average quotation was $137, and the Pennsylvania's two dollars more. On an average yield basis, Pennsylvania common returned 4.6 percent, and Central, 3.8 percent. As far as the investing public was concerned, then, the Central had better prospects than the Pennsylvania, for that was the only way to explain its higher price level in relation to earnings, dividends, and growth.

Investors interpret the term "prospects" in two different ways. During times of economic vitality and optimism, when indices are rising, they seek out companies that are rapidly growing. Speculators purchase their shares and so bid up their prices, with one result being a decline in dividend yields and an increase in the ratio of price to earnings. This occurred in the 1920s and the 1960s. It was the situation in the early twentieth century too, for this was a period of strong economic growth. The Dow Jones Railroad Average rose from a low of 73 in 1900 to a 1906 high of 138. On the face of it, these figures appear to indicate that the Pennsylvania should have sold at a higher price than the Central. And the reasons it did not were one of the most telling demonstrations that even then—in the midst of a stock market boom —there was a strong note of pessimism.

The eastern trunk lines were not aggressively expansionist in this period. Existing track would be improved to incorporate new technologies, and there would be changes in rolling stock. New terminals were always rising, and antiquated facilities scrapped. But the eastern railroads were not expected to make important new acquisitions, as they had under Morgan in the aftermath of the 1893 panic. Nor would they expand into new territories, for these did not exist in the settled East. The growth period in terms of trackage had ended; even had the railroads wanted to continue, the government might have stepped in to prevent large-scale mergers and combinations. The passage of the Hepburn Act was one sign of this, as was growing pressure from the ICC and congressional investigators, demanding new curbs on the railroads. They claimed the lines were powerful, and the major railroads had a hammerlock on the economy. It would have to be broken.

But the diagnosis was faulty, and if the true situation was not appreciated in Washington, it was understood in New York, at the Stock Exchange, and reflected in the prices of the Pennsylvania and the Central. In an optimistic period the former line would have commanded a higher price. But the Central seemed a safer bet during a time of decline.

Both companies were considered prudent and responsible. For years the Pennsylvania had boasted that for every dollar paid in dividends one dollar was set aside for improvements; and the Central was not far behind. But in 1906, the Central's trackage was far easier to maintain than that owned by its rival. The Central advertised itself as the "water level route," indicating that it had no important mountains or valleys along its routes. The Pennsylvania had to cross the Appalachians while dragging huge freight trains, a practice that was hard on equipment, and meant that it required larger and more expensive locomotives. This gave the Central an advantage in passenger traffic too. The Twentieth Century's route was seventy miles longer than the Broadway Limited's, and yet the two trains had the same running time. The Century's highest elevation was 920 feet, while the Broadway Limited had to overcome 2,192 feet along the way. In money terms, the Central expended $6,682 per mile—fairly low for the industry—while the Pennsylvania's charges were $11,463—close to an industry high. In a defensive period, this figure was deemed vital.

Then there was the quality of the business. The Pennsylvania carried nearly a quarter of the nation's freight—363 million tons in 1906. Its traffic density was twice that of the Central, as it had been for the past two decades. But there was some question as to the stability of this business, for the largest portion by far came from coal—the Pennsylvania accounted for over half the nation's total. And of all commodities, coal was most sensitive to economic dislocations.

Should there be a new depression like that of 1873 or 1893, the Pennsylvania might be crippled. President Cassatt had plunged the line into deep debt so as to pay for his additions and improvements. In such a depression, the debt might not be serviceable. The Central, in contrast, had a more varied carrying trade, and was considered better insulated from the damages that could be caused by depression.

This was why Central's common stock offered a lower yield than Pennsylvania's in late 1906. At that time, the country feared a depression, one that would be caused by the railroads themselves in their almost insatiable demands for new money.

In order to finance his many programs—including the erection of the Pennsylvania Station in New York and construction of the Hudson tunnels—Cassatt had to raise huge sums of money on Wall Street. Since his company was so well considered, and the price of its stock so high, he could float new issues of stock as well as bonds.* In 1899, the Pennsylvania had $129.3 million in common stock outstanding, and a funded debt of $88 million. The common stock in the hands of the public in 1906 came to $305.9 million, and the indebtedness, to $191.6 million. In seven years, the Pennsylvania's gross earnings had risen by 103 percent—but in the same period, capitalization had increased by 129 percent. Given Cassatt's plans, this tendency for financings to outrun earnings seemed incapable of being halted. His projects could not be long delayed, for important route alterations had already been started. Part of the money would come from earnings, but the rest would have to be raised on Wall Street. So long as the price of Pennsylvania common stock held and interest rates were low, there would be no problem. But changes in one or the other would be damaging, while a combination of the two together with a depression could cause the company to go into a tailspin.

The Central's position was somewhat more secure. In this period its capital stock outstanding rose from $115 million to $178 million, and the funded debt from $186 million to $231 million. The total capitalization advanced 36 percent, while the earnings went up by 70 percent.**

These were the kind of statistics that interested Wall Streeters, especially those who were forecasting a new crisis. The Pennsylvania was gambling that the prosperity would persist, and if it did, that line would continue to dominate the Midwest and its section of the East. If there was a depression, however, the Central seemed better situated for strong recovery.

A pattern had been established in the 1893 panic and depression. Those railroads that had gone into receivership had been reorganized, recapitalized, and in the early twentieth century were busily spending money to improve facilities, to take advantage of the national prosperity. The demand for capital was world-wide; bank rates were rising, and money getting tighter. Still the spending continued, for profits were high and the railroads saw no reason to retrench because of a few extra points in interest. The bankers would oblige them, and customers

---

*This was an important consideration insofar as raising money was concerned. The Erie Railroad, so debauched in the nineteenth century, was unable to sell additional stock, and even had trouble floating bonds. Lacking money, the line continued to decline, and so perpetuated the downward spiral begun by Daniel Drew—despite its fine right of way and good territory.

**These figures and others of the period can be found in Carl Snyder, *American Railways as Investment* (New York, 1907).

remained eager for the new issues. In early 1906, as Congress prepared to debate supplemental railroad control legislation, banker Jacob Schiff warned that "If the currency conditions of this country are not changed materially . . . you will have such a panic in this country as will make all previous panics look like child's play." Railroader James Hill spoke of "commercial paralysis," which might result if the expanding economy did not receive at least $1 billion a year for capital improvements and additions, and most of this would be required by the transportation sector—railroads. Along with others in the industry, Hill went to the capital markets in early 1907 to refinance bonds before rates rose even higher.

The collapse came that autumn; it was one of the sharpest in American history, and was not halted until the full force of the Morgan group had been brought to bear. But the panic was not followed by a depression, though it might easily have been without such banker intercession.

What might have happened had there been a depression—a period of poor economic performance, affecting freight and passenger traffic? Given three or four bad years, the railroads would not have been able to pay dividends, and then would have had to default on bonds—declare bankruptcy. There would be a rash of failures besides which those of the 1890s would appear minor. And in a future depression, there might not be a J.P. Morgan around to pick up the pieces. He was an old man, barely able to rise to the challenge of 1907. Soon he would be dead, and so great was Morgan's reputation that none could hope to fill his place.

Thus, the railroads were in a quandary. Continued spending on improvements would result in lower profit margins and perhaps place the lines in untenable financial positions during a business slump. A cutback on expenditures might lead to diminished service and prestige, a lower volume of business, an inability to borrow, and then collapse. The railroads appeared strong and confident as the last vestiges of the panic were cleared. But in fact they were becoming dinosaur-like—with huge bodies that moved sluggishly—and were vulnerable to attack from almost any quarter.

The Central's spending picked up soon after the panic had ended. The company projected new terminals for Utica, Rochester, Buffalo, Cleveland, Cincinnati, Indianapolis, and Detroit. Grade crossings were to be eliminated in Syracuse, Dunkirk, Rochester, Buffalo, and Cleveland. Additional tracks would be required for the Hudson division. Major renovations were planned at the Lake Shore, the Big Four, and the Michigan Central. The Manhattan freight terminal required modernization. The lines had been constructed in the nineteenth century; in the early twentieth they were being reconstructed. These projects would require at least $50 million a year for the next decade, perhaps more. This was not for acquisitions; the half a billion dollars would be used for maintenance and improvements.

Tight-money conditions obliged the Central to turn to equity financing. From 1906 to 1910 the company's debt rose slightly, from $231 million to $250 million, but its common stock outstanding went from $178 million to $223 million. Even with this massive effort, the Central still required additional sums in 1910. The company estimated its capital needs for the next five years at around $350 million.

How could such a sum be raised? In the decade ending in 1910 the Central had reported a net income of $340 million, and in its best year, 1910, $40 million had been earned. Clearly additional capital would have to come from outside sources. And there were interests willing to make such funds available.

Recognizing an opportunity to expand its empire, Standard Oil purchased shares and then asked for and received seats on the board for William Rockefeller and his banker, James Stillman of the National City. E.H. Harriman, too, was interested in the railroad. He instituted a small-scale buying campaign, but for the moment did no more, leaving Wall Street to guess as to his next move. Harriman knew he could not hope to dislodge the Vanderbilt-Morgan group, but given a general collapse, he might move in and take command. Both the Rockefellers and Harriman understood that the eastern railroads suffered from financial weaknesses although possessing substantial economic power. The thought of a raid would have seemed absurd at the turn of the century, but it was not out of the question in 1910, after the panic of 1907. In its maturity, the New York Central was reverting to what it had been in the early days of railroading, when Erastus Corning controlled the line: a vehicle for speculation as well as one for transporting people and goods.

The key to the Central was to be found in its capitalization, or so it seemed at the time. That it was a strong company could not be doubted; in most respects it seemed more secure than the Pennsylvania, though not as large. But it lacked the financial power to compete on an equal basis, and was in need of strong banker support. Morgan had provided this in the past, and new forces had joined him—the Guaranty Trust as well as the

National City. Now that they were in place, the scenario would be predictable. The Central would require money, and, unable to get it at reasonable rates through the issuance of bonds, would turn to stock offerings. Outsiders would purchase shares, and in time win representation on the board. But real power would remain in the hands of the Morgans and Vanderbilts, working in unison.

The Pennsylvania was in a similar financial position. Although the company had recovered quickly from the 1907 panic, President McCrea's spending programs—some of which had been inherited from Cassatt—required additional financing. There was a rights offering for 1.65 million shares in 1909 as well as several sales of convertible debentures. In 1906 there had been 6.1 million shares outstanding; in 1911, over 9 million were in the hands of the public.

Many of these were purchased by non-Philadelphians, as that city's grip on the line continued to slip. Henry Clay Frick, frustrated in his attempts to find a suitable role for himself in the steel industry, was a new factor here. He joined the board in 1906 and for a while was considered Cassatt's heir apparent. Frick was backed by Pittsburgh money—the Mellons in particular. He also had links with the Rockefellers, and with their help obtained large blocks of Reading stock, and was on the board of the Chicago and Northwestern. Frick was close to E.H. Harriman, and brought him into the Pennsylvania picture. In 1913 the company entered into negotiations with the Union Pacific, then seeking an important eastern ally. The Pennsylvania exchanged its blocks of stock in the B&O for the Union Pacific's holdings in the Southern Pacific, which gave it a toehold in the trans-Mississippi area. Under the proper conditions—political as well as economic—Harriman might reach to the Atlantic and the Pennsylvania to the Pacific. Again, Frick was the key; he was a power at the Union Pacific.

A new community of interests appeared in the making. The Harriman, Mellon, and Rockefeller forces—in loose and plastic alliance—would finance the giant lines, and combine to save them from disaster if and when a new panic and depression erupted, in much the same way as J.P. Morgan had functioned during the panic of 1907. Their price would be both large and audacious: Harriman would be granted his true transcontinental, Frick would obtain a major role on the business scene, and the Rockefellers and Mellons large dominions to enhance their empires. Given a favorable government attitude—and one was imaginable as a price for saving the economy—such a system and complex might have developed. The age of finance capitalism directed from New York could have been succeeded by one in which power was exercised by what amounted to economic nations, functioning as self-sustaining entities within the political structure.

But the government was opposed to further business expansion. There was no new panic and depression. There would be no giant community of interests. Instead, the railroads would have to operate on their own, and rely upon their bankers for additional financings.

Business economist A.M. Sakolski wondered whether the large roads could bear this financial burden for long. "New capital expenditures such as those contemplated by the New York Central undoubtedly tend to increase or to maintain earning power," he wrote in 1912. "The resulting additional income, however, may not, in some cases, offset the cost of acquiring new capital." If this was so, should not the Pennsylvania and Central have cut back on expenses—by foregoing the grandiose terminals, for example? Why have two trains on the New York to Chicago luxury run, when their returns on investment were bound to be low? Was prestige worth the price?

Even as he wrote, Sakolski knew the spending would continue; the competition between the eastern carriers made it inevitable. Once the Central had announced its plans for the Twentieth Century, for example, the Pennsylvania had to respond with the Broadway Limited, even though one set of trains could have accomplished the job more efficiently. The situation called for mergers, consolidations, or at least cooperation—but the government insisted upon competition, and in any case, neither railroad was interested in a merger at that time. Financial prudence dictated rate increases, but antibusiness sentiments were rising, and this was out of the question. So improvements were continued; for a railroad that did not take this path, wrote Sakolski, there would be a decline, and "this loss of business is the first step to receivership and reorganization."* In the parlance of a later generation, the lines were locked into a no-win situation.

The strain was felt in the post-panic year, when railroad earnings declined by 10 percent. In 1908 close to 3 percent of the nation's mileage was in the hands of receivers, a new twentieth-

---

*A.M. Sakolski, *American Railroad Economics* (New York, 1913), pp. 283-85.

century high. The Pennsylvania was far from distress, but its net income picture was not encouraging: $55.5 million in 1906, $55 million in 1907, and $53.3 million in 1908, while costs were rising. As for the Central, it reported income of $33.5 million for 1906, $34 million for 1907, and $33.8 million for 1908. Although both railroads noted an upturn in business in early 1909, they were in a minority, as additional carriers cut dividends, abandoned plans for improvement, and declared insolvency. Faced with financial stringency, many asked for rate increases, and, as expected, this resulted in demands for greater controls and investigations from shippers and reformers. The railroads responded that they required the funds in order to continue operations, improve upon them, and remain sufficiently solvent so as to be able to raise new money. But to many Americans who had blamed the industry for having precipitated the 1907 panic, it seemed the lines had decided to squeeze the nation in order to further enrich their treasuries and stockholders.

Buoyed by the wave of antirailroad sentiment, Congress prepared to frame new control legislation. President William Howard Taft, who had taken office in 1909, had for years distrusted the railroads, which he believed were engaged in conspiracies, and led by men who were "exceedingly lawless in spirit." A man of strong legalistic bent, Taft supported plans for a "commerce court," which would supplement the work of the ICC, and which would hear complaints against the lines and rule on rate increases. The commerce court was included in the Mann-Elkins Act of 1910, the strongest railroad control legislation yet signed into law. In the past the ICC could investigate rate increases after they had been put into effect; now the commission could suspend proposed changes for 120 days while holding inquiries, and then ask for an additional six months of delay if the time was required. The ICC could initiate rate changes on its own volition, and the commission was given control over freight classification.

Now the battle was joined. On the one side were the railroad men, arguing that without higher rates their properties would decline, and that such a situation was bound to harm all Americans. Their opponents questioned their sincerity and statistics, and suggested the roads were poorly run; economies, not rate increases, were demanded. In late 1910 President William Brown of the New York Central offered his testimony as part of the line's requests for higher rates. The Central paid an average dividend of 4.7 percent on the par value of its stock, he said, and was putting one-quarter of its profits into improvements. To lower the dividend would damage the Central's position on Wall Street, and make it impossible to raise money at low rates. In fact, the Central had just raised its dividend so as to be able to attract additional funds. True, the railroads had showed good profits since the end of the depression, but their rates had not kept pace with inflation. An increase was needed. Louis Brandeis, the ICC's lawyer, charged the dividend increase was proof the road was in good shape and did not need the higher rates. "We raised the dividend to the rate which a person could get on a first-class mortgage," responded Brown, to which Brandeis countered by charging the Central had been run inefficiently. He would bring in experts to testify to this and show how productivity could be raised. "When you find the men, send me a list of the first five or ten of them. . . . I will assure them a good position as soon as you can send them to New York," replied Brown. But in the end, the Central did not get its rate increase.

And the pattern continued, with the increases denied in a majority of the more important cases brought before the ICC and the commerce court during the next three years. Of course, some relief was granted, usually to the weaker lines that were able to demonstrate without a doubt that the increase would prevent utter collapse. But the more solvent lines, which wanted additional money for improvements, had a harder time of it. In 1913, when the commission denied requested adjustments for the eastern lines, Pennsylvania Railroad's chief counsel, George Patterson, attempted to demonstrate the seriousness of the situation. "The Pennsylvania system in three years has invested $207 million [yet] finds its net $11 million less. . . . In 10 years from 1903 to 1913 they invested $530 million upon which there was the munificent return of $2\frac{1}{4}$ per cent. And mark you, this was not in speculative enterprises . . . not in buying the stocks of other companies . . . not for building any lines into a new country. It was expended in the intensive development of the richest traffic-producing sections in the world."* The commission's majority rejected this argument. The American railroads were still mismanaged, their borrowing power had suffered from this and the unusually large demands being placed upon the credit markets, and both could be rectified without higher rates. There was talk of a new investigation of the railroads; in March 1913, just before he left office, Taft signed into law authorization for the ICC to make a comprehensive study of the lines. Some

---

*Albro Martin, *Enterprise Denied* (New York, 1971), pp. 209-10, 283-84.

reformers spoke of the need to nationalize the railroads; mere regulation would not suffice to make them more responsive to the public needs. And at this point, a handful of railroaders and their defenders agreed. Unless the companies were allowed to earn sufficient money so as to operate, they would collapse, and in the end nationalization would be required in the form of government management of the lines.

The economy was sluggish in 1913—today it would be called a mild recession. But the railroads had been in financial decline for several years. The expenses-to-revenues ratio had been 66.8 percent during the depression era of the 1890s, when it had appeared most of the nation's railroads would declare bankruptcy due to poor economic conditions. Then, in the prosperous first decade of the new century, the ratio leveled off, averaging 66.5 percent. There was no depression in 1908, but in that year the figure rose above 70 percent for the first time. So it would appear the situation could not be reversed, even in the best of times. Costs were outpacing revenues, and were increasing more rapidly than profits. They would continue to do so. There was little the railroads could do about expenses—this was an inflationary period, after all, and an increasingly complex technology commanded its price—while profits were being kept down by a variety of forces, most particularly the decisions of the ICC. By 1913, after a slight dip from 1909 to 1912, the expenses-to-revenues ratio rose above the 70 figure once more.

The coming of the European war in 1914 resulted in increased demands upon the American economy. Railroads in all parts of the country reported an excellent business, but the greatest advances were in the Northeast, the industrial heartland, whose factories received and filled large orders from the Allies. By 1916, total railroad revenues were $3.7 billion and net profits $735 million, both records. Clearly the railroads could not hope for more ideal operating circumstances. Yet that year the ratio of operating expenses to net revenues was 65.7 percent, higher than the 64.6 percent in 1902, when Morgan was in his prime and the railroads supreme. This meant that income continued to lag behind expenses.

There was another disquieting element. The ICC had prevented many major roads from obtaining rate increases, arguing that enlarged revenues from a more intensive use of facilities would result in bonanzas. But net return on invested capital declined at both the Central and the Pennsylvania in 1914. Both railroads were obliged to order new rolling stock so as to handle the additional business, and, lacking income sufficient for the task, had to make trips to the capital market, which already was showing sights of tightening. None but the most urgent improvement programs were continued. Even routine repairs had to be put off for a while. The railroads were shabbier in late 1916 than they had been since the turn of the century.

To some, then, it seemed the railroads had entered a new period of prosperity. But in 1916, over 37,000 miles of line were in receivership—almost one out of every ten in the nation. The golden age of railroading had ended, as the roadbeds became increasingly pocked by holes and the financial positions of major carriers worsened even while revenues advanced. The nation's railroads simply hadn't been prepared for the kind of volume they had to handle during the neutrality period, and the situation would darken in 1917, when America itself went to war. Increasingly expenses outran profits, with no end or relief in sight.

The industry slowed down perceptively. As late as 1913 over 3,000 miles of new track had been set down. In 1915, only 933 miles were laid; for the first time since the end of the Civil War the statistic was below the 1,000 mile mark. Close to 1,100 miles were built in 1916, and then the decline set in once again. This would be the last year the American railroads posted so high a figure. The industry's secular decay was evident by then. A combination of maturity, problems peculiar to the industry, and the demands of war had resulted in and hastened the decline. The activities of reformers had made an already bad situation worse, in large part due to a faulty diagnosis of the industry. Toward the end of the period even those who had opposed the 1910-13 rate increases were prepared to reconsider their positions. Former President Taft admitted his mistakes. "The inadequacy of our railroad system is startling. We have had many warnings from railroad men as to what would occur . . . their warnings are now being vindicated." And in late 1913, quietly, Congress abolished the commerce court.

Inadequacies but not vindication could be seen during the neutrality period. Many of the lines lacked the funds for required alterations, and could not adjust to the developing wartime economy. Costs were higher than ever, due not only to inflation and conversion charges but to a much larger labor bill because of the passage in 1916 of the Adamson Eight-Hour Act. Industrial profits had soared, and now the railroads came to Washington to ask for an overall rate increase on the order of 15 percent. Pennsylvania President Samuel Rea told the ICC that "the condition of the railroads today presents a menace to the country." If the major lines were to fulfill their economic roles, large rate increases would be required. Not to grant such requests would be to accept rapid decline and eventual paralysis.

The shippers opposed the increase. Clifford Thorne, one of their leaders who at the time represented the Shippers' National Conference, told the commission "the railroad presidents are patriotically rallying around the flag, saying, 'Give us more money. . . .' At a time like this the railroads should be satisfied with the profits of former years instead of demanding more. If they were really patriotic they would withdraw these tariffs, say the emergency they had anticipated had not transpired, and announce they were going to do their bit."*

The shippers and producers had far larger profits, and their requirements for reinvestment were smaller than those of the railroads. The emergency indeed had arrived. By 1916 New York port was exporting twice as much as it had in 1913, and the bulk of the additional freight arrived by rail. This affected all the eastern carriers, but the Pennsylvania felt it the most. Its pre-war programs were halted at great cost, and new ones—including expensive switching operations and the creation of new yards—were rushed to completion. The line's revenues did rise from $191 million in 1913 to $230 million in 1916, and earnings were good—$42 million to $52 million in this period. But without major rate increases, warned Rea, there would be a decline in 1917. The shippers won their point, but Rea was correct; the Pennsylvania's revenues in 1917 were $255 million, and earnings declined to $39 million.

The Pennsylvania's 1917 statistics were even more significant in the light of the commission's decision. "This record does not disclose the existence of a situation requiring so heroic a remedy," it wrote in rejecting the appeal. But the commission did find the rates on coal, coke, and iron ore to be insufficient, and permitted 15 percent increases on these. Even with this the Pennsylvania, the nation's leading carrier of these products, had a poor profits picture in 1917. Other roads did much worse. "I dislike to criticize any Governmental decision," said Rea, "but the people should know why it is impossible to provide adequate facilities and service, which are imperatively required for this growing country, and should know how unjustly the Eastern railroads are being treated."

This was the situation when the United States entered the war in the spring of 1917. Not only was there a car shortage but track

---

*K. Austin Kerr, *American Railroad Politics, 1914-1920* (Pittsburgh, 1968), pp. 151-52.

breakdowns had assumed record proportions, in part because of an inability to find the funds for repairs, but also due to the unprecedented use of facilities demanded by the government. There was a coal shortage in the East, caused by a lack of cars to carry the product from the mines to the coast. The railroad unions demanded higher wages for their workers, and threatened a strike unless important adjustments were made. In desperation, the government encouraged the leading eastern lines—the Pennsylvania, the Central, the B&O, and the Erie—to form a pool which would share surplus resources. The effort failed, primarily because such surpluses did not exist.

With the situation approaching the critical stage, President Wilson named a special commission to study the problem and return with solutions. Almost immediately thereafter, the railroads petitioned the ICC for a reconsideration of the 15 percent rate increase. Interest charges were rising, and so it was difficult for the roads to sell new bonds at reasonable rates. At the same time, the prices of railroad common stocks were declining—over 30 percent in all during 1917—and the railroads were unwilling to enter the equity markets. Even so, the rate increase was rejected. In its place, the ICC, with Congress's support, recommended the creation of a unified railroad operation for the duration of the war. The report reached Wilson's desk on December 5, along with a statement to the effect that a quick decision would be required.

It is important to understand that in the early twentieth century movements for nationalization of transportation and communication facilities had swept the western world. Throughout Europe, nationalization was viewed as a panacea, not only for railroads but telephones, telegraph, and water shipping as well. America had had its period of nationalism and state control—almost a century before, when men like Henry Clay and John Quincy Adams spoke of national roads and canals, supported by the government and following the general outlines of Gallatin's reports. Andrew Jackson had brought that period to a close. There had been a large measure of railroad coordination during the Civil War, but Thomas Scott could only persuade and recommend; there was no thought of operation and direct management. Harriman and Hill dreamed and planned for coast-to-coast lines later on, and even thought in terms of a global transportation system, but nothing of this kind transpired. J.P. Morgan had been able to erect communities of interests, but he wanted to obliterate differences and create industry-wide harmony, not lead a single transportation system. These individuals did not consider the European experience a worthwhile model. Only the Populists and Socialists had such ambitions, though even with them they were poorly defined, and in any case had no chance of being accepted.

Woodrow Wilson had pledged his administration to a strong antitrust policy in 1912. By 1917, however, that phase of his Presidency had passed. Now he considered several recommendations to suspend the antitrust laws for the duration of the war. The railroads were particularly important in his thinking, for if they faltered, the war effort would be severely damaged. Almost all of the proposals on his desk envisaged government control and operation; none suggested ownership. Most of the recommendations contained means by which the lines could obtain needed funds. Such plans had the support of a large number of reformers who considered operation and financing a first step toward nationalization. Others accepted railroad regulation and control as necessary elements of the war effort. Realizing they would receive no significant relief from the ICC, railroad leaders looked upon government intervention as their best possible solution. The large shippers needed the lines but didn't want to pay their rate increases; for them, government operation might provide an indirect subsidy, and as such would be welcomed. The railroad unions were wary. Was this a means of obliging them to forego wage increases? On the other hand, to openly oppose government ownership would seem unpatriotic, and the union officials wanted to avoid this. In fact, there was no organized opposition of any importance to government operation, in large part because there seemed to be no alternative worth considering.

On December 28, 1917, President Wilson authorized government operation of the railroads, citing the authority granted him under the terms of the Federal Possession and Control Act. Three months later, Congress spelled out the terms of the arrangement by passing the Federal Control Act. The railroads would be paid for the use of their facilities on a base equal to their average annual operating income for the three years ending June 30, 1917. Some of the larger lines protested the selection of this period as a base, for it included the unusually poor results reported in the second half of 1914 and through 1915. Even during the profitable period that followed, the railroads had been unable to finance operations out of retained earnings. In effect, the use of this base would only serve to perpetuate unusually low returns upon invested capital. The law provided for rate increases, however, and so the railroad leaders could at least hope that they would soon be granted.

Equally troublesome was the section of the legislation dealing with repairs and maintenance of equipment. The railroads were told their properties would be "returned . . . substantially in as good repair and in substantially as complete equipment as it was in the beginning of Federal Control. . . ." Congress authorized the establishment of a revolving fund of $500 million for this and other financial needs.

The legislation provided for a Railroad Administration to operate the lines, and Wilson had selected William Gibbs McAdoo as its director general. At the time McAdoo was considered one of the half-dozen most powerful men in Washington. In 1902 he had moved from Georgia to New York to become president of a predecessor company of the Hudson and Manhattan Railroad Company, and soon after he had helped construct the river tunnels. He became secretary of the treasury in Wilson's Cabinet, and in addition headed several key committees as well as the Farm Loan Bank. McAdoo was Wilson's son-in-law, and considered a logical Democratic Presidential nominee for 1920.

To McAdoo, progressivism was an archaic idea, one that had little to offer for the resolution of problems in 1917 and after the war. The United States could not function without the large corporations—steel was hardly a cottage industry—and tinkering with the complicated machinery could severely damage it. Rather, government should encourage businessmen to cooperate with one another, act as a mediator and go-between, and utilize friendly pressures rather than stern laws to lead businessmen to operate in a public-minded fashion. Somewhat reluctantly and in his own way, McAdoo had come to accept Morgan's concept of a community of interests, with the proviso that the government had a role to play as guardian of the public. Such a man, with such a background, did not represent a threat to the major lines.

New York Central President Alfred H. Smith knew McAdoo well; they belonged to the same clubs and were fairly close friends. Now McAdoo called Smith to Washington, where he served first as his temporary assistant and then as regional director for the eastern lines, considered the key to the entire system. Rea was troubled by this appointment, perhaps because he feared Smith would act so as to benefit the Central at the expense of the Pennsylvania. During the preceding two years the

Pennsylvania's operations had become tangled, due in large part to the fact that it bore the brunt of the increased war traffic. But Smith handled his decisions in an open fashion, and in fact the Pennsylvania received almost one-fifth of all the Railroad Administration's expenditures.

Under McAdoo's direction, the railroads cooperated in a large-scale effort at rationalizing operations. Repair work was standardized, and interconnections between lines developed and constructed. The Administration ordered 2,000 locomotives and 100,000 freight cars, all standard, which were to be distributed to the railroads where needed; in this way, McAdoo was creating a rational carrying system, and the new rolling stock would be distinguished only by names on the side, not style or preferences of managers. Wages were increased, but so were rates. In May 1918, McAdoo ordered freight schedules advanced by 25 percent, and he hinted that new appeals for adjustments to correct individual cases of inequities would be carefully considered.

The railroads welcomed the increases, and McAdoo was generally popular with industry leaders. Still, the adjustments did not cover wage increases, while maintenance costs rose four times as rapidly as rates. In 1916, the last peacetime year, the nation's railroads reported profits of $735 million; they were $442 million in 1918, the final wartime year, when the expenses-to-revenues ratio was 81.7 percent. The governmental additions to rolling stock could not keep pace with demands. Replacements due to intensive use were high, and inevitably the roads were obliged to operate with makeshift equipment.

The lines attempted to improve services after the wartime pressures ended. In 1919 the railroads spent $800 million on maintenance of ways and structures, more than twice the 1915 figure. Then, in 1920, over $1 billion was used for such work, a record that would not be broken for almost a quarter of a century, while equipment repair costs that year came to $1.6 billion, another record that remained until World War II. Such costs resulted in the establishment of an all-time mark that shocked the industry; in 1920, the expenses-to-revenues ratio was 94.3 percent. Not only was such a figure a sign of financial and industrial disease; it appeared to indicate that the malady might be terminal.

What had caused this situation? A handful of scholars noted that the railroads had been in trouble before 1917, and that wartime stringencies had only served to dramatize an already sorry condition. The government conceded the roads were in bad shape in 1919, but insisted they had been shabby when the Railroad Administration had assumed power. Those with long memories noted that this vindicated the railroads' position vis-à-vis the ICC and the shippers from 1910 to 1914, but it hardly answered the needs of the post-war period. Some of the companies charged the government had violated provisions of the Federal Control Act in that their properties had not been well maintained. The Railroad Administration denied this, and showed that it had spent over $4 billion on maintenance of Class I lines alone. Apparently it was not enough; during the next three years the railroads were awarded another $200 million to compensate for losses.

But even such a large sum could not bring the railroads back to where they had been prior to the government takeover. Both the Central and the Pennsylvania had altered their lines and constructed new facilities so as to assist in the war effort, while lines useful during peacetime were ignored and allowed to decay. Some though not all of the cost had been born by government. Now the railroads would have to pay for reconversion from their own treasuries. To further complicate matters, the economy went into a decline in 1919-20, and so the railroads would have a difficult time raising money for alterations and improvements. Most of the company presidents wanted government control to end as soon as possible. The managements of both the Pennsylvania and the Central agreed on this; neither had been satisfied with the way they had been treated during the war. In 1919, the Central earned 8 percent on its stock and paid its usual dividend of 5 percent, while the Pennsylvania earned 8.5 on equity and paid 6 percent—the margins were too thin for comfort. Not only were earnings below normal but they didn't take into account the massive deterioration of roadbeds and rolling stock. In all, the outlook was gloomy.

If the two lines looked forward to an end to the Railroad Administration, they could hardly expect benefits from the ICC. There was something to be said for federal regulation—even if the price was a measure of control. Some union leaders felt the same; McAdoo had been generous with them during the war. The shippers were pleased with the way they had been treated; rates had not risen as rapidly as they might have under private control and operation. Finally, men like McAdoo had been given their chance to demonstrate the workability of planning and economic coordination, and were convinced they had proven their points. By all means the railroads should be deregulated and "go private." But the benefits of standardization and integration should not be lightly discarded.

There seemed no doubt in early 1919 that the lines would soon be freed of governmental controls—there would be no nationalization of American transportation. Too, it was evident that Congress would discuss new railroad legislation, which would incorporate some of the wartime lessons.

Railroading was a mature industry by then. The great periods of growth had passed; consolidation of already existing operations was needed, along with the abandonment of lines that were no longer required. The statistics told the story. In 1911, there had been 1,312 separate railroad companies in the United States; there were 1,297 in 1914, and in 1919, 1,111. Nineteen eleven was the peak year in this regard; from that point on the numbers declined steadily. In 1920, as the railroads engaged in a massive rebuilding operation, only 314 miles of track were constructed, the lowest figure since 1836. There would be a recovery, but clearly the railroads had reached their ultimate point of expansion.

The executives understood this. They had no illusions about their positions. And they recognized that mature industries had requirements different from those of expanding ones, as well as other ambitions. So did many political leaders, for that matter, especially those who in one way or another had been involved with the Railroad Administration. A vocal cadre of experts in the universities was prepared to offer suggestions and make recommendations, and Congress was in a mood to listen. Technology also made its demands, both within the industry and without. Clearly the airplane and the automobile would alter the nation's transportation picture, as much as if not more than the railroad had in the 1840s and after. At the same time the railroads looked forward to electrification, and, if not concerned about expansion, hoped at the very least to retain a near monopoly of freight business and the bulk of passenger traffic. Because of these factors, it appeared the industry would soon undergo drastic alterations, which would involve rationalizations of existing systems and enhancement of their capabilities to meet the nation's needs.

The focus of such a change would have to be the Pennsylvania and the Central. The wartime experience had compounded the problems of the B&O and the Erie; both were on the decline, with no reversal in sight. With all of their problems, the Pennsylvania and the Central dominated transportation in an area which contained half the nation's population, freight, and passenger traffic, as well as being its industrial heartland. The leaders of both lines were certain their companies would retain their power and continue to perform as they had in the past. Financial problems would be met; Wall Street agreed, and the securities of both railroads held firm during the post-war recession. So survival was not an issue for these two companies. In 1920 they seemed strong enough and sufficiently flexible to meet any challenge. There was much talk of rebirth at the time, and grand plans for new facilities and trains.

The signs were deceiving. In retrospect, the 1920s may be viewed as an Indian summer for the Pennsylvania and the Central, one during which the options were fewer and decline beyond prevention by any political or financial force.

VI

Indian Summer

The nation's railroads were in decline during the immediate post-war period. Even the best of them appeared stagnant and insecure. The industry's leaders alternated analyses of their bright future—when trying to sell new stock and bond issues—with recitations of their woes—when conferring with the ICC or lobbying for legislation. The optimistic talks tended to be filled with generalities, vague ideas about high-speed trains, promises of new technologies, and hopes that service would improve. Pessimistic reports contained facts and figures, statistics indicating that equipment was old, the rolling stock in need of repair, the routes inadequate in some areas and overbuilt in others, and the financial situation close to being desperate. Clearly the pessimists were the more realistic. Perceptive observers could not have failed to notice this.

Those who traveled on the Twentieth Century or the Broadway Limited went in luxury, and similar trains on other major lines were up to pre-war standards in most respects.* But other travelers, those who took commuter trains or occasional trips on trains that were not showpieces, could see the signs of strain in peeling paint, unrepaired rolling stock, decaying roadbeds, and an air of mustiness where before there had been signs of fresh vigor and confidence. There were indications the companies recognized the situation and were trying to correct it. On occasion one might travel in a new passenger car, new locomotives were being pressed into service, and if one looked out of the window there were crews of laborers putting down new track

---

*Service on the Broadway Limited was halted during the war, while the Twentieth Century continued its runs. This gave the Central train an advantage it retained in the 1920s and after.

and repairing the old. The new and the old existed side by side; missing were tracks and rolling stock in between the two extremes, an indication of the effects of wartime usage on equipment.

Clearly a massive effort would be required to get the railroads back to where they had been in 1913 insofar as equipment was concerned. That was the kind of talk one heard in boardrooms during the post-Armistice period. The executives told the press they were looking ahead to a bright future, but in fact they were more interested in recapturing past glories and power and retaining present markets and customers than in setting new standards and records. This was a sign of a loss of nerve, recognition of a difficult situation, and a realization that no matter what they did, the glory days had ended and their mood could not be recaptured.

There was no single reason for this defensive attitude, but rather an awareness that the industry was being challenged on several fronts simultaneously. Railroading had been born at a time when it was able to fill recognized needs, and it developed as a result of the confluence of important economic, technological, social, and political streams. Close to a century after the formation of the first companies, all of these factors had turned against the major railroads and in the direction of new forms and structures.

Relatively few Americans traveled far from their homes in the early nineteenth century, and those trips that were undertaken utilized horses and wagons, coastwise ships, or feet. It was the commercial requirements of a developing economy that impelled the development and construction of turnpikes and canals, and the early railroads seemed an improved method of getting the goods to market. Yet the lines carried people, too—as has been seen, the upper New York railroads of the 1830s and 1840s were designed for that purpose and as feeders for the Erie. And the much publicized "romance of railroading" derived not from the hauling of coal and cloth but the carrying of people, even though both were important to the nation's economic development.

The railroads tied the major inland cities to one another, and all of them to the countryside and ocean ports. At first they supplemented the waterways, and then, to a degree, replaced them. Those who worked in the cities walked to their places of employment, then took horsecars, and by the early twentieth century, most arrived at their jobs by means of one form or another of railroad. To the urban Americans of this period, the vehicle was not a romantic wonder, but an accepted part of everyday life. Similarly, residents of small towns and farms had come to consider the railroad as a means of transporting goods and people, and not the awesome symbol of progress it had been in the 1850s. Both urban and rural Americans recognized its importance, but also saw its limitations.

Before the Civil War, Henry Thoreau had noted that the railroad gave Americans a new awareness of time. The locomotives ran on schedules, and tried to be precise in following them. Dictates of custom and business, as well as those of technology, required them to start and stop without taking into consideration the requirements of individual passengers. The arrival and departure of the Broadway Limited or the Twentieth Century were carefully timed, as were those of other great trains. This meant the traveler had to adjust to the schedule, and the shipper time his efforts to its demands. This was no great effort in the nineteenth century, given the social attitudes of the period. But the development of new technologies in the new century pointed up the railroads' limitations.

The automobile and truck awaited the owner-traveler, not vice versa. Given a decent road system, they could go where and when they pleased, not merely to the station closest to their destination when the train stopped there. Shippers who had been obliged to transport their wares to train depots, manufacturers whose decisions on plant location had been determined by railroad stops, and travelers who waited in dusty stations for trains and then had to worry about local transportation once they arrived at their destinations welcomed the automobile. This awareness of time and convenience worked to the new technology's advantage.

The automobile's flexibility was a decided asset, recognized by the government as well as private and commercial travelers. When the eastern railroads were troubled by bottlenecks and unable to reroute trains, the army used trucks to ship goods and men. In 1916 the Federal Aid Road Act, a modest measure, passed Congress and was signed into law. The following year the War Industries Board established a Highway Transport Committee, headed by automobile executive Roy Chapin. It helped coordinate motor traffic in much the same fashion as the Railroad Administration did for its sector, and in addition Chapin lobbied for additional aid legislation. This arrived in 1921, with the passage of the Federal Highway Act. Within a year, the federal government projected a system that would include all cities with populations of over fifty thousand.

The federal programs were modest, but the state and local governments mounted major efforts in road construction. In 1914, state expenditures for roads and bridges were only $75 million; fifteen years later the states spent over a billion dollars on such projects. In this period the nation's surfaced road mileage went from 256,000 to 662,000, while passenger car registrations rose from 548,000 to 4.5 million and those for trucks from 25,000 to 882,000.

The large motor buses that appeared in the 1920s usually charged lower rates than railroads and still showed higher profits on investments. The railroaders protested that the buses received what amounted to a subsidy in government-built and -maintained roads, while they had to pay for their tracks and pass costs on to consumers. But nothing was done either to raise bus taxes or lower those for railroads. The automobile in its various forms could not be withstood, and it became a major threat to railroads, not only for the carrying of individuals but freight as well. Just as the canals had been obliged to give way before what appeared to be a superior technology, so the railroads had to face the challenge of the motorcar in the 1920s. The locomotive's prospects for success were bleak.

Nor was this the only technological challenge, for aviation too threatened to take some of the railroads' business. The Post Office initiated airmail in 1918, and under the terms of the Kelly Act of 1925 the government established a transcontinental service based on private carriers, and helped them with technological services, weather information, and the construction of airports. This was still a minor part of the railroads' business, but the signs were disturbing, for toward the end of the decade there was talk of regularly scheduled passenger traffic as well as a small freight business.

As they had with the automobiles, the railroads complained about these direct and indirect subsidies, but to no avail. To further compound their problems, there was a revival of water transport in the 1920s, and the government assisted these shippers by dredging harbors and maintaining port facilities. Then there was the rise of petroleum pipelines, whose business more than doubled in the decade. These alternate transportation facilities threatened the railroads. Even in the area of folk heroes there was a switch of loyalties—from Casey Jones to Henry Ford and Charles Lindbergh.

The railroads were victims of their past as well. By 1920 it was clear to almost all informed students of the subject that the companies were in serious trouble, that organizational reforms would be needed if they were to remain viable. The companies disagreed as to tactics and strategies, however. On the one side were old progressives, now allied with a handful of railroaders, most of whom managed the stronger midwestern lines, who demanded competition, while on the other were those individuals whose wartime experiences had convinced them that competition was ruinous, and that the industry's only viable long-term solution rested in a major unification effort, under one or another master plan. The eastern lines agreed, but the habits of three-quarters of a century could not be broken easily. Each company wanted a dominant position in respect to the others; none would consent to advantages granted old rivals. Finally, there was the axiom of the industry, which by mid-decade had become a cliché: "Managements never merge themselves out of jobs."

The eastern lines had two sets of problems that were outgrowths of the new technologies and political developments. They could either fight their transportation rivals or in some way try to control them, possibly through a process of absorption and change. As for the government's merger programs, the railroads might cooperate or attempt to evade the concept of master systems. These choices could be perceived and isolated both in prospect and retrospect; they were as evident to observers of 1920 as to their successors a half century later. Decisions were required; equivocation and halfway measures would not do. Yet the nation's leading railroaders did equivocate, as well as seek other solutions to their problems, while wistfully hoping their difficulties would somehow be dissolved in the decade's general prosperity and euphoria.

The railroad leaders were in a quandary during the immediate post-war period. They disliked public operation and control and hoped to bring both to a rapid conclusion. So long as the government insisted upon retaining power, however, it had to assume responsibilities, and the companies hoped improvements would be made on tracks and rolling stock at public expense. These would be difficult to obtain once government control was ended. In addition, the railroads had no desire to return to the pre-war relationship with the ICC. They felt the agency had starved them, prevented meaningful modernization by holding down rates, and in general was an antirailroad organization. Too, the companies as well as the government had come to comprehend the virtues of wartime coordination even while realizing its limitations. Some way had to be found to retain the former while eliminating the latter. The administration appreciated the nature of the situation, and also knew that an already troubled peacetime economy would be dealt a severe blow if the newly freed railroads sank into debt and eventual bankruptcy due to a hasty and ill-prepared divestiture. Congress understood the delicacy of the problem, and in early 1919 the House Committee on Interstate and Foreign Commerce began hearings on a bill to restore the railroads to private control.

The railroad brotherhoods and a group of pre-war progressives also considered the situation, and concluded that nationalization was the only sensible way to resolve outstanding problems. They were led by Glenn Plumb, a lawyer who had been influenced by syndicalism before the war and then came to appreciate the efficiencies of coordination on a national scale. Plumb was general counsel for the brotherhoods, and in 1919 presented his plan to the House committee.

According to his figures, the nation's railroads were worth $18 billion. Plumb would have the federal government float bonds for that amount and then purchase the equity. The various companies would be unified and operated by a public authority, not unlike the Railroad Administration. The ICC would exercise rate-making powers and its work would be simplified by virtue of having to deal with only one management. Whatever profits existed by year's end would be divided equally between the government and the employees. This would encourage the workers to seek efficiencies and cut back on costs, and so result in better operations and perhaps even lower rates.

The Public Ownership League of America and the Plumb Plan League supported the measure. The former was organized and led by intellectuals, the latter by the brotherhoods. Had their plan been accepted, the railroads would have come to resemble public utilities insofar as actual operations were concerned. Whether or not the anticipated efficiencies would have transpired is questionable; other government operations weren't noted for them in 1920. Critics argued that subsidies would be required, that the railroads would become huge pork barrels under government ownership and operation. Farm organizations tended to view the Plumb Plan as a masked grant for the unions, and they distrusted its sponsorship. Shippers feared rate increases and preferred to play one railroad off against the others, clearly not possible under the Plumb Plan. The railroad executives could hardly be expected to welcome a proposal so contrary to their ideology and positions. McAdoo and his successors at the Railroad Administration spoke out in favor of the Plumb Plan, but they soon abandoned it when they realized it had failed to stir congressional interest. The proposal was rejected, and soon after, Congress turned to more modest plans.

The House committee hearings in 1919 and 1920 resulted in the framing of the Esch-Cummins Act, or as it was better known, the Transportation Act of 1920. This measure, which was signed into law on March 1, was designed to make the railroads financially viable and at the same time create a structure within which they could maintain such a position. In the first place, the railroads required protection by the ICC, not a return to the old opposition. The agency was expanded and empowered to set minimum as well as maximum rates so as to ensure the companies a return of at least 5.5 percent on investment, with the understanding that profits of over 6 percent would be recoverable. In order to ease the transition to private operation, the railroads were offered federal guarantees on a rental basis for the first six months—an offer that most accepted, and which cost the government a half a billion dollars. In these and related ways, the government sought to ensure financial liquidity for the railroads; there was a general recognition the industry was ailing, and would require help in order to perform its economic functions.

The second point involved mergers. Under the terms of the Transportation Act these would be encouraged so as to create major systems, each of which could survive in its territory. The ICC was given a mandate to come up with such a plan, and immediately contacted Professor William Z. Ripley of Harvard, perhaps the leading expert in the field. Ripley's report was delivered in early 1921. It was comprehensive in scope and more ambitious than any ever suggested by Morgan and his contemporaries. Ripley divided the nation into six territories, in which there would be erected sixteen major systems. The antitrust crusade against the railroads would have to be abandoned, and Ripley hoped the Supreme Court would reconsider its earlier antimerger stances. Progressive fears of and opposition to bigness were to be set aside, as were beliefs that the railroads dominated the economy. In 1920 these seemed outworn and not particularly useful. Before the war, Ripley's writings had been cited by those who had opposed large scale mergers. He too had changed. Now his plan became the basis for federal railroad policy, and was utilized by those who supported Morgan's concept of communities of interests.

The eastern territory was the key to the Ripley plan, for it remained the heartland of American railroading. Five major systems were to emerge: the Central, the Pennsylvania, the B&O, the Erie, and a combined Nickel Plate-Lackawanna. Ripley thought the consolidators would be pleased on learning that the smaller lines would be taken over by one or another of the five, while antimonopolists would be placated by the expected competition between them. But the plan also had unrealistic elements. The Erie and the B&O were weak systems in terms of rolling stock, finances, and prospects. The situation at the Nickel Plate was complicated by a new element in railroading. The line was controlled by the Van Sweringen brothers of Cleveland, who had purchased it from the Central in 1916, in a deal that had the blessings of Morgan and Company. The brothers expanded this base during the next two years. They acquired the Lake Erie and Western and a majority interest in the Toledo, St. Louis and Western—more familiarly known as the Clover Leaf. These properties were united through the formation of three holding companies—Vaness, Wester, and Clover Leaf, each of which sought additional properties. In 1922 the Van Sweringens further consolidated their lines through the medium of a fourth company, whose name indicated their goal: the New York, Chicago and St. Louis. The brothers knew relatively little about railroading, but were rapidly becoming adept at financial juggling. Together with their bankers, they planned to pyramid their holdings and continue to expand their base so as to create a major system.

The Pennsylvania and the Central took this into consideration when reviewing the Ripley Plan. It offered them little and demanded much. President Smith of the Central, now back in office after government service during the war, was particularly troubled. Not only had he sold the Nickel Plate to the Van Sweringens but Smith had introduced them to the Morgan bankers. "The control of the passageways must be in the hands that can make the best use of them," he told government investigators, and Smith made it clear he did not include the brothers in this group. Rea agreed. Both men and their companies were relatively secure in the early 1920s, for despite their problems, they were in better shape than the other major eastern carriers. Under the terms of the Ripley Plan, they would have to allow the Baltimore and Ohio and the Erie to obtain interests they never could have achieved in open competition. Smith and Rea were unclear as to where the Van Sweringens would fit into the program; clearly the brothers would be a fifth force, an openly expansionist one at that, the first important threat to eastern hegemony since George Gould had attempted to elbow his way into the area in the early twentieth century. At that time Wall Streeters had warned that there were five companies interested in the New York to Chicago run, but only enough business for two. The Central and the Pennsylvania dominated this route in the immediate post-war period, and it was considered the key to the region. Now the government, under the Ripley Plan, proposed to revive the other three. And the professor expected cooperation, even support, from the two major carriers. This was too much to bear. From the first, the Central and the Pennsylvania did all they could to block its acceptance.

The ICC went ahead with its program, hardly noting the dissatisfaction in New York and Philadelphia. In the summer of 1921 it presented a preliminary plan, based on the Ripley proposals. As might have been anticipated, Rea and Smith blocked the agency, and through delaying tactics and the presentation of alternate programs managed to prevent action that year. Other conferences followed, and all ended in failure. Then the companies met on their own, without ICC supervision and sponsorship, claiming their goal was compliance with the Ripley Plan. This was a ruse. While they talked, some of the companies scrambled to obtain additional properties. In time the ICC would tire of delays and then try to impose its own solutions upon the lines, and each wanted to be strong as possible when that happened.

The Van Sweringens took in the Chesapeake and Ohio, the Père Marquette, the Wheeling and Lake Erie, the Chicago and Eastern Illinois, and the Missouri Pacific—they even gained control of the Erie, making a shambles of the Ripley Plan. The B&O purchased shares in the Western Maryland, the Altona, the Buffalo and Susquehanna, and several other lines, while tightening its grip on the Reading. As for the Pennsylvania, it gained control of the Wabash, the Lehigh Valley, the Pittsburgh and West Virginia, and the Detroit, Toledo and Ironton, while accumulating shares of the Norfolk and Western. Rea conducted forays into the New Haven and the Boston and Maine as well, and the Pennsylvania consolidated its holdings west of Pittsburgh, in this way simplifying corporate structure in preparation for new opportunities should they present themselves.

As had been its policy since before the war, the Central concentrated on a few objectives rather than striking out in several directions simultaneously. After the heyday of J.P. Morgan it had ceded a portion of the anthracite trade to the Pennsylvania in return for a share of the bituminous traffic. Now it violated the agreement, deliberately, by purchasing large blocks of the Lehigh Valley. This caused a major rift with the Pennsylvania that for a while shattered any hope of a united front against the other companies and the government. The big four—the Central, the Pennsylvania, the Van Sweringens, and the B&O—behaved like feudal kingdoms in the 1920s, forming alliances and then breaking them so as to enter into new arrangements with other forces. They would unite temporarily against outside forces: The ICC would not be permitted to impose its solution on the industry, and in 1927, when there was some talk of a "fifth force" erected by West Virginia mining interests, the big four got together to prevent action.*

The Ripley Plan was a dead letter by the end of the decade. The ICC never did press forward; that part of the Transportation Act of 1920 was forgotten or simply ignored. Instead, four large enterprises consolidated and became still larger. The stock market was booming and interest rates were low, and both the Pennsylvania and the Central took advantage of this situation to obtain additional funds for improvements and expansion. The railroads had to be refurbished; there was no doubt of this. But expansion was another matter. Were it not for the easy-money atmosphere of the decade, the acquisitions might have been foregone, or at least been undertaken in a more modest fashion. In effect, some railroads accumulated new properties when the old were in need of pruning and development. The Van Sweringens ignored the ICC, organized the Alleghany Corporation—a giant holding company—and used it as a net to ensnare additional properties. The Pennsylvania countered with Pennroad, which was supposed to do the same. In 1930 the Central organized the New York Central Securities Company, never very active, apparently in order to keep up with the others.

The Van Sweringens were speculators, and their railroad empire was always shaky. But the Pennsylvania and the Central were among the oldest and most experienced companies in America. Their willingness to play the game by the new rules indicates the feverish atmosphere in railroading at the time. To what purpose did the Pennsylvania seek these additional properties? Several of them had insecure futures—the New Haven was in this category. The Central's new foray into anthracite could be justified on economic grounds, since for many years the

---

*The best source for the intricate maneuverings of this period is William N. Leonard, *Railroad Consolidation Under the Transportation Act of 1920* (New York, 1946), pp. 127-58.

Lehigh Valley had been a thriving concern and the coal-hauling traffic would not be challenged by the newer means of transportation. But many of the acquisitions and expansions resulted from a fascination with financial pyrotechnics and ill-founded dreams, not programs that took into consideration the industry's problems and potentials.

The ICC's stances compounded the difficulties. Before the war the commission had taken positions that had harmed many carriers, and had done so in the name of competition. There was a general recognition by 1920 that cooperation would be required to undo some of the damage, as well as create a viable industry. Even though the Ripley Plan had its flaws, the philosophy behind it was a sensible response to felt needs. The government wanted a federalized system in 1920, and this was reflected in the Transportation Act. But the law did not set a time limit upon deliberations, and so there were opportunities for delay. Had the ICC pressed ahead firmly in 1921, the Ripley Plan might have been put into operation, and at least a start toward regional cooperation could have been made. But it held back, and did nothing of importance in this area for the rest of the decade. Meanwhile the railroads went their separate ways, and there was less industry accord in the East in 1929 than there had been in 1914.*

The industry had failed to meet the organizational challenges of the 1920s. The companies would have to face the Great Depression divided and financially unprepared. Other industries that would suffer in the 1930s could explain their positions by arguing that the calamity could not have been predicted or anticipated, that they did not think their booms would ever end. This was not the case with railroading, for there had been no boom there. Even though railroad earnings rose by 40 percent from 1922 to 1928, this additional money did not cover increased expenditures, such as payments for acquisitions and, most important, the purchase of new equipment. And the industry was stagnant. In 1925, an excellent year for most sectors of the economy, more than 18,000 miles of track were in receivership, and abandonments of unremunerative properties became more common than ever before.

This should have been taken as a sign that railroading could decline precipitously given another depression. Statistics of the leading lines verified both the industry's status and the lack of

---

*"Evidence indicates that the Commission was strongly influenced (misled?) by the financial splendor of the 1920's and by the political philosophy of the times which looked askance at Government interference in business affairs." *Ibid.* p. 279.

understanding of it on the part of investors. The Central reported an income of $71.2 million in 1923 on revenues of $421 million, and its dividend was $5.00. In 1929, the Central's earnings were only $64.6 million, its revenues $396 million, while the dividend had recently been raised to $8.00. Yet in 1923, Central common stock sold for a low of $72^3/_4$, while the 1929 high was $192^3/_4$. In addition, the Central had $268 million in common stock outstanding in 1923, and through rights offerings and the conversion of debentures the amount reached just below $500 million on the eve of the Great Crash. Thus, the dividend was safer in the earlier year than in the later. The Pennsylvania's statistics were similar—stagnant earnings and revenues while capitalization and dividends were rising. Since the coal business was poor in this period, the company remained in a more vulnerable situation than the Central. Still, the price of its common stock rose from $40^7/_8$ to 110 in 1923-29. With declining profits in 1928, the company had no difficulty in selling 1.2 million shares through a rights offering, and another 1.4 million were placed in this way two months after the 1929 market crash—again, with little in the way of resistance. In this same period, the Dow-Jones Railroad Index rose from below 77 to close to 190.

Perhaps this kind of performance, these signs of investor confidence, encouraged the railroaders to enter into deals, form holding companies, and behave as though they were in an expanding industry. They might have believed their own propaganda, that the railroads were about to enter a new golden age, that the airplane and automobile could not replace them, even in passenger traffic. Still, some of the railroads did hedge their bets. They adapted themselves to new technologies, and demonstrated imagination and, on occasion, even daring in abandoning outmoded machines and track and purchasing the most modern equipment—though their efforts doubtless would have been more effective had their interests not been occupied by expansionist programs. More important, perhaps, some of the companies, the Pennsylvania in particular, recognized the automotive and aviation challenges and decided not to fight them but rather incorporate the two into their existing operations.

It appeared a replay of the 1830s, when the waterways had to deal with the new technology of railroads. Had the Erie Canal entered the field, there might not have been a New York Central, but instead a major transportation complex utilizing one or the other technology when the situation demanded it. Perhaps recalling this lesson, some of the railroaders of the 1920s seemed on their way to transforming their industry into a transportation operation, in which case it would have been more powerful than before—in fact, the materials were available to create transportation conglomerates in this decade, had the executives traveled along paths that were well marked and even explored. Here too, however, their interests were concentrated on railroad expansion; it was a major failure of imagination, but one that was understandable under the circumstances.

In 1920 motor carriers accounted for less than 1 percent of all intercity freight movements. Ten years later they took 4 percent of the business. In this same period the railroads' share declined slightly, from 77 percent to 74. Clearly the challenge in this sector was not serious yet, but the outlines of change were quite visible. The situation was more striking in commercial passenger traffic. There were few intercity buses before World War I, and most of these were in rural areas not served by trains. By 1930, close to one out of every five people who took commercial vehicles to go from the city used the bus, and all of this came at the expense of the railroads.

The Pennsylvania was one of the first railroads to appreciate the dimensions of this challenge, and beginning in 1922 the company purchased small motor carriers and established others. At first this was done in the name of economy; the Pennsylvania would abandon a little-used passenger line and replace it with a bus service, or, rather than constructing a spur into a developing territory, it would use buses until the traffic made trains economically feasible. There were obvious economic advantages to this approach, as well as an important political one: at the time the buses did not come under ICC regulations, even though they were engaged in interstate commerce, and the same held true for trucks.

At first the Pennsylvania's efforts in motor transportation were exploratory and supplemental. Then, in 1927, the company embarked upon a more ambitious program. It organized small passenger bus companies with impressive names, but, for the moment at least, little in the way of equipment—Pennsylvania Virginia General Transit, Pennsylvania Indiana General Transit, Pennsylvania Illinois General Transit, and the like. These companies operated buses that serviced small communities as well as taking over existing Pennsylvania bus operations within their territories. Two years later the company organized American Contract and Trust, a wholly owned subsidiary, which served as a holding company for these and related enterprises. Then it purchased the People's Rapid Transit, which operated a scheduled service between Philadelphia and small towns in New Jersey. This was followed by the acquisition of the Buffalo Interurban Bus Lines, the largest factor in that city. More important, the Pennsylvania took an equity position in the Motor Transit Corporation, which had just begun carrying passengers between New York and Chicago. Clearly this was not a threat to the railroad yet, but the Pennsylvania was looking ahead to a time when such carriers might offer lower rates to long-distance travelers. Shortly thereafter, the company changed its name to the Greyhound Corporation, and projected an ambitious expansion program that would challenge the eastern railroads for economy fares. This would require additional financing, and the Pennsylvania was willing to provide it. Furthermore, the two companies joined to form the Pennsylvania Greyhound Lines, which within a year had 8,000 route miles and small terminals in most of the eastern cities. The Greyhound buses were not as fast as the passenger trains, partly because they were really trucks with special bodies, but also due to the lack of good roads. Both would improve over the years, and Greyhound expanded rapidly. Other railroads suffered financially because of a loss of passenger business; the Pennsylvania was able to recapture part of the loss through its bus operations.

The company followed a different approach regarding freight service. It purchased several trucks for use within Pittsburgh in 1923. Now the Pennsylvania could offer additional services to small shippers, who would pay a modest fee to have their goods delivered direct to their destinations rather than have them picked up by a different carrier at the terminal. The services were expanded to other cities soon after, a practice imitated by rival railroads. In 1926 the Pennsylvania purchased Scott Brothers, a major trucking company in the Philadelphia area, and two years later took interests in similar firms in Baltimore and Pittsburgh. By 1930, the company had trucking operations in Buffalo, Cleveland, Toledo, Dayton, and other cities of their size and rank. In addition, the Pennsylvania experimented with hybrid railroad-truck transportation. Specially designed containers were loaded on flat-cars and carried to the terminal closest to their ultimate destinations. There the container would be transferred intact to a truck, which would take it to the receiver. The container operations afforded obvious efficiencies and economies, and had the further benefit of confusing the ICC, which for a while wasn't certain whether it had jurisdiction over such means of transportation, and if so, how much.

A more interesting though less profitable form of hybridization concerned aviation. Few Americans traveled by air in the 1920s, and the planes carried little in the way of freight except mail. No one was really certain as to the future of commercial aviation, or what form it would take, although several companies were in the field and, given strong backing from Wall Street, making ambitious projections. The Lindbergh flight in 1927 gave credence to at least some of these and resulted in the formation of several new companies. One of them, the Transcontinental Air Transport, began operations in early 1928 and announced its intention of providing a coast-to-coast service—New York to Los Angeles in forty-eight hours. The company was backed by Curtis Aeroplane and Wright Aeronautical, as well as several other aviation companies. The Pennsylvania was intrigued by some of Transcontinental's plans, and purchased a one-fifth interest in the company for $500,000.

Transcontinental envisaged a system that bore a closer resemblance to the old Pennsylvania Main Line than to modern air transport in that it combined two forms of transportation in an effort to obtain benefits from both. Passengers would board a Pennsylvania train in New York in the early evening, and from there go to Columbus, Ohio. Then, in the early morning, they would take a plane to a western terminal of the Atcheson, Topeka and Santa Fe, and arrive there by dusk. They would eat on the train, sleep, and awaken in New Mexico, in time for a day flight to Los Angeles or San Francisco.

It was a cumbersome system—sleeping on trains at night, flying on Ford Trimotors by day—and chances for missed connections were considerable. After several organizational changes the service was put into operation in 1930, but wasn't very popular—and certainly no challenge to the all-rail trip with a single change at Chicago or St. Louis. Transcontinental underwent some additional alterations before emerging as Trans-World Airlines in the mid-1930s. The Pennsylvania retained an interest in the new company, but sold the last of its shares in 1926, at which time scheduled coast-to-coast air travel was feasible, but still believed commercially impractical.

The railroads modernized rapidly in the 1920s; according to some estimates, half the nation's rolling stock in 1930 was less than ten years old. Even while diverted by mergers and financial manipulations of various kinds, the managers understood that without improved service their profit margins would decline, and in the end, the companies would falter and perhaps even enter the lists of the insolvent.

Many of the changes at the Pennsylvania and the Central

resulted from the resumption of programs that had been interrupted by the war. Both companies completed their terminal-construction programs; toward the end of the decade the new ones tended to be smaller but more efficient than the pre-war giants, this a result of additional economies and a realization that travelers and shippers were more interested in costs and schedules than frescos and columns. They encouraged their suppliers to design and construct larger freight cars, and dispatchers were put on notice to concentrate on adding to the number of cars per freight train. This program was successful; at the Pennsylvania the net tonnage per freight train rose by nearly 25 percent in the 1930s, advancing steadily in most years, while the Central's net tonnage increased by slightly more than 20 percent in the same period.

As had been the case earlier, the Pennsylvania's modernization efforts were more dramatic than those of the Central, due in large part to its difficult terrain and size. Although the Central operated slightly more miles of first track, the Pennsylvania's were utilized more intensively, and it was the most important American railroad by almost any measurement. At the end of the decade the company carried one out of every five railroad passengers, and accounted for well over 10 percent of the nation's freight, locomotives, employees, revenues, and net railroad investment.

Leadership played a role too. Alfred Smith of the Central died in an accident in 1924 and was succeeded by Patrick Crowley; both men were more concerned with management and finance than with modernization. Under their leadership the Central repaired the war damages, added new rolling stock and locomotives, and initiated important schedule changes so as to reflect the developing needs of its territory. These men were similar to Rea of the Pennsylvania, who concentrated upon political affairs and acquisitions. Rea delegated a good deal of his authority over management to Vice-President William W. Atterbury, who before the war had been the company's operations chief as well as serving as president of the American Railway Association. Atterbury had entered the army as a general in 1917, and served as Pershing's director-general of transportation. By 1920 he was one of the nation's most prominent railroad figures and spokesmen, and an acknowledged expert in technology. When Rea retired in 1925, Atterbury was named as his successor and immediately accelerated important projects he had begun several years before.

The Pennsylvania was particularly proud of its electrification program. The company had been one of the earliest advocates of electrification, having helped develop the technology and actually using it on several minor roads in the late nineteenth century. The company insisted that electric railroads would be more efficient, cleaner, quieter, faster, and more economical than the familiar steam locomotives. In addition, the Pennsylvania knew it could not run the coal burners in its Hudson tunnels for fear of asphyxiation. Indeed, the Pennsylvania owned and maintained more long tunnels than any other American railroad, and its engineers, who believed that future alterations in routes would be simplified by new tunneling, had urged the line to consider electrification.

The debate between advocates of steam and electricity stirred considerable interest. Even now there are defenders of steam who claim it had been killed by short-sighted executives who knew little of technology. Then there are the critics who charge the companies delayed the transformation from steam to electrics and diesels because they were more concerned with manipulating securities and properties than with their real business, transportation. Neither judgment is fair or accurate. In the 1920s the eastern railroads did embark upon major electrification projects. Rather than rebuild their old, worn tracks, the companies ripped them up and replaced them with electrified ones. The entire system—except terminals and stations—had to be revamped, for electric engines could not run over tracks designed for steam. Although many key railroad statistics looked poor in the 1920s, construction expenses rose rapidly, especially in the early years of the decade as the companies replaced and repaired worn-out equipment and paid for the electrification programs. Then, in the second half of the decade, the roads were ready to take delivery on the new engines and put them into operation.

The number of engines in service actually declined in the 1920s, from 69,000 in 1920 to 61,200 in 1929. This was due more to efficient operations than a loss of business. In addition, the figures are distorted as a result of the electrification program. In 1920, there were only 388 electrics in service, and in 1925, 379. The new tracks were ready by then, and the lines received their electrics and put them into service. In 1929, the railroads used 621 electrics, and the fleets expanded even during the depression, for there were 900 in service in 1940. In contrast, the number of steam locomotives declined steadily, from 69,100 in 1920 to 60,200 in 1930 to 44,300 in 1940.

The Central was of two minds as to the benefits of electrification. It was one of the nation's major haulers of bituminous, the kind of coal used by steam locomotives. This market would be harmed by the electrification effort. On the other hand, there was no doubt that the coal burners were dirty, a fact that bothered passengers—the Lackawanna converted from bituminous to anthracite and created the figure of a young lady for use in advertising campaigns: "Phoebe Snow/dressed in white/rides the road of anthracite."

If the Central wanted to retain its long-distance passenger business and appear modern, it would have to replace the steam engines. In retrospect, it might be argued that the Central made the wrong choice for the right reason—that it should have gone directly to diesels and had no reason to prefer the electrics. But in the 1920s, as its rival electrified, the Central thought it wise to follow suit. By 1930 it had 146 electrics in service. Then it halted, unable to continue due to the depression.

In contrast to the Central's occasional wavering, Atterbury emerged as electrification's most enthusiastic supporter. He spoke out on the subject, prodding other railroaders to take the plunge. The fact that the Pennsylvania was the nation's leading carrier of anthracite, the kind of coal used by electric utilities, may have been a factor in this, but far more important was Atterbury's own convictions. His major project and showpiece was the Washington to Philadelphia run, work on which was begun in 1926 and completed two years later, at which time Atterbury announced that construction would soon start on the tracks between Philadelphia and New York. Meanwhile he electrified the passenger lines in the Philadelphia area and began a similar program for the Long Island Railroad. These projects cost well over $300 million before completion. By the late 1930s, the Pennsylvania had 2,000 miles of electric track, more than one-sixth of its total.

In 1930 the Pennsylvania had 99 electrics, two-thirds that of the Central, but it was expanding while the Central was not. By 1933, the company owned or leased 115 electric locomotives, and in 1935—Atterbury's last year with the Pennsylvania—it had 203, more than any other American railroad. Of these, 63 were freight carriers, almost all delivered that year. In the midst of the depression, the Pennsylvania continued to expand its electrification program, though at times its budget was strained to do so and other programs were delayed. Atterbury's ambition had been to set the company well on the way to electrification, and so he did—in this respect, his administration resembled the single-minded drive of Cassatt in expanding the Pennsylvania's reach.

Was it a wise move? Since Atterbury was viewed as a master of technology, his decision certainly must have been carefully considered and undertaken. Still, other lines did hold back, not so much because they had faith in steam locomotives but rather due to the development of a third technology—the diesel.

These locomotives had been known in Europe before the war, if only on an experimental basis. While Atterbury was pushing ahead with electrification, several small American lines considered the diesels, and in 1925 one was tried out on the Central Railroad of New Jersey, but only for switching operations. By then several manufacturers were busy developing a diesel-electric. These new locomotives were powerful, but expensive—more than twice as much as steamers. But they were highly efficient, even more so than most of the electrics, and used small amounts of fuel. Furthermore, they utilized a simple technology—diesels could run for weeks without major overhauls, and they rarely broke down. They were easy on tracks and clean. In fact, the diesels had almost all of the advantages of the electrics combined with those of the steam locomotives—they could run on the old tracks as well as the new.

In 1929 there were only 25 diesels in America, with 52 more on order. Little was done in the next few years as railroaders considered their options and assets during the depression. Several western lines, which had been interested in electrification, now turned to diesels instead, attracted by their advantages but also aware of the costs of electrifying entire lines. The Burlington and the Union Pacific led the way. In 1932 there were 80 diesels in operation, and in 1934, when the Burlington turned to them, 104. Then the floodgates were loosened. The lines reported 639 in service in 1939, and in the following year there were 967, more than electrics for the first time. The trend was well established by then. The all-electrics had reached their peak and would slowly decline, while the diesels continued to replace the steam locomotives.

Atterbury's great drive to electrification had been poorly timed and oversold, but this could not have been seen in prospect, only in retrospect. Clearly changes were required, and electrification offered solutions that were both attractive and plausible. Given another decade of prosperity, the all-electrics might have won the day, with the diesels used only to complement them and on lines that could not afford the massive construction programs. A steam locomotive might be replaced by a diesel, which, though it cost more initially, made up the difference with operational efficiencies. In contrast, the electric required an entire new system. This impelled the railroaders toward the diesel in depression America. It was a sensible move; the new locomotives performed well and those who made the choice had little reason to regret it. As for Atterbury, he might have been ahead of his time. For although the diesels were efficient, they did burn petroleum, while the electrics could be powered by energy derived from coal, water power, or any other source. This meant next to nothing in the 1930s and for the next three decades, periods of cheap oil. But it would make a difference in the 1970s, though by then this was one of the railroads' less important problems.

On the eve of the Great Depression, the Pennsylvania and the Central both were considered in fine shape. All the bond-rating agencies gave them high marks. Their stocks were viewed as investments safe for widows and orphans. Even with the advent of the motorcar age, the railroads were considered an indispensable part of the nation's economic infrastructure. And so they were. But the entire economy was due for a rough period, and the railroads—burdened with debt, unable and unwilling to enter into mergers that would result in greater efficiencies, and crippled by generations of antagonism on the part of regulatory agencies, as well as being victims of their own technological flaws—were in a poor condition to face the new challenges. In 1929, only 5,700 miles of track were in the hands of receivers; the figure was 22,500 in 1932. The railroads reported a net income of $977 million in 1929; in 1932, they had a deficit of $121 million, the first since such figures had been gathered. Most of the major companies—those not in bankruptcy—were able to pay their bondholders, but dividends were cut and, in some cases, eliminated. In 1929, the railroads paid a total of $561 million in dividends, and in 1932, $151 million.

Like the others, the Pennsylvania was badly shaken. From its 1929 high of 110 Pennsylvania common fell to a 1932 low of $6^1/_2$. But despite its expansionist programs, the Pennsylvania was still a strong railroad, one with a heritage of conservative finances. With the exception of the Cassatt years, it had always attempted to finance expansion through retained earnings. To be sure, Rea's acquisitions and Atterbury's electrification programs had been costly. They ate up the surpluses and cut into reserves. It was for this reason that Atterbury had sold large common stock issues in 1928 and 1929, and he would have continued to do so were it not for the onset of the depression. As it happened, the crash came at a rather fortuitous time for him. Atterbury was obliged to cut back on electrification, and eventually completed the program with the aid of New Deal agencies, the Works Progress Administration in particular. By 1932 the acquisitions had been digested, and were not a serious burden. Pennroad collapsed and almost went out of business, but its finances were separate from those of the railroad company, and so were not reflected in its earnings statements. Still, the Pennsylvania's net earnings were only $1.03 a share, and there was talk of passing the dividend so as to preserve capital. But in the end Atterbury authorized the payment of $1.00 a share, more out of a respect for tradition than from sound financial management.

The Central was in a far more dangerous position. Before the war it had enlarged its debt in order to pay for improvements and acquisitions. Then, during the 1920s, the company engaged in a reconstruction and electrification program while at the same time attempting to contain its indebtedness. In order to do so, the Central had sold far more common stock than had the Pennsylvania. This meant greater security for bondholders, but a somewhat precarious situation for the stockholders.

The Central was a major firm within the industry, but then, as before, was not as carefully managed as the Pennsylvania. With its excellent terrain and well-developed territory, it had lacked the challenges its major rival had to overcome. The Pennsylvania responded to these challenges by leading the way in technological development, innovations, and careful expansion. More often than not the Central followed, and to investors this indicated a more conservative attitude—later it would be perceived as a lack of initiative. True, the Central was capable of imaginative moves, such as the introduction of the Twentieth Century, but the Pennsylvania usually recovered quickly, and in any case its freight business, though less glamourous, was far more important in terms of earnings than such dramatic touches.

Finances were the most important consideration in the early 1930s, and here the Central was clearly in second place. In 1932 the company reported operating revenues of $293 million against the Pennsylvania's $331 million. Yet its funded debt was $670 million while the Pennsylvania's was $626 million. Its smaller revenue base and larger debt were disturbing in the depression atmosphere, and were reflected in the price of its common stock, which had sold for 130 as late as the spring of 1931, and which fell to below 10 by autumn 1932. In a desperate move to preserve working capital, the Central ordered an end to any new construction, and even repairs were cut back, so that the rolling stock became run down, while road beds declined to where they had been during the World War I period. There was a difference between 1918 and 1932, however. During the war Americans believed the situation would be rectified given a period of normal economic activity. This sentiment was absent in 1932.

The reasons could be found not only in the general pessimism of the time but in the performance of such strong companies as the Central. Earnings, dividends, and the price of its common stock had risen in the 1920s, as has been indicated, but while industrial production increased by more than 25 percent from 1923 to 1929, the Central's revenues actually declined slightly. In the past railroading had been a cyclical industry, alternating good times with bad, using the earnings of the former period to tide the companies over rough spots. If there was one major lesson to be learned in the 1920s, it was that even in the best of times, railroad performance would be lacking in vitality.

The Central reported earnings of $0.49 a share in 1931, when it tried to obtain financing for several projects and failed to do so. The regular $2.00 dividend was paid in February, even though it hadn't been earned. There was a deficit in the second quarter, and the dividend was cut to $1.50. Despite continuing losses, the Central paid another $1.50 in August, and $1.00 in November.

President Frederic Williamson, in office less than a year, attempted to float new bond issues, and was rejected by his bankers. Morgan and Company turned him down with deep regret. But given the state of the economy, the situation in the financial world, and the Central's deficits, there was nothing else it could have done. Private capitalism, which had done so much to create the railroad systems, was itself in deep distress in 1932.

Williamson then turned to the government—the Reconstruction Finance Corporation—to ask for a $7 million loan for its West Side reconstruction project. Vanderbilt would have spurned such an idea, and Morgan would have considered such a sum a comparative trifle, but their days were over, and the railroad felt no shame in asking for federal assistance. This required some negotiation, for the RFC did not make a practice of lending money to dividend-paying corporations. Still, the Central had passed its February dividend, and appeared about to do the same for its May payout. Did this mean the company would put an end to its long-time record, established by Erastus Corning, of never letting a year go by without a dividend? Wall Street was fairly confident there would be a payout, if only as a bow to tradition.

Discussions with the RFC continued, and in late March the

agency announced the loan of $4.4 million to the Central. Soon after, President Williamson announced that the company had a first quarter deficit, and indicated there was no hope for a turnaround in the near future. He released figures to show that the Central, like all other major railroads, paid out more in taxes than in dividends, and he asked the government for some form of relief. It was only a gesture; Williamson and other railroaders knew such help would not be forthcoming.

On May 11, the Central issued a press release stating it would not pay a dividend that year. The story was buried on the financial page. Given the circumstances of the nation that spring, it wasn't worth more than that. Still, the passing of the Central dividend was a significant symbolic event for both the railroad and the industry. For well over a half century the Pennsylvania and the Central had been considered reference points for the industry, operations other lines measured themselves against, and their securities had been among the safest investments. Railroading was a sick industry in 1932, far more than most. Its great decline was well under way, even though Williamson and his colleagues regularly proclaimed that the bottom had been reached. The Central survived; it did not file for bankruptcy. There would be deficits in 1933 and 1934, and the company would barely break even in 1935. But the railroad would never regain its old status. Nor, for that matter, would the industry.

VII

Decay

The dramatic performance of the economy in the interwar period—great prosperity in the 1920s followed by even greater depression in the 1930s—masked the decline of the railroads in both decades. The good times buoyed the industry, giving many lines an outward appearance of health while their balance sheets told a different story. Similarly, the industry's problems in the 1930s were blamed on the depression and not what were becoming chronic ills of American railroading. Outsiders continued to predict the companies would recover when the rest of the economy moved upward.

Industry leaders often believed their own press releases; many corporation presidents held to the turn-of-the-century notion that the well-being of the economy and that of the industry were intertwined, that without prosperous railroads the country would be crippled, and that it was only a matter of time before Washington would come to appreciate this.

Their reasoning was alluring. When the economy soared, the railroads were needed to transport ever-increasing amounts of freight and numbers of people; in depression times the railroads were far more economical than any other form of transportation, and so would draw traffic from trucks, buses, cars, and airplanes. Given the opportunity to compete with highways, waterways, and airways on an equal basis—which meant an end to government subsidies and tax advantages—the railroads would conquer their rivals.

To be sure, company presidents and chairmen of the boards recognized the increasing threats of alternate means of transportation, and realized that even during the best of times many major railroads would lack sufficient capital for modernization and maintenance. Rates would not be raised to meet costs and provide profits, for even if the ICC permitted increases, competition with rival methods of transportation would keep them down. Still, the industry's leaders made a good case for their position, and some lines made large wagers they were right.

In the mid-1930s, railroaders would compare the economies offered by one of their 160-car trains of over 12,000 tons to those of a fleet of trucks carrying the same freight. A regularly inspected and maintained steam locomotive might travel over 100,000 miles a year; trucks and buses of that period required major overhauls every 25,000 miles or so. Before the war it had been assumed that steam technology had reached its peak. There were improvements in the 1920s, however, and by the 1930s the steamers were more powerful, dependable, and rapid than ever before. In 1936—a year when it appeared recovery had begun—the American railroads placed orders for 435 steamers, more than twice as many as had been contracted for during the previous six years. In addition, the diesel revolution continued throughout the decade; 937 of them were sold in 1941, and more orders would have been accepted were it not for the coming of war. It may have been the era of the automobile, but General Motors' Electro-Motive Division, the nation's largest manufacturer of railroad diesels, grew at a more rapid rate than any other branch of that corporation.

The industry proclaimed that if Americans wanted the most modern and efficient form of transportation, they would find it on the railroads. The Association of American Railroads compiled statistics to prove that highway costs were far greater than those required to maintain road beds and tracks, and of course it was much less expensive to improve existing lines than to construct new highways at public expense. "Renting a ride on the railroad" was more sensible than purchasing an automobile and then having to pay for repairs, obsolescence, and insurance. Railroads were safer than automobiles, and accidents on the tracks were rarely fatal.

Throughout the decade the railroads presented these and similar arguments. Most were sound and logical; some were rather fanciful and exaggerated, but this was to be expected. And still the industry declined.

The nation had 700 railroads in 1933, or half as many as had been in operation during the Theodore Roosevelt administration. One hundred of these either went out of business or merged in the next six years. The Department of Commerce reported that exactly one mile of new track was set down in the

United States in 1939; the following year there were nineteen. Over 1,000 miles of track were abandoned in each year from 1932 to 1943, and in 1942, close to 3,000 miles were set aside. There would have been more were it not for ICC disapproval of many abandonments—a new role for the agency, which for so long had prevented the companies from expanding. By then the nation's railroads operated slightly less than a quarter of a million miles of main track, and the figure was contracting each year; the industry had reported the same figure in 1912, when expansion was in the air. Thus, an entire generation of growth was wiped out, with more to come.

Increasingly the railroads were ignoring, or at least trying to ignore, their passenger business. There were 10,000 fewer passenger cars in service in 1937 than in 1932, a decline of 20 percent. The freight car fleets tended to remain stable, although there was some falling off which was compensated for by the larger sizes of the replacements. The bulk carriers hit bottom in 1932-33, and then rebounded, their tonnage doubling in the next decade. In 1933, only 9 new passenger cars were put into service in America, while 2,163 freight cars were delivered. The railroads acquired over 340,000 new cars and gondolas of various descriptions in the 1933-41 period, and only 2,625 passenger cars.

Of course, the freight fleets had always been by far the larger of the two, and due to the rough treatment given the bulk carriers, they did not last as long. Still, in the pre-World War I heyday of railroads, the nation had required over 1,000 new passenger cars per year. Over 3,500 of them were put into service in 1914, and as recently as 1929, close to 2,500 were delivered. In contrast, 81,590 freight cars were put into service in 1929, and 80,263 in 1941. Yet passengers did not desert the railroads in the 1930s; the figures for commuters stabilized and then rose after 1932, while total passenger miles went from 17 billion in 1932 to 29 billion in 1941, and then shot up to 54 billion in 1942, the first full year of war.

The railroad companies spoke of retaining the loyalty of old passengers and winning new ones, but in fact most of them made the decision to concentrate upon freight. It was sensible from their point of view. The companies simply could not afford to do otherwise. Freight business had always paid better than passenger. Freight tracks could be used around the clock, while commuters used the railroads twice a day, and occasional travelers took trains at their convenience, not that of the railroads. Late freight deliveries were unfortunate; delays in passenger service could be most damaging. A coal train could meander along a poor roadbed on rails that should have been replaced years before, while passengers demanded good rails and equipment. Before the depression the carriers could afford to fight for both passengers and freight—this was the situation in 1923, when the industry spent over a billion dollars for additions and betterments. In 1932, such expenditures took slightly more than $100 million, and most of it went into the freight lines. Increasingly in the depression, passengers were treated like bulk packages. The railroads abandoned them before they gave up on the lines. Given the economics of the situation as distinct from the propaganda, this could not only have been anticipated but was to be expected. The railroads might fight a holding action against the trucks, and could make an attempt to do the same against the interurban buses. But even during the depression, the automobile gained ground on the locomotive, if only by default.

This forced decision had implications more important than the abandonment of rails and passengers. It meant the railroads would woo the shippers far more than they had in the past, and tend to play down public relations geared at passengers. The Twentieth Century and the Broadway Limited, as well as their counterparts on other lines, were fossilized relics of a previous age. The railroads could not discontinue such flagship operations out of embarrassment and the need to placate the ICC. But these baubles would only be maintained, not added to or improved. The same was true for the showplace terminals, although work on several already under way would be completed. Later on, old-timers would claim that the coming of the diesels ended the romantic age of the railroads. This was only partially true. Far more important than the abandonment of the old steamers was the abandonment of the passengers. There was romance in a long-distance trip on a modern passenger train, complete with roomettes, bars, dining cars, and observation platforms. This could not be found in boxcars that carried potatoes and heavy machinery.

The New Deal has been called a social revolution of widespread consequences. Whether or not this was so is questionable, for most of those who were on top of the social and economic pyramid in the late 1920s were still there when America prepared for war in 1940. Still, the depression had crippled the power of the large investment banks, while New Deal legislation imposed restrictions upon how they exercised whatever of it remained to them. The sudden decline of the Wall Street banks was compensated for by the expansion of Washington's financial and economic power. This had important implications for the eastern railroads, which for a half century had been led and often dominated by the House of Morgan and Kuhn, Loeb and Company, and their allies.

The era when Morgan and Harriman would battle for railroad domination, when important tycoons hoped to gather major railroads as keystones for their empires, had ended. The great capitalists were dead, and their places taken by competent but often faceless bureaucrats; Wall Street was a financial desert in the early 1930s; and the railroads were no longer prizes. But the government in Washington did not reject Morgan's old philosophy regarding the industry, although the New Dealers had quite different reasons for advocating it. The bankers had sought to create communities of interests and foster cooperation, in return for which they would provide the companies with needed capital. While they had opposed aspects of the Ripley Plan, it was more out of a dislike for the ICC and fear they would give up more than they would get than an inherent dislike for unification. In their times, Morgan, Schiff, Harriman, and the rest had planned for unitary systems. Now the New Dealers spoke in the same terms, only they called it nationalization and rationalization, harking back to the Plumb Plan in some instances and McAdoo's concepts in others.

This confluence of philosophies could be seen in the origins of the New Deal's Emergency Transportation Act of 1933. The previous year, Republican banker Frederick Prince had proposed dividing the nation's railroads into seven great systems, a drastic version of the Ripley Plan. There would be two companies in the East, one headed by the Pennsylvania, which would include the B&O, the other a union of the Central and the Van Sweringen interests. The ICC was to bless these unions, and permit the new companies to abandon whatever trackage was necessary in order to become economically viable. The Emergency Transportation Act supported this concept, though not in detail or by name. A federal coordinator of transportation was to be named who would promote reorganizations and mergers, offering federal aid and support to those companies that accepted his recommendations. But the railroads were not interested in the plan, which in 1933 appeared both socialistic and unnecessary, while Federal Coordinator Joseph Eastman lacked the power to compel their cooperation. Instead, the Pennsylvania and the Central joined others to back a set of proposals put forth by Pennsylvania Vice-President A. J. County, who called for the creation of a unified eastern system, including both roads and coordinated by a board consisting of representatives of all the major lines. Under the terms of the County Plan, each road would retain its own identity—managements would not be fired—but would cooperate on improvements and share some rolling stock. The proposal was considered worthwhile by the companies involved, but received little attention from the Roosevelt administration, which in 1934 was more interested in several nationalization schemes. During the first phase of the New Deal, then, nothing of substance was accomplished. Several of the eastern lines received RFC assistance, usually continuations of loan arrangements worked out during the Hoover years, and some cooperated with the Public Works Administration in using unemployed workers to help in construction work, this despite opposition from the unions. That was the extent of intervention in 1933-34.

The situation changed in 1935, with the final collapse and liquidation of the Van Sweringen empire. More a product of financial legerdemain than railroading economics and management, the holdings had been in trouble since 1930, and would have fallen sooner were it not for constant help from Morgan and Company. But in September 1935 the brothers' business holdings were auctioned and their various railroad components passed into new hands.

This liquidation prompted Senator Burton K. Wheeler of Montana, chairman of the Interstate Commerce Commission, to begin an investigation into the Van Sweringen case and others like it. His subcommittee hearings lasted for four years, during which time they became the focal point for congressional railroad policy. The companies were carefully examined, and much of the time was spent on unraveling the affairs of the eastern carriers. Little in the way of new information was uncovered, but Congress and the public were instructed in the interconnections that had developed between the railroaders and the bankers, the existence of communities of interests, lobbying efforts, and financial manipulations. The railroad presidents came to testify, and on several occasions Williamson of the Central and Martin Clement of the Pennsylvania defended their companies against attacks. But the critics of the railroads received far more attention, even though they were describing the situation as it had been in the late 1920s, not what it was in the mid-1930s. The companies were weak and hardly in any shape to pose a threat to the political structure. Yet the reformers talked as though they were still powerful.

Given the mood of the period, it perhaps was inevitable that Wheeler would advocate sweeping changes for the industry. Federal Coordinator Joseph Eastman, who supported the idea of government-industry cooperation, was overruled by the subcommittee majority. A long time antibusiness crusader, Wheeler held center stage. And in April 1935 he called for the establishment of a new federal corporation, to be known as United States Railways, which would assume ownership and operation of the industry after proper indemnification was made. Wheeler won Eastman's cooperation for this version of the old Plumb Plan, and told reporters he expected it to pass Congress and be ready for Presidential approval sometime in early 1936.

It was not a revolutionary concept. Municipal and state governments in America had organized and run railroads, while the Canadian National Railway was a national enterprise. Given the mood of the time, talk of nationalization was not considered radical in Washington. Still, the Association of American Railroads condemned the concept, and led the opposition to what it viewed as an alien philosophy. The Central and the Pennsylvania, the twin bulwarks of the Association, joined in the chorus. Clement spoke of the great concentration of political-economic power that would be created under the Wheeler proposal. Williamson was more direct. "Politics lives on jobs," he said. "It is obvious that under a government which is based on the political party system, the railroads under a system of government ownership would be administered primarily for the need of that system. Under government ownership the job of every one of a million railroad employees sooner or later would become a political prize, with merit and experience taking a back seat."

The debate continued for two years. On the one side were Wheeler and legislators elected on antibusiness platforms, along with a segment of the New Deal's left wing, while on the other side were the major railroads, now unified in a new organization known as the National Committee for Prevention of Government Ownership of Railroads. Wheeler was able to keep the idea before the public; the industry mobilized opinion and rallied its congressional supporters in votes against several nationalization measures. Thus, there was a stalemate, and throughout the

Great Depression Washington lacked a rational railroad program.

Other aspects of American business showed marked improvement during the first Roosevelt term. The railroads continued to decline, with the number of miles of line in bankruptcy increasing sharply. In 1933 there were 42,000 miles in the hands of receivers, and in 1936, 70,000; two years later 77,000 miles were in this position. Every important industry leader agreed that something had to be done to salvage the systems, for if this trend continued, there would be no need for a Wheeler Plan—most of the railroads would be bankrupt, and then the government could assume power over them through court actions, not legislative enactments. The eastern lines continued to press ahead for programs of consolidation under private ownership and petitioned the ICC for permission to abandon uneconomical lines. Wheeler and his supporters never deviated from nationalization and criticized the industry for its opposition. The legislators viewed the railroad leaders as robber barons, while the railroaders considered Wheeler a dangerous and irresponsible radical. Clearly they could not work with one another.

Yet both agreed the old system was outmoded, that competition in the railroad industry had become harmful, and that, like the telephone and electric utilities, railroads in the 1930s were natural monopolies. In fact, the only major point of difference was in the question of who should own and who should manage. As many students of business were observing at the time, ownership and management, once united, had become separate functions. The owners of securities wanted income and capital gains, not a direct voice in management, while the administrators owned relatively small amounts of the common stock in their corporations. Some method of exchanging corporate securities for government bonds might have been agreed upon—Wheeler put forth several, and all were rejected by the industry. The administrations might have been kept on, to work for the government corporation as federal bureaucrats, and since many had taken salary cuts in the early 1930s, their incomes would not have declined by much, at least when taken in the aggregate. In other words, there was room for compromise between the two points of view. But the men involved could not accept one another, not only as individuals, but as symbols. The twin images of the progressive, antirailroad reformer and the rapacious tycoon, created in another age, were still alive in the 1930s, a period when American capitalism was prostrate and the railroads crumbling. Thus passed another opportunity for a major alteration of the industry.

The New Deal was the most reformist administration since Andrew Jackson's. Yet it was unable to develop a program to bring a large degree of order to the railroads. The Emergency Transportation Act of 1933 did just what its name indicated it would—it dealt with an emergency, and not very effectively at that. There was no permanent plan, nor even a coherent philosophy. Andrew Jackson had contradicted himself, but insofar as transportation was concerned, he usually opposed federal largesse, and policies formulated during his Presidency had set the railroads along the course they eventually took. The lack of action and philosophy in the New Deal era confirmed them on the road to paralysis.

A new war appeared inevitable in 1939, and so the Roosevelt administration abandoned its reformist posture and assured the business community that nothing further would be done to harm its vital interests. Not only were the various Wheeler proposals dropped but New Dealers sought out prominent railroaders to make certain their lines were being readied for a national emergency, one that might be more serious than that of 1917. In those cases where the lines were in need of repair, financial aid was offered through the RFC and construction help in the form of WPA contracts. But the industry was not restructured, and there was no new Railroad Administration.

The Pennsylvania, the Central, and other major lines had won their battles against government figures who wanted them to integrate and unify. But was their objective a sensible reflection of economic and technological realities or an automatic reaction against federal power, a heritage of the Theodore Roosevelt years that made little sense thirty years later? Independence for its own sake made little sense, except in the personal dimension, and still it was pursued by companies which for half a decade had skirted bankruptcy.

The Central's reputation had outlived its performance, at least insofar as public opinion and governmental attitudes were concerned. After experiencing a sluggish recovery during the early New Deal period, the company slumped badly in the 1938 recession. That year operating revenues fell below $300 million, thus wiping out all the post-1932 increases.

As had been anticipated, passenger travel declined, in part

due to the nature of the economy and the continued growth of the automobile and bus but also because the Central pursued an aggressive policy of abandonments.* Beginning in 1934, the company led an informal alliance of New York railroads seeking ICC permission to eliminate unprofitable passenger spurs. The agency was sympathetic, perhaps in fear of causing a complete collapse. Ironically, the abandonments began along the old Buffalo-Albany route, which had formed the original New York Central over eighty years before. The small towns that had grown along the Erie Canal and which later organized short passenger lines were now threatened with a loss of their service. The Central's argument for doing so was sound. These towns now had highways, and increasingly their populations were leaving the rail for the road. The ICC supported abandonments there, and in 1937 over 200 miles of New York track, most of it passenger lines, were cut. The small towns lost important parts of their economic bases; switching facilities, stations, and small repair operations were closed down, and jobs were eliminated. Some of the towns—Oneonta and Canandaigua among them—were so severely crippled that they never recovered, victims of not only the depression, but the interrelated factors of automobile development and railroad collapse.

The decay continued in upper New York and other parts of the old Central empire. It was as if a long-range, almost unnoticed economic and technological revolution had taken place and was continuing, one that had implications almost as far ranging as those of the New Deal. An automotive infrastructure had been superimposed upon the old railroad networks, taking what it wanted and could absorb, and discarding the rest for the time being. The long-haul western lines were not badly hurt, for they could still compete successfully against the trucks. The situation was different in the short-haul East, and at the Central in particular. In the past the line had prided itself on its wide diversity of customers, from truck farmers to shirt manufacturers; unlike the Pennsylvania, it did not have to depend upon a single product—coal in this case—for its prosperity. While it was true that the company's forays into the Pennsylvania soft coal fields had made that product its most important freight item, it never amounted to more than a quarter of total commodity revenues. But while the mine owners continued to ship their products by rail, manufacturers and many farmers had turned

*Charles R. Cherington, *The Regulation of Railroad Abandonments* (Cambridge, 1948), is the best source on the subject.

to trucks, and so the Central was severely hurt. Each time it abandoned a commuter spur, it also did away with a line which carried some manufactured goods to market, and hastened its own decline. The Central pruned and trimmed and withered, and then pruned some more, seeking an ultimate fall-back position, but never certain where it might be. So it was that the railroad shut down more than 500 miles of main track in the 1930s in its continuing search for stability, and in each year earmarked additional trackage for elimination.

The company reported a net deficit of over $20 million in 1938, its poorest year thus far, for a loss of $3.13 a common share. It was a bad time for the economy as a whole—the nation's industrial index fell by 30 percent in 1938. In contrast, the Central's decline of 25 percent seemed a sign of strength. It was not; instead, the slower fall indicated the company was already scraping bottom. In 1937 the industrial index had been at a post-1929 high, while in the same eight-year period the Central's revenues had declined by half. Its performance was worse than the average of all Class I railroads, not surprising in itself considering that the average had been boosted by the output of the western lines. But the Central also was among the poorer acting of the eastern lines. The company had showed declines in the ratio of its operating revenues to total industrial production in every year of the past fifteen—in 1938 the ratio for the Central was 50, for all Class I's, 57. That year too the company's income had covered less than 60 percent of the bonded interest; it had to go deep into reserves to meet obligations. Although new financings were required, they could not be considered due to the Central's increasingly poor reputation on Wall Street. The common opinion there was that the company was on the skids, and that management never again would be able to bring down costs or raise income.

Such a view may have been justified, but to a degree was unfair. The Central's territory, which had seemed ideal a half a century before, was more than almost any other a victim of the automobile and the depression. And like other Class I eastern lines, the railroad was saddled with a redundant labor force, which it was unable to prune due to the powers of the brotherhoods. Tracks would be abandoned after prolonged negotiations with the ICC, and schedules would be slashed. Equipment would be permitted to grow shabby. But the workers remained, to be placed in positions where they hardly had to do more than report in order to receive paychecks. Featherbedding had always plagued the industry, and in the 1930s it seemed a final blow that would destroy the Central. The statistics told the story most graphically. In 1929 the Central had revenues of $57,000 per mile and costs of $44,000. In 1932, after the company cut back on maintenance and repairs, revenues were $17,000 and expenses, $20,000. During every year of the rest of the decade, expenses per mile were higher than revenues. Yet the Central had as many people on its payroll in 1940 as had been there in 1934, and in this period the company's wage bill rose from $141 million to $183 million.

There was nothing management could have done about this, considering the strength of the unions and the support organized labor received from Washington. Thus, from an enterprise whose primary task once had been to provide transportation required by customers, the Central had evolved into one that was at least as interested in maintaining the jobs of those who worked there. The Central had become a self-serving and self-justifying operation, a not unusual condition in the industry or among mature enterprises plagued by intense competition. Nor was this situation confined to the organized workers, for management was just as intent on retaining its positions. In 1934 the Central had employed 878 executives at $4.4 million; in 1940, there were 887 in this category, with salaries of $5.2 million.

These statistics were distressing, not only in the light of the decline of railroading but in that the Central was falling more rapidly than most of the other eastern carriers. In 1929 the company had accounted for 9.4 percent of the total operating revenues for all Class I lines. In 1938, the revenues were 8.4 percent of the total. In the same period net income declined from 8.3 percent of all Class I's to 4.2 percent.

By the late 1930s, Wall Street had concluded this decline could not be arrested, that the Central had been stricken by a fatal ailment and would not easily recover. Old-timers found it difficult to accept the situation. Every consolidation program offered for the Northeast contained a proposal whereby the Central would acquire several weaker roads. A half century earlier the Central and the Pennsylvania had shared power at the C&O. In 1938 that railroad offered a plan whereby it would acquire the Central.

Toward the end of the Great Depression the Central appeared hopeless. Two out of three of its locomotives were over twenty years old, as were half its passenger cars. Over 40,000 of the Central's freight cars had been put into service before 1920; less than 800 had been added from 1930 to 1935. The Central would have required investments in the billions of dollars to bring its equipment to the point where it could lure passengers and freight, and in the late 1930s it could not raise millions on the capital markets, while its common stock sold far below 10. The Vanderbilts and representatives of the Morgans still sat on the board, but they too lacked the power and prestige they once had possessed, and the former group became interested in the arts and society, the Morgans in industrial securities—especially those involved with aviation and autos.

The gap between the Central and the Pennsylvania widened considerably in this period, so that the latter company was the clear master of eastern railroading by the time America had to prepare for a new world war. Its revenues and income declined, but both appeared more than satisfactory when set beside the statistics for other Class I lines, the Central in particular. For example, the Pennsylvania's operating revenue as a percentage of all Class I's fell but slightly from 1929 to 1938, going to 11.11 from 10.87. Then it rose sharply, while the Central remained moribund. Operating income, the most significant indicator of efficiency for this period, showed the Pennsylvania rising from 10.6 of all Class I's to 15.3 percent, while the Central's share was cut in half. The Pennsylvania reported profits for every year of the 1930s, though only $0.84 a share for the disastrous 1938 recession. But it held firm for investors insofar as dividends were concerned, although in four of the depression years it payed a token $1.00.

This was accomplished by a combination of developments. The lines had been aggressively modernized in the 1920s; the electrification program had almost been completed, so that no major capital expenses were required. In addition, the company was in good financial shape in 1929, and so better able to meet the crisis than most railroads. Though troubled by competition from pipelines, the Pennsylvania was able to fight off the challenge of the truck due to the nature of its territory and the kind of freight carried. Because of this, the company's rate schedules held firmer than those of most lines, including the Central. For the same reason the Pennsylvania could take a stronger stand against the railroad brotherhoods, and although employment remained higher than might have been desirable, wages were lower and hours longer than at the Central, while worker productivity was better. Due in large part to these reasons, management was able to cut operating costs from $493 million in 1929 to $227 million in 1933, and from that time until the coming of the war, income increased at a more rapid pace than expenses.

Another important factor in the Pennsylvania's cost-cutting program derived from its position in regard to passengers. The company remained the largest passenger line in the nation, with the Central a distant second. In addition, if one were to include the Long Island in its total—and that company was really a Pennsylvania subsidiary—it carried more commuters than the next two lines combined. Therefore, its approach to this part of the business, which was a money loser in the early 1920s, was extremely important.

The Central had responded to losses in this area by petitioning for permission to abandon part of its service. So did the Pennsylvania, but not in so vigorous a manner—the company cut back on less than 250 miles of track in the 1930s, half that of the Central. More important, however, it tended to ignore the needs, demands, and complaints of passengers, the only exceptions being those along the Philadelphia Main Line, and even there service was not up to the level of the 1920s. Meanwhile, the Pennsylvania concentrated its attention upon the industrial and mining areas. Passengers demanded clean cars—new ones if possible—and schedules established to meet their needs. Coal and iron shapes could be hauled in old, unwashed cars, which cost a fraction of that required for passenger carriers, and could do without cosmetic repairs and maintenance. The same was true for locomotives. By the end of the decade over two-thirds of the Pennsylvania's locomotives were more than twenty years old, and when one considers that the electrics were in the other one-third, it can be seen that the Pennsylvania's steamers were among the oldest in the nation. In the 1930s the company prided itself on its modern repair shops, and the general public didn't consider that such a company, with such a policy, would require up-to-date repair facilities to take care of its antiquated rolling stock. But the difference showed up in the balance sheets, which made pleasant reading for the stockholders.

Unlike the Central, the Pennsylvania was in a position to review alternatives and select from among them. In the 1930s the company decided to concentrate upon heavy hauling, to cast its lot with the possibility of economic recovery, one that would be fueled by coal and erected from steel and iron—and during which an increasing number of Americans would own automobiles. The passengers would be carried and serviced. The Pennsylvania would petition for rate increases and continue its public relations program. But for the most part, the passengers would be made to understand, in various subtle ways, that their needs were not of primary importance at company headquarters. There was little for travelers to choose between the Central's abandonments and failure to upgrade equipment and the Pennsylvania's program, but the decisions indicate the inability of the Central to control its own destiny and its growing sense of futility, and the Pennsylvania's attempts to come to terms with its situation and make the most of its position and strengths. The rolling stock of both companies was in bad shape toward the end of the decade, the Central's because it could not afford to do better, the Pennsylvania's because it decided it was best to proceed in this fashion.

Still, the Pennsylvania was little more than a *status quo* operation, fighting to retain what it already had, and not particularly interested in expanding much beyond that. Although the truck and bus operations were profitable, the Pennsylvania added few new units in the late 1930s. The airline venture was dropped, in part because the company cared even less about transporting people by air than it did by train, but due more to continued losses with no end in sight. Given the Pennsylvania's circumstances, the nature of the industry and the period, this approach was not only understandable but also sensible.

Old travelers who recalled the glory days of the Twentieth Century and the Broadway Limited thought the Pennsylvania was on the decline, and some even switched to the Central in protest. But the Philadelphia aristocrats took a different view of it all. Their great-grandfathers had hoped to create a railroad which would never embarrass them. The Pennsylvania proved to be just that, for in the 1930s embarrassment involved finances, not performance. Owners of Central common stock had no income from their holdings. The Pennsylvania's shareholders—especially those in the Philadelphia area who held thousands of shares each—could at least count upon an annual return. They blessed the old railroad, and then took part of the money and purchased large Packards.

The experiences of the railroads during World War II were strikingly different from what they had been in the first war. This was more the result of alterations in the industry's status and capabilities than any major ideological shift, although this too had taken place.

Due in part to his World War I experiences in the Wilson administration, Franklin Roosevelt was sympathetic to the plight of the railroads. In addition, he had a lifelong affection for the trains. The President supported the Transportation Act of

1940, which not only placed water carriers under the ICC for the first time but committed the nation to a unified transportation policy. The underlying hope was that the railroads would be helped by the government to regain a part of their old position. Thus, Washington finally realized that railroading was not only a sick industry but one that merited federal nurturing. But it was a vague law, and little was done to implement its provisions because of the coming of the war.

While Congress debated the act, Roosevelt established the Council of National Defense, which included an advisory committee, one of whose members was to represent the transportation sector. Ralph Budd, an aggressive western railroader, was named to the committee, and soon after became commissioner of transportation, charged with coordinating all forms of travel and transport in preparation for America's entry into the war. Immediately Budd clashed with several prominent New Dealers, who charged him with using his office to assist the railroads at the expense of other carriers. Since he had long claimed that railroads had been discriminated against, it was not a difficult accusation to document, and Budd did spend most of his time with that industry.

Under his direction the companies commenced a large-scale program of track upgrading as well as placing orders for new rolling stock. Over 80,000 additional freight cars were put into service in 1941, the most since 1926, and in the next three years the companies took delivery on 138,000 more. The output of passenger cars was a secondary consideration. Still, over 1,000 new ones were delivered in 1944, more than any year since 1930, while many old cars were renovated for the transport of servicemen. Locomotive deliveries were far less satisfactory—the plants that produced them were converted to the fabrication of tanks and other war-related vehicles. Still, 1,047 were built and put into service in 1941, the most since 1926. In all, the railroads took delivery on over 4,000 locomotives during the war, and the large majority of these were diesels—in 1944, for example, the lines ordered 74 steamers and 680 diesels. Old steam locomotives were renovated and put back into service, literally saved from the scrap heap at the last minute. The companies enlarged their repair shops, put on additional personnel, and did the best they could under difficult circumstances. They accomplished the task, as many of the antique steamers traveled well over 100,000 miles a year in 1942-45. By the end of the war, the nation had 2,000 more locomotives than had been in service in late 1941, and in net terms all were diesels. In this way, the wartime period saw a revival of the conversion effort that had begun in the 1920s.

Budd left his post in mid-1942, when Roosevelt established the Office of Defense Transportation and selected Federal Coordinator Joseph Eastman for the post. Eastman was considered a moderate reformer and in addition was an experienced Washingtonian; under his leadership relations with the critics improved. Although he had often disagreed with prominent railroad executives in the past, Eastman got along well with them during the war, and had no difficulty completing the job Budd had begun. In order to prevent several strikes that could have paralyzed the nation, Eastman permitted wage increases. Then, to compensate the companies, he approved rate advances, especially on government-contracted work. If the lines had been undercompensated for their efforts during World War I, they made up for it in World War II.

The comparisons between the status of the industry in 1917 and 1941 indicate that this was not done for the sake of justice but rather because there was no other way by which the industry could have met the demands made upon it. The railroads had expended well over $6.7 billion for capital additions, replacements, and repairs during the 1920s. Electrification and dieselization programs during that decade were well publicized, and indeed were indications that the lines were making every effort to modernize. But these were slowed down or actually halted on most lines during the 1930s. Thus, the rolling stock on the nation's railroads was older in 1941 than in 1917, and many important road beds in worse shape. The statistics for rolling stock were particularly striking. In 1941 the industry had a quarter fewer freight cars than in 1917, while the passenger fleet had been cut by a third, as had the number of locomotives. In part this decline had resulted from the increased capacities of the cars and the greater power of the locomotives, but the impact of the depression and the advance of the automobile were at least as important. Truck registrations rose from 391,000 in 1917 to 5.2 million in 1941, and in the same period passenger car registrations went from 4.6 million to 29.6 million.

In 1917 the Class I lines still were strong, though on the decline, while in 1941 the same companies were in the process of recovering from the disasters of 1938. In 1917 there had been 17,000 miles of track in receivership, and in 1941, 70,000. Operating revenues had increased from $4.1 billion to $5.4 billion between 1917 and 1941, with large jumps taking place toward the end of the 1930s when America began to prepare for war. But expenses had risen too, from $2.9 billion in 1917 to $3.7 billion in 1941. Net income actually declined, from $658 million to $558 million. In 1917 stockholders received $456 million in the form of dividends; in 1941, they were paid $239 million.

The war effort of 1941-45 was more complete in most respects than had been that of 1917-18. The actual American involvement lasted longer, and the fighting took place on two major fronts as compared to the European stress of World War I. Of course, all aspects of the second war were on a larger scale—costs, men involved and killed, and industrial production. Necessarily, there were greater demands made upon transportation. The truck, bus, and auto played important roles, as did the airplane and ship. But shortages of rubber and gasoline made truck and bus transport undesirable, while German submarines limited the use of coastwise shipping. The large-scale movements of people and materials required the intensive use of railroads, and the lines enjoyed their last major boom period. In 1938, total railroad ton-miles had been 292 billion, against 1918's 409 billion. In 1944, the figure was 741 billion, and headed upward. Total passenger mileage in 1942 was a quarter above that of 1918, and double the World War I average for each of the next three years. Railroad operating revenues went from $7.5 billion in 1942 to $9.1 billion in 1943, $9.5 billion in 1944, and were only slightly below the $10 billion mark in 1945—twice as much as they had been in 1918.

Revenues rose more rapidly than wages early in the war, so that in 1943 net income was $992 million, twice that of 1918. Due to increased employment and higher wages, income fell sharply later on. But the decline was not as serious as it appeared, for most railroads were squirreling funds away into depreciation accounts, and charging them against current income.

By almost any measure, the railroads performed well during World War II. Furthermore, they emerged in 1945 far stronger than they had been in 1941. The Class I companies used their earnings to repay bonds and increase dividends, and in general position themselves well for the expected return of hard times as well as the necessary reconstruction effort. The lines would have to refloat bonds and sell additional equity in the post-war period, and use the money to revive the modernization programs in an attempt to retain at least some of their wartime gains. The improved financial positions would be a lure to potential investors, or at least this was the hope and expectation.

Management was in a better frame of mind in 1945 than had been the case in 1939; worn-out executives had been transformed into relatively secure individuals. Their companies had demonstrated they could compete with automobiles and airplanes, and certainly with trucks; they still were a key ingredient in the nation's transportation complex, one that could not be permitted to decline. Some of the companies went so far as to predict a revival of the passenger business. The new diesels would soon be shifted to middle-distance passenger service, and the growth of the suburbs appeared a favorable sign for the commuter lines. What was needed, they said, was an indication of favor from the government.

This came in 1948, with passage of the Reed-Bulwinkle Act, which permitted the railroads to enter into agreements on rates, subject to ICC approval. This meant that should the commission decide it was in the public interest, it might suspend the antitrust acts insofar as the railroads were concerned. A half century before, the companies had been severely criticized for having formed communities of interests and for engaging in conspiracies to avoid competition. Now Congress approved a measure that would encourage Morgan-like communities, and even invited the railroads to cooperate in rate fixing. President Truman noted this in his veto of the measure. A member of the Wheeler Committee while in the Senate, he had long distrusted the powers of the railroads. Congress overrode the veto, and the Reed-Bulwinkle Act became law. This too encouraged the railroaders and enhanced their hopes for continued revival.

Such men did not ask for federal aid or permission to merge so as to save dying firms. Rather, they demanded that the airlines and automobiles be taxed at the same rate as the railroads, that no special privilege be afforded any form of transportation. The Association of American Railroads spoke often of the emerging transportation industry, as distinct from railroads, automobiles, and aviation—in effect, calling for a wedding of all three, under the leadership of the major railroads. Such were not the approaches and perspectives of businessmen who felt themselves unimportant. "The railroads want no subsidy; they want equity," said Pennsylvania President Martin Clement. "They are a heavily taxed industry competing with subsidized industries and all they ask is equality of opportunity."

Clement had reason to be confident, for the Pennsylvania had come out of the war in good condition. Unlike most of the Class I companies, it had been unable to obtain rate increases sufficient to compensate for high labor costs. Still, through the intensive use of facilities the company was able to show good results from 1941 to 1945. In this five-year period it earned a total of $28.71 a share, ranging from a low of $3.98 in 1941 to a high of $8.17 the following year. Over $300 million was added to surplus accounts. Current assets rose by over $150 million, while current liabilities in 1945 were only $74 million higher than they had been in 1941. During this period the Pennsylvania invested a total of $284 million in roadbeds and equipment, after depreciation accounts were taken into consideration, for an average of $57 million a year—as recently as 1939, the company had expended only $16 million for these purposes.

The Pennsylvania was in a good liquid position, necessary since in 1946 it announced another modernization program, one that would include diesels—at the time the company was the only important American railroad without them. The stockholders had reason to celebrate too, for in 1942 the Pennsylvania paid a dividend of $5.00 a share, after having increased the payout by $1.00 a share each year from 1939 to 1942. The $5.00 dividend held for the rest of the war, and in this period the price of the common stock rose from a low of 17 to a high of 47. Thus, the company was positioned to go to the capital markets after the war.

Furthermore, it had a well-considered program, a heritage from the 1930s. The Pennsylvania's major concern was freight, and its position in its markets appeared secure from competition. The company was interested in some of its commuter lines too; in 1945 Clement announced the purchase of 395 new coaches, most of them for selected routes, and in the following year the company initiated a station-renovation effort. The Pennsylvania of the mid-1940s may have lacked glamour and excitement, but it was a strong company, and gave the impression of confident though middle-aged power.

In contrast, the Central seemed flashy and erratic. It had not done as well as had the Pennsylvania during the war, and in fact was far below the average for the Class I lines. By 1943 the company's tracks were being used to their capacity, and some traffic had to be diverted to other carriers while the Central struggled to improve road beds and rolling stock. Still, after depreciation is taken into consideration, the Central invested only $137 million in road and equipment, an average of $27 million a year against 1939's $11 million. With slightly more miles of track than the Pennsylvania, the Central spent less than half as much for this purpose.

Williamson resigned in 1944 and was succeeded by Gustav Metzman, an experienced Central executive, who had previously served as vice-president. Both men agreed that the company's financial position had to be strengthened considerably, and they gave this priority over all else. The Central had good earnings during the war. In 1939 it had reported $0.70 a share, and in 1940, $1.75 a share. During the next three years earnings were $4.07, $7.61, and $9.73. In the 1941-45 period the Central earned a total of $30.75 a share, more than $2.00 a share better than the Pennsylvania, though on a much smaller equity base. In line with company policy, the Central reduced its long-term debt with much of this money, so that it declined from $601 million in 1941 to $494 million in 1945. Current assets increased by $193 million and liabilities by only $62 million. The company did restore the dividend in 1943, to $1.50 a share, but all indications were that payouts would be sacrificed if the financial upgrading program demanded it. Wall Street understood this, and investors approved. As recently as the early spring of 1942, Central common stock could be purchased for below 7. By the end of the war, it was at 35.

At the time the Williamson-Metzman approach appeared sensible. The Central was an institution as well as a company, and the path to recovery appeared to begin on Wall Street. This was in the company's tradition. For more than a half a century the Central had been dominated by financial interests, the House of Morgan in particular. George Whitney, one of its partners, was on the board of directors in 1945, and most of the others were his allies. Far longer than that a Vanderbilt had appeared at the meetings, and Harold Vanderbilt was the current family representative. Traditionally the annual meeting took place in Albany, but corporate headquarters were close by Vanderbilt Avenue, on the west side of Grand Central Station.

The Philadelphians continued to dominate the Pennsylvania, having fought off challenges by outside interests. Now they were secure in their positions. Of the company's seventeen directors, twelve were Philadelphians, most from old Main Line families. A century before, the founders had determined that the Pennsylvania should be a solid, well-managed road, one that would help them regain power from New York. This did not happen, but the Pennsylvania was still a Philadelphia operation, and as such looked askance at the flighty New Yorkers.

Much had changed since then, but at least this seemed permanent.

It was different in New York. In late 1945 there were rumors on Wall Street of a raid on the Central. These were discounted, but they persisted, and after a while it became evident they had substance. The contest for the Central began the following year.

At first it seemed an unorthodox but not unusual happening—there had been raids in the past, after all, and such events had to be expected in the future. There was more to it than that, however, for this challenge was not only one for power but for philosophy as well, though none of the participants could have understood the full implications of his words and actions at the time.

With this raid opened the final act in the drama.

Intermission

There is a serendipitous quality to much of human existence. This is not to say that happenstance rules our lives, though a case might be made for it. Rather, individuals talk and write a good deal about resolving major, long-term issues, but in fact most of their activities consist of dealing as best they can with specific, limited, often mundane, short-range problems. In time small decisions can pyramid and create major difficulties. This can rarely be seen in prospect, though afterward traceries and regrets are quite common, and almost expected. On such occasions one asks, "Where and how did the condition develop?" Usually it was the unexpected by-product of a series of solutions to old problems.

This is worth keeping in mind when considering the situation of the eastern railroads in the aftermath of World War II. All had to face major challenges, while at the same time responding to immediate and pressing demands upon capital and personnel. There were political and economic pressures as well, and finally there was the cake of custom that could not be broken, for it had been built up over a century, layer upon layer, and gave the appearance of petrifaction.

In this period the American Association of Railroads, attempting to remind the nation of the importance of its members, promulgated the slogan: "If the Railroads Did Not Exist, They Would Have to Be Invented." Perhaps. But by then automobiles, trucks, and buses could have done much of their job, and a generation later a contentious school of economic historians would claim that the railroads had not been as vital to America's economic development as had been previously believed, that waterways could have performed the tasks of carrying people and goods almost as well, and that the nation would have been better off without the gigantic construction effort.* Of course, these conclusions were contested, and in any case it was the view of the present looking to the past. To those Americans who embraced the railroads in the second quarter of the nineteenth century, the vista was quite different.

Still, the issue was and is important, and the AAR slogan merits more than a passing thought. Perhaps it was valid—perhaps America needed and still requires railroads. Even if this is so, it does not mean the structure of the industry was and is sensible, rational, and well considered. Few important organizations are. They evolve, retaining forms and ideas long after they have become outworn, and are amalgams of large and small decisions, reactions and ideologies, in which the personalities of men mix with the need to solve and meet new problems and opportunities.

Railroading is concerned with transportation, of course, with the moving of goods and people from where they are to where someone wants them to be. This was not much of a problem in the American eighteenth century. The would-be traveler or shipper required a vehicle, personnel to man it, and the expertise to get it to its destination. Furthermore, few people required transportation; self-sufficiency was not only considered desirable but more often than not was the only option open to those who lived in rural areas and made up the large majority of the population. If for some reason a person wanted to go someplace else or send his goods there, he would seek the most convenient vehicle, as well as the least expensive. For most this meant waterways—oceans, rivers, and lakes—which did not require maintenance. If there was no waterway in an unsettled area, the traveler might hack his way through the wilderness, and in time this might result in the establishment of a path, and then a road. Like the waterways, such roads were thought of as being "natural." They were not mapped, and there was no charge for their use. Constant utilization would make them broader, while disuse resulted in disappearance. Needless to say, such roads were not maintained, by either private concerns or governments. That came later.

*In particular, see Robert Fogel, *Railroads and American Economic Growth* (Baltimore, 1964), and Albert Fishlow, *Railroads and the Transformation of the Ante-Bellum Economy* (Cambridge, 1955). Fishlow believes the use of railroads in 1860 added some 5 percent to the gross national product—no more. Even afterward, the maximum addition was in the area of 10 percent. But also see Peter McClelland, "Railroads, American Growth, and the New Economic History: A Critique," *Journal of Economic History*, XXVII (March 1968).

Canals and turnpikes were outgrowths of this natural form of waterway and highway. The canals were considered extensions of the rivers and lakes, and the turnpikes permanent forms of already existing roads. Their originators had limited ambitions, goals, and capital. They would not create a market or change the economy of their locality but instead serve what already existed. Thus, a canal might be dug to a minehead, and a road that washed out every spring would be paved and maintained for the use of local farmers and travelers.

The roads utilized coaches and wagons, and the canal boats were little different from most river boats except that they had shallower drafts. They were not intrusions upon the landscape, and although the canals were considered major projects, they did not require a large leap of imagination, either on the part of shippers or travelers. In addition, they were natural monopolies within their own technologies. There was no need for two roads between points that were only a few miles apart. Similarly, only one canal would be required to connect a mine to a river. Should there be a canal and a turnpike between the two points, they might compete with one another. Such a situation was rare, however, since the presence of the first would discourage businessmen and governments from constructing the second.

These simple early turnpikes and canals were followed by more ambitious ventures with different objectives and impacts. To those who knew little of such things, they didn't appear so—they seemed only longer, larger, and more costly. But they were, and the difference represented a giant leap of imagination on the part of the organizers. The small turnpikes and canals were attempts to respond to needs created in the past and which were troublesome in the present. The larger ones came into being to create a different kind of future, often to alter that future or hasten its arrival so as to assist those who organized, financed, and constructed them. Earlier, man adjusted to nature and the economy; later, man tried to control both.

Such was the case with the Erie Canal and the National Road. Neither would have been undertaken without government encouragement and aid, since their profitabilities and need were in doubt. The promoter of a short local canal might anticipate a great deal of traffic the first day it opened for business; Governor Clinton had faith in the Erie and believed it would be a money-maker, but he couldn't be sure it would draw enough traffic to pay its bills. Certainly the Buffalo to Albany traffic in the early 1820s did not merit the construction of such a canal, nor, for that matter, even a turnpike. But there were other considerations. The canal would make land in western New York more valuable. Towns and cities might develop along the route. The trade of the upper Midwest would be opened to the Hudson River Valley and New York City. The canal would enhance the state's economic and political positions. Similarly, those politicians who supported the National Road thought it would help bind the nation together, and accelerate the settlement of the West. Like Clinton, they wanted to manipulate the future, not react to the present.

Most turnpikes and canals were economic failures. Pennsylvania and Ohio politicians wrecked the finances of their states by voting appropriations for ambitious canals when geography and the economy militated against them. Finally, since these enterprises did not respond to particular needs, they invited competition from others who had the same dreams of a prosperous future. In some cases a canal might have succeeded without competition by drawing upon what business already existed and developing new customers. The mania would wreck it, by encouraging other canal builders to compete, and in the end all would go bankrupt. The combination of overcapacity and heavy fixed costs was too much to bear.

The canal and turnpike experiences both anticipated and molded those of the railroads. Their failures ensured that the early lines would not receive much in the way of government aid—had the Erie's success been multiplied throughout the nation, governments might have participated in the construction of the railroads, and the history of the industry would have been drastically different. Total economic impact and political considerations, not profit and loss, would have ruled, as they did in the early days of the National Road. The reaction against the government-business nexus was such as to prevent this from happening. Jacksonian Democracy, that complicated and convoluted movement, was clear on this point: The government would not get into the transportation business. There were some municipal railroads, and the states did assist them indirectly, but for the most part, the lines would be created by the private sector.

Despite the startling new technology they embodied, the origins of the New York Central were in the pattern set down by the early canals and turnpikes. That is to say, they responded to definite, perceived need: supplementing the work of the Erie: The Mohawk and Hudson and the other upper New York lines were designed to carry passengers more efficiently than could the canal, while some were originated in order to haul freight to the waterway from inland locations. Later on they were united by Erastus Corning, who used the railroad as part of his personal conglomerate, as a vehicle to enhance his banking, mercantile, and manufacturing businesses. Corning and some of his allies, most notably Dean Richmond, had emerged from the world of inland waterways, and they conceived of a large-scale hybrid transportation system that would connect New York City to Chicago, using lake boats and river steamers as well as locomotives. Given the capital needs of such a system and the nature of railroading, they had to build in anticipation of business rather than in recognition of an already existing market. But it was no great risk, for the seeds of business were already planted, awaiting the coming of the railroad to grow.

The Pennsylvania Railroad's origins were more political and emotional in nature. The state's clumsy Main Line system had cost the taxpayers over $16 million, more than twice as much as New York had contributed to the Erie Canal, and it was a major failure—in fact, the most expensive blunder in American canal history to that time. In addition, Philadelphia saw its political and social leadership slipping away during the Jacksonian period, while New Yorkers were coming to dominate the Midwest by virtue of their canal. Finally, New York's new railroads not only augmented the waterway but were drawing additional business to Manhattan. So the Philadelphia aristocrats organized their railroad, hoping it would be a money-maker and pay dividends but more in order to preserve and enlarge their trade position and retain their prestige.

The Pennsylvania Railroad was as great a success as the Main Line system had been a failure. Within a decade of its organization, the railroad was led by professional managers, President J. Edgar Thomson at their head, while the Philadelphia aristocrats appeared content to collect dividends and other benefits. Thomson was the leading railroader of his day, and nothing if not a rational one. Systematically he drove westward, making certain the new markets were there and could be captured, and then ensuring the Pennsylvania had the best routes and equipment. The company had to be financially solvent; the Philadelphia aristocrats had insisted upon this, and Thomson and his successors were pleased to oblige them. More than any other Class I line, the Pennsylvania was able to remain independent of banker control, although toward the end of the century external financing was needed.

Cornelius Vanderbilt took over at the Central shortly after

Thomson had consolidated his position at the Pennsylvania. Vanderbilt was an empire builder, a man of vast ambitions, an investor and speculator, perhaps even a business genius, but he was not an engineer or a railroader. In the New York Central and Hudson River, as it was then called, he had a line with good rolling stock and roadbeds as well as fairly conservative finances. Thomson had to overcome major topographic problems in constructing the Pennsylvania, for the routes went through fairly rugged territory, and in addition he had to satisfy the Philadelphians that the company's finances were secure. In contrast, the Central had a water level route most of its way, and so Vanderbilt could afford to leave the actual running of the line to subordinates while he concentrated upon expansion. The Central did expand, often ahead of its markets, at times making uneconomical acquisitions and in general taking a far more ebullient stance than did the Pennsylvania. This program called for huge amounts of money, far more than could be generated through depreciation and earnings. Only Wall Street investment banks could raise such sums, and so the Central turned to them. The Vanderbilts remained the largest single stockholder group, and members of the family sat on the board. But the House of Morgan was the dominant force at the railroad in the last years of the nineteenth century.

By then the great age of expansion in the Northeast had come to a close. The railroad systems had exploited the prime areas within their territories. Additional business might be obtained by extending lines into marginal areas, and of course the companies would grow as their regions developed. There was the temptation to challenge other companies for their business, to engulf and even acquire them. Railroad wars had existed before then, but in comparison to those of the late nineteenth century they had been mere skirmishes.

Morgan and his colleagues understood the situation and the way it had developed. Competition in railroading may have made sense in the early days, when the companies turned from satisfying existing needs to creating new ones and then exploiting them. In such times, the fruits of the contest encouraged vigor and growth. That period had ended; competition was becoming ruinous, and those who understood this called for its elimination. That their programs conflicted with their philosophies did not appear to trouble the major bankers, who were ever ready to jettison doctrine in order to establish sensible business practices. They presided over communities of interests, organized mergers, encouraged coordination, and all the while insisted upon an end to what already was known as cutthroat competition.

The critics of such business practices opposed these moves, though they could not get together on a basic approach or program. Most of them saw the railroads as masters of the economy, their leaders among the major robber barons and malefactors of great wealth. If they perceived their weaknesses and understood the reasons for their actions, they said and did little to indicate it. The flaws in the areas of organization and perception were soon obvious. Instead of controlling and curbing the major lines, the first reform impulse actually aided them. The railroads approved of the ICC as a political means to achieve an economic goal. The bankers and railroaders hoped to regulate themselves; if the government wanted to join in, through the vehicle of an agency dominated by men friendly to the business point of view, it would be welcomed, though in a discreet fashion.

Some of the more radical reformers had a different approach. They would nationalize the lines, in much the same fashion as was being done in parts of Europe. The businessmen strongly opposed nationalization—here ideology would not be abandoned. Still, such a program was not essentially different from Morgan's. By the turn of the century, almost all important groups dealing with railroads realized that coordination would be required in the future. It was then—when the northeastern lines were still healthy, when railroading was the dominant form of transportation, when the nation's political and business elites were traveling along parallel paths—that rationalization would have taken place. Insofar as the Pennsylvania and the Central were concerned, they had different origins, but their territories abutted upon each other's, and in some cases overlapped. Politics, economics, and history had created two separate lines; all three might have been seen as militating in favor of their unification during the Age of McKinley.

This did not occur, of course. Instead differences among railroaders, the mounting of a new antirailroad crusade, and several tactical errors on the part of the industry's leaders, combined to permit the moment to pass. For the next half century and longer, the railroads would consider mergers and combinations, but these usually were defensive in nature, reactions to external threats.

The times were ripe for either large-scale mergers on a regional basis or nationalization. The economics and the logic of the situation demanded one or the other. But tradition and ideology opposed both. There was no solution. Instead, congresses and government agencies acted in ways that starved the railroads of needed funds, while their executives continued expansion and modernization efforts which did not add sufficiently to net profits. As a result the companies were obliged to broaden their equity and debt bases, and these would prove heavy burdens in leaner times. The politicians attacked when they should have defended; the businessmen embellished when they should have pruned.

Both reactions made sense at the time. In retrospect, they may be seen as major blunders.

The industry's problems were compounded during World War I. On the one hand the Railroad Administration did its job well—this should have indicated that unification could work—while on the other the major lines came out of the war short of capital and long on repair and modernization requirements. By then almost all important students of the subject recognized the need for unification, and several plans were put forth to accomplish this. None were accepted, in large measure due to ideological and personal differences. The automobile, truck, and bus made their inroads on railroad business, and still the industry was unable to develop a rational program, one that would meet the new technological challenges while at the same time enhancing the service and profitability of their constituent companies. Weaknesses in various systems were masked by the general prosperity; they were seen for what they were in the depression of the 1930s, and by the end of the decade it seemed evident that the industry no longer had the vitality to recover.

Throughout all of this, the Pennsylvania and the Central remained the twin pillars of the industry. The western lines may have had the glamour, but these two giants, operating in the richest part of the nation, possessed the largest share of revenues, cargoes, passengers, and, in good years, profits. The Pennsylvania was better managed, both in terms of carrying efficiency and finances. The Central was in constant financial difficulties during slumps, which were broken by almost spectacular profits in the few good years.

Most of the consolidation plans set forth in the first half of the century were based upon the survival of the Central and the Pennsylvania. All the other lines might vanish in mergers, but not the Central and the Pennsylvania, whose positions in the industry were unique. This too was a victory of tradition over pragmatic analysis. It was as if the idea was unthinkable. In 1946 the Pennsylvania celebrated its one hundredth anniversary. It had originated as a rival to the New York Central, and so it remained. That this situation would continue seemed an immutable law of American railroading.

The railroads came out of World War II in better financial shape than they had been in at any time since the early 1930s. Their excellent performances during the conflict demonstrated that under the proper conditions they could compete with other forms of transportation and secure their positions. All that was required, said their executives, was equal treatment in the area of taxation and government aid.

The Pennsylvania was a strong road and company in 1946. Its freight business was profitable and in little danger from the automobile. Passenger operations were another matter, and an important one since the Pennsylvania was the leading carrier of people in the nation. The company's executives knew they had several options in this area. They had the money and the confidence to compete with the automobile for commuter business, and perhaps even retain a profitable portion of the long-distance trade against the challenge of the airplane. In any case, the Pennsylvania was in far better shape than the Central, especially in the matter of morale.

That company had been badly shaken during the depression, and remained on the defensive psychologically. Management was concerned with liquidity in this period, and had utilized the wartime prosperity to put its balance sheet in order. Not only was this a prime requisite for survival but what might have been expected from a company that was controlled by investment bankers. But to what end was this being done? Would the Central use its stronger financial position to enhance its operating record? Or would it continue to fall back in the face of perennial assaults from rival forms of transportation? The Central had been a sick and dispirited company before the war, and in 1946 there seemed little hope for substantial and permanent recovery. Clearly drastic alterations of one kind or another were demanded. It was as if management had determined that the company either would collapse or decline, and had selected the latter option. Only the threat of revolution—the ejection of the old ruling group—could change this, and the threat was made in the mid-1940s.

The old ruling groups at both the Pennsylvania and the Central seemed to agree that theirs was a mature industry. The Pennsylvania had evolved methods of coming to terms with this situation, while the Central had not. The federal government finally had recognized the railroads no longer could shake the economy to its foundations, although lingering fears and old ideologies died hard. Many spoke of the possibilities of a rebirth, but few within the industry believed it. Had the choice been theirs to make, the old patterns might have remained intact; the Pennsylvania could have consolidated its fall-back position, while the Central would have solvency as a reward for accepting a secondary position in eastern transportation. Prudence dictated such courses of action—neither company could hope to fight the new technologies and win.

A new force entered the picture at this point. Fresh men claimed that rebirth was possible—in effect, they hoped to reinvent railroading, and in such a way as to return the lines to their old glory. Such an idea may have been overly ambitious and even unrealistic, but the new men stirred the industry into action; the challenge evoked a response, in fact several of them. And with this, the Pennsylvania and the Central were set upon altered courses, no longer certain of their destinies.

In the mid-1940s, the cake of custom began to crack.

VIII

The Coming of the Barbarian

Oris Paxton and James Mantis Van Sweringen were opportunists in the sense that they knew how to grab the main chance when it came their way. The brothers were rather ordinary-looking men, often mistaken for twins though Oris was two years older than James. Bachelors, they lived together in a modest Cleveland house shortly after the turn of the century, and worked out of the same office as real estate salesmen. They were personable, open-hearted, and without guile. Potential buyers and sellers trusted the Van Sweringens, even when their knowledge of properties was flawed and incomplete. Both had an instinctive talent for friendship, so necessary in their line of work. So they did quite well, and after a while decided to go off on their own. For a time they concentrated upon sales, then entered construction, and from this they learned about financing. Finally, the Van Sweringens became developers, and their major project, Shaker Heights, continues to this day as their monument—at least for this phase of their joint careers.

Shaker Heights is located on the outskirts of Cleveland, and in the days when automobiles were still fairly novel was connected to the central city by streetcars. The brothers knew their property would be worth more if it possessed a better transportation system. Accordingly, they explored the possibility of constructing an electric line to Cleveland. The brothers had no idea of what this entailed nor even the implications of such a move. So in late 1915 they sought advice from Alfred Smith, one of their many friends and a neighbor, who the previous year had become president of the New York Central.

At the time Cleveland's transportation was dominated by the

Nickel Plate, which in turn was controlled by the New York Central, and that company of course was a jewel in the Morgan crown. The Central had purchased the Nickel Plate in order to end competition between that company and its own line from Chicago to Buffalo, and ever since had hoped to find some way to sell it to friendly interests. Too, the ICC was also pressing for divestiture. Smith saw in the Van Sweringen plan a way to satisfy all parties. After several conversations with Thomas Lamont of the House of Morgan he offered to sell the Central's interest in the Nickel Plate to the brothers for $8.5 million.

Oris and James were interested, but they only had $500,000 in cash and another $500,000 from a group of close friends. Morgan and Company helped them raise the rest. The bankers organized Nickel Plate Securities Company, and then sold a portion of its shares to the public, using the money to pay for the railroad. The brothers retained the rest, which carried control as well. In this way they entered the railroad business.

Out of such a chance encounter was born a convoluted and complicated empire, which at its height ran more miles of main track than any other eastern line. Additional holding companies followed—General Securities, Vaness, Chesapeake, Alleghany, and smaller units—all financed by Morgan and its satellite, Guaranty Trust. Into the empire went the Erie, the Missouri Pacific, the Chesapeake and Ohio, and other major roads as well as a score of minor ones. On paper the Van Sweringens were among the most powerful men in the industry, commanding railroads with a book value of well over $3 billion. Their empire was financial, however, and not operating. Its major product was to be capital gains, not the hauling of freight and services to passengers. Afterward it became evident that the brothers had no clear idea of what they controlled, owned, or even how their empire had been erected.

This conglomeration was hard hit by the 1929 crash, but Morgan and the Guaranty rushed in with loans to keep it afloat. Other crises followed, and each time new loans were forthcoming. The bankers believed they had no choice in the matter; to withhold the money would result in a collapse, in which case their bonds would be worthless. But even the bankers could not prevent the securities from sinking on a depressed market. By 1932 several Van Sweringen units were in bankruptcy, while the common stock of the major holding companies sold for a few dollars a share. Still, these corporations did not default. The Guaranty, Morgan, and other financial institutions would make loans to the companies, which would then use the funds to pay interest on bonds—thus returning most of the money to whence it had come. The bankers hoped this record would encourage outsiders to purchase new bonds, but this did not occur. However, the Reconstruction Finance Corporation did lend the Van Sweringen interests some $75 million, almost all of which was eventually lost.

There was no mystery regarding the bankers' actions. Their primary concern was to extract their loans. The common stock and control of the railroad operation were of secondary importance. And so the empire drifted, more a financial pump than anything else.

The cycle continued well into 1935, by which time the Missouri Pacific and several other Van Sweringen railroads were in bankruptcy. Now the bankers concluded that further injections of money would be wasted; the patient was beyond help. Hoping to salvage something from their holdings, they foreclosed on their loans. Bankruptcy was announced in late August. On September 30 the assets of the various Van Sweringen companies were auctioned off in New York, not far from Wall Street. Whatever money could be obtained from the sale of packets of securities would go to satisfy creditors. The Van Sweringens were to receive nothing. To most individuals interested in such matters it seemed the brothers were defenseless.

This was not so. James was ill and could not attend the auction, but Oris was there, seated across the room from George Whitney of Morgan and George Roosevelt of the Guaranty. Neither banker spoke to Van Sweringen, who even then was looked upon as a relic from the previous decade. But at Oris's side was Colonel L.P. Ayres, a director of the Alleghany and a staunch Van Sweringen ally. Ayres had spent most of the previous month in discussions with seventy-three-year-old multimillionaire George Ball, founder of the mason jar fortune, who also was a close Van Sweringen friend. Ball had cared little about railroading in 1932, when Oris had persuaded him to accept a seat on the Nickel Plate board. But he did dislike easterners in general and bankers in particular—for this reason among others he had refused to sell securities in his company during the 1920s. Ball was convinced his friend had been duped, and he was there to protect his interests and also to strike a blow against the bankers.

With Ayres's help, Ball had organized a holding company, Midamerica, whose purpose was to salvage as much as possible of the Van Sweringen interest. This was to be accomplished through their control of Alleghany, the largest railroad holding company in America and the key to the empire. The bankers knew of the plan and approved. The Midamerica group would pump additional funds into the operating lines and see them back to prosperity. If they succeeded, Alleghany bonds would be redeemed at par. The brothers would purchase the common shares from Midamerica at a price that would insure Ball a substantial profit. All would benefit. So Whitney and Roosevelt sat by and watched while Midamerica bid for and won a packet containing 2 million shares of Alleghany common and 34,000 of the preferred. The total cost was slightly below $3 million. For this, Ball received a holding company that operated more miles of main track than existed in Great Britain and had effective control of several major lines, the most important of which was the C&O. For that sum of money Morgan's heir relinquished control of a company that was as large as the old man's domain at its peak. Such was the situation in America in the mid-1930s, and such was the status of railroading.

Who had control? James Van Sweringen died in December, and Oris followed less than a year later. George Ball had invested in friendship, not railroads, and with their passing he lost all interest in Alleghany. He gave the presidents of the constituent lines a free hand in operations, and seemed to have written off the investment. Ball let it be known that he was prepared to sell to the right group at the right price. But he wouldn't talk with Wall Streeters or bankers—not that they wanted to discuss Alleghany in this period. Few financiers had an interest in a nearly defunct railroad holding company, no matter what its prospects.

Robert Young was interested, and George Ball was willing to talk with him. At the time Young was not quite forty years old, and, although well known within some business circles, was hardly considered an important figure. Born in Texas, he had dropped out of school after a series of clashes with his father, married, and took a routine job at du Pont. Unable to live on his salary, Young speculated in stocks, using a small inheritance from his grandfather as a stake. He lost everything in the stock market crash of 1921, but became intrigued with finance and manipulation and turned to their study. Young took an office job at General Motors, and by the end of the 1920s was managing several accounts for stock speculators there. He did well for himself too, especially after selling short on the eve of the 1929 panic. Young purchased a New York Stock Exchange seat in 1932, forming a partnership with Frank Kolbe, himself a former General Motors financial analyst.

Young, Kolbe and Company did well at a time when most brokerage firms considered themselves fortunate to break even. The partners retained the business of many General Motors executives, and in addition traded for their own accounts. They specialized in finding undervalued stocks with a decent chance of recovery, not a difficult thing to do at the bottom of the crash. Young became interested in Alleghany preferred in late 1932 and began accumulating it for himself, the brokerage, and his clients. The following year he asked for representation on the board, not unusual in itself since by then Young either owned or controlled a large block of shares. The Van Sweringens turned him down. Young withdrew, but continued his purchases. The following year he met Allen Kirby, heir to the Woolworth fortune, and Kirby too obtained shares through Young, Kolbe. This continued even after the bankruptcy sale and the deaths of the Van Sweringens.

Why was Young so interested in Alleghany? That the company had potential was obvious, but for what? In the past it had been a management operation, headed by men who were more adept at comprehending securities than depreciation schedules. Yet it also might become a railroad. Cut down to proper size, given sufficient capital and the blessings of the ICC, Alleghany might merge several of the companies it controlled and so create a giant eastern carrier, one that could rival the Pennsylvania, not to say the Central. It would center around the Chesapeake and Ohio, the dominant force in West Virginia and eastern Kentucky, one of the nation's leading coal haulers, which operated some 5,000 miles of track. The C&O owned a southerly route to Chicago and a line between that city and Buffalo, and so abutted upon Pennsylvania and Central territories. Professor Ripley had thought the C&O might become the nucleus for one of the surviving eastern lines, and the idea persisted in the 1920s and afterward, even though the railroad carried few passengers. The Morgans had toyed with the idea, and the Van Sweringens had based their empire upon it. Robert Young might have had the same ambitions in 1937, when he approached George Ball to discover his price for the Alleghany common.

Or he might have been seeking a speculative vehicle. Young knew almost nothing about railroads and showed little inclination to learn. He did understand speculation and stock values, and the way Wall Street operated. He had the confidence of powerful men at General Motors and du Pont, but only in the area of investments. Young had never operated a company in his life. Perhaps he could obtain the Alleghany shares at a low price—Ball was eager to sell—and then make some cosmetic changes in the company to cause it to appear attractive. The price might rise, and Young's group would unload, thus obtaining a large profit. This was the kind of operation Young understood and in the past had carried off with little trouble and much profit. It may not have been what he had in mind at the time. Certainly this was the intention of his group. The General Motors and du Pont executives had no desire to enter the railroad business, particularly in the depression year of 1937, when a new wave of bankruptcies had hit the industry and Alleghany securities scraped bottom.

In fact, the economic decline caused some members of the group to question Young's judgment. For three years he had invested their money in Alleghany securities, and they had nothing but losses for their trouble. Furthermore, Senator Burton Wheeler had taken note of the Young-Ball negotiations and had said some ominous things about an unhealthy nexus of General Motors and the railroads. Was this an attempt to end competition in transportation? Wheeler meant to find out, and the General Motors people, anxious to avoid an investigation and in any case beginning to feel the Alleghany foray had been a blunder, notified Young of their desire to sell out. Others followed, so that in the end Young was on his own, with only Allen Kirby remaining of the original group. Negotiations with Ball had reached a critical point, and hesitation could kill the deal.

Young was obliged to make an important decision. If he proceeded with the plan, it would involve all of his money in addition to a series of promissory notes. Should Alleghany recover, the securities would rise in price and Young would be a multimillionaire. A poor performance, on the other hand, would result in his personal and business bankruptcy. Mere investment and manipulation would not do, considering the stakes. If Young did move into Alleghany by purchasing the Ball holdings, he would have to do so as an active manager, and not merely as the absentee owner. He would have to take a series of crash courses in railroading, absorb the vocabulary of the business and its politics, as well as economics and finance. Young would have to cultivate relations with the ICC and other government agencies, learn the ways of state legislatures, and how to deal with his bankers. Of course, this would be a major challenge, an exciting adventure, and Young must have liked that. In the past he had dealt with paper; assuming command of the Alleghany would make him the master of the Nickel Plate, the

C&O, the Missouri Pacific, the Père Marquette, and other important railroads whose names still had a romantic sound to them in the late 1930s.

Young could not resist. The negotiations with Ball were concluded successfully. The aged manufacturer would receive $6.4 million for his holdings—more than twice the price he had paid for the securities two years before—with $4 million in cash and the rest in two-year notes secured by Alleghany stock. Kirby supplied most of the money, while Young was to take care of the guarantees. He knew that if he could not meet the deferred payments, Ball would reclaim Alleghany and so wipe him out. In a short period of time, then, Young had to salvage several troubled and deficit-ridden lines, or at least convince investors he was well on the way to so doing.

Young believed part of this could be done, but not in the manner by which such things had been accomplished in the past. For the past half century no important railroad had been able to function without strong backing from investment bankers. Tradition and common sense dictated a continuation of the pattern, so Young traveled to pay court to Thomas Lamont of the House of Morgan, to convince him and his fellows that Alleghany would remain a responsible member of the community. With Morgan and Guaranty on his side, prepared to purchase his bonds and finance his activities, perhaps Young would be able to succeed. Should he fail to win their confidence, however, all would be lost. This was the conventional wisdom.

Young went to see Lamont soon after taking command. The meeting did not go well. In his usual understated way, Lamont made Young understand that he expected to have a major voice in determining Alleghany's policies, while Young was equally firm in saying that he planned to run the company his way. Although the Morgan partner did not say as much, he implied that Alleghany would find it difficult to obtain financing without such cooperation. In a studied fashion, Young responded that he was sufficiently aware of Wall Street tradition to appreciate the meaning of his actions, and was prepared to work the consequences. With this, the meeting ended, and as far as Young was concerned, a new chapter in American railroading had begun.

No railroad could operate for long without a financial constituency. Wall Street banks were one part of that constituency, while the RFC and other New Deal agencies were another. But not all the banks were in New York, and an anti-Wall Street stance would not be without benefits in Franklin Roosevelt's Washington, especially in 1937, when the New Dealers blamed business for the new recession. Senator Wheeler had an innate distrust for most businessmen, but he came to trust Young, expecially after Young appeared to break loose from the bankers. Several major investment bankers in the Midwest also noted the conflict. Harold Stuart of Chicago's Halsey, Stuart and Company had long spoken of how his city could replace New York as the nation's financial center. In the 1920s he had worked with Samuel Insull to try to seize utilities underwritings from Morgan and other Wall Street firms. Now he met with Young and pledged his support. So did Cyrus Eaton of Otis and Company, a Cleveland investment bank. These men had allies too, and although they were hardly as powerful as the Wall Streeters, they did have the resources to finance Alleghany.

The idea was intriguing, from a prestige as well as a profits viewpoint. For close to a century the eastern railroads had been run from New York and Philadelphia. If Young could unite the operating lines controlled by Alleghany into a single system, a Chicago-Cleveland axis might defeat the easterners.

Young needed the political reformers and the "provincial bankers," but the situation and his personality demanded a third force for his army, and that was the public itself. Railroaders and bankers had been accustomed to catering to portions of the public—shippers and important purchasers of securities, for example. But the bankers had never seemed to care much about the opinions and even the actions of small investors and those who held no securities, while the railroad executives were prepared to sacrifice passenger traffic to the needs of freight. In an age of reform, the arrogance of a Vanderbilt—"the public be damned"—and the high-handed methods and attitudes of the elder J.P. Morgan were recalled by antibusiness writers who assured their readers that little had changed. Small investors had been crushed by the depression, and they tended to view Wall Street as the origin of their distress. Such people could be rallied by antiestablishment businessmen allied with progressive politicians who promised to operate in their interests. A few years later Wendell Willkie would assume this stance in politics. Young intended to fill the position in railroading.

It was not a sudden decision, nor one that was plotted in advance. Young was a free-wheeling opportunist, using whatever elements of power were available in order to achieve his objectives. Under different circumstances he could have worked well with the Morgans—after all, he had been an ally of the General Motors hierarchy only a few years before. In the

1920s, an age of stock market speculation, Young had been a speculator. During a period of reform, he would be a reformer.

The Chesapeake and Ohio was the key to his plans, for without it there could be no new major eastern carrier. Young knew it, and so did the bankers. In late 1937, the Guaranty fired its first blast at Young. It controlled large amounts of C&O bonds, under the terms of which certain collateral had to be maintained. The line's collateral was inadequate, and so the Guaranty announced its intention to foreclose—to oust Alleghany and assume command at the railroad. Litigation followed, with both sides knowing such matters usually took years to decide, and that unless Young could meet his payments schedule, Ball would regain control of Alleghany—and the bankers would be back in their old position.

Young asked for and eventually obtained a temporary injunction restraining Guaranty from voting any impounded stock. This meant that the small shareholders held the key to control, and with the election approaching, Young and the Guaranty initiated drives to obtain proxies. This was Young's first direct experience in dealing with the general public. He sent a series of letters to stockholders, all of which reflected his growing anti-Wall Street point of view. By then his former General Motors clients had joined the Guaranty forces, and so it was relatively simple for him to portray himself as a champion of the "little man" against the "interests." Young won a plurality of the proxies, but due to technicalities the contest ended in what amounted to a draw.

Now he took a different tack. Still a major influence at the C&O, he insisted that the company's next series of bond offerings be thrown open to competitive bidding. Lamont and the Guaranty were shocked; they had handled the C&O financings for decades, and had assembled a syndicate headed by Morgan, Stanley and Kuhn, Loeb that was prepared to continue. Now, with Young's backing, Halsey, Stuart and Otis made a bid for a $30 million issue at lower rates. They won the underwriting, but Young had an even bigger victory. Not only had he dealt a blow to the Wall Streeters but he had convinced small investors that he was their defender, while the New Dealers were more certain than ever that the New York bankers had milked the railroads dry of funds, and were continuing to do so even in the late 1930s. Thurman Arnold, the crusading head of the Department of Justice Anti-Trust Division, had just opened a massive assault upon monopolies; he became a Young ally and promised to explore the situation carefully. Now the contest was broadened, with Arnold and the ICC investigating competitive bidding and worrying the Wall Streeters, while Young attacked on the other flank by informing the shareholders of developments and offering them his interpretations.

Meanwhile, Young was unable to meet his payment to Ball, and in mid-1939 was obliged to surrender 1.2 million shares of Alleghany common to him. Still, Young retained a position in the company—some 800,000 shares—and launched a new attack. Charging Ball with having manipulated prices prior to the 1937 recession, he initiated a $5 million suit against the aged manufacturer. The government was brought into the action, since Young charged Ball with violations of the Securities Act of 1934. On its face the suit had little merit, but Ball would be unable to vote his Alleghany shares until it was decided. Thus, Young retained control of the company. Disgusted with the situation and probably wishing he had never met the Van Sweringens, Ball contacted Morgan and the Guaranty to ask for advice and assistance. The bankers were busy defending themselves against the Young-inspired charges of rigged bidding, and they too had tired of the fight. Together with his governmental allies, the interloper had succeeded in forcing the most powerful financial groups in America to the wall.

In the end the bankers were obliged to accept competitive bidding, while the exhausted Ball agreed to an out-of-court settlement whereby he surrendered almost all the Alleghany stock in question to Young and his group, and in addition reimbursed them most of their original purchase price. Young was the master of the Alleghany and the C&O and prepared for the next step, the merger of most of the lines owned by the holding company. In 1945 the directors of the C&O, the Nickel Plate, the Père Marquette, and the Wheeling and Lake Erie met and approved of a merger. But the plan was opposed by a group of Nickel Plate preferred shareholders who threatened to take the case before the ICC unless they received a better rate of exchange for their holdings than Young had offered. This was a conventional ploy, hardly a serious obstacle, but it placed the financier on the defensive. This time he was not fighting the powerful Wall Street interests; instead a relatively small group of minor stockholders had challenged him, the stakes being a few hundred thousand dollars' worth of stock. Young might have won the contest. Even had he capitulated it would not have been a major defeat, either financially or in terms of prestige. So it seemed rather strange when he announced that the four-way merger would be delayed. In fact, it never took place.

Some of Young's intimates later claimed he had withdrawn because he did not want to be placed in a position of fighting groups of small investors, after having expended so much time and effort in establishing himself as their champion. Certainly he would have been out of character in such a contest, which the press surely would have covered. More likely, Young had tired of the struggle. Or he might have decided that the merger no longer was as desirable as it once had seemed. By then Young had become interested in other aspects of the industry too. Cynics claimed he had begun to believe his own press releases, which put Young forth as a man intent on saving the railroads from extinction. Friends said he had a morbid fear of aging, took his fortieth birthday in 1937 very hard, and had turned to the business crusades in an attempt to sublimate dark fears. His only child died in an accident four years later, and Young's periods of depression lengthened and became deeper.

Then too, perhaps the man found himself, by chance, in the right industry and struggle but for the wrong stakes. The various clashes revolving around Alleghany and the C&O had made a public figure of the onetime wheeler and dealer. Prior to these contests, Young had worked with and against cliques of speculators and investors, usually behind the scenes. Now he was a celebrity, the subject of articles and interviews, and he liked the excitement, the notoriety, along with the salving thought of public service. But what was it for? Had he succeeded in putting together a major system based upon the C&O, Young would be master of a large freight carrier, with a comparatively minor stake in passenger travel—human beings. This was necessary and even vital, but hardly glamourous or of a magnitude to engage such a man for long. Increasingly he talked of the need for better passenger travel, and the railroads' mission in this field. He hoped to lead the fight for a reborn industry that would challenge the automobile and the airplane for travel business. Whatever the reason for this change, Young liked the idea of devoting himself to such a cause and engaging himself in such a struggle. It was a role he would fill and play for the rest of his life. Young required a proper and dignified excuse to ease himself out of the C&O situation, and this was provided by the stockholder suit. Next he needed a vehicle with which to enter the passenger field, and his sometime ally, Thurman Arnold, unknowingly gave one to Young in the early 1940s.

Arnold was convinced the railroads were one of the most powerful forces in American business. He knew little of the industry's problems or even the close to hopeless state of some of the major carriers. His enemies were Vanderbilt, Morgan, and others like them—men long dead—and not the faceless executives in charge of their lines. After the 1937 recession, President Roosevelt became certain big business was preventing recovery and would have to be harshly curbed. Arnold was to be his instrument in what was the most vigorous antitrust campaign ever mounted. The Assistant Attorney General scattered indictments like so much buckshot, and one of his blasts struck Pullman, Inc.

By any measure Pullman was a monopoly. It owned Pullman-Standard, which was the only important manufacturer of sleeping cars, and in addition owned the Pullman Company, which operated sleeping cars for all the railroads that used them. J.P. Morgan had been instrumental in achieving the monopoly and, as was customary, meant to extract his price. He insisted that the large lines be given seats on the Pullman board, and that his company, the New York Central, have a major role in setting company policy. As had been past practice, each railroad would sign separate contracts with Pullman so as to avoid charges of monopoly. This meant that a passenger traveling from New York to California would have to make a complete change—Pullman included—at Chicago or St. Louis. Such was the case in 1940. Harold Vanderbilt and "Jack" Morgan were directors, and travelers disembarked in midcontinent, while redcaps unloaded and reloaded baggage. It was a strange sight, and irrational, since the railroads regularly permitted the rolling stock of rival carriers on their tracks. But an exception was made for the Pullmans. Within a generation, however, few recalled the origins of this tradition.

Arnold issued his antitrust complaint in mid-1940, and the case started on its way through the courts. Three years later a three-judge federal court found Pullman to be in violation of antitrust statutes, and promised a divestiture plan the following year. The judges also spoke of how the public interest had been violated and of changes required in this area. In particular, the revamped operations would have to offer travelers a through service, with sleeping cars switched from company to company as were freight cars. What J.P. Morgan had shied from doing at the turn of the century, the court mandated in 1943.

The following year the judges informed Pullman of their decision; the company would have to divest itself either of its manufacturing or service unit. It was no surprise. Pullman promptly opted to retain its manufacturing operation, and informed the client railroads of the coming divestiture. President D.A. Crawford suggested that the companies organize a jointly owned subsidiary which would purchase Pullman Company and then operate it in the interests of all. The New York Central was eager for such a solution, and indeed its representatives on the Pullman board had recommended it. But some other lines, led by the Pennsylvania, feared domination by the Central group, and so rejected the suggestion, announcing they would operate their own services. Negotiations dragged on, with no solution in sight. The judges admonished Pullman to sell; Pullman cited its attempts at compliance; the Pennsylvania held firm. It was a stalemate, and with the court insisting upon an alternate plan, Robert Young entered the picture.

Several of Alleghany's lines used the Pullman service, and so Young could claim to be an interested party. The New York Central had been unable to organize a pool, he said. Perhaps Alleghany could do so instead. Crawford rejected Young's suggestion; he was a Central man and eager to see that line succeed. A short period of fencing followed, and then Young petitioned the court for permission to submit a bid for control of the Pullman Company.* If and when he gained control, he pledged to spend a half a billion dollars to upgrade equipment and so make long-distance railroad travel competitive with rival forms of transportation. The new passenger carriers would be quite different from the old—Young carefully did not use the generic term "Pullman," a hint that he might let contracts to other manufacturers. He spoke of library and motion picture cars, of how the basic design of sleeping compartments hadn't changed in a generation. Young thought payments could be made by means of a credit card, and since the airlines had a no-tipping policy, he would institute one too.

It was a dramatic presentation, which was widely reported in the newspapers. Now Young was on the front pages as well as the financial section. While the judges considered his offer, Young contacted the heads of the major railroads to ask for meetings where he would present his plans. As might have been anticipated, the Wall Street bankers sent out the word, and the major

---

*Young's petition was handled by the law firm of Arnold and Wiprud, which was headed by Thurman Arnold, who had left the Attorney General's office for the federal bench, tired of that, and opened a private law firm in Washington. His associate, Arne Wiprud, had formerly been head of the transportation division of the Anti-Trust Division of the Justice Department.

lines refused to acknowledge Young's existence. All did so, that is, except the Pennsylvania. Never dominated by bankers, and retaining its suspicion of the New York crowd, that line was willing to listen to what Young had to say. After all, the Pennsylvania had been the first to oppose the industry-wide plan to purchase the Pullman Company, and had long been considered something of a maverick. President Martin Clement informed Young he could have his meeting, and the financier traveled to Philadelphia, first making certain the newspapers knew of it.

The conference was short and to the point. After Young had repeated his many ideas, Clement informed him that the Pennsylvania was committed to owning and operating its own fleet of sleeping cars, saw little economic gain in spending huge sums of money on new equipment, and was not interested in further discussions. Still, the two men had taken the measure of one another, and neither was displeased with the encounter. Clement had been distant and proper, but clearly did not consider Young the moral leper he had been labeled by the Wall Streeters. In a way, this inconclusive meeting was one of the most important railroading events of the decade, or at least it would seem so twenty years later.

New York Central President Gustav Metzman rejected Young's overtures, and vowed never to grant him an audience. Instead he called in his financial vice-president, Willard Place, and assigned him the task of eliminating Young from the Pullman picture. Place did meet with Young, the two men and their allies sparred with one another for a while, and that was all. Shortly thereafter Place told Metzman that Young was a serious contender, and that unless the industry acted quickly he might be able to win important political allies. Spurred on, Metzman abandoned attempts to woo the Pennsylvania, and put together a purchasing group charged with coming up with a firm deal for the Pullman board to consider. He knew the board would be sympathetic to such an offer and recommend acceptance. So did Young, who, as expected, went to Washington seeking political support. Other purchasing groups appeared—at one time there were at least five of them—so that by late 1945 the bidding had become heated. On the surface at least it seemed passenger railroading had a bright future. If this were not so, asked onlookers, how could one explain such eagerness in obtaining control of the Pullman Company?

In the end the contest came down to one between Young and the Central's group. Metzman stressed tradition and experience, and asked the government to approve the purchase by his syndicate on the grounds that it would ensure continuity of operations at a time when the nation was undergoing the stresses of conversion from a wartime to a peacetime economy. His purchase price came to slightly more than $60 million. This sum was based on complicated depreciation schedules and was to be made through deferred payments. For his part, Young repeated his plans, and toward the middle of November told the court he was prepared to pay $75 million in cash for the Pullman Company. The Wall Streeters announced they would match the bid, and Young responded that he was prepared to go higher. In addition he charged the Pullman directors with acting in bad faith, noting that they were intimately tied to the Metzman syndicate. Finally, Young initiated a public relations program in the hope of winning national support for his program. "Invisible Lines Divide America," noted an advertisement he placed in newspapers throughout the nation. If he gained control of Pullman, it would be possible to travel coast to coast without changing sleeping cars.

Of course, the court had indicated it would insist upon this no matter who won, but the advertisement had the effect Young knew it would. The Wall Streeters were placed on the defensive, and their only response was to note that Young lacked the funds necessary to make good on his promises, and as chief executive officer of Alleghany and the directing voice at the C&O and other lines, he would favor them at the expense of their rivals. To this Young replied that he would relinquish control of all railroads in which he had an interest if permitted to purchase Pullman—although he did not say how this would be done. Still, in mid-December the court decided that the parent company should be allowed to sell the Pullman Company to whomever it wished. This appeared to be a major, final victory for the Metzman group.

Not prepared to concede defeat, Young attacked on four fronts simultaneously. First he told reporters that he would lodge an appeal with the Supreme Court. Then he insisted upon being allowed to join the Metzman group, basing his demand on his position at the C&O. Young accelerated his advertising campaign, and some of his new broadsides were masterpieces, still cited as such by textbooks on the subject. One showed a smiling pig standing in a freight car doorway, holding a cigar, while a sorrowful human family looked on from the side. "A Hog Can Cross the Country Without Changing Trains—But YOU Can't!" was the headline. Readers and editorial writers were impressed, and Young's fame increased. But the ICC considered it a vulgar display. Commissioner Charles Mahaffie and Assistant Finance Director C.E. Boles had long thought Young a bad influence within the industry, had him under investigation, and now came out in favor of the Metzman group, indicating he would support it before the Supreme Court.

The fourth front was the most important of all. The Guaranty, Morgan, and other major Wall Street banks and trust companies appeared to have gained a key victory over Young, the Alleghany, and the midwesterners, using Metzman's New York Central as their rallying point and vehicle. Unable to defeat the combine, Young decided on a bold stroke. He would raid the Central.

New York Central executives of the immediate post-war period often talked of the company's glorious past. Most of them had grown up during the great railroad age, when the Central had been a major force in a vital industry. During the day they were surrounded by artifacts and symbols of that time—on their office walls were pictures of famous trains, and large oil portraits of their predecessors stared down from between the hangings in the boardrooms. The solid Edwardian majesty of Grand Central Station, with its statue of Commodore Vanderbilt in front, was a monument to the great company. There was a strong feeling of secure power about the place. One could not help being impressed when standing in the middle of the terminal, beneath the blue and gold ceiling that was studded with stars, surrounded by the cool marble, listening to the echoes of the trains arriving and leaving, and the noises of passengers. Even the smells were intoxicating; they seemed to recall the past in their combination of dust, lubricants, and musty cloth and leather.

The executives believed the Central had a promising future as well. Like most railroads in this period, the company turned out many presentation brochures, filled with architects' drawings, diagrams, paintings of trains still in the planning stage, and glowing paragraphs designed to stimulate the imagination. Bound in plastic and printed on fine paper, these brochures had a mixed readership—executives who either knew such projections rarely came to fruition or who wanted to delude themselves, and the general public, hardly interested in such matters. There was talk of new diesels that would cut travel time to Chicago by half, lightweight passenger trains that would reduce costs, increase revenues, and enhance enjoyment of train travel.

Dome-topped observation cars, oak-paneled saloons on wheels, and luxurious but compact roomettes would await the passenger, while terminal improvements would enable redcaps to get luggage to waiting taxis before the arrival of their owners. It was an enticing vision.

The New York Central had a magnificent past in 1945, as well as the promise of a glowing future. It was the present that provided all of the headaches.

The company filled an important economic role. Without it the region would undergo great hardship, perhaps even paralysis. The line expected to lose passenger business now that the war was over and restrictions on automobile production and travel were ended. The Central had little more than a faint hope for a renaissance of the commuter business, since the territory it served already was laced with good highways and roads, awaiting an automobile-hungry population. Young might dream of a revival in this area while Metzman and his colleagues gave it lip service. But the Central management knew that the company was destined to rely more heavily on freight than it had in the past. Such had been the drift during the interwar period. Passenger traffic had picked up in World War II, but only because travelers had no alternative in most cases, while military personnel had no choice in the matter. If nothing else would kill long-distance travel, the wearisome journeys in overcrowded antique cars could be counted upon to do the job.

Bituminous coal was the Central's most important freight, as it had been for over a generation, and in 1945 it accounted for only a quarter of the total. As before, however, the line had a wider variety of cargo than most major eastern companies—slightly more than 40 percent of the Pennsylvania's freight was coal, for example. Various manufactured goods were the Central's largest single category; the products of factories took more than half the carloadings that year. Military sales were important, and these would decline, but management had great expectations for the automobile industry; Detroit traditionally preferred the Central's water level route for its shipments to eastern markets. Just as the automobile had crippled the passenger business, so services to that industry helped bolster the line's freight revenues. Given a booming auto market, as was anticipated in 1945, the Central could expect to do very well in this segment of its operations.

The remaining quarter of the freight business came from petroleum, ores, produce, and a wide variety of miscellaneous products. Pipelines could deprive the Central of the petroleum business in time, and the company expected this would be the case. Produce could be shipped to local markets by truck, and this had been the tendency before the war, but refrigerated railroad cars were still required for long-distance hauling. The ore business, of course, was at least as secure as coal.

The Central was confident it could outperform most truckers within its territory on a cost basis, and the truckers agreed. But they were planning to change the situation. Already Detroit was turning out refrigerated trucks, and by early 1946 it seemed the Central's profitable milk business would be lost. More important, however, was the activity of various automobile lobbying organizations which attempted to win support for a federal highway program. In 1923 the Bureau of Public Roads, headed by Thomas MacDonald, had set forth the idea that the nation needed a network of arterial highways that would enter every American city with a population of more than fifty thousand. Now this idea was revived, with MacDonald, still at his post, talked about a major interstate system that could cost in excess of $50 billion before it was completed. Before the war the state of Pennsylvania, with help from the RFC and the WPA, had constructed the first link of the Pennsylvania Turnpike, 160 miles of which were opened in 1940. Now that the war was over the state intended to complete the line, which would run across the state, where it would connect with the Ohio Turnpike, then being planned, and the New Jersey Turnpike, then being discussed. Such a system would compete with the Pennsylvania Railroad for passengers and freight, but the railroad didn't expect to encounter much trouble in retaining its coal-hauling business, was prepared to concede marginal freight to the trucks, and cared little about long-distance passenger travel. As yet there was no hard proposal for a New York Turnpike, but the Central knew that if and when one was constructed, it would travel along the New York-Albany-Buffalo route. Such a road could attract shippers and cut deeply into the Central's revenues—in much the same way as the Central itself had helped vanquish the Erie Canal a century earlier. Still, in 1945 such a road was a distant threat and no more.

Although the Central's roadbeds and terminal facilities were in decent shape in 1945, its equipment was outdated and worn through wartime service. Ten out of every thirteen freight cars were over fifteen years old; one in four had seen service during both world wars. Close to half the Central's 3,600 locomotives had been on the line when Woodrow Wilson left office in 1921. At a time when several western lines planned to have all-diesel, service by 1947, six out of every seven Central locomotives were steam, and the company had no plans to change the situation drastically.

Long-distance passenger travel no longer was pleasant. Four of every five dining cars were over twenty years old and they showed their age. Few had been equipped with air conditioning, and passengers complained that the once-famous Central cuisine had become third rate. The company had blamed most of its troubles on the war, but there were no material improvements now that the fighting had ended.

The Central was inefficient in its use of labor. In itself this was not unusual, for the railroad unions for many years had insisted upon featherbedding and no-cut clauses in contracts. Still, within the industry the Central was known for its inability to keep costs under control. In late 1945 the company had 124,000 employees—more than at any time since the late 1920s. A record number were occupied in the maintenance and repair of roadbeds and equipment, long ago one of the most inefficient of all railroad operations. Metzman tried to defend the situation, claiming it was necessary if the Central were to be ready for post-war demands. In fact, the company had lost control in this area, and had no clear idea of how to regain it. Some cuts were made in late 1945 and early 1946. But at the same time new union contracts guaranteed jobs, increased wages, cut hours, and had little impact upon productivity. Other railroads were in the same situation but many—the western carriers, for example—could bear the strain. The Central could not—at least not for long.

Some special aspects of the corporate picture offered hope, however. During the Vanderbilt-Morgan era the Central had purchased shares in several railroads, most of them coal haulers, in order to extend the company's reach. These stocks were still in the portfolio, and some paid regular and good dividends. For example, in 1945 the Central received close to $3 million from its shares in three lines—the Reading, the Mahoning Coal, and the Pittsburgh and Lake Erie—while its 70 percent ownership of the Cleveland Union Terminal provided an additional $1.3 million. Other terminal income added to the total. But the most interesting contribution in the category of nonoperating income came from rentals of various properties, many of which were in midtown Manhattan. Over $1 million after taxes and costs came in from this source alone, in a year when the Central's rail operations provided slightly less than $50 million before taxes and other deductions. In all of their discussions and projections, neither Young nor Metzman gave evidence of considering this to be of major importance for the company's future.

In fact, the Central was one of New York's most important realtors. Everyone knew it owned Grand Central Station, of course, as well as the thirty-four-story New York Central Building directly behind it. But the company also owned a large block of land bounded by Madison and Lexington avenues to the west and east, and Forty-fifth and Fifty-first streets to the north and south, a parcel as big as and even more valuable than Rockefeller Center. The area had been used as railroad yards before the construction of Vanderbilt's terminal, and afterward some of the land had been leased to private builders. When they defaulted in the 1930s, the Central assumed ownership of the buildings as well. Most urban planners agreed that this area would be the site of major change in the post-war period, and that land values were bound to increase.

The Central owned many hotels, among them the Biltmore, the Commodore, the Roosevelt, the Chatham, the Barclay, and even the Waldorf Astoria. Some had outlived their usefulness and would have to be razed, but the land beneath them was valuable. The company had land holdings elsewhere as well. The Cleveland and Chicago operations were thriving, as were real estate parcels in White Plains, Yonkers, Buffalo, and other cities and towns along the route.

Those properties not directly or indirectly connected with railroading were carried on the books as a $40 million investment, at a time when the Waldorf Astoria alone might have fetched as much on the open market. This figure did not include the Central's West Side terminals between Thirtieth and Thirty-third streets on Eleventh Avenue. These were being consolidated, and there was some thought that part of the holding might be sold to private interests. Such a transaction could return to the company more money than it might earn from railroad operations in several years. The Central might have been a moribund railroad in the mid-1940s, but it had the makings of a vigorous real estate company.

Nor was this all. Like the Pennsylvania, the Central had invested in bus services, and in 1945 owned more than a quarter of the Class B shares of Central Greyhound, which operated throughout its territory, from New York to Chicago. The Central held close to half the shares of United States Freight, a holding company engaged in freight forwarding, and which competed with Railway Express and Parcel Post. It was still a small operation, but possessed great promise—more than railroading, in any case.

Thus the wheel had turned full circle. Land speculators had been a major force in planning and financing the Erie Canal. Such individuals had roles in constructing the small upstate railroads that were later brought together by Erastus Corning to form the New York Central. Corning himself was an important land speculator; the railroad was designed to help provide him with profits in this area. But like the rest of the northeastern trunk lines, the Central came into being without important land grants of its own, such as those that would be acquired by the major western transcontinentals. After World War II several of the western lines would become interested in mining and farming their properties, as well as selling plots to land developers. In time, the Union Pacific, to name one such company, might evolve into a firm in which railroading was secondary to minerals. The Central could not do the same, of course, and for this reason such potentials escaped Metzman and Young. But its urban real estate holdings, acquired as a by-product of terminal building and the development of rights of way, did exist, and in some ways they were even more valuable than the mineral rights of the Union Pacific. In other words, the Central was sitting on a real estate empire, growing in value all the time, but which in 1945 was still underdeveloped.

Neither of the contestants in the various struggles of the late 1930s and 1940s was able to make this leap of imagination, an essential precondition for such a change. A generation later new businessmen—the conglomerateurs—would do so with great aplomb. A man with the imagination of a James Ling, for example, might have seized the Central through a series of share exchanges with existing stockholders, and then divided the company into its component parts. Most of his attention would have been devoted to the healthy operations. As for the railroad itself, it would be isolated and on its own, allowed to decline, even given away if that were possible, or await a government bailout.*

No such individual was on the railroad scene in the immediate post-war period. Metzman and his group were railroaders, born

---

*Such a solution is not as far-fetched as might appear. Conglomerateur Ben Heineman took control of the Chicago and North Western a generation later, and after returning it to prosperity used its common stock to obtain a series of firms in nonrelated areas. Then he divested himself of the railroad by giving it away to its employees, in return for which the remaining company, Northwest Industries, received a huge tax write-off. Today Northwest is thriving, as a leading manufacturer of underwear and cowboy boots, among other things.

and bred, their lives dedicated to the industry and their line. Given a free hand they would have made the best of the situation, attempting to enhance freight operations and slowly leaving long-distance travel to other means of transportation, concentrating their efforts in this area on remaining commuter operations. Young was not a true radical in the same sense as the conglomerateurs would be later on. Rather, he was a convert, a mild heretic at most. Young believed the railroads could be saved, not only for coal, ores, and other freight but for passengers as well. More to the point, he was convinced the tasks could be accomplished by private enterprise of the traditional variety; he never spoke of the need for government subsidies and did not consider nationalization a viable alternative. Young envisaged an altered industry, not one that was transformed or reborn. For years he had advocated managerial, organizational, and technological alterations. He had a flamboyant style and was an outsider, and when compared to the entrenched industry powers he did seem somewhat unusual. But in fact he was scarcely more revolutionary than Ripley and other men who had suggested a reshuffling of the systems in the past. Certainly he was not to be compared with Glenn Plumb in terms of advocating major changes. Still, to the traditionalists at Central headquarters he seemed a menace from the provinces.

A few years later, historian Arnold Toynbee would write of the decay of civilizations. When they became too self-satisfied and lazy, unable to meet new challenges, they invited attack, he wrote. Usually this came from the outside, from barbarians who lived on the periphery and watched hungrily. In time they invaded, clashed with the established powers, and eventually triumphed. The newcomers did not want to destroy the civilization but rather to assume its leadership and share in its power and prestige.

The established business elites tended to view assaults by outsiders in such terms, and they reacted viscerally against newcomers with the "wrong" backgrounds. Just as George Ball distrusted the Wall Street bankers, so they considered him a crude outlander. Investment bankers like Harold Stuart and Cyrus Eaton spent a good deal of their business lives contesting the old order for power, and they thought in terms of civic pride and moral values as well as economics and finance. Now Robert Young of Texas, a self-styled populist and anti-New York reformer, had appeared to hurl his challenge at a leading citadel of the old order, the New York Central. The press portrayed Young as a Lochinvar out of the West, while Metzman and his colleagues were old-fashioned defenders of a system that no longer worked. It may have been exciting symbolism but this was not the situation, for Young was no barbarian, and Metzman could hardly be compared to the evil robber barons. Still, it was the general viewpoint as the struggle for the Central began, and lost in the verbiage was the real issue involved: the need or the lack of it for drastic change at the railroad.

IX

Under New Management

The New York Central enjoyed heavy passenger traffic in December of 1945, as Americans traveled to winter resorts and visited their families to celebrate their first post-war Christmas. The seasonal pattern had become traditional at the Central, as it had with other trunk lines, and extra trains were placed into service to handle the travelers. Management knew this bulge would continue for a few years more, but then decline as automobiles became available once again and air transport ceased to be exotic, expensive, and occasional. The situation demanded foresight, preparations to meet the new challenges. Would the Central be up to them?

Passenger revenues that December were close to $20 million, a record that still stands and is not likely to be broken, and the Central handled the travelers in fine style, with scarcely a hitch, despite having to use worn-out and marginal equipment. But it was the only bright spot in the company's picture that Christmas season. Freight revenues were $26.6 million, continuing the steady decline that had begun even before the end of the fighting in Europe. This was the key statistic and trend, for the Central had little hope for passenger business and, despite the record, expected no net profit on operations. Earnings were supposed to come from freight and other activities, some of which were not related to railroading. The severe post-war economic and social readjustments were bound to result in dislocations, and management wasn't certain how to deal with them.

That December the Central reported a net loss for the month on combined passenger and freight operations of $556,000. The previous December it had earnings of $4.2 million, and in 1943, they had been $8 million. In December 1942, when the economy had been straining to meet war demands and railroads were operating at above full capacity—seemingly impossible, but it was done—earnings reached $11.1 million. The last monthly deficit had been reported in March 1938—$37,000—while in the bleak December of 1937, the bottom of the Roosevelt recession, the Central had lost close to a million dollars.

Those bad times had not been forgotten during the war, even when profits were high. Central's management had to face the possibilities of a new recession during that Christmas season of 1945. The figures appeared to indicate that one was in the works. The company could do little to prepare for the decline; fixed costs, including servicing of debt, could not be cut by much, while management claimed that further economies in other areas were next to impossible.

Operations returned to the black in January 1946 and remained there in February, but in March the Central lost $1.5 million. The old pre-war pattern seemed to have reasserted itself. Railroad operating costs remained high—this was a capital intensive industry, after all—in average years the Central would do well to break even on combined passenger and freight business, while in poor times there would be a string of monthly deficits. But these costs would rise steadily in boom periods, while revenues increased, often substantially, so that the profits picture would seem excellent. Accountants and financial analysts called the phenomenon "leverage." It had always been a hallmark of railroading as an industry, and the Central offered as close to a perfect example of it as might be found.

Like all railroad men, Gustav Metzman had learned its lessons early in his career, while leverage was fundamental to Wall Street speculators such as Robert Young. Both understood what the other was talking about in this area, but though their principles were the same, they expected to exercise them differently. At the Central, Metzman was contending with a railroad that had a substantial passenger business, something he believed could not be made profitable, and so he hoped to stress freight. He thought in terms of longer trains, of freight cars with larger capacity, with each extra dollar of revenue transformed into ninety cents or so of profit. Robert Young controlled the C&O, most of whose business was in freight, but he dreamed of a revival of passenger travel. The fare paid by an incremental passenger on a scheduled train would be added, intact, to pre-tax profits.

Metzman had devoted his entire business life to the Central, and wasn't going to change his base of operations and loyalties in the twilight of his career. Young faced a different situation and possessed a different personality. By 1945 he had become a strong advocate of the passenger train, and had waged war against the Central, its bankers, and the railroad establishment in general for the better part of a decade. In retrospect his move to seize the Central appears both logical and inevitable, but at the time the relatively sedate railroading and banking communities looked upon it as a daring act.

Railroad revenues and profits were poor in 1946. Passenger revenues declined from $1.7 billion the previous year to $1.3 billion, while freight went from $6.6 billion to $5.9 billion. Due to the workings of leverage, net income fell sharply, going to $335 million from $502 million. And as had become traditional, the Central felt the squeeze more than most Class I carriers. In 1945 the company had earned $24.4 million, which came to $3.79 a share, and in 1946 it lost $10.5 million, $1.62 a share.

The Central had revived its dividend in 1942, paying $1.00, and it was raised to $1.50 in 1943. The dividend was passed in 1946, and Metzman refused to speculate as to when it might be restored. Investor confidence was badly shaken, and the price of Central's common stock began to slide; during the first ten months of the year, half the equity value was wiped out, and by November the common was selling for around 15.

It was in this period that Robert Young began his campaign to seize power at the Central.

Rumors of a raid appeared in the financial pages and in the business press in late 1946, although there had been talk of such a challenge earlier. The stock inched upward, reaching the 20 mark before Christmas as speculators moved in, hoping for a massive buying effort by the principals that would send the price still higher. Young refused to confirm or deny the rumors, but by then there seemed little doubt they were true. Still, he did not appear to have the financial power to gain complete control. For eight decades the Central had been a Vanderbilt property, and Harold Vanderbilt and his family certainly wouldn't sell.

On January 8, Alleghany notified the ICC that it had purchased 162,500 shares of Central common for the C&O. The size of the holding was surprising. The Vanderbilts owned around 100,000 shares, with more than half of them in the name of Harold Vanderbilt. Together with the Morgan group they had an additional 200,000, enough for control, though the company had 6,447,000 shares outstanding. For the moment they did nothing, while Young continued his purchases, and the price rose. By the end of the month Allagheny had 250,000 shares, impressive but insufficient to challenge management. Still, Young approached Metzman in February and demanded a seat on the board. This was "taken under advisement." Two weeks later the Supreme Court decided against Young in the Pullman case, and the Central's group was permitted to take control of that company. By then, Alleghany owned 400,000 shares of Central, and Metzman knew he would have to consider Young's request for representation seriously, while at the same time developing a new strategy aimed at denying him power.

Clearly the Central's management would need allies, for banker support would not suffice in this case. With the Pullman experience fresh in his mind, Metzman decided to turn to the ICC. The leaders of that agency had developed a strong dislike for Young and many of those around him, and the financier made little attempt to disguise his belief that the commissioners and lawyers were allies of the Wall Street bankers. So Metzman announced that Young and Robert Bowman, the chairman and president of the C&O respectively, would be granted seats on the Central's board—subject to approval by the ICC.

This meant that Young would have to petition the agency for a review in order to obtain the desired permission. Furthermore, he would have to expose himself to examination by railroad officials as well as by unfriendly ICC leaders. Jacob Aronson, one of the Central's counsels who had helped negotiate the Pullman purchase, would be there to contest the seating of C&O officials, charging that the action would violate provisions of the Interstate Commerce Act that forbade interlocking directorates. Did Young plan to merge the Central and the C&O? If so, this would be a violation of Section 7 of the Clayton Anti-Trust Act in that it would lessen competition. And what of the impact of the creation of a community of interests upon other railroads? The Virginian Railway Company serviced a section of the West Virginia coal fields and had long sent part of its freight northward via the Central's tracks. A Central-C&O nexus might work against its interests, and President F.D. Beale would be there to challenge Young's seating on the Central's board.

The strategy was obvious, as was the goal. Let Young purchase all the Central shares he wanted, but prevent him from voting them or in any other way exercising power at the railroad. In time he would tire of the situation and sell the shares, in this way removing himself from the picture after suffering still another defeat.

The hearings were scheduled and conducted, and worked out

pretty much according to plan. Central and Virginian lawyers cited the statutes, while C.E. Boles of the ICC, who had clashed with Young in the past, not only agreed with them but characterized Young as a dabbler and adventurer, who had purchased Central stock "for the purpose of indulging a hobby," and who had demonstrated "a willingness to take great risks with the company's funds." Boles doubted that Young truly spoke for small investors, and threw down a challenge. Why not seek a proxy contest? If Young wanted a merger, and could get enough proxies, he could file for one, which would then be considered on its merits. By purchasing Central stock through Alleghany, Boles implied, Young was using muscle to overwhelm the small investors who had little use for him.

For his part, Young spoke of the benefits of cooperation, cited his successes in making railroads under his control more profitable, and criticized the Central's management for its past performance. He also lashed out at the bankers and their law firms, which made huge profits from their positions, implying they were bleeding the industry dry. On more than one occasion he noted that the Virginian was controlled by the Mellon family, which was part of the old money clique which had led the eastern lines to ruin. As before, he looked upon himself as a clean outsider representing new forces—among them small investors—whose coming to power would benefit the industry and nation. There was nothing wrong with railroading, then, that a general housecleaning of managements, bankers, and law firms couldn't rectify. Finally, he included government agencies in the list of his opponents, citing several scandals and hinting at ICC collusion with existing managements.

All of this was well reported in the press and resulted in appearances on radio shows. Young was front-page news, and once again he seemed a maverick reformer prepared to enter into combat with "entrenched interests." In some ways the drama of this contest masked the complexities of the issues involved. For most Americans railroading was a dull subject—the glamour age had ended by 1948—but a personal struggle for power was something else. This suited Young, who looked upon it as a moral as well as a financial crusade. Clearly withdrawal from such a fight would be next to impossible.

Probably Young knew even before the hearing began that he hadn't much of a chance of victory. This would explain his inflated rhetoric and willingness to polarize the situation more than was necessary. He was not surprised when, on May 10,

1948, the commission denied his request for representation at the Central. The initial attack had failed; now he readied himself for a long siege.*

It began with a series of diversions. Young told reporters of a projected three-way merger. First he would purchase control of the Virginian, and then bring it together with the Central and the C&O. Young also initiated legal action seeking to obtain the right to vote his shares in the Central. There was no chance of obtaining a large block of Virginian shares—the Mellons certainly wouldn't sell—and the ICC would have stopped the merger, while the courts had not proven sympathetic to those seeking to overrule ICC decisions. But both forays would keep the Central and its allies occupied for the time being, while Young worked behind the scenes to organize his major assault. At the same time, he mounted a new advertising campaign, criticizing railroad managements and politicians unable to run their companies and the country with any degree of efficiency. This served to keep his name and voice before the public and solidify his image as the defender of the public against the tycoons and their allies.

Meanwhile, Young cemented his friendships with old allies and sought new ones with others who had similar interests. As before, Allen Kirby could be counted on for support, as could the anti-Wall Street investment banks of the Midwest. To them he added Sid Richardson and Clint Murchison, two Texas oil millionaires, who also had close relationships with important figures in the Eisenhower administration, and who were convinced they could beat the New Yorkers at their own game. During the late 1940s and early 1950s these men engaged in several joint speculations, drawing together as Young prepared for a new attempt at winning the Central and defending his interests in other railroads, the Missouri Pacific in particular, against attacks by the ICC.

The plan was simple enough, never hidden from the public or disguised so as to throw the ICC off guard. Young would accept Boles's challenge, though in a modified form. Members of his group purchased Central's shares on the open market, in small lots for the most part, retaining their stock in street names.** At

---

*This phase of the contest as well as other aspects of Young's career are well covered in Joseph Borkin, *Robert R. Young, the Populist of Wall Street* (New York, 1969).

**One keeps stock in street names by leaving them at the brokerage, in Young's case Merrill Lynch, Pierce, Fenner and Beane. They would be so registered on Central's books, and so the railroad would not know their true owner. Central realized Young had been purchasing shares, but the device of street name registry masked his actual holdings.

the same time Alleghany added to its already large block, in the end reporting ownership of 800,000 shares. When all was ready and the Missouri Pacific situation clarified, Young would challenge Central's management to a proxy contest. He would not seek a merger with the C&O as Boles had recommended, however; Young knew he had little chance of success, given the climate at the ICC. Rather, he would promise to divest himself of all interests in other lines when he gained power at the Central.

This campaign took six years to prepare and construct. Then, on January 16, 1954, Young contacted Harold Vanderbilt to inform him of his program. He expected to seek the chairmanship of the Central that year, after defeating management in a proxy contest. He told of all his plans, not saying exactly how many shares he already controlled, however. The details of the conversation were relayed to the Central's leaders. Though the confrontation had been expected, Young's boldness was somewhat surprising and unnerving—was he so certain of victory that he could afford to signal his intentions in advance? Three days later Young and Kirby resigned their positions at the C&O, while Alleghany sold its holdings in that railroad to Cyrus Eaton. Thus, Young put all of his chips on the table. If defeated at the Central, he would no longer be a major force in American railroading. And with this, the proxy contest began.

The financial press announced the opening of what was considered the second round in the fight, a continuation of the struggle that had ended, temporarily, with the ICC decision against Young in 1948. But this was not the case. For the situation in eastern transportation had changed dramatically in the intervening years, and in such a way as to make Young's dreams of the 1940s outdated and all but destroy any chance he might have had to revive passenger transportation in that part of the country.

Although he never said as much, Young's hopes for a passenger train revival and talk of efficient and comfortable coast-to-coast service had been based upon convincing Americans that the renting of a seat or compartment on a safe and proven train made more sense than the purchase of an automobile or the perceived risks of a flight on an airplane. Americans of the 1920s rarely took automobile trips of more than a hundred miles or so without considering the dangers of a breakdown, wear and tear on the car and its driver, and the uncertain quality of roads, while aviation was a chancy industry and the planes often unreliable. In the 1930s, of course, the depression held back both automobile and airplane travel, and so the passenger trains could at least survive and retain most long-distance travelers. Ingrained habits, a shortage of automobiles, and poor roads might have encouraged Young to believe that the passenger train could compete successfully with autos in the post-war world, while aviation remained exotic in the late 1940s.

The situation had changed by 1954, however. Airline route mileage, which had been only 39,000 in 1945, was 114,000 ten years later, and in the same period revenue miles flown went from 32.6 million to 131.5 million, and passengers carried from 475,000 to 3.4 million. The slow, small, and uncomfortable two-engine propeller craft of the pre-war period had been replaced—at the major lines, at least—by larger, faster, and roomier giants, while the carriers talked confidently of jet planes, traveling at high speeds above the weather, that would make their appearances in the next few years. In the late 1930s a DC-3 could take a passenger across country—with several stops for refueling and taking on or landing passengers—in the better part of a day, assuming weather conditions were good. In this period a passenger might make the trip by sleeper train in little more than three days, and go in comfort and even luxury most of the way. By 1954 the DC-6 made the coast-to-coast run, nonstop, in less than seven hours, and on a regularly scheduled basis. Meanwhile the railroad carried passengers in pre-war sleepers, and the service was not as good as it had been in the 1930s.

The airlines had revamped operations and had prepared for the boom that was not long in arriving. They were able to utilize aviation technology developed at government expense during the war, while they received federal aid for airports and other services. The railroads had none of these benefits, and so they declined. In 1945, domestic aviation revenues were $214 million, against $9 billion for the railroads. Ten years later aviation revenues were $1.2 billion, and railroad revenues, $10.2 billion. Clearly the gap was narrowing rapidly. But the change was even more dramatic insofar as passengers were concerned. In 1945 three out of every four people who traveled between cities went by rail, while only three of every hundred took airplanes. Ten years later the railroads' share was one in three, while aviation accounted for one-quarter of all intercity travel.

Robert Young's talk of a true transcontinental passenger service appeared attractive in 1947, but the idea had lost a good deal of its original appeal by the mid-1950s, as the airlines captured the long-distance trade. Perhaps it would have happened in any case, for the new technology clearly had more advantages than the old. Still, the contest had been decided by default; the railroads had not mounted their best efforts, and possibly had given up too much too soon.

The automobile posed an even more serious threat, and of course its potential had been recognized by some railroaders shortly after the turn of the century. The key elements here were automobile sales and roads, and there had been booms in both areas during the 1920s. Sales were poor during the depression 1930s, but after a slight dip total registrations rose, while bus transportation actually benefited from the hard times. Governments on all levels improved existing roads and added to the total mileage. Many roads were constructed in order to find work for the unemployed; there was no great demand for them from the driving public. Thus the pace of construction was not as hectic as it had been in the boom years of the 1920s.

Slightly more than 2 million private autos were sold in 1938, against more than 4.5 million in 1929. Total registrations rose slowly in between, going from 26.7 million to 29.8 million. Only a handful of cars were produced during the war, and these for the military, as the industry converted to the manufacture of armed vehicles, airplanes, and the like. Automobile usage declined drastically; gasoline rationing and the unavailability of tires resulted in keeping people at home or obliged them to take trains and buses. Production and sales soared after the war—6.7 million cars were sold in 1950, and even then the industry was unable to meet all demands. But there was a decline during the Korean War, after which the boom resumed.

Road building expanded shortly after V-J Day and quickly became a major industry. The Federal Highway Act of 1944 authorized the expenditure of $1.5 billion on roads for the three years following the end of the fighting, while the states proceeded on their own to develop plans for toll turnpikes. The eastern states had been impressed by the Pennsylvania Turnpike's pre-war performance. Not only had it proved a financial success, but the road had attracted new business to the state. Soon after the war's end Pennsylvania projected a large-scale improvement program, including extensions to Ohio in the west and New Jersey to the east. Work on the New Jersey Turnpike began in 1946, the same year New York debated its thruway—which was to run parallel to the Central and the old Erie-Hudson waterway. The New Jersey Turnpike was completed ten years later, with an extension to the Lincoln Tunnel and New York

City and another linking it to the Pennsylvania Turnpike. By then the New York Thruway was open from New York City to Buffalo, while an extension was being constructed from the latter city to the Pennsylvania border. Meanwhile the Ohio Turnpike, the Indiana State Toll Highway, and the Illinois State Toll Highway were being completed or already operating. It was possible to travel from New York City to Chicago along the New Jersey, Pennsylvania, Ohio, and Indiana toll roads. New York, Pennsylvania, and Ohio planned a toll system from Buffalo to Cleveland, but only part of it was completed, the rest being constructed as a superhighway with federal funds. In this way, two giant highways ran from New York to Chicago, one an automobile equivalent of the Pennsylvania Railroad, the other running close by the Central's famous water level route.

All of this was coming to fruition as Robert Young opened his new assault upon the Central. He repeated old promises to deliver better passenger transportation. Yet even as he maneuvered for control, the states and the federal government were putting together this massive highway-turnpike system. Within three years a person would be able to drive from New York to Chicago in less than two days. The same trip on the Central or the Pennsylvania could be made in less than one day, while the cities were three hours apart by air. Given the costs of motels, additional meals, and tolls—as well as repairs and wear and tear—the automobile was the more expensive form of transportation, even if it carried one or two passengers along with the driver. Still, Americans had renewed their romance with the car. They enjoyed the turnpikes and superhighways and the freedom of individual travel, and so took to the road anyway.

There was more to come. Three months after Young had issued his challenge, Vice-President Richard Nixon told the annual Governors' Conference about the administration's new federal highway program. He talked of "a grand plan for a properly articulated system that solves the problems of speedy, safe transcontinental travel," and said the federal government was prepared to spend $5 billion a year over a ten-year span in order to achieve a national system—this in addition to the $700 million per annum already being spent by Washington on roads. Detroit was delighted and the railroads dismayed. Once completed, it would be possible for a driver to go coast to coast without ever leaving a turnpike or a major highway.

Young had long advocated transcontinental railroad travel. When he first talked of it, trains carried most of the passengers going from New York to California. The situation had changed drastically by the mid-1950s. In the future, the trip would be made by airplane, auto, or bus. Even the staunchest railroaders, the bitter-enders, had to concede that the train had lost the long-distance customers and that they would never be regained. But as far as the Central and the Pennsylvania were concerned, the key to it all was that 837-mile stretch between New York and Chicago, on which rolled trucks and buses as well as autos. Watching the vehicles speed along, they might have reflected on the sentiments of the canal men of the 1840s as they saw the railroads speeding through central New York or Pennsylvania, sucking people and freight from the flat boats. Robert Young had lost the most important battle before taking command of the Central. No matter what he did at the line, there was no way to restore passenger travel on a large scale once the turnpikes and highways were completed.

Young moved his pieces into place in late January and early February of 1954. Counting the Alleghany shares together with those he and his associates had purchased for their own accounts, Young owned or controlled over a million shares of Central common, more than 15 percent of the company's equity. Since he was no longer an officer of either Alleghany or the C&O, Young presumed the ICC would permit those companies shares to be voted in the next election, which was scheduled for May 26, and of course he was certain Cyrus Eaton would support him in anything he wanted. Thus armed, he went to the Central and asked for representation on the board, indicating that unless two seats were granted, management could expect a proxy fight. The request was denied, with President William White speaking for the members. White had become chief executive officer a year and a half earlier, when Metzman retired and moved up to the chairmanship. His election had come as something of a surprise, since the company had a tradition of promotion from within, and White had been president of the Delaware, Lackawanna and Western at the time. In his eleven years there he had managed to transform a broken-down, deficit-ridden line into one which was solvent, profitable, and constantly improving. White was no miracle worker, hardly a showman, and certainly no match for Young in the area of public relations. But he was a solid and at times imaginative railroader, who might be able to provide an appearance of freshness at Central headquarters. Management and its bankers knew that this ingredient would be required if Young continued to press for power. White was charged not only with improving performance, but creating confidence in the railroad, so that the price of its common stock would rise. Without this, Young would be able to gather supporters from among the dissident stockholders.

White's regime began auspiciously. As might have been anticipated, he spoke of the need for tighter controls and of the company's plans for modernization of facilities and improvement of services. Additional funds were earmarked for dieselization, stations were painted, and a new public relations staff taken on to spread the word of the new look at the Central. More important, however, was the fact that 1953 was a good year for the economy, and railroading shared in the prosperity. Continuing the recovery which began with the Korean War, net income of the nation's railroads rose to $940 million, which, excepting the World War II years, was the best performance since 1929. The Central did well, reporting earnings of $34.1 million and $5.27 a share against 1952's $24.7 million, or $3.83 per share. As though to reward the faithful, White doubled the $.50 common stock dividend and hinted at further increases should earnings continue at that level. Central's common stock rose only slightly in 1953, however. This was considered satisfactory, for although the economy was strong, the end of the Korean War and the advent of the first Republican President since Herbert Hoover raised fears of a new recession. Stock prices marked time while earnings advanced. Brokers and analysts argued that a new bull market was in the making, and political observers noted that the firmness of the market was more a tribute to Eisenhower's popularity than anything else.

For the nation would have its recession. Beginning in the second half of 1953 the economy slowed down, even while earnings remained high. The Central felt the impact in September, when for the first time that year monthly revenue figures fell behind those of 1952. The decline continued into early 1954, so that by the time of Young's challenge there seemed little possibility of a dividend increase. Revenues for February, when Young asked for seats on the board, were $57.1 million, against $64 million for the same month in 1953, while income stood at $1.1 million, down from $4.7 million in Febraury 1953. There would be a revival in March and then another decline in April, while in May 1954 the Central would report a deficit of $5.2 million, the first in more than two years and the worst showing since the end of the post-war readjustment. That the Central's performance was poor was known at the time. Even those who had little interest in the matter were informed of the fact by Young's broadsides, published in advertisements, reported in news stories, and aired on television interview programs. Understandably the stockholders held management responsible for their losses. Young was able to blame the Central's leaders for matters they could not have controlled as well as for actual mistakes and failures. From his point of view, the timing of the proxy fight could not have been better.

The contest began in early February, when Young invited White and his old nemesis, Willard Place, to lunch. His group had no argument with White, said Young, and under certain circumstances he could remain in the presidency—but not as chief executive officer—after the proxy fight had been won. Even Place might be retained as financial vice-president, though his major concern since the Pullman contest had been the elimination of Young from railroading. Both men would have to remain neutral in the struggle, and in addition Young insisted on being given the Central's list of some 44,000 stockholders without having to go through the courts to get them. Young got the list, but White and Place opted for participation on the side of management. "If anyone should start a proxy fight, the New York Central board and management would also start soliciting proxies," said White, to which Young responded with a reiteration of themes which by then had become familiar. "The real issue is whether the owners of the properties are going to be made to continue to submit to a Morgan non-ownership board with its countless conflicts of interest or whether they are going to enjoy what every honest business under our American system must have if shareholders and the public are to be served instead of the be damned...."

With this, what perhaps was the most dramatic proxy contest in corporate history began.*

The campaign revolved around legal manipulations and a public relations contest. Since Alleghany was restrained from voting its 800,000 shares, the company sold them to Richardson and Murchison, in such a way that the two Texans did not have to put up funds for the acquisition. The Central's bankers and lawyers protested, several Alleghany shareholders initiated suits, and the matter dragged through litigation until the very eve of the election. There was no way of knowing whether the shares could tip the balance, but clearly such a sizable block was important, not only for its own sake but the way the decision

---

*The campaigns are well covered in Borkin, *Robert R. Young*, pp. 132-210.

would affect independent shareholders. In the end the Central's protests were rejected, and the 800,000 shares were voted for Young's slate of candidates. Meanwhile, White and Young campaigned for support in the fashion of political candidates. They met with shareholder groups, hired public relations advisors, appeared at press conferences—including television shows such as *Meet the Press*—and attempted to win support from financial writers. Campaign buttons were distributed, with slogans like "Win with White" and "Young at Heart" inscribed in bold letters. Each man went to Grand Central Station to meet the trains, shake hands with passengers (and possible shareholders) and pose for photographers. The Central spent $1.2 million on its campaign, while Young used $1.5 million of Alleghany money for the contest. Sid Richardson owned a vacuum cleaner company; his sales force of three hundred was diverted to ringing the doorbells of Central shareholders and selling Robert Young. There was much hoopla and little serious discussion regarding the industry and the company. Newspapers and trade journals speculated on the results; each side authorized polls and released their findings when they helped its cause. Young and White set forth rival platforms, the former noting that at one time Central common stock sold for 275 and paid an $8.00 dividend, while White promised a higher payout in the future if returned to office.

Tide magazine, an advertising trade publication, took a poll of leading marketing executives and then released the results. By a two-to-one margin these individuals guessed White's group would win the contest, but they thought Young had done the better job of getting his message across—the vote here was five to three. Some of the reasons given for supporting management were: "White is a railroad man's railroad man." "Big blocks of conservatives as well as widows and orphans are afraid of Young." "The Street resents attempts to push it around." Those who bet on Young said: "He's rough, tough, used to winning—and he's pretty right on his ideas." "Young has enough influential backers to unseat White." "Young has been and is a terrific power in railroading." Here, too, there was no discussion of issues, only of the personalities of leading actors. This was politics and show business in the media age, not economics and railroading. But given the nature of the contest and its inherent drama, it was to have been expected.

Young won the contest by more than a million proxies—thus, he didn't need Richardson's and Murchison's 800,000 votes. His slate of candidates took its place as the new board. Young announced he would serve as chairman for a salary of a dollar a year, and that his board would waive all fees until a $2 dividend was achieved.

This was a major shift of power. In the past such giants as J.P. Morgan and E.H. Harriman had battled for control of major railroads, but not since James Hill had come out of the West to do battle with the easterners had such a dramatic turnabout taken place. Even then, Hill had taken relatively minor lines, certainly none of them as prestigious as the Central. Robert Young, who described himself as a stock speculator and securities analyst, and not a railroader, now sat in the seat of power once held by the Vanderbilts and the Morgans, and before them Erastus Corning. To old-timers it appeared a cataclysmic transfer of power.

The shift took place at the proper moment as far as Young was concerned. The nation started to come out of the recession shortly before the ballots were cast, and the pace of activity on the nation's railroads quickened. In May it had appeared that the company could be insolvent before the year was out. By day White spoke of dividend increases, while at night he pored over Place's reports, and ordered the legal department to investigate alternate actions under the bankruptcy laws. Papers for such an eventuality were prepared and ready for implementation even while the campaign reached its final stage. White and his group wanted to win the contest, but the loss must have offered them some relief, for others would have to meet the crisis while they were in comfortable retirement, on the sidelines.

The economic upturn changed all this. The Central earned $2.6 million on railroad operations in June, and results improved each month for the rest of the year. The December traffic approached the record for that month, and by then it was evident to all that the company would have no trouble with its cash flow. Despite losses in the first half, the Central was able to show a net profit of $9.2 million for 1954. If Young had any fears of tipping over into the abyss, he gave no sign of them. Instead he took credit for the improved performance and promised to do even better in 1955. As he told it, the railroad was on the verge of rebirth, with the $2 dividend in sight.

For all his reputation and talk, Young remained ignorant of many aspects of the industry. This had been one of the reasons he had been so conciliatory to White and Place earlier in the year. He knew they were experienced and able railroaders, the kind of men he would need when he took command. In the early stages of the proxy contest he had taken care to separate the managers from the board, attacking only the latter as representatives of the "damnbankers." Professionals such as Robert Bowman and Walter Tuohy of the C&O had taken care of operations, while Young had planned grand strategy and public relations campaigns. Often Young spoke rashly, promising more than his companies could deliver. On such occasions the managers would inform him of the facts and dimensions of problems and urge him to back down. Meetings and telephone calls would follow, Young would receive a further education in railroading, and then, most of the time, he would quietly accede to their arguments. This practice was known within the industry and on Wall Street, and during the proxy fight White had often spoken of Young's inexperience. But as far as the general public was concerned, Young was the operating officer, with the faceless railroad executives there to put his plans into action after working out details.

Young did not delude himself in this area; he was no egomaniac. From the first he knew that he would require a superlative manager if and when he captured control of the Central. Although on good terms with the C&O management, he did not want to bring one of that line's executives to New York, both in order to avoid charges of creating a community of interests and to make a dramatic appointment. Several men were considered, but Young had a favorite from the first, Alfred Perlman of the Denver and Rio Grande Western.

This was an interesting selection, one bound to cause discussion within the industry, and Young must have relished the prospect. At that time most railroad executives had fairly undistinguished academic careers, receiving their real educations at their companies. The industry had long since stopped producing men like Harriman and Hill, and instead was noted for its solid plodders. In contrast, Perlman had been considered a prodigy at MIT, where he received his degree at the age of twenty, and he then went on to study railroading at the Harvard Graduate School of Business Administration. There he worked under William Z. Ripley and others who were helping create federal railroad policy, and several of Perlman's papers on reorganization were considered classics in their field. Ever since he had been a teen-ager, Perlman had worked on the railroads, at first during summer vacations. Later, as a graduate student, he had helped Ralph Budd rebuild the Burlington, all the while being called in by other lines as a consultant. Perlman went to the bankrupt Denver and Rio Grande Western in 1936 on what he thought would be a short-term assignment and remained for eighteen years. The company operated some 2,000 miles of track from Denver and Pueblo in Colorado to Salt Lake City and Ogden in Utah. It was an important coal hauler, and in addition a significant carrier of transcontinental passengers. The company had outmoded and often broken-down equipment and a poor worker-productivity record when Perlman arrived; its credit was nonexistent.

Perlman scrapped everything but the rights of way. First he convinced the bankers that the company could be made profitable once again, and obtained new sources of credit. Then he began a dieselization program and at the same time ripped up old tracks and set down new, often supervising the work himself. Workers were reassigned to more productive tasks, and efficiency rose sharply. The company was back on its feet by the time war came, and it earned a good return on investment during the emergency, using the money to pay off old obligations and further strengthen its credit. The Denver and Rio Grande Western embarked upon a new modernization program in 1946, made possible by large loans readily granted by its bankers. In 1947 the company paid a dividend, only 15¢, but impressive considering that the line hadn't been able to meet its bonded interest in 1935.

The Perlman strategy was simple enough, though its implementation required great skill and knowledge. His line would have the most efficient equipment possible, to attract business and so cover the heavy fixed charges and show a profit. Wherever possible Perlman replaced workers with automated equipment, and he spoke of trains that operated with small crews aboard, and these more for safety and to conform with union requirements than anything else. The familiar engineers, brakemen, and conductors would be gone, and in their places would be staffs of technicians at electronic consoles, directing the entire network from a series of command posts. He knew that the airlines and autos would soon take his transcontinental business, and that buses could take care of local transportation. This was all to the good, for Perlman had little use for and interest in passenger travel. The Denver and Rio Grande Western would concentrate upon freight in a growing area, and Perlman planned for the day when his long, efficient trains would move from siding to siding, making money on each trip. In time the company might merge with others, for Perlman was one of the industry's leading advocates of combination, and had been since having worked under Ripley in creating ICC policy in the 1930s.

Before going to the Denver and Rio Grande Western Perlman had been considered a brilliant theoretician, and used as such by railroad executives, who liked to think of themselves as practical men. After his success as an operating president Perlman's reputation grew, but at the same time he came to be considered an oddity. From the first, railroad presidencies and chairmanships had been reserved for Protestants who had risen to power after long apprenticeships at their companies. These men formed a brotherhood; each knew the others and felt comfortable with one another at conventions and congressional hearings. A small handful of Catholics had managed to find their way to the executive suites, but as of 1954, no Jew had ever headed a Class I railroad, and as far as anyone could recollect, none had ever been considered for such a post. Perlman, an eastern Jew with an academic background, could not have hoped to obtain the presidency of even the Denver and Rio Grande Western, a medium-sized line by industry standards, were it not for that company's desperate position. Within a few years he was considered one of the best railroad men in the nation, but still the other executives felt somewhat uncomfortable in his presence, the product of an anti-Semitism that for the most part was genteel and appeared permanent. Perlman had accepted this—he really had no choice in the matter—knowing that had his religion been different, had his academic credentials not been so impressive, he would have been snapped up for the presidency of one of several Class I lines. Now, in 1954, he was asked by Robert Young to take over the management of the New York Central, one of the two most prestigious lines in the industry. On the surface it seemed a replay of the Denver and Rio Grande Western situation—a troubled railroad was turning to an outsider because it was desperate, and could not afford to play the game by the old rules. But there were important differences. Young was also an outsider, even more so than Perlman, and so were his principal backers. Each man in his own way had been obliged to fight the old guard, and each had won. At the Central they would have the opportunity to deal with an enterprise that had long been the symbol of an older America that had denied them access and opportunities.

The two men met for the first time in late May, shortly before the proxy vote. By then Perlman had learned of the Central's difficulties and also knew he would be offered the presidency. Whatever their preconceptions, the eastern academically inclined Jew and the largely self-educated wheeler-dealer Texan found they liked one another, and in fact shared some of the same ideas. The meeting was harmonious, and Perlman indicated that he would accept the presidency once Young was in a position to offer it to him. The victory was announced on June 14, and at the same time Young told reporters that Perlman would take over White's job.

It did not take Perlman long to realize that the Central was close to collapse. Thomas Lamont and other bankers told him there was little hope, and some urged immediate bankruptcy, after which reorganization would be possible. Then, with a clean financial slate, the Central might be able to stage a comeback. But Perlman's pride would not permit him to begin his New York career in this fashion, and in any case he thought the situation could be salvaged. Within the next four months he cut some 15,000 workers from the payroll, mostly from the clerical and professional staffs, long one of the more inefficient areas at the company. Some services were cut back temporarily in order to save money, even though Perlman knew they would have to be restored once the ICC received complaints and acted upon them. Still, these actions would have accomplished little had not the economic revival taken place. Young understood this, as did Perlman, but the chairman was accustomed to personalizing such events, and he did so in this case. "Miracles can still happen with an ownership board and a good all-around organization wrapped up in one man—the president," wrote Young to Perlman that October, when it seemed clear the crisis had passed. From that point on Perlman was the master of the Central, while Young spent most of his time on public relations and long-term strategy.

This was important, because the two men had differing ideas as to the future of the company. While it was true that Perlman and Young both favored modernization, the president showed less interest in passengers at the Central than he had at the Denver and Rio Grande Western, while the chairman continued to talk about a revival of this business. Within a few months, however, Perlman had convinced Young that there was no possibility of a profitable transcontinental run, and that even within its own territory the Central could not hope to make money on this business. Curtailed service and abandonments, not purchases of new passenger cars and upgrading of stations, was the answer. Perlman wanted to divert all profits into modern freight technology. If the Denver and Rio Grande Western could make money in its territory, the Central should be able to do so by drawing upon the booming industries along its line. Soon after taking office and making certain the company would survive,

Perlman toured the line and saw evidence of decay and misuse. Repairs and alterations began at once. Young would continue to speak about the passenger trains of the future, but in 1955 the New York Central devoted itself to freight.

The two men did agree that the Central should seek mergers and consolidations, though, again, for different reasons. Young had always wanted to unite the great passenger lines to eliminate changeovers. Perlman was concerned with competition for the freight business by rival forms of transportation. In particular he was convinced that the New York Thruway possessed the potential to destroy the Central by diverting the traffic of New York from railroads to highways. Perlman noted the potential of the St. Lawrence Seaway, another Eisenhower-era project then in the works. When completed it would open the Atlantic sealanes to Great Lakes shipping, thus making ocean ports of such cities as Chicago, Cleveland, Erie, Detroit, and Buffalo. No longer would Detroit's autos and Chicago's grain be shipped to New York via the Central and from there reloaded for overseas destinations—with the Seaway, those cities and others would turn to liners that docked in their ports. If Henry Ford's work indirectly destroyed the passenger business, Dwight Eisenhower's programs seemed to be doing the same for the freight operations of the eastern trunk lines.

In Perlman's view, this meant the Central and other eastern railroads would soon suffer from overcapacity to an extent that would overshadow that of the Great Depression. Not only would passenger business be crippled but trains carrying freight might be forced to operate far below their potential. What sense would there be in creating efficient systems if they were not to be utilized fully? The only answer was consolidation, to a greater extent than even Ripley and others of his generation had discussed. For a while, Young had talked of a merger of the Central with railroads in adjoining areas whose operations dovetailed with his, the object being improved passenger services, greater usage, and, in the end, higher revenues and profits. Perlman had no such ambitions. In the first place, he would not consider mergers and combinations until he had revamped operations, so the Central could enter negotiations from a position of strength. Then he would seek out lines within his territory, or at least those whose territory overlapped that of the Central and so served the same customers. Mergers with such companies would enable him to end freight competition, eliminate duplicate services, and abandon rights of way. Perlman was not so much interested in increasing revenues as he was in cutting costs. He envisaged a lean company, operating fewer but more modern and efficient trains around the clock, seven days a week. This would enable him to cut down on cost per freight mile, to an extent that would make the railroad cheaper to use than trucks and ships.

Young wanted the ICC to help make his line a leading passenger railroad, and he used many arguments in working for a merger with the C&O. Perlman would petition the agency for permission to leave the passenger business to others. At one point, while pleading for the right to abandon a particularly unprofitable line, he claimed the Central would be better off purchasing autos for each passenger than continuing services. Once the revival had taken place he might seek out merger partners.

The logical conclusion to a Perlman strategy would be the unification of the Central and the Pennsylvania. He did not say as much in 1954—how could he?—but in retrospect this appears to have been his ambition. If and when negotiations were begun, the Central would have to function as an equal partner, and not the object of a salvage operation. If Perlman succeeded at his new post, he might emerge in a few years as the most important influence in American railroading, and perhaps the chief operating officer of one of the most powerful combinations in the nation.

Obviously the railroad could not pursue both the Young and Perlman strategies at the same time. Given its limited assets, it would have been fortunate to survive intact, and the two men spent most of their time in late 1954 attempting to ensure survival. Capital expenditures that year were cut to $35 million, the lowest level since 1944—in contrast, White and the old administration had spent $140 million in 1952, when the Central rushed completion of its dieselization efforts while at the same time expanding its freight car fleet. By early 1955, when there seemed little doubt that the company would avoid bankruptcy, management was able to chose between the Young approach and that put forth by Perlman. By then the new president had the confidence of all at headquarters, and even the chairman had to concede that passenger travel could not be revived and that concentration upon freight was the only sensible course to follow. Young delivered the $2.00 dividend, the reward he had promised stockholders for having supported him the previous year. He remained the official spokesman for the company, and continued to appear on radio and television shows. But Alfred Perlman was the real master at the New York Central.

He set about his tasks with a ruthlessness that surprised even his oldest associates. Employees who were not productive and not covered by strong union contracts were fired. To the 15,000 given their severence in 1954 were added an additional 10,000 in 1955-57. The maintenance departments were especially hard hit, and Perlman also fired crew members on passenger trains. Under White the Central had done all within its power to maintain standards on the commuter lines. Perlman simply let them fall apart. Commuters screamed that the service was irregular and declining, that the cars in which they rode were filthy and in need of repair, and that the roadbeds were ramshackle. The Central denied all, and did as little as possible to change the situation. Commuter operations worsened appreciably under Perlman. The president was deaf to all protests, and in fact used an auto to get to work, even though he lived near a commuter station. In his actions if not his words, Perlman invited commuters and other travelers to switch to autos and buses. The money he saved by ignoring passengers was used to improve freight services.

Perlman explored the potential of the Central's securities portfolio and its land holdings in Manhattan and elsewhere. He sold marginal land and some securities, not only to obtain additional funds but so as to realize tax advantages—in 1955 alone the company obtained close to $9 million from this source. Perlman launched a renovation program at several of the Central's hotels, and in the process increased the profits from them by 50 percent in four years. He was not interested in the company's equity position in U.S. Freight and the Reading, and disposed of a large portion of the holdings in 1956 and 1957 by distributing them to Central's shareholders in lieu of the cash dividend—at the same time he avoided paying capital gains taxes, saved money that might otherwise have gone to shareholders, and was able to claim that he had raised the cash value of the dividend to $2.70 in 1956 and $2.73 the following year.

As a result of these operations and the improved national economy, the Central reported earnings of $8.78 a share in 1955, and in 1956, $6.58. Perlman's critics charged him with manipulating the figures, to which management noted that most of the increase in earnings had been derived from railroad operating income, which had reached a post-war high. Perlman used these funds to improve the Central's financial position, in this way assuring the banking and investment community its stocks and bonds were once again prime holdings. This accomplished, he borrowed funds at favorable rates and initiated his freight operations improvement program. Capital expenditures took $37.6 million in 1956 and $75.3 million the following year. This was only a fraction of the amount White had spent in his last years, but the former administration was interested in expansion, while Perlman used his funds to contract operations. He scrapped old freight cars and steam locomotives and purchased new, modern, efficient cars and diesels. By 1957 the Central had only 123,000 freight cars, 25,000 fewer than in 1953, but a majority of them were less than twenty years old. The number of locomotives in service in 1953 had been 2,873, and in 1957, 2,132, but, again, the fleet was modernized by the latter year—at least insofar as freight was concerned. Perlman opened new freight facilities in Buffalo and Youngstown as further indications of his intention to give other means of transportation a battle when it came to the freight business. His most impressive new facility was in Elkhart, Indiana. Completed in 1958, it was named the Robert R. Young Yard.

Young had little to do with the company after the 1954 crisis had passed. Naturally he was delighted by the company's fine showings in 1955 and 1956, and as the Central's common stock rose to the $50 level, he predicted it would soon double and go to par. Young purchased additional shares, while many of his friends, convinced that he indeed had turned the railroad around, did the same.

Perlman had saved the railroad and initiated a sound program of change, but he hadn't performed a miracle. The nation was struck by a new recession in 1957, and the Central suffered, as did most other railroads. That same year the New York Thruway reported a better than anticipated volume of business, and there was no doubt it had taken a good deal of the railroad's freight business—Perlman predicted that unless the railroad received relief in one form or another the Thruway would destroy the railroad.

Together with other leading railroaders, Perlman petitioned Washington for help. In particular he wanted permission to eliminate all unproductive passenger lines or, failing that, as many as possible. During the previous eight years, he told a congressional subcommittee, the Central had lost over a half a billion dollars on passenger services, and had been obliged to continue the service at low rates due to the rulings of state regulatory commissions. "We can be nibbled to death in 49 places at once, and no one is responsible when the patient dies," he said. The great railroads would not collapse, but rather decay, noticed by a relative few. "Unless you take steps now, don't expect to wave a magic wand when emergency or catastrophe is upon the country and expect to have up-to-date, modern and efficient railroads to do your bidding. Then it will be too late."

The congressmen had heard such talk before. They did nothing this time, and the decline ran its course, wrecking Perlman's hope for a revived New York Central.

If Perlman was discouraged, Young was crushed, and his black moods came more frequently than before. After having won the Central he had come to realize that he had loved the battle more than the prize. With Perlman in command he even lacked the satisfaction of having his own hand at the tiller. Young possessed the forms of victory, not the content, and it wasn't enough. He had other problems too. Several of his former associates had quarreled with him about investments, and law suits followed. Young's control of Alleghany was challenged, and there were continuing complications arising out of his dealings with Richardson and Murchison in the C&O matter. Central common stock declined to below 15 that winter, and while Young lost a fortune, the wipeouts of his friends hurt at least as much.

He had no new ambitions or interests, and perhaps considered the old ones had been poorly selected. The past decade or so had been filled with victories and ironies—had the fights been worthwhile? Certainly he had defeated the bankers and the old guard, but what had been accomplished, who had gained from the struggles, and in what ways? He had been told by Gustav Metzman that passenger railroading could not be revived, that the Central would have to concentrate upon freight. William White had said the same, and also stressed modernization and the need to work in harmony with the bankers. For all of his unique and unusual qualities, Alfred Perlman had more in common with these men than he did with Young. He shared their outlook regarding the freight business and the need to eliminate passengers, and he often told Young of the importance of obtaining lines of credit from major Wall Street houses. When Young had begun his crusade, the Central was on the decline and its stock sold for around $15 a share. Twelve years later the company was still failing, and the stock was back to the 1946 level. Had the years been wasted?

Young felt superfluous. On January 25, 1958, he walked into the study of his Palm Beach mansion, picked up a shotgun, and killed himself.

X

The Mood to Merge

The economy slowed down in mid-1957, and before the year was out it had become evident that the United States was in a new recession. Like all of its predecessors, this one had several causes, the more important of which were rising interest rates, the Eisenhower administration's tight-money policies, and a decline in private investment. The launching of the Soviet space satellite on October 4, 1957, was a blow to national self-confidence, and may have contributed to this, the most severe economic downturn between the times of Franklin Roosevelt and Richard Nixon.

Manufacturing was particularly hard hit; industrial production fell by 13 percent between August 1957 and April 1958, while the gross national product fell by close to 4 percent. Auto sales plummeted, and led the decline. But though a painful experience, the recession was not long lived. Unemployment bottomed out at 7.5 percent in September, after which most of the indices bounced back, and the year ended on a strong note. As a result of this recovery, America's gross national product actually rose slightly in 1958, going to $444 billion from 1957's $440 billion and $419 billion in 1956.

Many of the nation's railroads did not recover so rapidly, or indeed at all. Their earnings declined by 10 percent in the June 1957-April 1958 period, while net income fell by 17 percent. Dividends were cut and additional companies went into receivership. The situation was particularly serious in the Northeast, where turnpike revenues were on a rising trend in 1957 and 1958, and the federal highway program was accelerated as a countercyclical measure. The twin blows of the recession and the road building led many staunch Republican railroaders to complain that Eisenhower had dealt them crueler blows than had any New Dealer, and they demanded relief. The presidents of major lines predicted paralysis unless drastic changes took place, and the figures bore them out. Talk would no longer do, they said, and they asked for severe curtailment of passenger services, tax relief, and even subsidies in order to keep operations afloat.

Thus stirred, the ICC opened hearings on the requests in late 1957, and a few months later a subcommittee of the Senate Committee on Interstate and Foreign Commerce met to listen to industry representatives and their critics and, in the end, make suggestions and recommendations for new legislation.

The hearings lasted for three and a half months, during which time the company representatives complained about declining profit margins, increased costs, and the tax advantages and subsidies provided other forms of transportation. It was in this period that Alfred Perlman emerged as a leading spokesman for the eastern lines, for while others had his grasp of the figures, none was able to present them in so dramatic a fashion. "Since 1946, the Central has invested a quarter of a billion dollars in passenger service equipment and facilities; it has spent $14 million promoting and administering its passenger service; and it lost about half a billion dollars providing this service," he said. "Let's go from Albany to Buffalo on one railroad. On one side is the Erie Canal, built by the State of New York, dredged by the State of New York, maintained by the State of New York. Right next to it is the new superhighway built by the State of New York, and on the other side of it is the St. Lawrence Seaway being built. I would say that if the New York Central Railroad were given the money that the Seaway is going to cost the taxpayers, we would be very happy, with that money, to carry freight that is going to be carried on the Seaway free. So, when you say, what is happening in the other forms of transportation compared to the railroad, there is a picture of the New York Central."

Perlman's charges of unfair competition were easy to document. As had been the case for decades, the federal and state governments had subsidized rival forms of transportation while collecting taxes from the railroads. In 1958 the federal government spent $431 million in supporting the airlines and airports, with the state and local governments adding a quarter of a billion dollars for airport construction and improvements. National highway expenditures that year were $10.3 billion, with $2.5 billion of the sum coming from Washington. The federal government provided $561 million for waterways, and in addition granted subsidies totaling $202 million to the merchant marine with another $219 million going to the Coast Guard. That year the private railroads spent close to a billion dollars on maintenance, $232 million on construction, and paid federal, state, and local taxes of $180 million. Perlman told the senators that the Central alone paid New York City taxes equal to $2.50 per share of common stock. Part of that money was used to construct public bus and truck terminals which did not pay taxes. He claimed the two New York airports represented an investment of $200 million. "These airports are taxed at a rate of $450,000. And with the values that are put upon the land out there, if that same tax were applied to us, we would be paying $4,000,000 instead of $450,000." The heavily subsidized motor vehicles, ships, and airlines drew business from his line, while the regulators refused to permit the Central to abandon unprofitable operations.

Perlman indicated that three alternatives existed, each of which involved greater freedom for the industry. The lines might be allowed to shut down routes on which they could never again hope for profits. Failing this, they could be granted subsidies, on the order of those given rival forms of transportation. Or the ICC and Congress could encourage large-scale mergers which would enable surviving companies to effect economies. Without one or all of these, he said, the Central and other eastern carriers would be unable to survive for long.

From the first it seemed clear the subcommittee was sympathetic to the railroads' plight, and would recommend relief measures. Even while the hearings were taking place, the Central was granted permission to eliminate its Putnam Division, while the Lehigh Valley's request to become an all-freight carrier received a friendly hearing. But Perlman and his colleagues were disappointed with what they obtained under the terms of the Transportation Act of 1958. There would be no subsidies; instead the federal government would provide means by which the railroads could obtain loans. In addition, several excise taxes were eliminated, while the companies were granted greater leeway in setting their rates. The legislation said nothing about abandonments and mergers, which the railroads considered to be the best solution to their problems. Behind the scenes, however, the corporation executives were given to understand that in the future the ICC and Congress would look favorably upon such a policy. So the railroads proceeded on their own, and even before the hearings were adjourned began jockeying for position and seeking allies. The huge pieces of the northeastern railroad puzzle were moving into place. But in 1958 it was not certain which companies would link with one another. The partnerships were as much a function of personality as economics, as the courting dances began.

There were approximately 150 railroad companies in the area serviced by the New York Central and the Pennsylvania, but only four others besides them could be categorized as real and symbolic powers, whose presence in a merger would create both economic impact and front page news. In places their operations intertwined like spaghetti; the managements of all six appreciated the fact that mergers would create opportunities for important economies. The companies competed with one another, to be sure, usually on ground rules set down a half century earlier and still obeyed. Together the firms had created a community of interests. At one time or another during the past century each of the six had considered mergers with one or more of the others. In 1958 they were of two minds as to combinations; naturally each line hoped to survive, guarded against a takeover in which managements would lose jobs, while fearful of being left out of some master combination dreamed up by two or more of the community members.

The Erie seemed both the most likely merger candidate and the company bound to vanish once combination had been achieved, and for this reason its management remained aloof from discussions with the other five. Squeezed between the Central to the northeast and the Pennsylvania in the southwest, the Erie never had been able to develop its full potential in the nineteenth century, and the situation was further complicated by rapacious and indifferent managements. This was not without benefits, however. Since the Erie lacked the funds to compete with the Pennsylvania and the Central in the area of passenger travel, it concentrated upon coal and freight instead. In 1958 these accounted for over 80 percent of revenues, with the Erie making every effort to retain old shippers of heavy equipment.

By then it had become a conservative company, due more to lack of opportunity than anything else. Once the wildest of the eastern lines, in 1958 the Erie was the most prudent, modernizing at a slow rate, guarding its cash position, and viewing deficits with horror and husbanding its few resources. The Erie reported revenues of $132 million in 1954, and had earnings of $6.4 million. Revenues were the same four years later, but the company had a deficit then of $3.7 million. Management was deeply troubled, for it saw little hope of revival in the turnpike era. In addition its territory was decaying, while stronger rivals were seizing part of its customer base. So it sought a merger partner, one smaller than itself so that management could continue. Perhaps the new company would be able to effect economies that would enable it to do what the Erie had done for the past half century—survive.

EASTERN RAILROAD STATISTICS, 1958

(millions)

Company	Common Stock Shares	Working Capital	Senior Capital	Revenues	Earnings Per Share	Mileage
Erie	4.7	$15	$346	$229	$1.75 (d)	3,200
B&O	2.5	32	546	383	5.37	5,900
C&O	8.2	55	387	356	6.36	5,200
N&W	7.4	55	114	204	7.57	2,700
Pennsylvania	13.2	87	685	844	0.27	9,900
N.Y. Central	6.5	41	768	659	0.62	10,300

The Erie found a mate in the Delaware, Lackawanna and Western, a Pennsylvania company that had terminals and other facilities in some of the cities serviced by the Erie. In addition, for a distance of 125 miles their lines ran parallel, and so abandonments would be possible. Discussions opened in 1958 and resulted in a merger two years later that was approved by the ICC. The new company, known as the Erie-Lackawanna, was stronger than either of its components, but remained a chronic invalid and a candidate for bankruptcy. This merger bought time, and not much more.

The Baltimore and Ohio was a much stronger railroad, and its survival was never in doubt. Its two main lines, one to Chicago, the other to St. Louis, went through rich coal and steel areas which the B&O had helped develop; there were shippers along the lines who had used the railroad for more than a century. Like the other major eastern railroads, the B&O lost money on its dwindling passenger services—close to $20 million in 1957 alone—and regularly petitioned for permission to abandon marginal lines, some of which had lost more than half their passengers in the post-war decade. A merger with a passenger line would enable the new company to close down duplicate operations without an appreciable loss of services but with a dramatic reverse of deficits, while a link with a freight hauler would provide the B&O with revenues to offset such losses.

The B&O was the most highly leveraged Class I railroad in the East, with the largest fixed costs per mile, and so was subjected to wide swings with the rise and fall of the business cycle. Its bonded debt in 1952 was $660 million, with only $2.6 million common shares outstanding.* That year the B&O earned $27 million on gross revenues of $442 million, which came to $9.74 a share. In 1957 the company earned $8.53 a share and in late summer the stock soared to close to 60. This changed with the coming of the recession. The B&O reported sharp earnings declines, and in early 1958 the common stock was selling for 23. By then the company was ready to listen carefully to serious merger proposals.

One was already before the board, for in the summer of 1957 Walter Tuohy of the Chesapeake and Ohio had approached B&O Chairman Roy White with the idea. The C&O was on its own by then, for the links with Alleghany and the Central had been severed. Chairman Cyrus Eaton and Tuohy had long been comrades of Robert Young, but Young was dead, and neither man got along well with Perlman. So the idea of a merger between the Central and the C&O was dropped, and Tuohy turned instead to a connection with the B&O.

The Chesapeake and Ohio was one of the dozen or so strongest railroads in the nation. Less than 5 percent of its revenues was derived from passengers; the company had no worries from this source. Instead, it serviced the bituminous coal fields and highly industrialized areas in the Midwest; the C&O was the largest hauler of bituminous in 1957, and its other business was growing at a steady rate. The company was in good financial shape, its rolling stock was modern, and prospects were fine, even during the recession. True, earnings declined to $6.36 a share in 1958 from $8.34 the previous year. But the C&O maintained its $4.00 dividend, business recovered that summer, and after a brief dip the common stock went on to reach its old high.

A merger of the "two Ohios" seemed both logical and inevitable in 1958. The managements were compatible with one another, and preliminary surveys indicated that there would be no difficulties with work forces and rolling stock. Both railroads were major factors in the West Virginia coal fields, and after the

*In contrast, the Pennsylvania had one of the lowest fixed costs per mile, and on revenues of over a billion dollars had $831 million in debt and 13 million shares outstanding.

merger the new company would not only be the dominant force there but realize great economies by eliminating duplicate facilities. Was such a merger in the public interest, however? Would it not tend to lessen competition? While the answer to the first question was moot, it was certain there would be fewer carriers if the linkage took place. The Norfolk and Western, then the second most important coal carrier in the area, might easily have raised the issue, but it remained silent, perhaps as part of an understanding that involved C&O-B&O acquiescence to its own ambitions.

If the Erie was the most marginal railroad of the six, the Norfolk and Western was the strongest and healthiest. Other lines thought in terms of contraction and elimination of unprofitable routes; the Norfolk and Western wanted to expand and showed profits on most operations. At a time when other railroads were concerned about their ability to borrow money, the N&W had one of the lowest debt-to-capital ratios in the industry. In 1958, for example, the company's debt was slightly more than twice its working capital, while the B&O's ratio was seventeen and the Erie's, twenty-three. The Erie reported a deficit that year, when most of the nation's railroads were in decline due to the recession. The N&W, in contrast, showed $7.57 in profits, down only slightly from 1957's $7.75, and had no difficulty maintaining its $4.00 dividend.

The N&W was a coal hauler, with close to 90 percent of its freight coming out of the West Virginia fields. Its modern, efficient trains ran westward from Norfolk to Columbus and Cincinnati, while a system of long spurs went southward as far as Durham, North Carolina. This business was marked by stability, and relatively immune to the kind of business slowdown that took place in 1957-58. Operating income rose to $44.6 million in 1957, from the previous year's $41.3 million, and then declined slightly to $43.8 million in 1958. At the time of the slowdown the N&W was in the midst of a dieselization program, which required large outlays of capital. Rather than cut back, the company accelerated purchases, a sign of confidence, so that by the end of the decade all of its diesels were less than ten years old, and the rolling stock considered the best maintained and utilized in the East.

Stuart Saunders became president of this efficient and well-managed company in 1958. A Harvard Law School graduate who had joined the N&W nineteen years before as an assistant general solicitor, Saunders had worked his way up the corporate ladder rapidly, and was only forty-eight years old at the time.

This steady progress was as much a tribute to his personality and social graces as anything else. Though he was intelligent and conversant with many aspects of the business, Saunders was most comfortable in the boardroom or the country club, dealing with fellow executives and politicians rather than with engineers and technicians. The actual running of the railroad was left to others, and this was not unusual, for there were no major problems at the N&W. While other railroad presidents were troubled by new financings, outworn equipment, deficit-ridden operations, and angry commuter groups, Saunders had none of these worries and instead spent a good deal of his time solidifying his contacts and preparing the way for mergers with less fortunate lines.

At one time the N&W, like the B&O and the C&O, had been controlled by the Pennsylvania. When Morgan ruled and Cassatt held sway, the N&W was looked upon as a useful but hardly vital line—a well-placed pawn rather than a knight or bishop. The situation was quite different by 1958, when the Pennsylvania was troubled and worn, while its former subordinate lines were in far better shape. The C&O and B&O shares had been disposed of before World War I, and most of the other Pennsylvania investments in railroads had been sold off soon after. But the Pennsylvania still owned a large block of N&W common, while its wholly owned subsidiary, the Pennsylvania Company, was a major holder of N&W preferred.

At the turn of the century it appeared that the Pennsylvania might absorb the N&W, which had only recently emerged from bankruptcy. There was no chance of this taking place in 1958. Not only might such a move be opposed by the ICC, but the other N&W shareholders would have protested, since they had no desire to see their top-grade investment watered down through a merger with the Pennsylvania. Such was the change in railroad fortunes in half a century. So the Pennsylvania contented itself with an informal community of interests and collecting dividends. The alliance of the two firms remained strong; Saunders's appointment was ratified in Philadelphia before being announced in Roanoke, while Pennsylvania Railroad executives sat on the N&W board.

The following year Saunders approached the Virginian Railroad with a merger offer, and this too had been approved in Philadelphia. It was not an unexpected move, for the N&W had sought such a merger since the mid-1920s. Saunders carried it off in fine style, and the result was an even stronger railroad.

The two managements meshed well together, with a minimum of personality conflict. Together they worked out a plan to abandon duplicate facilities and consolidate terminals. Revenues and profits rose in 1959, aided by the economic recovery. Saunders increased the dividend to $4.70 a share, and the common stock soared to over 100, more than double its 1958 low. He was hailed as an industry leader, and cited as man of the year in railroad publications. The Philadelphians appreciated this performance, and even then he was singled out as heir apparent to the Pennsylvania's presidency—assuming he wanted it.

The Pennsylvania no longer was the blue chip it had been as recently as the late 1940s. The railroad long had suffered from organizational difficulties, a heritage from the time when Thomson had established the Pennsylvania Company to handle the western business and subsidiary empires in other regions of the territory. But technological leadership combined with a fine service area masked such problems. Now they could no longer be ignored, and management bent every effort in the 1940s and 1950s to simplify corporate structure and eliminate waste. Much had been accomplished, but still more had to be done in the late 1950s before the line could be as efficient as its rivals.

Even had the organizational problems been resolved, the Pennsylvania would have been in trouble. The freight business was strong and profitable; in 1953 this brought in a record $787 million, more than the combined totals for the B&O and C&O. Had the Pennsylvania been able to relinquish all other operations, it would have been almost as sound as the freight lines to its south. But the passenger business remained a drain on its profits. Ironically, the Pennsylvania was suffering from Cassatt's success in capturing passenger operations and taking over such large carriers as the Long Island Railroad. In 1958 the Pennsylvania was the nation's most important passenger line, a status it had occupied for half a century and longer. One-fifth of its revenues came from passengers that year—$142 million, at a time when the N&W's total revenues were only slightly more than $200 million. And it was a losing proposition with no hope of reversal.

As had been the situation at the Central, the Pennsylvania made good profits on passenger business during the war, and operations were in the black in 1946 and 1947 as well. But there was a deficit of almost $45 million in 1948, which broadened during the next few years, as competition from automobiles and airplanes increased. The 1951 deficit was close to $72 million, while the Pennsylvania's net income was $26.7 million. Coming as it did when the Pennsylvania's total business was declining, the deficit was increasingly dangerous.

After years of careful study the Pennsylvania still lacked an effective method of meeting the problems. It favored abandonments, but understood that the ICC would prevent them in most instances. Along with other eastern lines the Pennsylvania fought the highway and turnpike interests on the basis of the belief that the trucks would take a portion of their freight business. But the same roads would draw even more passengers, thus deepening the deficits from such operations. This situation would strengthen their arguments before regulatory agencies, but still there was no assurance abandonments would ever be permitted to an extent the lines deemed necessary. And, of course, there was no hope of subsidies.

In 1952 the Pennsylvania embarked on a program to meet the problem, though realizing it could not be resolved. Attempts would be made to effect economies by cutting down on some services, by eliminating lightly patronized runs. At the same time—in part to convince regulatory bodies of its sincerity—the Pennsylvania added trains to peak-hour operations and promised to order modern coaches. The ICC cooperated, and losses did decline—perhaps more an indication that the Pennsylvania was in need of reorganization than anything else. By 1955 the deficit had been pared to $50 million. Then, as a result of new labor contracts and an inability to obtain necessary rate increases and further schedule adjustments, the deficit rose once more. In March 1958 management announced that the losses on passenger operations in 1957 had been $57 million. The board offered no hope for an early reversal of the trend, and in fact the deficit climbed in the first two months of the new year.

Like the Central, the Pennsylvania was a declining railroad, and its fall was all the more dramatic since it had long occupied a higher status within and outside the industry. Operating revenues in 1958 were $844 million, continuing the decline from the 1953 peak of more than $1 billion. Net income was $3.5 million, and that included over $18 million from the government in settlement of a claim for retroactive mail pay. This came to $0.27 per share; without the special payment the Pennsylvania would have lost more than a dollar a share. In 1947 the company had earned $1.45 per share and had a dividend of $1.25. Now the dividend was slashed to a quarter, and that issued only so as to keep the skein of unbroken payments alive.

The Pennsylvania had always prided itself on its liquid position and strong balance sheet. As recently as 1951 its debt was less than five times its working capital. By 1958, however, the ratio was eight and increasing at an accelerating pace. The company's working capital that year was $87 million, a twentieth-century low, and there seemed no way to staunch the monetary outflow.

Alfred Perlman's New York Central was the sixth northeastern railroad power. Like the Pennsylvania it had suffered a decline, and Perlman knew it could never return to the turn-of-the-century glory days. In 1958 the Central reported earnings of $4 million on revenues of $659 million, which came to $0.62 per share. But like the Pennsylvania, the Central included its settlement for retroactive mail pay in its figures. This came to $13.7 million, while an additional $1.8 million was derived from income tax adjustments for previous years. In reality, then, the Central lost over $11 million that year, around $2.00 per share.

The Central passed its dividend in 1958; Perlman saw little sense in retaining payments under the circumstances, for unlike the Pennsylvania leaders, he had no intention of memorializing the past. He and the management teams brought in during the past year thought the company's fortunes could be reversed, and that railroading itself could be reborn as a vital occupation and service. Perlman's reforms were taking hold; the company was being run more efficiently than ever before, and freight hauls that once were marginal now showed fine profits. What the Pennsylvania was attempting to accomplish in the way of consolidation and cost cutting the Central had already come a long way toward realizing. Perlman's bright young men were out to revolutionize the industry, and as they pored over old accounts they found errors and bungling that amazed them. From their point of view, the Metzman and White administrations were filled with incompetents who had permitted excellent opportunities for profits to elude them while running the road to ruin. And all the while they cast glances at the Pennsylvania, in their view an archaic line managed by mossbacks who were cousins of the Central men of the pre-Perlman era. The two companies continued to compete for freight business, and the Central's management teams felt confident that within a few years at the most they would be able to capture a good deal of territory from competitors and in the process make the Central the dominant force in eastern railroading. As they saw the situation, the Pennsylvania was headed downward while the Central was rising; soon the curves would intersect, and afterward their movement upward would accelerate. That the Central's new management felt this way was no secret. It was discussed at conferences and bandied about over lunches and dinners. The Pennsylvania managers came to admire the efficiency of their Central counterparts, but they also resented their attitudes and disliked them as individuals.

The Central's administration and board had worthy ambitions, but the company lacked the financial muscle to achieve them. Working capital in 1958 stood at $41 million, less than half that of the Pennsylvania, while the company's bonded debt was $789 million, $117 million more than that of its rival. The Central's finances were highly leveraged, and if Perlman's ambitions were realized, the company could report huge profits. But he needed time and money, and he lacked both. Many of the Central's bonds would come due in the mid-1960s, and at that time Perlman would have to enter the capital markets in force. If the company seemed solvent and growing by then, he would have no difficulty. But if the Central faltered, if the reforms either failed or were too little too late, or if the nation was in a recession that caused a dip in railroad earnings, the company would face a severe cash-flow crisis. So the element of risk was high. Perlman wanted the Central to merge with another line, and in such a way as to assure its survival and the continuation of his own power. Could this be done, and if so, how? Perlman had a limited time to make his deal. The clock was ticking in 1958, and he—and others within the industry—knew it.

These, then, were the six pieces of the northeastern railroad puzzle—the Erie, the B&O, the C&O, the Norfolk and Western, the Pennsylvania, and the Central—and their views toward mergers and acquisitions. For all practical purposes the Erie absented itself from the picture. Union with that moribund railroad offered little of value to the others, and in any case the Erie management wasn't interested in overtures. So there were five companies involved in the wooing, and within the group several interesting possibilities.

The possible mating of the C&O and B&O has already been mentioned, and talks between the two managements continued after the ice was broken in 1957. Had these failed, the C&O might have turned to the N&W as a counterweight. The two railroads serviced the same geographical area, the West Virginia coal fields, and for decades had competed for customers. More than any other possible combination it would have resulted in consolidations, integration, and higher profits. On the other hand, both were strong lines hardly in danger of faltering. Neither management had any intention of bowing to the other;

Walter Tuohy and Stuart Saunders were ambitious men, and each expected to come out of a merger in command of a still larger operation. Too, the N&W had important ties with the Pennsylvania, while many of the second-echelon men at the C&O retained emotional attachments to the Central; they would not mix well. Finally, the ICC could hardly have been expected to approve such a merger as being in the public interest. All parties appreciated the situation, and so the combination was never considered seriously.

Under the proper conditions the N&W could be united with the Pennsylvania. The ICC might be won over if the Pennsylvania could demonstrate that without such a merger it would be forced to the wall. As for the N&W stockholders, they could be bought out via a tender offer or satisfied by a substantial premium in exchange terms. Managements would offer no problem, since the Pennsylvania people already dominated the N&W board, and Saunders would have been accepted as the leader of the combined company. The N&W's coal-hauling income would help offset the Pennsylvania's losses from passenger travel, and the two companies' rolling stock would mesh well. Still, such a merger would only be a holding operation. Of all the possible combinations this one would have offered the fewest economies, the least opportunities for consolidation. And if it were brought before the public, the Central could be counted upon to protest, claiming it would give the Pennsylvania an unfair advantage in the eastern market.

The Central considered the ramifications of a merger with the B&O. Major economies might be realized—Perlman estimated them to be on the order of $70 million a year, against the $40 million in savings from a B&O-C&O combination. The Central's accountants pored over the B&O figures, and planned on how to utilize the company's leverage effectively, while Perlman's managers demonstrated how relatively small expenditures could result in significant savings. The Central's traffic men superimposed the maps of the two lines, and slashed away at duplicate terminals, freight yards, and tracks. On paper at least, thousands of miles of right of way could have been abandoned. As for top management, White could become chairman and Perlman president and chief executive officer, while some prestigious line or staff position could be found for B&O president H.E. Simpson. Even now there are those at the Central who claim that such a merger, if entered into in the early 1960s, would have served both the public interest and the needs of the companies involved. The B&O management felt otherwise, as might have been expected, while the stockholders would have had to receive a considerable bonus for accepting the plan. The Central lacked the resources for a tender offer; merger would have to come about through overtures from the B&O or the intercession of a third force, and neither possibility existed in 1958.

What this meant, then, is that each of the five railroads had two possible merger partners. The B&O could have united with the C&O or the Central; the C&O with the N&W or the B&O; the N&W with the Pennsylvania or the C&O; the Central with the B&O; and the Pennsylvania with the N&W—and finally, to complete the circle, the Pennsylvania could have merged with the Central.

Exploratory conversations on this last merger, which if effected would have created a company with over 20,000 miles of track—approximately one-tenth of the nation's total, or more than exists in Germany today—opened in September 1957, when Pennsylvania Chairman James Symes broached the subject with Robert Young, then in the last months of his life. Young was interested. The two men hit it off right away, and on November 1 the Pennsylvania and the Central announced that merger talks were under way. Though not completely unexpected, the news did come as somewhat of a shock. These century-old rivals were planning to come together—it was as though France and Germany had indicated their intention to seek political union ten years earlier. But it was a sensible move. Both railroads had suffered badly during the recession, and each knew it could hardly continue functioning as it had in the past for much longer. This was not an engagement entered into through love but rather necessity. Symes put the matter simply: the Pennsylvania and the Central would merge "in order to halt deficits."

In making the announcement Young and Symes were also conceding defeats and swallowing their pride. The Central's chairman had come to the end of his string. Young's personal fortune had melted, and his dreams of a viable passenger railroad had been discarded by the very men he had selected to head the line. In 1957 railroaders often quoted James Hill's views of passenger trains: "Like a male tit, they are neither useful nor ornamental." Young must have felt the same way when announcing the merger decision.

Symes's failure was far less dramatic but equally poignant. Sixty years old at the time and five years away from retirement, he had come to the Pennsylvania in 1916 to clerk in the traffic department, at a time when the railroad was powerful and confident, at the dawn of the automobile age. The son of a Pennsylvania baggage master, he was a railroader to the core, and one whose entire life had been devoted to a single company. The Pennsylvania was, after all, the most traditional of American railroads, accustomed to promoting from within. Ever since the days of J. Edgar Thomson, Pennsylvania presidents had come up through the ranks, either to die in office or soon after leaving the helm. Symes was very much in this pattern. As was customary, he lived along the Main Line, had memberships in all the proper Philadelphia clubs, and found his friends among the leaders of the city's banks, trust companies, industrial corporations, and charitable institutions. Symes had not inherited his position; few Pennsylvania executives did. But like all of his predecessors, his social status and role at the company were closely linked. In 1957 he occupied an important place in the Philadelphia pecking order, one he expected to turn over to whoever succeeded him. This too was in the nature of things.

Now, through no discernible fault of his own, Symes was obliged to announce merger negotiations with the despised New York Central. And his partner in the talks was to be Robert Young, a Texas speculator who was not a true railroader at all. Behind Young was Alfred Perlman, an arrogant Jew, who hardly could be fitted into the Philadelphia society which even then restricted memberships in important clubs to genealogically sound Protestants. How could Perlman be explained to individuals who had gone through their lives thinking of Jews as retainers, sharpsters, and—even after World War II—somehow alien to the American scene? Still, necessity was the mother of friendships as well as invention, and by early November Symes and Young were getting along reasonably well together. This concord did not extend to Perlman, who grew more distant from Young and made no secret of his opposition to the merger and dislike of Symes. But Young was the major force at the Central, and Perlman could do nothing to alter this.

Symes and Young hoped to unite and so overcome their opposition. It was a formidable array, including elements of the ICC, the Justice Department, congressional antimonopolists, executives of other eastern railroads, the trucking interests, and those within their own ranks who for sound or frivolous reasons wanted to block the merger. They would have to respond to challenges from antique reformers, who talked as though the Central and the Pennsylvania were still the dominant forces in eastern transportation, and of politicians certain to make capital from fighting the "entrenched interests." Still, the two men had reason to anticipate success, if not in 1958, then surely soon after.

Perhaps the resulting combination could have survived its difficulties had the merger taken place then, on the eve of an economic boom which enhanced railroad earnings along with those of almost every other industry. In 1958 the components were somewhat compatible, their operations fairly similar. But this was not to be. There would be a merger, but not in 1958. Instead, ten years would pass before the final union, and by then it was too late for prosperity or even survival as a railroad. Too, the companies had altered greatly in this interlude, oppositional forces had time to become entrenched, and the nation itself changed dramatically, and not in a way to benefit the merged company.

Acting together, Symes and Young might have carried it off—they could have created a viable railroad, concentrating upon freight but also serving commuters, and turning a profit on operations. These two very different men found that their ideas were close enough to make this come about, even while ambitious younger executives within their organizations opposed them. This last chance faded three months later, with Young's suicide. Now it was an entirely different kind of situation, and what might be called "Perlman's fandango" commenced.

Alfred Perlman did not favor a merger with the Pennsylvania at that time. This did not mean he wanted to go it alone. Rather, he realized that should the two companies come together the Pennsylvania would be the senior partner, to dictate policy and programs, with its executives in positions of power. Perlman had not come to New York in order to bow before the Philadelphians. At least not yet, or perhaps never.

He continued to play for time, telling Young and the others that such a giant system—it would be the seventh largest corporation in the nation—"might not be in the public interest." In this way, Perlman indicated that he anticipated governmental challenges, and implied that he might welcome them. Still, he agreed to join the Pennsylvania in a study of possibilities, which was completed in less than a year, and showed that savings on the order of $100 million annually might result from a merger. By then Young had died, however, and Perlman was in his place as chief executive officer. The merger too was as good as dead.

Things were looking up for Perlman and the Central in 1959.

The railroad's revenues and earnings advanced, due in large part to the general economic revival but also in response to the introduction of new operating methods. There was talk in Washington of federal legislation to aid the railroads—the industry's decline during the recession had frightened congressmen who had visions of their areas losing services. In January Perlman announced that while he was still interested in talking about a merger with the Pennsylvania, the creation of three or four major systems in the East might better serve the national interest.

Finally, Nelson Rockefeller took office as governor of New York, and he was committed to aiding the railroads and eager to begin work. In February he met with Governor Robert Meyner of New Jersey and New York City Mayor Robert Wagner to discuss ways of helping the commuter lines. There was a Public Service Commission inquiry, followed by a flurry of activity. First, the railroads were granted $15 million per year in tax benefits, and an additional $20 million was loaned to the Central, the Long Island (still owned by the Pennsylvania), and the New York, New Haven and Hartford for the purchase of new passenger cars. The Port of New York Authority was authorized to float a $100 million bond issue, the proceeds to go for railroad assistance in various forms. Rockefeller pressed on, recommending changes in full crew regulations and other ways of increasing railroad income. "The obligation of the state to take action to preserve our transportation system arises from the recognition of the public necessity for rapid, mass transportation into and around metropolitan areas," he said. "This public dependence necessarily created a degree of public responsibility."

If Rockefeller could deliver on his intentions—and in late 1959 it seemed that he could and would—then the Central's passenger deficits might vanish, subsidized as they would be by the state. Meanwhile, Perlman's reforms and the economic recovery would enhance freight earnings. Little wonder, then, that the Central drew away from the Symes-Young merger proposal. There would be time for that later on, said Perlman's managers. Within a few years, if all went well, a merger might take place, and with the Pennsylvania—but one in which the Central would be the senior partner. Perlman had broken off discussions with the Pennsylvania in January of 1959; at year's end it seemed a good move.

This is not to say that Perlman was disinterested in combinations, but that he rejected one in which the Central would not be the dominant force. He saw a possibility of such a creation in early 1959. During the past year and a half, Presidents Tuohy of the C&O and Simpson of the B&O had held merger talks, and these seemed about to mature. Now Perlman entered the picture, suggesting that the Central join in the plan, in this way creating what he called "a counterweight to the Pennsylvania." Tuohy and Simpson were not interested, and proceeded on their own. In May 1960 the boards of both railroads announced their approval of a merger in which the B&O stockholders would obtain a substantial bonus for accepting a tender offer, while the C&O would emerge as the surviving firm. Perlman was angered; he had not been informed of the arrangement. By then he had come to think of a tripartite merger as being in the Central's best interest, and so he did what he could to foil the union.

This took the form of a proxy fight for the B&O. The Central purchased shares on the open market, and soon had 20 percent of the common. He then flew to Switzerland to convince the banks there, which controlled another 17 percent, to oppose the C&O merger and instead support a B&O-Central combination. Tuohy fought too, shoring up his allies, and in the end he won. Then both men issued their tender offers to B&O shareholders, and once again Perlman was defeated.

With this, the Central abandoned the idea of a relationship with the B&O. ICC hearings followed, and the B&O-C&O merger was approved in late 1962 and accepted by President John Kennedy a year later. Bowing with as much grace as he could muster, Perlman sold his shares of the B&O to the C&O, and Alleghany Corporation followed suit. Tuohy was now head of an 11,000-mile system—larger than the Central—and by 1964 was able to report a saving of $35 million per year. Other coal haulers were added—the Western Maryland, for example—and the new entity, then being restructured and soon to emerge as the Chessie System, was both strong and solvent, a tribute to the magic of merger.

While Perlman and Tuohy fenced for control of the B&O, Stuart Saunders of the N&W made plans to enlarge his prosperous company through a consolidation with the Nickel Plate and a lease of the Wabash. This smacked of a Pennsylvania-inspired marriage, for the N&W was dominated by the Pennsylvania, and the Wabash almost completely owned by it. If approved, the new line would extend the N&W's grasp to Chicago and New York, while its substantial cash flow could be employed to invigorate the somewhat moribund Nickel Plate, and perhaps enable it to compete more equally with the Central in the area of freight haulage.

Perlman was most distressed by this move, which he correctly gauged as an attack upon his territory. Originally the Nickel Plate had been built as a counterweight against the Central, and for this reason Washington had forbidden the two lines to unite, even after Vanderbilt had taken command of both. Now the N&W was proposing to take it over, to create a major giant in Central territory which would be controlled—in part at least—by the Pennsylvania. What would be the next step? Already there were rumors of an eventual gathering of all the Pennsylvania companies to create a huge eastern network, to come after the N&W plans were realized. At the head of it all would be Stuart Saunders, for by then the N&W leader was considered a virtual certainty to succeed Symes.

Even as Perlman maneuvered to block the C&O-B&O merger, he petitioned the ICC for permission to join in the N&W-Nickel Plate-Wabash combination. This may not have been a serious move on his part. Rather, Perlman wanted to block the merger and so stymie whatever plans might have been hatched in Philadelphia. Saunders was angered, for he recognized the Perlman move for what it was. Although the two men hardly knew one another, already they had arrived at a mutual dislike. To Perlman, Saunders was an insubstantial railroader who had spent his professional life at a company so wealthy it could have run itself. As for Saunders, he viewed Perlman as a troublemaker, an arrogant newcomer not really fit for the comradeship of the eastern railroad leaders. Saunders vigorously opposed inclusion of the Central in his merger plans, and so did Symes. Whether or not the Pennsylvania's leader hoped to unite with the enlarged N&W is impossible to say, but he must have known that any move in this direction would be certain to arouse Perlman to a state of frenzy, not to mention the reverberations in Congress and at the ICC. So Symes held back and instead accused Perlman of wasteful maneuvering and of ignoring his only true merger partner, the Pennsylvania itself.

The Central lacked the resources to challenge the N&W, and so Saunders was able to proceed without much in the way of interference. By the time his proposal reached the ICC in mid-1963, the merger had been expanded to include the lease of the Pittsburgh and West Virginia and the purchase of the Akron, Canton and Youngstown, along with that of the Sandusky line of the Pennsylvania. Approval was granted, and accepted by the Kennedy administration at the same time permission was given for the B&O-C&O merger.

The enlarged Norfolk and Western operated some 7,500 miles of main track over a domain as large as the Central's, and in fact overlapped it in several key areas. Now that the N&W had turned to new interests, its rivalry with the C&O for domination of the coal fields became less important, and the two giants cooperated more fully with one another than ever before. This was evident in 1963; two years later the companies had created an informal community of interests, and in 1966 they petitioned the ICC for permission to merge.

By then the merger movement not only had accelerated, but was driving to a climax. The Pennsylvania still owned a major slice of the N&W, which was in the process of drawing closer to the C&O. To further complicate matters, several chronically sick lines—including the Erie-Lackawanna—were exploring means of uniting with the N&W, even while that strong railroad rebuffed all overtures.

The outlines for such a chain were there to be seen in mid-1961. Once the C&O and B&O came together, the other pieces would fall into place. Perlman had wanted time, and it was running out. Unless he acted soon, the Central would be left alone. Symes also understood the situation; he knew Perlman would have to accept his offer once it was made. So while testifying before the ICC on the C&O-B&O merger, he indicated that the Pennsylvania was prepared to reopen negotiations with the Central. If Perlman knocked on the door, he said, "the door would not be closed."

Perlman was a realist. He met with Symes that October, and talks were reopened. Within weeks a draft proposal was ready for consideration. The Central's shareholders would receive 1.3 shares of stock in the new entity, while the Pennsylvania shares would be exchanged on a one-to-one basis. Since the Pennsylvania had close to twice the number of shares outstanding than did the Central, the new company would be dominated by its stockholders—on roughly a 60-40 basis. In a concession to the Central, the new board would have fourteen Pennsylvania directors and eleven from the New York railroad. The Central was to sell its holdings in the B&O, while over the years the Pennsylvania would divest itself of its N&W stock. Of course, there were other proposals, but these were the main ones. And it boiled down to one thing as far as Perlman was concerned. The Central was to be merged into the Pennsylvania; it would disappear into the Philadelphia company, no matter how the fact was disguised. Whatever role he was to have in the new company—and there was some doubt there would be any—it would have to be that of a stepson, not a legitimate heir, and the same would be true of his new technocrats, some of whom later said they felt like Cinderellas ready to meet their stepmother and stepsisters.

The true inheritor made his appearance in late 1963. With all the parts falling into place, Symes felt it possible to retire, and as had become traditional at the Pennsylvania, he helped select and then present his successor. As expected, it was to be Stuart Saunders. Now he and Perlman would have to bring the merger into being, and the two men still disliked one another, disagreed on strategy and tactics, and in fact on what the function of the new corporation should be.

The augeries were not favorable.

XI

A Recipe for Disaster

Stuart Saunders had inherited a diverse business empire and a set of strategies. Symes had completed the dieselization and electrification programs as well as refinancing and reducing the debt. Still, the empire was disorganized and in need of overhaul—a chronic circumstance at many large railroads. The Symes strategies had been opportunistic in the best sense of the term, but also were overly timid and unrealistically bold at the same time, and in any case incomplete. While pushing for the merger he had tried to set the Pennsylvania's affairs in order. Saunders was supposed to complete both tasks.

From the first the new chairman knew that these two strategies contradicted one another. So did Perlman. Yet Saunders set out upon both roads simultaneously, hoping perhaps that the combination and intelligent improvisation would result in success. In addition, he had several new ideas of his own. Like Perlman, then, he was a gambler for high stakes.

In order to prepare the way for a viable merger, Saunders would have had to truncate the Pennsylvania so that it would be prepared to absorb the Central; it would have been the corporate equivalent of the docking in space of two vehicles, one American, the other Soviet, for that was the view each management had of the other. Several years of preparation would have been required to decide which duplicate facilities would be abandoned and how the remaining ones would function, to ascertain means of harmonizing the operations of fleets of passenger and freight cars and locomotives, and especially of labor forces and managements. The Central had embarked upon a large-scale automation program, while the Pennsylvania had a smaller one. Saunders and Perlman would have to combine them after the merger, and no one seemed to know if this was possible. New schedules would be required. This seemingly minor item could take months to complete, and if not done well would result in chaos and the loss of tens of millions of dollars. So if the merger were to take place, the Pennsylvania management would have to plan ahead. Government approval was anticipated by the mid-1960s. There wasn't much time.

What might occur should this approval be withheld, or eventually denied? Then Saunders would require an entirely different strategy, and one did not exist. He would have liked to expand upon the diversification program and spend little time, effort, and money on the railroad, but this was not possible, for the Pennsylvania was cash-short and the ICC would be certain to protest any further curtailment of services. The railroad would have to be returned to a measure of solvency, and this would mean expenditures that could dash the expansion program in other areas. Saunders would have had to trim antique facilities and divert resources to more profitable ones, so as to have a smoothly operating railroad and ancillary operations. This was what Perlman had been attempting to do at the Central, and if Saunders didn't particularly admire his opposite number, he did respect some of his programs. With little in the way of resources and capital, Perlman had developed several of the properties he had inherited to fashion a major real estate subsidiary, free from ICC controls, which contributed importantly to the firm's income. At the same time he had cashed in on outmoded properties, selling them off intelligently and at the proper time. The rents and capital gains then had been plowed back into the railroad and remaining properties, creating additional income and enabling the transportation operations to become more efficient, and perhaps eventually turn a decent profit as well. Perlman remained convinced the Central could survive on its own. He was not so sure about the Pennsylvania.

Saunders's line had fewer income properties, though on the surface at least it appeared in better financial shape with greater resources. There seemed no reason why it could not acquire nontransportation subsidiaries and so imitate the Perlman strategy—Saunders would not consider this imitation, of course, but instead imaginative diversification. Some of this had been done, and the movement was accelerating. It was in the best interests of the Pennsylvania. But would it prove beneficial for the Penn Central—assuming there was to be such an entity?

Symes had spent his last years in office working for the merger while at the same time preparing the Pennsylvania to receive the

Central. Perlman had opposed merger, but toward the end of the Symes period had come to accept it as inevitable. Now he had Saunders to deal with, a man more concerned with acquisitions of non-railroad properties than unification with the Central. In other words, priorities were reversed at the Pennsylvania, and Perlman almost welcomed the arrival of a kindred though antagonistic soul.

So the two managements continued on the path to unification, while doing little to guarantee success if and when it took place.

Symes had initiated a diversification program of sorts. He had joined with the Madison Square Garden Corporation in planning a new arena, to be erected on the site of Pennsylvania Station in New York. The landmark terminal was to be razed—this would require a great deal of delicate maneuvering, since it was a major historic building—and the railroad operations would continue as before below street level. A twin office tower complex would be constructed to complement the Garden. In effect this was to be urban renewal, so dear to the wishes of city planners of that time. The final cost of the project was estimated to be slightly more than $100 million, with most of the money obtained through the sale of new securities. In return for its properties, the Pennsylvania was to receive a new, modern terminal, smaller and certainly less impressive than the old, but large enough to handle the reduced business. More important, the company received a quarter interest in the complex, at almost no cost.

Symes planned similar operations in Philadelphia and Chicago. The old Broad Street Station was razed, and in its place was constructed Penn Center, a joint venture of the Pennsylvania and Uris Brothers. Work on this complex of office buildings, a hotel, and a shopping center had begun by the time Saunders took office, and several apartment buildings, garages, and even a bus terminal were soon added. With Tishman Realty and the Chicago, Burlington and Quincy Railroad, Symes leased air rights over several downtown Chicago properties and planned for the construction of a $100 million office building complex, ownership of which was to be shared by the three firms. It too would be financed by the sale of bonds, and so the Pennsylvania would receive a substantial equity position in a potentially lucrative project at almost no direct cost.

Other ventures seemed promising. In the 1962 annual report Symes noted that the Pennsylvania owned close to 11,000 acres of land and meant to develop it intensely. Several coal mines were opened in the early 1960s, and a major salt deposit along the Ohio River was discovered; Symes planned to invest in the mines, and perhaps organize a chemical subsidiary or enter into joint ventures with established firms within the industry.

Saunders accelerated development of the New York and Philadelphia projects. He renegotiated the Chicago operation, helped create the framework for what became the Gateway Center, and obtained a half interest in it for the Pennsylvania. New urban redevelopment operations were set into motion, the most important being in Pittsburgh and Washington. The program initiated by Symes and continued and broadened by Saunders resulted in the reconstruction of downtown areas in major cities, with the Pennsylvania leading the way. When completed, the railroad would have a large share in several profitable real estate complexes—or at least, this was the hope in the mid-1960s.

Saunders planned an even more ambitious redeployment program. Symes had tended to work with what he had and maintain the railroad at the center of all his plans; the new chairman looked outside the company for opportunities; to him the railroad was only the most important of many holdings. Saunders was intrigued with the development of conglomerate corporations such as International Telephone and Telegraph, Litton Industries, Ling-Temco-Vought, and Gulf and Western. These began as small companies which, through the acquisition of other firms, became large. Some had even changed the basic nature of their business in the process—Textron had been a textile company, and had been transformed into a huge conglomerate with many interests, none of them related to fabrics. The conglomerates had glamour, the kind afforded the railroads a century earlier. They were exciting, venturesome, and aggressive, and these qualities could hardly be ascribed to the railroads of the early 1960s. Within Saunders's mind there grew an idea. Why not turn the Pennsylvania Railroad into a conglomerate? Ben Heineman was doing as much at the Chicago and North Western, a road that operated even more miles of track than the Pennsylvania, and was accomplishing the task through the purchase of shares in other firms outside of the industry. In the end, if all went well, Heineman would transform the old railroad into a new conglomerate, just as a caterpillar became a butterfly. Saunders wanted the same fate for the Pennsylvania.

His vehicle for this transformation would be the old Pennsylvania Company, which had been organized by J. Edgar Thomson in 1870 to take control of those tracks west of Pittsburgh. So it remained until 1918, when Samuel Rea, attempting to streamline operations and make them more efficient, transferred all leases from the subsidiary to the parent firm. What remained was a diverse bundle of securities—property deeds, shares in small water and electric companies whose facilities were used by the railroad, a handful of shares in industrial concerns carried for investment purposes, and the like. From 1918 to 1963 the Pennsylvania Company officials did little but clip coupons, accumulate dividends, and then transfer a trickle of earnings to Philadelphia.

This changed in 1963, when Symes and Saunders began using the Pennsylvania Company as their vehicle for expansion. The incoming chairman seemed interested in transforming the old Thomson operation into a captive conglomerate—which in time might become larger and more important than the railroad itself.

The diversification began with the acquisition of a one-third interest in the Buckeye Pipe Line Company. It took slightly more than $28 million in cash and a new issue of preferred stock, and over the next two years Saunders bought out the rest of the company for an additional bundle of preferred stock and cash.

It was a sound investment and acquisition. Buckeye was the eighth largest processor of crude oil in the nation, one of the most important suppliers of jet fuel to the airlines. A stable money earner with good growth prospects, Buckeye could be counted upon to provide funds that would enhance the Pennsylvania's earnings statements. This might serve to boost the price of the parent firm's common stock, which then might be utilized to make further acquisitions. Such had been the path taken by Litton and other conglomerates. Apparently Saunders hoped the same magic would strike the Pennsylvania.

The following year Saunders purchased a 60 percent interest in the Great Southwest Corporation, a land-development operation with several properties, the most important of which was an amusement park situated between Dallas and Fort Worth known as Six Flags Over Texas. The following year Pennsylvania purchased another 20 percent of the firm, and Great Southwest acquired land near Atlanta for the construction of Six Flags Over Georgia. This was a time when Disneyland became the centerpiece of the Disney empire, and similar amusement parks were planned for other parts of the nation, including a Disney World in Florida. The Six Worlds operations were in this tradition, and by investing in them it appeared that Saunders was making a wager on the future—amusement—to help salvage the past—railroads.

Then the Pennsylvania purchased a 51 percent interest in

Arvida Corporation, a Florida real estate firm that had been founded by aluminum tycoon Arthur Vining Davis. Arvida owned approximately 100,000 acres of land and was buying more, using it to form retirement and leisure-oriented communities.

Macco Realty, a large residential real estate company based in southern California, was acquired next. Macco already had begun work on its first community, and after the takeover projected seven more, as well as purchasing additional acreage in Orange County.

Finally, Saunders acquired the Strick Holding Company (a manufacturer of aluminum trailers and containers with an interest in mobile homes), made loans to Executive Jet Aviation, an operation which hoped to develop a large charter business, and increased holdings in Madison Square Garden. Pennsylvania was on the prowl for other investments and acquisitions in the 1960s, and there seemed little doubt this policy would continue whether the merger with the Central took place or not. In fact, some of those at the Pennsylvania Company came to view the Central as simply another addition to their portfolio. The Pennsylvania was on its way to becoming one of the nation's leading land developers. The Central's New York properties would fit into their plans nicely. As for the railroad, that was of secondary interest.

This was the problem, at least insofar as the merger was concerned. The Pennsylvania had expended close to $200 million on all of these non-railroad acquisitions. With the exception of Buckeye, all were future-oriented firms, which not only wouldn't pay much in the way of dividends for many years but would require additional expenditures for expansion. Each dollar used for this purpose would be one less available to the merged railroad later on. Huge sums would be required to coordinate the facilities of the Pennsylvania and the Central. Saunders knew this in 1963, when the buying spree commenced. Yet he proceeded along the path for the next four years. Symes had left the railroad in good financial shape. Saunders emptied the treasury, changed accounting procedures so as to mask deficits, and diverted funds from the railroad to the newly acquired operations.

In 1965 Saunders engineered a *coup*. He sold most of the assets of the Long Island Railroad to the Metropolitan Commuter Transportation Authority, a New York State agency, for $65 million. Thus he divested the Pennsylvania of an invalid line that could not help but run deficits, while at the same time obtaining a large sum of money for his acquisitions program. Other assets were disposed of, as the Pennsylvania seemed intent upon ridding itself of railroad properties to purchase real estate developments.

Saunders acted not out of perversity or a lack of understanding of the problems merger would bring. Rather, he truly believed that the future Penn Central would be stronger with the pipeline and real estate firms than it would with the money. Why plow funds into a railroad when they could be used for more profitable and promising ventures? It had been different at the Norfolk and Western, whose net income as a percentage of operating revenue had been close to 25 percent in 1961, an industry high that was twice that of the Union Pacific, its nearest competitor. In contrast, the Pennsylvania's return that year had been 1.5 percent, while the Central reported a loss. Saunders had gone from a money maker to a marginal operation, and so he adopted a new approach and program to fit the circumstances.

Saunders knew that the securities of a railroad—even a giant such as the Penn Central would be—could expect little attention on Wall Street, while that of a budding transportation-real estate-amusement empire would be prized. He hoped to transform the Pennsylvania into just such a conglomerate. All of this was faintly reminiscent of the contest at the New York Central in the 1860s, when Erastus Corning, that man of many parts, was ousted by Commodore Vanderbilt, a convert to railroading. This time, however, Saunders, whose views were similar to Corning's, was on the ascendent, while Perlman—more in the Vanderbilt tradition—would have to play a subordinate role. That this was so was due as much to the nature of the economy and the times as the relative positions of the two companies. It meant that the personality clash between the two men would be reinforced by elementary disagreements as to tactics, strategies, and, most important, goals.

Despite these differences, Saunders and Perlman had concluded that railroading was a declining industry, and that their individual lines had been slipping rapidly, and so were in need of drastic change. While clearly preferring to go their own ways, the two men saw benefits in a merger—always assuming it took place in the proper way, though this was defined differently in Philadelphia and New York. Together they strove to overcome opposition from outsiders, even while doing little to stifle contention within their own organizations.

Those who argued against the merger could be divided into

several categories. First and most prominent were antique reformers more concerned with past abuses and theories than current realities. To them the Pennsylvania and the Central were giants, dominating their areas, sitting astride the nation as they had a half century before, now hoping to realize the ambitions of J.P. Morgan and his kind. Senator Estes Kefauver, who headed the Subcommittee on Antitrust and Monopoly, saw in the creation of the Penn Central the birth of a supercorporation that might come to create a supergovernment. "Let no one be misled as to what the creation of giant power, such as the Pennsylvania-Central, may mean in the American economy," he told his subcommittee. "On the board of that massive road will sit policy officials from some of the country's largest and most powerful banks, insurance companies, steel companies, aluminum companies, public utilities, coal companies, and other companies." He warned of the "possibilities for discrimination, rate control, traffic diversion, reciprocity with suppliers, and actual influencing of the pricing policies of shippers by that road. . . ." Leon Keyserling, who had headed the Council of Economic Advisors during the Truman administration, thought that the nation was about to be set upon a major economic upswing which would increase railroad revenues and profits. The Central and the Pennsylvania were in better financial shape than was commonly believed, he said, indicating that the lines were hiding profits and assets through dubious accounting procedures. "The railroads as a whole are in no financial crisis justifying a frenzied move toward mergers accompanied by contraction," Keyserling concluded. The two lines favored the merger because they wanted to maximize profits at the expense of services. Throughout this period Keyserling and other longtime opponents of big business spoke of the rapacity of railroaders, indicating this was the major, if not the sole, reason for the merger application.

Other critics harkened back to the plans set down by Ripley and others after World War I. Those aimed at creating a balanced railroad map in the East in which the benefits of both competition and consolidation would be realized. The Penn Central would crush smaller lines operating within its territory as well as cripple even the larger ones. Professor William Leonard of Hofstra College, author of the definitive work on implications of railroad policy in the 1920s, feared for the future of the Erie-Lackawanna, for example. "What will be the fate of the New Haven and seven other New England roads not designated for any particular eastern system? Will they be left to decay and die? Or might they be grouped into a regional system? The public interest requires that the ICC, in considering the reconstruction of the eastern rail district or area involved in these merger applications, take into account and make definite plans for the future welfare of these New England carriers." Leonard opposed nationalization and the continuation of present policies, but he wasn't certain the Pennsylvania-Central merger was in the public interest, and he recommended a moratorium until such matters were worked out.

Although these criticisms persisted, they were not too serious, and in any event easily disposed of. While it was true that the two lines had been healthy giants prior to World War I, this was no longer the case, said Symes, Saunders, and Perlman. In fact, both companies had shrunken considerably since that time. "The Pennsylvania had more employees than the two have now," said Symes in 1962. "It had more freight cars, more locomotives, produced more ton-miles of freight, more passenger-miles of passenger service, and about the only thing in which the Pennsylvania was not as big as both are now was in the miles of railroad track." Saunders and Perlman produced documentary evidence of declines in profitability, losses on passenger service, and even when using Keyserling's projections, were able to show that the railroads could not hope to achieve the same rate of profitability on assets as might be obtained from insured bank accounts. In other words, there was no incentive to invest in railroading, and unless this was changed—by means of the merger—the lines would have to continue their downward slide, and eventually be taken over by the government.

The Leonard criticism was somewhat more difficult to respond to, for it was evident that the New England passenger lines were troubled and might go under. Was this the responsibility of either the Pennsylvania or the Central, however? Perlman suggested that all of these lines be brought together into a major New England line, which might include the Boston and Albany, which was affiliated with the Central. "I am willing to give up that asset to have balanced competition in New England," he said, somewhat disingenuously, since the B&A was a deficit-ridden operation, the very kind he was hoping to abandon. But the scarred and embattled New York, New Haven and Hartford petitioned for inclusion in any Pennsylvania-Central merger, and its administration could not be dissuaded. Furthermore, the New Haven had impressive allies—most of New England's congressional delegation and a majority of the ICC members favored a takeover of the line as a price for approval.

The New Haven, which operated more than 1,500 miles of track, had been a promising property at one time. Before World War I the Pennsylvania had purchased control of the line as part of its attempt to invade Central territory and then go on to New England. But the company had fallen victim to the automobile, truck, and highway—ironically, its last great spurt of profitability came in the 1950s, when it hauled the materials used to construct the Connecticut Turnpike, which ran parallel to its lines. By the early 1960s the New Haven was a hopeless invalid, having lost most of its freight business to the Turnpike while commuter operations resulted in always increasing deficits. The company applied for a $50 million disaster loan under the Defense Production Act, but was turned down in 1961. So it filed for bankruptcy in 1962. That year the New Haven reported a deficit of $12.7 million, which fell slightly, to $12.3 million in 1963, and then rose to $15 million in 1964. There was no turning back. The 1968 deficit would top $22 million.

Perlman and Saunders understood the situation, and at first agreed to reject any merger that included the New Haven. The Central chairman thought the company should be liquidated, its outmoded rolling stock scrapped or sold to satisfy creditors, its property sold to real estate developers. Saunders was less vehement but equally determined to exclude the New Haven. But when Congress and the ICC indicated they would take them at their word, Saunders backed down. Perhaps the New Haven could be revived, he thought, probably with more faith than analysis. In the end, over Perlman's strong objections, he agreed to permit the New Haven to join the Pennsylvania-Central. And with this, Saunders satisfied the last major objection put forth by the antique reformers.

Serious opposition came from those groups whose futures would be affected by the merger, and of these, none was more important than the railroad brotherhoods. More than Symes and Saunders, they appreciated the fact that the merged line would employ fewer workers than were once on the Pennsylvania payroll. In 1920, when there had been more than 2 million railroad employees, the Pennsylvania had a work force of 280,000 and a payroll of $527 million. There were only 700,000 railroad workers in 1962, when the Pennsylvania's payroll included 66,000 workers who received $428 million in wages and salaries. That the decline would continue was not in doubt. The merger would accelerate the layoffs, for as management slashed away at duplicate facilities, men as well as capital goods would be declared redundant. For this reason the unions stepped up their lobbying activities in Washington, their representatives testified against the merger, and the nation's labor movement as a whole frowned upon it, thus uniting with the antique reformers in this regard.

Saunders and Perlman had experience with such matters, and appreciated both the stakes and the options involved. In previous mergers the unions had been bought off with promises of security; such had been the case when the Norfolk and Western absorbed the Virginian. Now Saunders indicated a willingness to be most generous to the workers—more, perhaps, than was necessary, for he wanted to stifle the opposition before it developed. In May of 1964 he agreed to offer lifetime protection to any worker employed at the time of the merger. Perlman protested; the pattern in the other mergers had been protection for four years, and he felt Saunders was giving away too much, and in such a way as to cripple the merged giant. Furthermore, any employee dismissed between the conclusion of the agreement and the merger would have the right to be rehired, while all those fired—even for cause—would receive a year's severance pay. In return for this the unions agreed that the work force could be reduced by a maximum of 5 percent per year, and that workers could be transferred to new positions if they agreed to do so, and if the company paid moving expenses. Finally, the railroad brotherhoods agreed to drop all opposition to the merger.

The Merger Protective Agreement of 1964 removed a major obstacle to the unification, and was hailed as such by Saunders, who increasingly was becoming the spokesman for it in the press and in Washington. Perlman said little, for he realized that the inability to cut back on the labor force had crippled his plans for a spare, efficient transportation facility and had given a boost to Saunders's projections for a conglomerate. Other Central executives said as much, as did members of the board, to no avail. In the end they were proven correct, for the agreement was one of the more significant factors in the crash.

The merger presented political problems which transcended party and geography within the Washington-Philadelphia-New York triangle. The Kennedy administration had doubts regarding the wisdom of unification, and neither Perlman nor Saunders had influence with those close to the President. Governor David Lawrence of Pennsylvania, a Kennedy confidant, spoke of the overwhelming power of such a combine, while Democratic Mayor of Philadelphia James Tate made no secret of his opposition to the merger. Then Kennedy was assassinated and his place taken by Lyndon Johnson, who, among other things, was one of Saunders's closest friends. The word came down from Washington in January of 1964, as Saunders negotiated with the brotherhoods. Tate reversed his stand. Pennsylvania's new Republican Governor William Scranton gave the merger his blessings, after some friendly nudgings from influential publishing millionaire Walter Annenberg, who also was a major stockholder in the Pennsylvania and a Saunders ally. Other political figures of both parties fell into line, the only important exception being Milton Shapp, a Kennedy advisor who was seeking the Senate seat held by Republican Hugh Scott. Not only did Shapp claim the merger would be detrimental to business in Pennsylvania but he went on to charge the line with exercising an unhealthy influence upon the state's politics, one that would intensify should the merger be accepted.

Shapp and the handful of antique reformers that remained could not block the merger once the unions and the White House sided with Saunders. In late March 1965 the ICC examiners recommended approval to the commission. Further hearings and delays followed, so that it took another year and a month before the full ICC gave its approval as well. This did not mean the merger would take place, however, for several last-ditch opponents of the wedding had filed objections against both lines in state and federal courts. These wended their ways upward through several jurisdictions, reaching the Supreme Court in late 1967. Not until January 15, 1968, did the high court rule in favor of the combination.

This was the last step, and the removal of the final obstacle. Merger Day was selected: February 1. The staffs in New York and Philadelphia made the final preparations; many could scarcely believe the merger was really going to take place, for they had awaited it for so long, while others talked of it as though about to enter a marriage with an unwanted partner, arranged by parents. In the field the yard crews began painting the words "Penn Central" on equipment and buildings, along with the new logo. Throughout the country economists and other observers of the business scene issued proclamations about the biggest merger in American history, the most talked about since the creation of United States Steel close to three-quarters of a century before.

It was to be one of the most unusual years in American history, as well as one of the most unhappy of times, the initiation of an era of troubles. The nation would undergo repeated shocks during the next three seasons—the Tet offensive in Vietnam,

A Recipe for Disaster

announcement that President Johnson would not seek reelection, campus disorders, the assassinations of Martin Luther King and Robert Kennedy, and finally the riots at the Democratic Convention in Chicago and the surrealistic political campaign that followed. Such news made the merger seem of minor importance, and so it attracted little press coverage after February. This was important, for had it not been for these more dramatic and significant events, the difficulties and birth pangs might have been more carefully analyzed and discussed. As it was, the news was shoved to the back pages and the business sections of the nation's newspapers and magazines. We now know there were troubles from the start, difficulties that had been foreshadowed during the courtship and debates, but shoved aside once the merger had taken place. But they remained. Not until two years had passed would they resurface and be recalled.

Some of the signs could be discerned in the annual report, released in late March. This was rather unusual, since the new entity was less than two months old at the time. Clearly parts of the report had been prepared prior to the merger, and by the Pennsylvania staff. It was a glossy, thirty-three-page affair, and, since there was little upon which to base analysis, seemed more a prospectus and public relations brochure than anything else.

The publication came out of the company's main headquarters in Philadelphia. Saunders would remain there to initiate programs and direct strategy, while Perlman would stay in New York to take care of day-to-day railroad operations. Even then the two antagonists would have little contact with one another. To Perlman and others of the old New York Central, it had been less a marriage than a conquest and capitulation. The Pennsylvania staff agreed, and in a not too subtle fashion celebrated their triumph on the cover of the brochure. It was subtitled: "121st Annual Report," and not presented as the first. Thus—unofficially, at least—the new company would date its origins from April 13, 1846, the day the Pennsylvania received its charter. The Central's heritage would be minimized.* This was a symbol, said some at the Pennsylvania headquarters, of which partner would dominate the union.

The letter to stockholders reflected the Saunders approach

---

*Soon after the merger, the name of the New York Central Building was changed to the New York General Building, and the etched letters "C" and "T" were changed to "G" and "E" in a skillful fashion, so that few noticed it at the time.

rather than that of Perlman. Although there was some talk of improvements of rail properties, most space was devoted to diversification and non-railroad operations. "As a diversified company, we are broadening our base of earning capacity in order to achieve a more satisfactory rate of return on investment," it read. "We will continue to emphasize this diversification program which is making a growing contribution to consolidated earnings." Further on the letter talked of "one of the great strengths of the Penn Central," and this did not refer to railroads but "the fact that we are uncommitted to traditional approaches." The longest paragraph dealt with the company's role in "cultivating the profit potential of properties and air rights over railroad facilities in the major cities we serve."

The earnings statement, the so-called "bottom line," reinforced this attitude. "Penn Central's consolidated earnings for 1967 of $71.4 million (before extraordinary charges) reflect a growing contribution to profits by non-railroad subsidiaries, but a sharp decline in railroad net income. It was a poor year for the entire railroad industry, and particularly those in the East."

The report went on to sketch the outlines of a giant enterprise, with total consolidated income for 1967 of over $2 billion, and assets of $6.2 billion, with the railroad properties alone valued at more than $4.5 billion. The Penn Central operated 20,000 miles of main track of the nation's 340,000, or one in seventeen. It owned one of every eleven locomotives, and the same proportion of freight cars.

These were impressive figures, and certainly the Penn Central was the largest transportation complex by far, as well as a major corporation by almost any criteria. But it certainly wasn't in the same league with the nation's leading industrial concerns. Penn Central's revenues could not compare with those of General Motors ($22.7 billion in 1968) or Standard Oil of New Jersey ($14 billion). Rather, it was in a class with Firestone, Armour, and Woolworth. Its net assets were close to those of Sears, Roebuck, U.S. Steel, and IBM—but far behind the $40 billion of American Telephone and Telegraph, the $16.7 billion of Standard of Jersey, or General Motors' $13.9 billion. The Penn Central was the dominant eastern railroad, and as such filled a vital economic role, but at the time of its birth was a minor force as an industrial operation. And this was Saunders's problem and the paradox. In those areas in which the Penn Central was needed, profits were low or nonexistent and opportunities almost impossible to realize, while investment opportunities were good in the fields where the corporation was not really required. Saunders was intent on moving the Penn Central out of the first category into the second. If transportation was as important as the government said it was, he implied, let Washington bail us out. Lacking that, we will go in search of opportunity—like the managers of Litton, ITT, Gulf and Western, and other conglomerates.

All of this was implied in the rhetoric of the annual report. It also created the impression that Saunders and Perlman were masters of one of the movers and shakers of the American economy, a supergiant that had resulted from the most far-reaching merger in the nation's history. This assessment was exaggerated, as would be most of the same kind of material emanating from Penn Central headquarters over the next two years.

This was not unusual for the times, however. The Penn Central had been created at the pinnacle of the great bull market that had begun in the early 1950s, and the investment atmosphere was euphoric. To some analysts, the Penn Central represented a new kind of capitalism, and in it they saw the ability of American business to adjust to radically new circumstances. One research report called the corporation "a giant learning to walk." The Penn Central was "on its knees," and would soon begin to "struggle to its feet" and then take "huge strides ahead." The railroad operations would be troublesome, to be sure, but in time could be made profitable—several Wall Street houses were even moderately hopeful that the New Haven would prove a worthwhile acquisition. But the key to the Penn Central, they thought, were the real estate and pipeline operations and the kind of entrepreneurship that enabled a railroad company to develop into a conglomerate. The stock was selling for around 60, and investors were urged to purchase shares before the merger-related difficulties were resolved. Once these were out of the way, so the conventional wisdom had it, Penn Central common stock would double and then double again.*

To even informed onlookers the Penn Central appeared most impressive. It was structured with three levels of ownership and operation, with room for more. At the apex was the Penn Central Transportation Company, which owned and managed all

---

*From the first the Penn Central was a symbol of sorts, and portrayed as such later on. Just as it was organized at the peak of investor enthusiasm, so it went bankrupt at a time when American capitalism seemed to be falling apart. The kinds of individuals who saw in the sinking of the *Titanic* a shattering blow to Victorian self-confidence and a prelude to World War I would make of the Penn Central failure a symbol of the dead end of American business. This subject will be explored further in the last part of this work.

the railroad properties as well as several minor subsidiaries. In addition, the Transportation Company was charged with developing railroad-controlled real estate. Finally, it owned all the stock of the old Pennsylvania Company, a second tier of operations. This entity in turn owned shares and directed activities of acquired non-railroad corporations—the third level —which included Buckeye, Great Southwest, Macco, and Arvida. The organizational chart dispelled any lingering doubts that the merger was not really a Pennsylvania takeover. The new Pennsylvania Company was the same as the old, both in operations and management. The Transportation Company now included the New York Central and its subsidiaries, as well as the New Haven, along with the Central's real estate empire.*

Most of the Central's executives worked for the Transportation Company, at the New York headquarters. Thus they had little to do with the Pennsylvania Company, which Saunders directed from Philadelphia and which he considered the key to the corporation's future. As president, Perlman had a voice in decisions regarding operations on all three levels, but in practice he rarely was consulted regarding affairs outside of transportation, and showed little inclination to alter the situation.

In fact, only two men were to have an overall grasp of the entire company. Saunders insisted upon retaining the final say on important policy decisions made by executives, and in the beginning at least made an effort to understand the situation at the New York headquarters. Increasingly, however, his time was taken by other matters, politics included, and so he tended to delegate authority to staff members. This enhanced the power and prestige of the second man in the chain, Chairman of the Finance Committee David Bevan, and toward the end he functioned as much as *de facto* chairman of the board as anything else.

An old Pennsylvania hand who had come to the company in 1951 after serving as treasurer for the New York Life Insurance Company, Bevan had little use for the Central's properties and leadership, and had opposed the merger. He was an aggressive, arrogant, and often brilliant railroader, and so quite similar to Perlman. As might have been anticipated, the two men clashed from the first, and Bevan came close to quitting in 1968 rather than serve with such a man. During the next two years they would fight over authority and power, and toward the end were no longer on speaking terms.

*The New Haven merger, which was completed on the last day of 1968, was costly. The Penn Central paid out $8 million in cash, $23 million in bonds, and 950,000 shares of common stock for a line that proved a major drag on earnings.

If Bevan disliked Perlman, he had contempt for Saunders, who he felt was ignorant of railroading and little more than a public relations man. At one time Bevan had been led to believe he might succeed Symes, and the thought of having been passed over for Saunders rankled. To make matters worse, Saunders insisted upon invading Bevan's preserve—finances—something Symes had never done. Since he had to deal with Saunders on a day-to-day basis, Bevan had to maintain appearances. But he rarely went beyond that, and then at the cost of personal anguish.

Bevan's interests extended beyond the Penn Central, to include leadership of the Penphil Corporation—or perhaps it would be more accurate to say that Penphil had an intimate though indirect connection with the Penn Central. Organized in 1962, Penphil was an investment operation which sought out undervalued situations, made commitments to them, and in the case of several, sold the securities at a handsome profit to the Pennsylvania Railroad. Among the companies whose shares were sold in this fashion were Great Southwest and Kaneb Pipeline. The Pennsylvania and Penphil had coordinate dealings in other issues, including Continental Mortgage Investors, Tropical Gas, and National Home. Had Bevan used his position at the Pennsylvania to enhance the profitability of Penphil? If so, was this accomplished through inside and confidential information, or had he recommended that the Pennsylvania purchase shares in which he had an interest?

Penphil had twenty-six members, some of whom were Pennsylvania officials and members of the board, who throughout the 1960s seldom referred to its operations. Afterward, when the existence and activities of the company were revealed, Bevan characterized it as "a small, informal investment company set up by a number of us who were linked by friendship to invest for capital appreciation." It surely was more than that. In the summer of 1967, Bevan wrote of its future to Charles Hodge, a partner in the investment banking house of Glore Forgan, Wm. R. Staats, Inc., whose firm handled much of the purchases and sales, and whose wife was a charter member of Penphil. "We are thinking of having a large number of shares of Penphil outstanding and going, you might say, public ultimately with Penphil and turn it at the same time into an aggressive acquirer of other companies so that we can build it up into a very substantial conglomerate holding and operating company." Already he had formed a second company, Florphil, which was to invest in Florida properties, and was manipulating to consolidate it with

Penphil and several other companies.* This would leave Bevan at the head of a major conglomerate at the time when such firms were the darlings of Wall Street. But the mergers didn't take place; instead the Penphil partners decided to continue along the path with the Pennsylvania which had already been so profitable, and which promised even more once the merger had taken place.

Bevan had made a total investment of $16,500 in Penphil. Within eight years this grew to realized and paper profits of approximately $1,750,000.

Saunders and Bevan could not have planned and executed the merger were it not for the strong support they received from segments of the banking community. Of course, no major railroad or other capital-intensive enterprise can function for long without an intimate relationship with its bankers—such had been the case in the late nineteenth century when men like Morgan and Jacob Schiff had ruled Wall Street between them, and it was no different in the 1960s. Generally speaking, the more troubled the railroad—the more it required financing—the greater would be the banker influence. Perlman knew well what this meant, for he had operated in such a manner at the Denver and Rio Grande Western. By the time he had left that line it was in the black, with little in the way of short-term debt, and with long-term obligations structured in such a fashion as not to be a burden upon finances. Thus this road did not have to rely upon bankers for assistance. Nor would it require bank services to effect mergers and acquisitions, for the Denver and Rio Grande Western under Perlman was a transportation operation and no more. This was what Perlman had hoped to do at the Central. If it could be transformed into a profitable railroad, the bankers would be servants and not masters of the line.

Conditions were different at the Pennsylvania, and Perlman knew it immediately. Saunders and Bevan relished the banker connections. To them the Pennsylvania was a shell which was to be used for other, non-railroading ventures. These men and their allies were not so much railroaders as they were manipulators, and since this was an age of manipulation, they appeared quite modern. The bankers approved of their actions, just as they viewed Perlman as old-fashioned and their natural enemy. In the mid-1960s Perlman, Chairman Kirby, and a few others at the Central—the most important of whom was Robert Odell of

---

*United States Congress, House of Representatives, Committee on Banking and Currency (92nd Congress, First Session), *The Penn Central Failure and the Role of Financial Institutions* (Washington, 1972), pp. 245-49.

San Francisco, the president of Allied Properties—opposed merger for that reason. The future Penn Central would be led as much by bankers as by management; it would be less a railroad-centered enterprise than a vehicle for banking profits and brokerage commissions.*

The leading bankers serving on the Central's board supported the merger, often in conjunction with their Pennsylvania counterparts. Isaac Grainger of the Chemical Bank and Seymour Knox of Marine Midland led the pro-merger forces. Perlman tried to get along with them and went so far as to accept Knox's invitation to join the Marine Midland board. But both sides on the board knew he had little love for bankers, and that his delaying tactics were inspired in part by the desire to put the railroad's affairs in order and so lessen their influence.

The Pennsylvania bankers appreciated the situation and offered their help to the New Yorkers. One of these was Howard Butcher III, a Pennsylvania director whose family had a traditional involvement with the railroad. Butcher also was head of the investment house of Butcher and Sherrerd, which in turn had significant connections in the Philadelphia and Manhattan banking communities. He owned a block of Central stock, which along with his Pennsylvania holdings would appreciate should the merger take place. In addition, he could expect more brokerage business from the newly formed company.

Butcher served as chairman of International Utilities Corporation, the president of which was John Seabrook, who in turn was on the board of the Provident National Bank, a major holder of Pennsylvania Railroad bonds and notes. Seabrook knew Bevan—also a member of the Provident board—and was considered part of the Pennsylvania family. In 1965, Butcher used his influence to place Seabrook on the Central board as well, where he acted as a rallying point for the pro-merger forces. Afterward Seabrook succeeded Butcher as chairman of International Utilities and was a charter member of the Penn Central Board, along with Grainger and Knox.

From the point of view of Perlman, Odell, Kirby, and others at the Central, the Pennsylvania under Saunders had been a banker-ridden operation. The Central's bright young men understood what the management there had done. Later on the

*This is not to suggest the bankers were acting in an underhanded fashion. But such men could not be expected to have much enthusiasm for railroading, while their interests in arranging mergers and acquisitions had been whetted by the conglomerate movement. And, of course, a reborn Penn Central would safeguard their investments in the two rather shaky railroad companies.

Pennsylvania's accountants would be charged with "cooking the books." This was not so. Rather, they had used many of the devices available under commonly accepted accounting procedures to maximize the railroad's earnings. This was done by changing the basis of consolidation to include the earnings of subsidiaries even when these were not remitted to the parent corporation. Thus, the Pennsylvania added the earnings of Buckeye, Macco, Great Southwest, and other satellite firms to its own, even though these funds were not deposited in its treasury. Bevan admitted as much, and saw nothing wrong with the practice, since it was being used by many of the conglomerates and other "go-go companies" which he and Saunders were hoping to emulate.* Thus, the Pennsylvania's 1966 earnings per share without unremitted subsidiary revenues was $3.87, but when these were added, the figure came to $6.44. That year the Pennsylvania paid a $2.35 dividend, continuing the steady increase in payouts that began when Saunders had taken over in 1963—at which time the dividend had been only $.50. In 1967 the company earned $0.67 per share and reported $1.01—but after extraordinary charges of more than $11.00 per share, the corporation showed a deficit. Still, the generous dividend policy continued, rising to $2.40 per share. Again, none of this was secret, but the basis of consolidation was squirreled away in the back of the annual report, and so the general public—and even many stockholders—received an erroneous impression of the Pennsylvania's financial progress and situation.

The Central's management understood what this meant and implied. As far as the public, the stockholders, and even many financial journalists were concerned, the stronger Pennsylvania was merging with the troubled New York Central. In fact the cash-short Pennsylvania had several reasons for wanting the merger, and one of these was the hope of using the Central's assets to bolster its weak position—and to effect additional non-railroad takeovers. Bevan said as much to Saunders in 1966. "Over the short term today the New York Central earnings as

---

*In a November 21, 1966, memo to Saunders, Bevan wrote: "A policy may be instituted of attempting as far as possible to keep net income and cash flow as closely together as possible without regard to what the immediate effect is on earnings. Up to several years ago, this was basically the policy pursued by the Pennsylvania Railroad. The policy may be instituted of maximizing earnings to the greatest extent possible within the limits of good accounting practices. In the last several years this has been done on the Pennsylvania in accordance with your expressed desires. It does mean, however, that we tend to create a wider and wider difference as between reported income and cash flow. Today the cash flow of the Pennsylvania Railroad is substantially less than its reported income...." *The Penn Central Failure*, p. 27.

reported are much more real and tangible from the standpoint of an ability to pay dividends than are those of the Pennsylvania. Virtually all of their earnings are actually available for the payment of dividends. . . . On the other hand, much of the Pennsylvania Railroad's income is in the form of income of subsidiary companies which, in turn, have their own requirements for the plough back of money."*

This was what Perlman had hoped to avoid. He knew that the merger would deal a crippling blow to eastern railroading. At first he fought it as best he could and then, unable to do so any longer, he resigned himself to a subordinate role at the much-heralded Penn Central, while knowing it had little chance of success.

This, then, was the uneasy and flawed triad of power at the Penn Central. There was a chairman more interested in political maneuvering and non-railroad activities than the supposed central business of the corporation. Despite his successful tenure at the N&W, Saunders was not a railroader in the accepted sense of the term. But he was impressive at board meetings and before stockholders, and had a record of results. More than a century earlier the Philadelphia aristocrats had granted full powers to J. Edgar Thomson, with the understanding that he show profits, pay dividends, and run the line in such a way as never to embarrass them. Under Saunders's leadership the dividends had been increased and the price of the common stock rose by more than 500 percent in four years. As for the matter of pride and integrity, however, there had been changes over the years. Washington Butcher, president of American Steamships, served on the board during the Thomson years. He understood the words differently from his descendent, Howard Butcher III, who resigned from the board after having been accused of using secret information to sell 81,700 Penn Central shares, and been made the object of a stockholders' lawsuit in the bargain.

The Penn Central had a chairman of the finance committee with outside interests that conflicted with his main job, and on occasion there were questions as to whether he was working for Penphil, Penn Central—or himself. That Bevan was able and intelligent was beyond doubt. But he would not use his fine qualities for the Penn Central alone. And like Saunders, he had little interest in railroading or the transportation operations.

Finally, the corporation had a president who was conceded to be one of the three or four top men in the industry. It would be

*Ibid.

his task to bring together two huge operations and staffs. The railroads had developed independently for more than a century, and so the welding would be difficult and costly. The Philadelphia management cared little for Perlman's problems and had no desire to finance his massive programs for railroad rehabilitation. He would have needed Saunders's support and Bevan's resources for the successful completion of the task, and he lacked both.

The Penn Central had a chairman who didn't like his president or trust his chairman of the finance committee. For his part Perlman had always opposed the merger and thought of Saunders as a lightweight and Bevan a shady rival. Finally, Bevan was barely on speaking terms with the other two men. Saunders had the Pennsylvania Company, his embryonic conglomerate, and Bevan was involved with Penphil, which too was a conglomerate. Neither had anything to do with railroading, at least in the direct sense. Perlman stood for the railroad—alone most of the time, isolated by personality, interests, geography, and religion and social class.

Taken as a whole, it was a recipe for disaster.

XII

The Dead Phoenix

Saunders, Perlman, Bevan, and the other officers appeared at the annual stockholders' meeting on April 1, 1968, to tell of their plans and field questions. Presumably all of those present had read the optimistic annual report and knew of the glowing forecasts. Saunders was in top form, charming the audience, demonstrating his grasp of problems, indicating his plans for future profits while acknowledging current difficulties.

Most of the trouble was at the railroad. The wedding of the Pennsylvania and the Central had not been smooth, but this had been anticipated. The Penn Central had established a special fund of $275 million to provide for the changeover, the retirement of equipment and personnel, and all other dislocations. Saunders believed this was more than enough money for the tasks, and he implied that the new corporation that emerged after the changeover would be bold in design but prudent in financing.

The railroad had been hurt by the economic recession; operating revenues had fallen from $1.7 billion to $1.6 billion (on a consolidated basis), while return on investment from railroad properties had been .8 percent, compared with 2.7 percent in 1966. But once the needed economies had been effected and national prosperity returned, Saunders said, the Penn Central's railroad operations would become profitable.

Bevan offered few comments. But in answer to one question, he conceded that the railroad's income was "alarmingly low in relation to our investment in transportation facilities," and he implied that unless the turnaround took place soon, the corporation would be in a cash-flow bind.

Perlman said little, and some reporters noted that he

appeared uneasy throughout the session and left soon after, to return to New York on his special Pullman car.

At the time of the meeting the corporation had a cash balance of $31.9 million, a cash deficit of $10.5 million, and a negative cash-flow of $44.9 million. By the end of April the balance was down to $30.3 million, the deficit had risen to $16.6 million, and the negative cash-flow to $61.5 million. Almost all of this red ink was due to the railroad, which lost $27.8 million in the first quarter of the year. Real estate operations provided $5.3 million, while the sale of properties added another $8.4 million. Dividends and credits from subsidiaries fetched $12.9 million that quarter, while $2.2 million came in from interest and securities transactions. In all, the company earned slightly more than $1 million. But the Pennsylvania's bookkeeping practices enabled it to add contributions by subsidiaries in the form of unremitted earnings, and these came to $12.4 million. This practice enhanced the bottom line that was reported to the general public. As far as casual readers were concerned, the Penn Central earned $13.4 million. Outsiders might have concluded that the Penn Central was doing well, that Saunders was delivering on promises to create a large, well-managed, profitable corporation. Few bothered to analyze the statement or even to seek additional information, and those who did made little noise outside of the financial press. There were no front-page stories about problems at the Penn Central that April and May. But the quarterly report told the story to those sophisticated in reading such statements.

The Penn Central was bleeding profusely from its railroad operations, and this condition would worsen once the New Haven was absorbed.* Earnings from real estate and dividends from subsidiaries could not cover the railroad losses. Were it not for the sale of properties, the corporation would have reported a deficit. Since there were limits as to how much railroad property could be disposed of, management had to face the choice of conceding losses or selling off additional properties, perhaps some from affiliated companies, which then would remit the funds to the parent corporation. The situation recalled the railroad epics of early silent motion pictures, when in order to keep the locomotive going, firemen ripped the coaches apart and used the lumber to feed the engine. Throughout its history, the Penn Central would be obliged to dispose of assets in order to

*The New Haven's 1968 deficit was $22.3 million. Afterward its figures were incorporated with those of the Penn Central, but it certainly continued to perform poorly and show losses in 1969-71.

obtain funds for the railroad. The sale of a portion of the Norfolk and Western holdings resulted in a reported profit of close to $20 million in 1968, for example, and $23 million the following year. Saunders and the ICC had agreed to the sales as a precondition to merger, and so they caused no great surprise.*

Others did. In January 1969 the corporation formed the Penn Central Company. This entity acquired the common stock of the Transportation Company on a share-for-share basis, adding yet another layer of management. Saunders said he would use the Penn Central Company as a holding company, an umbrella beneath which the Transportation Company, the Pennsylvania Company, and future acquisitions would be gathered. There was more to it than that. Throughout 1968 the Penn Central had sold off income-producing properties at an accelerating pace, and some were the kind Saunders had hoped would provide the company with a new image. The Bryant Ranch and Six Flags Over Georgia were sold in 1968, and they returned a profit of $16.5 million, while Six Flags Over Texas, the most successful of the Penn Central's amusement parks, was disposed of in 1969, resulting in another profit, this of $17.5 million. In all, such real estate sales brought in close to $40 million in profits during these two years. And while Bevan arranged for the sale of assets in order to provide funds for ongoing railroad operations, Saunders sought investment opportunities elsewhere and delivered glowing speeches on the corporation's future.

Bevan's major occupation was juggling all of the balls—keeping both Saunders and Perlman provided with funds. It was a difficult task, one that could not be accomplished by relying upon sales of property and cash-flow alone. Bevan might have tried to sell additional shares of common stock or float new bond issues, but he held back, perhaps because he didn't want involvement with the Securities and Exchange Commission. Had the SEC made even a cursory investigation of the Penn Central at this point, and had investors read the prospectus with any degree of care, they would have learned just how shaky an operation it had become. So Bevan used a different approach.

In this period many industrial corporations borrowed funds by means of selling commercial paper to banks. These were nothing more than pledges to pay that were not based upon collateral or earnings, but instead on the general credit of the corporation. Bevan asked the board for permission to sell such

*The best study of this subject is United States Congress, House of Representatives, 92nd Cong., 1st Sess., Committee on Interstate and Foreign Commerce, *The Financial Collapse of the Penn Central* (Washington, 1972).

notes, short-term obligations that would mature in less than a year, and use the proceeds to pay for ongoing expenses. Prudent corporate policy would have dictated the sale of bonds to pay for capital expenses, and notes to finance temporary deficits. Bevan would use the money to cover both long- and short-term debts, to service the capital and expense budgets, as it were. It was a chancy policy, but there were no alternatives. The board agreed, Bevan notified the rating agencies of his plan, and the National Credit Office, without investigating the company, gave the paper a prime rating. Then the request went before the ICC, which with no significant investigation authorized the Penn Central to issue $100 million in commercial paper. This was sold to the banks—almost all of which had representation on the Penn Central board—in July and August 1968.

So the banks obtained another major stake in the corporation. This is not to say they lacked one in the past, but rather they undertook to provide the Penn Central with financial props, as much to save their own investments as anything else. They also learned how serious the situation at the railroad had become, and certainly leading bankers knew then if not before how risky an investment they had made. Other financings followed. Bevan arranged for a $50 million Eurodollar loan in November. In January he met with representatives of the International Bank for Reconstruction and Development and other world banking figures, asking for advice and help so as to save the company from financial embarrassments. Two months later he petitioned the ICC for permission to raise the commercial paper limit from $100 million to $150 million, and the request was granted. In May he was unable to meet payments on old commercial paper, and asked the ICC for the right to increase its revolving credit agreement from $100 million to $300 million, with the understanding that some of the new bank borrowings would be used to redeem commercial paper. The ICC agreed, and the banks went along with the new loans. Bevan was walking a financial tightrope in 1969, and the performance continued into 1970. In January, for example, he approached the First National City Bank with a request for a $100 million "bridge" loan—a short-term borrowing in anticipation of revenues—and although rejected, continued negotiations until the very end, six months later.

From the first, then, members of the board, the major banks, and even the ICC knew of the Penn Central's financial distress. No one said anything to the public. The banks did all they could to lessen their obligations to the corporation. While purchasing short-term notes, they sold long-term obligations and common stock.

In effect, the banks were reorganizing their Penn Central holdings. Their plans were clear enough. Over time they would eliminate all equity and bond positions, keeping the corporation alive through the transfusion of short-term money. Then they would try to oblige the Penn Central to "kick the habit," by renewing only a fraction of the short-term notes. The "rollovers" would continue for as long as possible—or long enough to enable the banks to bail out. In the end, if it were done right, the banks would own little in the way of Penn Central bonds and stock and a small portion of commercial paper; they would have sold the long-term obligations and equity to those investors transfixed by Saunders's oratory.

Nor were the banks alone in this practice. Most of the Penn Central's officers did the same. Even while he labored to find funds to keep the company going, Bevan liquidated much of his portfolio. On March 11, 1968, he owned 33,904 shares of Penn Central common. Bevan sold regularly throughout 1969. On June 19, 1970, two days prior to the bankruptcy, he sold 4,900 shares, leaving him with 13,246. Two months later Bevan's Penn Central holdings were completely liquidated.* Taken as a group, the officers sold over 20,000 Penn Central shares in 1968, 39,000 in 1969, and 19,000 in the first half of 1970. Those brokerage houses affiliated with the corporation continued to issue glowing reports, while their leaders cleaned out their portfolios as quietly as possible.

Saunders persisted in beating the drum, even when rumors of problems filtered down to the general public. On January 30, 1969, he issued a preliminary earnings report for 1968, which showed a decided improvement over 1967. Earnings were approximately $90.3 million, he said, against $71.4 million the previous year, and the prospects for the future were never brighter. This provided the backdrop for Bevan's attempts to win new credits from the banks and permission to do so from the ICC. On February 20, Saunders told reporters that the corporation had "turned the corner," and that quarterly earnings reports would make pleasant reading in the years ahead. The annual report was released in late March. In it, Saunders noted that earnings were 27 percent above those for 1967, and that this increase had been produced "by our investments in pipelines,

*Perlman was one of the few board members not to engage in such practices. On February 1, 1968, he owned 2,860 shares. His only sale prior to the collapse came on April 1, 1970, when he sold 500 shares. *Ibid.* p. 259.

hotels, industrial parks, air rights developments and other non-railroad enterprises." He went on to praise Great Southwest and Macco—the very subsidiaries whose holdings were being sold—and noted, sadly, that the railroad operations had shown a loss of $2.8 million. The line had problems, Saunders conceded, but these were nonrecurring. With what must be considered unusual brazenness, he spoke of the New Haven acquisition, which was to be "rejuvenated" so as to transform the decayed road into a "viable and productive part of our system." Finally, the report noted the progress being made by the Metroliner, a new service operating between New York and Washington. "We expect to get the entire 50-car fleet into service this summer."

The rhetoric was not unusual; it followed the pattern set down long ago by such documents. "We have complete faith in the wisdom of our merger and in our ability to achieve, much quicker than originally anticipated, the projected merger economies and efficiencies." This, at a time when the special $250 million fund was melting rapidly, and Perlman complained of a lack of capital. The cash balance at the end of March stood at $55.3 million, up from January's $26.1 million as a result of new short-term borrowings, but the cash deficit that month was $26.9 million, twice that of the previous month.

The statement of consolidated earnings told the story, far better than did the rest of the report. In 1968 the Penn Central took in $769 million, and of this only $226 million came from earnings and depreciation, while $457 million was acquired as a result of Bevan's short-term financings. Of this amount, $280 million had been used to reduce the long-term debt—to pay off banks and others who held bonds, some of the same people who helped finance the short-term obligations. The New Haven acquisition took $128 million, while other railroad activities—new equipment, repairs and renovations, operating losses, and the continuing effort to unite the two systems—accounted for an additional $306 million.

This was the problem. Saunders's cheerful projections to the contrary, the railroad could not be turned around. Under the most favorable of circumstances, given harmonious and talented leadership, the Penn Central still would have suffered from the same kinds of difficulties that had resulted in the decline of eastern railroading since the 1920s. To these were added the special problems at the giant enterprise. Together they crushed the corporation in little more than two years.

The long-term decline of American railroads continued in this period, as automobiles and airline activities expanded, and new turnpikes, trucks, and buses, airports and jet liners, attracted travelers and shippers. Noncommutation income for all railroads declined from $443 million in 1964 to $291 million in 1968 (the first full year for the merger) and in 1970, they stood at $248 million. Commuter income rose slightly, not as a result of the number of riders but rather the growing willingness of regulatory bodies to grant rate increases. Freight income advanced for the same reason; the number of revenue miles originated in 1970 was approximately the same as it had been in 1964.*

The Penn Central shared in this stagnation and decline. Revenues there rose at a slightly more rapid rate and revenue miles declined a particle more than the regional averages. Shippers and travelers were not excited about the merger. To them a railroad was just that—a rail road—whether it was called the Pennsylvania, the Central, or the Penn Central. By the late 1960s they tended to compare railroads with alternate means of transportation, and not one line with the other. And in fact, some of the shippers, especially those in the long-haul business, had reason to prefer the old operations to the new.

The difficulties on this level derived from the nature of the staffs and networks of the two carriers. Neither meshed well with the other.

As has been indicated, Perlman's Central managers prided themselves on having developed a modern operation, while viewing the Pennsylvania as a mossback railroad run by bankers and antique types. Prior to the merger these differences appeared to be based upon personalities and attitudes toward modernization. Afterward both the Central and the Pennsylvania men came to understand that their differences were far more serious, and derived as much from the natures of the two roads as from anything else.

Despite its significant coal-hauling operations in the south of its territory, the Central for decades had concentrated upon serving the manufacturing corporations of the Midwest and upper New York. It carried a wide variety of manufactured goods from there to markets in the East, and to businessmen involved in international trade. The Central's personnel in the yards and on the trains understood this. A train carrying a cargo of Chevrolets had to arrive in a certain city before a certain time. Delays would result in angry telephone calls from General

*These and related statistics can be found in Association of American Railroads, *Statistics of Railroads of Class I in the United States, 1964-1974* (Washington, 1975).

Motors to New York, and instant actions which quickly reached those responsible. Efficiency and speed were prized, long before Alfred Perlman took command. Generations of Central employees appreciated the economics of the automobile, appliance, machine tool, and related industries. Perlman built upon this base; he did not create a tradition, but rather revived it and added his own touches.

The Pennsylvania, in contrast, had derived most of its freight revenues from the carrying of coal and various ores. Its trainmen and yard personnel knew that one carload of anthracite was not much different from another. Thus, the delay of a cargo was not particularly important, for another could be substituted with no one the wiser, or, for that matter, caring much about the switch. The Central's leaders were astonished at the Pennsylvania's apparent slovenliness and backward attitudes. For their part, the Pennsylvania people were angered at what they considered efficiency for its own sake and the high-handed treatment they received from their Central counterparts. They would substitute one carload of washing machines for another, seeming not to care that each had a different mix of models, colors, and features. They measured their success in terms of volume. Saunders had wanted trains that could carry larger amounts of freight, and had been willing to sacrifice speed to get them. Perlman had to be concerned with customer satisfaction. He had spent tens of millions of dollars on computer systems and switching facilities that made certain the right car arrived in the right place at the right time. Each railroad suited the requirements of its customers, and had done so for decades. But their attitudes were quite different, and were bound to cause friction.

Perlman's job was to bring the two methods and groups of men together. It was a task for a diplomat, a man of sophistication who was flexible, and one who considered the job worthwhile and capable of being accomplished. Perlman was a harsh man who angered quickly, was convinced the Pennsylvania operations were outmoded and would have to be refashioned along the Central lines, and who had never really believed in the merger. Now he had to work with those men who came to New York from Philadelphia, and who viewed Perlman as an arrogant martinet.

The chief operating officer of any large corporation needs an executive vice-president for operations with whom he can work in harmony. At the Central Perlman had one in John Kenefec, a veteran who not only admired his chief and after a while could anticipate his reactions but also disliked the idea of a merger—so much so that he quit his post shortly before the union to go to the Union Pacific. Kenefec was replaced by Robert Flannery, who understood that a Pennsylvania man would come in after the two corporations were brought together.

Perlman's operating vice-president at the Penn Central was to be David Smucker, who had joined the Pennsylvania in 1929, fresh from college, and was devoted to the line; if anything, he disliked the merger more than did Perlman or Kenefec, and made no secret of the fact. But he was sixty years old, close to retirement, and felt he could get along with Perlman for a few years. As for Flannery, he became vice-president for systems development, with one eye on Smucker's job.

Smucker was a tough and able man, who had come under fire as one of the trustees of the Long Island. For ten years he had served as president of the Pennsylvania's captive line, the Detroit, Toledo and Ironton, and at one time had been considered as Symes's replacement. He was not the kind of person who would take well to Perlman's plans. These involved the elimination of duplicate facilities and methods of operation in order to create a harmonious whole. To Smucker this implied the substitution of Central men and procedures for those in force at the Pennsylvania—an open criticism of the work of his lifetime. Both men knew there would be troubles. Yard managers who had become accustomed to the pace and routings of their railroads now would have to learn an entirely new set of procedures, and deal with different customers.

From the first there were foul-ups, misroutings, bottlenecks, and, in some yards, utter confusion. Entire trains were sent to the wrong cities by managers who didn't know what to do with them, but who had to clear the tracks for other trains. Some were "misplaced," lost for days, only to turn up hundreds of miles from their destination. This was unfortunate for coal shippers and users and a disaster for the manufactured goods sector. One such client complained the new company had combined the worst features of the Pennsylvania and the Central, and vowed to use trucks in the future. "We started mixing up the people, and problems were inevitable," said a railroad executive. "All of a sudden dispatchers were getting orders to run trains to West Jockstrap."

Who was to blame? Smucker thought it was the Central men, trying to lord it over their Pennsylvania counterparts, and he became a rallying point for his old colleagues, whose disaffection increased as the breakdowns continued. Perlman complained to Saunders that Smucker either was sabotaging operations or simply not up to the job. He had never thought much of the man—in a pre-merger meeting Perlman had exclaimed that Smucker was "running a wooden-wheeled railroad," and neither one had forgotten the encounter. Now Smucker withdrew into a shell while Perlman worked through Flannery, who by early 1969 was the *de facto* operating vice-president. The old Central crews looked upon this as a victory, while the Pennsylvania people lost whatever enthusiasm they might ever have had for the company. The matter came to a head in late January. Perlman asked Saunders to fire Smucker, and the request was denied. Then Perlman threatened to resign unless Smucker was replaced. Saunders bowed to this. Smucker left the Penn Central, and Flannery took his place.

In a corporate sense, the merger indeed had been a Pennsylvania takeover of the Central. But at the railroad, in the area of operations, the reverse had occurred.

Smucker was not the only Pennsylvania man who gave Perlman trouble. There was Henry Large, the Pennsylvania vice-president for marketing, who like Smucker was close to retirement at the time of the merger, and had spent his working life at the railroad. Large was a traditionalist, which in industry terms meant he knew most of his important shippers by their first names and was accustomed to a relatively informal way of conducting business. His Central counterpart, James Sullivan, was younger, more aggressive, and attuned as much to computer studies as personalities. In a development parallel to the Smucker-Flannery situation, Large became executive vice-president for marketing while Sullivan remained on, reporting directly to Perlman. The differences in opinions and approaches were equally striking. Large continued to strive for increased volume—the Pennsylvania way—while Perlman and Sullivan had their eye on profits. By the summer of 1969, Perlman was insisting that Saunders fire Large, claiming he was partially responsible for losses as a result of poor pricing policies. Saunders protested that the shippers liked Large, and grumbled that Perlman had taken a dislike to the man. "I do like Henry Large," said the president. "He's a great big lovable St. Bernard." That was the trouble: "He's giving away the railroad." Did the shippers like him? Of course. "Who doesn't like Santa Claus?"

Saunders would not fire Large. To do so would signal a complete capitulation to Perlman in railroad matters, and he could not afford such a show of weakness. It was then that Perlman once more considered throwing his resignation on the table.

Perlman was a railroad man, both in the old and new senses of the term. This meant he understood the need to spend huge sums on operations, maintenance, improvements, and additions. In the automobile age it also implied an ability and willingness to work with shippers, to demonstrate that railroads were more efficient and cheaper to use than trucks. Perlman had revamped the Central at a cost of well over a half a billion dollars, and still the job had not been completed at the time of merger. As president of the Penn Central he hoped to continue the task, and enlarge its scope to include the Pennsylvania. Little wonder, then, that he clashed with the Pennsylvania management, hardly as dedicated to railroading as he, and certainly not attuned to the requirements of competing with trucks. The conflicts with Saunders over Smucker and Large were surface manifestations of a deep philosophical gulf.

So were Perlman's fights with Bevan. The president needed hundreds of million of dollars to establish the Metroliner service between Boston and Washington. New trains would be required all along the line, and automation programs put into place. If this were done, Perlman swore, the Penn Central would have a profitable operation. It would take time and money. Perlman told the board that for 1968 alone, he would require $1.5 billion for the Metroliners and other expenses.

Bevan was outraged by the figure, but even more by the offhand way it was presented. Perlman had not separated capital spending from operating costs, had offered no indication of contingency requirements, or indicated what future capital needs might be. From an accounting point of view the presentation seemed irresponsible, and he said as much. Somewhat subdued and realizing he had gone too far, Perlman backed down and soon returned with a more detailed statement. Capital spending for the first year would be $300 million, he stated. Bevan said he would try to provide that sum, as well as funds for ongoing expenses. Soon after, however, the board learned that Perlman had badly underestimated costs. Operating results were poor that year, and were getting no better. Due to inefficiencies in the yards and on the tracks, costs rose and revenues did not meet projections. Leasing charges increased sharply, as the Penn Central used its rolling stock badly. And all the while, Perlman kept coming back with new requests for funds, adding program upon program, with hardly a thought as to how the money was to be raised.

Bevan complained about Perlman's unrealistic capital demands, but by late 1968 relations between the two men had deteriorated to the point where they barely were talking to one another. Saunders understood what was happening; no less than Bevan he resented Perlman's capital spending, since they not only siphoned funds from the corporation but obliged him to delay his acquisitions programs. He had never thought Perlman was the right man for the job, and now he looked for ways to oust him from the presidency.

Saunders began with the board. Making certain secrecy would be maintained, he complained that the railroad was in a shambles due to Perlman's inability to manage it. He spoke of the president's insatiable demands for additional funds, and observed that the corporation could not afford such deficits. There was some debate, but the Pennsylvania people did control the board, and in early 1969 Saunders obtained permission to conduct a discreet search for a successor.

If Perlman knew of this, he gave no hint of such knowledge. Rather, he continued his program of replacing Pennsylvania people with his allies and seeking new capital. Meanwhile Saunders approached the head of the Northern Pacific, Louis Menck, and offered him the position. Menck decided to remain where he was, so Saunders looked elsewhere, to the automobile industry in particular, poring over lists of vice-presidents at General Motors and Ford.

Bevan, who was not a member of the board, may have been unaware of what was happening, but given his connections within the company he should have had an inkling that something was up. In June he struck. Bevan presented Saunders with an ultimatum: either get rid of Perlman or accept my resignation.

Meanwhile, Perlman persisted in his efforts to fire Large, threatening again to resign unless the marketing vice-president was retired and replaced by Sullivan. Now Saunders had two resignation threats on his hands. Although nothing would please him better than to get rid of both men, he knew he needed Bevan's expertise at raising money. As for Perlman, his lack of results had made him redundant months earlier.

Saunders tried to mollify Bevan, telling him that should he remain, he would receive additional power and be invited to take a seat on the board. Furthermore, several of his protégés would be elevated—to positions then held by former Central men. In effect, the Pennsylvania would take the railroad away from the Central. For the moment, Saunders said nothing about Perlman. It wasn't necessary. Bevan agreed, convinced that his work had been afforded proper recognition at last.

As for Perlman, the president asked for an additional $25 million which would be used to refurbish freight cars. Saunders protested, and Perlman insisted. Either give me the money, he said, or accept my resignation. By then, of course, Saunders had become quite accustomed to hearing the word "resignation." He accepted Perlman's with alacrity. The president was beyond retirement age anyway, and so his departure could be disguised as an ordinary leave-taking. Perlman would be provided with an office and an honorary position, that of vice-chairman, which carried a liberal salary and fringe benefits. He accepted, perhaps with a sense of relief. For by then Perlman had come to realize that the railroad could not be revived.

The nature of American transportation, the situation at the Penn Central, government policies, and the timing of the merger—all were wrong. The automobile and the airplane had already won the battle for passenger transportation. The railroads knew this but the ICC behaved as though it did not, and refused to permit widespread abandonments. Large segments of the public still thought of railroads as major economic powers rather than what they had become: vital parts of the economic infrastructure which, though at times unprofitable, were required to insure the health of the nation. Leaders at the Pennsylvania and the Central supported this view, but they could not work together. The most tactful and diplomatic of leaders would have had trouble in this area, and Perlman was short on both attributes.

Like most American railroads, the Pennsylvania and the Central had followed the curves of the business cycle for the past half century, showing good profits in boom eras and meager ones during recessions and depressions. The Penn Central would never have the opportunity to demonstrate what it could do during a period of prosperity. For in 1969-70, and into 1971, the economy and nature combined to provide additional blows to the tottering colossus.

Richard Nixon had campaigned for the Presidency in 1968 promising to end the Vietnam War with honor while resolving the dislocations caused by that conflict. To some, it seemed a faded replay of the Eisenhower approach of 1952, when the general said he would conclude the Korean War and bring an end to economic controls. The two wars were quite different in nature, of course, and so were the economic difficulties. For in 1968 the economy was out of control, superheated, with the

American people suffering through the most rapid inflationary spiral in two decades. The solutions these two men offered were similar, however—a cooling off of the economy by means of fiscal and monetary measures. Just as Eisenhower had precipitated a recession in 1953, so Nixon would do the same in 1969.

Stated in terms of constant 1958 dollars, America's 1967 gross national product had risen from $675 billion in 1967 to $706 billion in 1968. The rapid expansion continued into 1969, but by early summer it was evident the decline had taken hold. Still, for the year as a whole the GNP was $725 billion. By December, however, the economy was sliding, unemployment rising—but inflation hardly abating at all. While Federal Reserve Chairman Arthur Burns increased the money supply so as to stimulate growth, Congress passed the Economic Stabilization Act of 1970, authorizing the President to institute controls to halt inflation. Nixon had opposed the measure and refused to utilize its provisions, placing his faith in the less stringent medicine of monetary and fiscal policies. Meanwhile the nation struggled through a bewildering combination of inflation and recession. Construction and manufacturing were particularly hard hit, along with related industries, railroading in particular.

The story could be told in statistics. The net operating income for the nation's railroads fell from $678 million in 1968 to $655 million in 1969, and then plummeted to $489 million in 1970. Income after fixed charges showed an even more disastrous picture—$603 million to $545 million to $257 million. There was a continued slow decline in passenger traffic, while freight offered a mixed picture. For example, coal shipments and revenues held up well, the result of continued demands by utilities. But the machinery sector performed poorly. There the decline in shipments was sharp—from 6.5 million tons in 1969 to 4.6 million in 1970—as the effects of the recession combined with the continued competition from other forms of transportation to shrink railroad usage more rapidly than might otherwise have been the case.

The problems of inflation and recession were compounded by the weather. Snow began falling in late November 1969, covering most of the Northeast and Midwest, remaining on the ground as frigid air came down from Canada. Additional storms followed, and much of the Penn Central's territory had subfreezing temperature for weeks on end. As is usual in such cases, manufacturing enterprises were hard hit. And the railroads suffered breakdowns, yard jams, and power losses due to fallen wires.

Saunders's 1969 report to stockholders noted these difficulties, and the chairman wrote of how they affected the railroad. Due to inflation, wages had risen by 7 percent, and this cost the company an additional $74 million. "Total employment costs consumed about 59¢ of each railroad revenue dollar." Thus, the generous contracts signed with the unions prior to merger were taking their tolls. In addition, material costs rose by 5 percent, or $9 million, while increases in interest charges accounted for another sizable sum. "We estimate the impact of inflation on the railroad at $100 million for 1969," said Saunders. The chairman did not estimate losses due to recession, but did note that the economic slowdown had "a significant effect" upon revenues and earnings. As for the weather, "the winter of 1969 and early 1970 was the most severe in nearly a century throughout a large portion of our operating territory." Later on Saunders would tell the Senate Commerce Committee that the railroad had been paralyzed for more than three weeks. "We couldn't get a car through Selkirk yard for days. As I say, it was worse than a strike." Saunders estimated that the bad weather had cost the Penn Central "at least $20 million."

Transportation revenues for 1969 came to $1.9 billion. According to the annual report, railroad costs and expenses were about the same. Thus, as far as the casual reader was concerned, the Penn Central's railroad operations just about broke even, and under trying conditions. But lower down on the earnings statement was a special item, an extraordinary loss, most of which was due to "investment in long-haul passenger service facilities," which came to $126 million. This looked like a charge against merger operations, something stockholders and analysts had come to expect. Such was not the case, however. Late in the year Bevan had decided to write off that amount against the complete depreciation of old passenger cars and stations. Since it was reported as an extraordinary item it did not affect earnings. But it did reduce depreciation charges by more than $4.5 million, which was reflected in the final earnings statement given the shareholders, and so made the company appear better run than really was the case.

Bevan also had several important subsidiaries remit special dividends to the parent company. This enabled the Penn Central to show decent earnings, while stripping the subsidiaries' treasuries. Merchant's Despatch Transportation, a trucking company, reported a 1969 profit of $2.8 million and remitted $4.7 million to the Penn Central. Another trucking subsidiary, New York Central Transport, had profits of $4.2 million, and yet paid $14.5 million in dividends to the parent firm. When these items and the unremitted earnings of the major subsidiaries—Great Southwest, Macco, and Buckeye—were added in, the Penn Central showed earnings of $.18 per share. But the extraordinary items accounted for a loss of $5.22, and so there really was a net earnings loss of $5.04 per share. Were it not for the tricky bookkeeping, the deficit would have been at least double that sum. Yet the Penn Central still paid a dividend— $1.80 per share in 1969, against $2.40 in 1968. Saunders apologized for the cut, but pledged to restore the old rate once conditions improved. While so acting, however, insiders were selling Penn Central shares and bonds, bailing out before all was lost.

What did this mean? Inflation might be moderated, and the economy returned to a growth stance. One could not predict weather conditions, but surely 1970 and 1971 would not be as unfavorable as 1969. But the industry itself could not be so rapidly transformed, or the essential elements of the Penn Central's railroad operations and finances. In March 1970, Saunders spoke of a restructuring of passenger services, including the termination of several unprofitable long-haul passenger trains. He hoped that through the redesign of the system's trackage the Penn Central would be able to eliminate some 5,800 miles of track—more than one quarter of the total. How long would this take, and at what cost? In 1969 the ICC had allowed the Penn Central to abandon 422 miles, and this only after lengthy hearings and with great reluctance. Nor was the agency willing to grant necessary rate increases. In November the Penn Central was permitted a 6 percent boost, which didn't even allow the line to keep pace with inflation, and several commissioners implied that this was all that could be expected for the next year or so. The Metroliner was plagued with chronic operating difficulties; the New York to Washington run was not profitable, though Saunders wasn't ready to abandon hope.

Finally, there was the problem in Washington. In the past Saunders had been able to evoke the name of his great and good ally Lyndon Johnson whenever he needed bureaucratic assistance. Johnson was gone in 1969, and in his place was a man who spoke the language of competitive capitalism, even while he made exceptions for his favored supporters. Richard Nixon was no particular friend of the Penn Central, or for that matter of railroading in general. He had no stake, personal, political, or professional, in the operation's success. A man whose major interests had always been in the foreign policy area, Nixon had never developed a well-informed view of the actual workings of American capitalism, even while serving as a Wall Street lawyer in the 1960s. To him, big business seemed a form of diplomacy, and important matters could be ironed out in meetings of chief executive officers and their retinues. The operations behind these men do not appear to have interested him. At a time when the Penn Central might have benefited from having a man in the White House who had an understanding of economics and railroading, none was there.*

Nor did the Penn Central have a chief operating officer who fully understood the industry or the company. Failing to lure a major railroader to fill Perlman's position, and unable to come to terms with an executive in the automobile industry, Saunders turned elsewhere in his search. In late September 1969 he announced the selection of Paul Gorman, who had just retired as president of the Western Electric Company, the manufacturing subsidiary of American Telephone and Telegraph. Gorman had no railroad experience, and certainly no knowledge of the Penn Central operations. The job came his way by chance; Gorman and Penn Central director Charles Hodge belonged to the same country club, and Hodge—who knew Gorman socially—recommended him to Saunders. He had accepted the post without first examining the situation carefully, and during the next three months—Gorman didn't assume office until December 1—he read Penn Central reports and held conversations with Saunders, who revealed little of the company's serious problems.

Why did Gorman take the position? He was sixty-two years old at the time and knew he hadn't a chance of winning the AT&T presidency. Like so many other important executives, he had hoped to cap his career by directing affairs at a major corporation. Now he would have the chance to do this at the Penn Central—or at least, this was his expectation. As for Saunders, his new president had a reputation as a cost cutter, a stickler for efficiency, and as a man with no industry experience would be free from allegiance to either the Pennsylvania or the Central faction. After close to two years with Perlman such a person would be a relief. Where Perlman seemed to spend money in a reckless and unrealistic fashion, Gorman would trim expenses

---

*Of course, very few American Presidents had ever shown much knowledge of economics or a detailed understanding of American business. Of all American Presidents, only George Washington and Herbert Hoover could be categorized as businessmen. Still, Nixon demonstrated less understanding for and sympathy with the business community than might have been expected from one with his supposed ideological proclivities.

while at the same time bowing to others—Saunders and Bevan in particular—in all other matters.

Gorman did clean house. Among others to go was Henry Large, whose marketing job was taken by Illinois Central veteran Edward Kreyling, Jr., a man with a reputation for efficiency. Perlman was gone, but his approach was accepted by Gorman, and in this respect at least the drive for a New York Central-type operation continued. In the months that followed, additional Pennsylvania executives would be replaced with outsiders who hewed to the Perlman philosophy. But there was a difference in structure which made these changes less meaningful than might have been expected. Gorman did not have control over accounting, a rather unusual situation, given his mandate. Rather, all financial matters, both internal and external, were in the hands of David Bevan, whose grip on the railroad was stronger than ever before.

Perhaps this was to the good—the effects of the recession and the winter storms were being felt, and fiscal demands had to be met—but it assured that Perlman's plans to reconstruct the railroad would be scrapped. It would have happened in any event, for survival was the key consideration in late 1969. But with Bevan and the former head of an electrical manufacturing firm in charge of the nation's largest railroad, whatever remained of a hope for a revivified transportation company came to an end.

Perlman's departure in December 1969 was a signal moment. Both the Central and the Pennsylvania had been organized by financiers who soon after either turned the line over to engineers and professionals or did all they could to transform themselves into railroaders. Perlman was the last of this group. Now the Penn Central was once more headed by financiers, and this provided the final cachet for what Saunders and his group had believed from the first. The Penn Central was not really a railroad. It was, rather, a property, led by men with no real or deep commitment to that form of transportation.

On December 1, Saunders hosted a staff luncheon for the incoming president and spoke of the need to change direction at the railroad. "We are at a critical point in the history of our company," he began. "We face an urgent need to produce merger benefits of increasing quantity and quality. We must make money on this railroad, and in the process improve our service, lower our costs, and enlarge our volume of profitable traffic." This was, of course, hyperbole—what executive doesn't want to lower costs, enlarge profits, expand volume, and make money? But it was vital that all of these be done at the Penn

Central, where costs were skyrocketing, deficits deepening, and volume stagnating. "It is entirely possible that the next six months will be the most critical in the history of our railroad," said Saunders. This was somewhat surprising, for the chairman had long been famous for his optimism. Now he could no longer ignore the drift of events. "Frankly, our customers are apprehensive about whether or not Penn Central can meet the test of adequate service during the winter months," said Saunders, referring to the winter foul-ups, and he urged the new management to improve the record of the old, and to do so with less money and other support from the parent corporation. It was an impossible task.

Several directors understood the situation, and hoped something could be done about it. One of these, Robert Odell, had been Perlman's ally in opposing the merger but nonetheless had joined the new board after the formation of the Penn Central. Odell also was on the board of the Pennsylvania Company and, unlike the directors of many corporations, took his duties and obligations seriously. After a while he began investigating what he considered unusual corporate procedures. Through 1968 and into 1969, Odell watched the board approve of highly questionable financing practices. He knew that many directors had little faith in the company's future, and he had heard rumors that the banks were trying to save the Penn Central long enough so as to provide themselves with a cushion before the crash. In November 1969 Odell voiced his fears and suspicions, and called for a general corporate reorganization. Specifically he wanted top management to step down—Saunders and Bevan in particular—or, lacking that, be fired. Then Perlman would be restored to power and given a chance to turn the railroad around.

Not only was Odell's request rejected, but the board refused to discuss it, looking upon it perhaps as the last gasp of the Perlman faction. Soon after, however, Odell was joined by a new director, E. Clayton Gengras, who, like Gorman, was a friend of Charles Hodge. Gengras headed the Security Insurance Company of Hartford and had a reputation for acquiring and then reorganizing poorly managed corporations. Already he had purchased some 200,000 shares of Penn Central for Security, and the word was that he would help turn the company around, which in turn would lead to higher stock prices and a large profit for his firm. Gengras soon was named to the board of the Transportation Company as well, and was shocked by the lack of information given him and other directors. Together with directors Louis Cabot and William Day he asked for specific statistics on deficits, operations, and in particular, financing methods. Saunders replied that he would give the matter consideration, but did nothing concrete in the way of providing information.

All of these men suspected the Penn Central was in financial distress, but it was not until November, when Saunders asked the board to approve the omission of the regular quarterly dividend, that the members began to comprehend the seriousness of the situation. Saunders urged the board to be patient; he was certain Gorman would turn the railroad around. When Day asked for full financial disclosure, Saunders wrote, "If we go too far in this regard, we also get ourselves in greater trouble so far as our financing is concerned. I am, however, in complete accord with you that the Board should have all the facts."*

What were the facts? Bevan's financial manipulations, and in particular his virtuoso performance in selling short-term paper, were only suspected toward the end of 1969. There was no warning from the firm's auditors, Peat, Marwick, Mitchell & Co. (whose 1969 fee had been $600,000), which certified that the accounting was in accord with commonly accepted principles. The ICC voiced no criticism. Nor did the Securities and Exchange Commission, then busy at work helping Wall Street firms survive, with little time left for the Penn Central. At the railroad there was a failure of operations, due to long-term trends and short-term problems, both of which eluded solutions. And there was growing evidence of financial erosion at the parent corporation, although the board remained ignorant of much of this.

Odell remained disturbed by the situation. Unsatisfied with the way Saunders had handled his requests for information and critical of the overstating of earnings by several subsidiaries, he submitted his resignation in February, with the understanding it would take effect in May. Fred Kirby, another old Central director, left in April. But neither man spoke of the reasons for his departure.

Without David Bevan's speculative and manipulative skills the corporation might have collapsed in early 1970. The previous year he had written off assets, sold properties, and remitted special dividends from subsidiaries in order to keep the line afloat. Gambling on Gorman's abilities at holding expenses down, hoping the economy would recover, and that money markets would remain open to him, Bevan had entered 1970

*Financial Collapse of the Penn Central Company, p. 166.

knowing that unless all three conditions were met the corporation would collapse. Then Saunders would have to take his case to the federal government. And if help were denied, bankruptcy would become inevitable.

The campaign for survival began in early March, when business was stirring, even while expenses continued to climb and revenues fall. On March 12, when the outside auditors came to review the books, Bevan assured them all would be well. He conceded that railroad operations would continue to be poor for the rest of the quarter, with losses running upward of $100 million. In order to minimize the losses, however, he would arrange transfers of assets so as to provide the Transportation Company with a paper profit, though in fact this would have no net impact upon the corporation as a whole. In addition, Bevan updated an exchange of N&W stock that provided a second paper profit, which would appear in the first quarter's report. This was in accord with commonly accepted accounting procedures—or, at least, so Bevan claimed. Peat, Marwick agreed. The auditor signed a favorable opinion letter, qualifying it only by a note that the Penn Central had failed to provide a reserve for federal taxes.

Gorman was shocked by all of this; obviously manipulations of this kind were not tolerated at Western Electric. Also, he didn't understand the reasoning behind the move. "Why do we bother with those kind of things?" he asked. Again, Gorman didn't comprehend Penn Central procedures. If the general public, and the Wall Street community, realized how dangerous the situation had become at the Transportation Company, whatever confidence remained in the Penn Central would be smashed. The company had to be kept afloat until the banks and board members had liquidated most of their holdings.

Gorman protested these and similar activities at the next board meeting. According to the minutes, "The President then stated that he was deeply concerned about a number of management practices, although there was no indication that they were illegal or had not been approved by outside counsel and outside auditors." Gorman asked that such bookkeeping gimmicks be done away with. "He stated that he had followed this code for over 40 years and did not intend to change at this stage of his career and that he would like to discuss certain matters with the Committee to determine whether the practices would be continued in the future."*

---
*Ibid. pp. 54-56.

Nothing was done. Almost to the end, Gorman failed to comprehend the nature of the situation at the Penn Central, which after all was so alien to everything he had experienced in the past. Gorman strove to cut expenses and had his eye on the railroad, while the bigger picture eluded him for several more months.

Meanwhile, Bevan continued his search for funds, and in the process used every technique known to modern treasurers. Basing his request upon the Peat, Marwick statement, he petitioned the ICC for permission to float a $100 million bond issue for the Pennsylvania Company. This subsidiary would use the money to purchase three properties from the parent company. Thus, the Penn Central would receive a substantial infusion of cash in return for the transfer of assets from one box to another. The underwriters—Glore, Forgan, Salomon Brothers & Hutzler, and First Boston—understood Bevan's operation. There was nothing illegal about it—though the properties involved had cost the Penn Central less than $30 million, and clearly had been overpriced. Bevan had been aboveboard with the bankers. He even conceded, privately, that the Penn Central well might be on the verge of bankruptcy. Despite all of this, the underwriters agreed to put forth their best efforts—to try to sell the bonds to their clients.

It is difficult to imagine a worse time in the past thirty years in which the securities might have been offered than the spring of 1970. In the first place, the paper undoubtedly was of questionable merit, and although it carried a premium coupon—10.5 percent—the risks were greater than the possible rewards. Too, there was the gimmickry involved, certain to frighten any speculator or bargain hunter who might have read the prospectus. Most important, however, was the nature of the market at the time. The previous March the Dow-Jones Industrials had stood close to 950. It fell below 900 in June and crossed the 800 mark in January 1970. By late April, as the prospectus was being readied, the Dow Industrials was below 750 and headed downward at an accelerating rate and with higher volume. Wall Street was close to panic. President Nixon's business advisors urged him to take action to restore confidence, but he held back, perhaps because he didn't perceive the situation as being that critical, or due to a lack of plans to meet this kind of emergency.

The problems of the Penn Central seemed minor compared with those facing the entire American financial apparatus. Yet the underwriting plans continued. On April 28, the investment bankers contacted some of their best customers to "test the water." It was icy. Bevan was informed that there was almost no hope of marketing the issue, and that he should seek alternate means of obtaining funds. But there were no alternatives—at least not in New York. Bevan had reached his own dead end.

Saunders was working on a different level. He had spent part of the past month at ICC headquarters, attempting to win concessions on freight rates. No action had been taken, but even had rates been raised immediately, the cash-flow problem would have remained. Higher rates might take care of future needs. In April, the Penn Central needed funds to survive into the summer.

Saunders and Jonathan O'Herron, one of Bevan's assistants, had met with Secretary of Transportation John Volpe on two separate occasions in March to explore the possibilities of federal aid. In particular they wanted subsidies for passenger travel, additional track abandonments, freight-rate increases, and permission to diversify into other forms of transportation. Volpe was reluctant to act; he certainly didn't receive the impression the matter was urgent, for such talk had gone on for years. He suggested that the railroad might qualify for help under the terms of one of several national security acts. Volpe steered Saunders and O'Herron out of his offices and into those of the Department of Defense, and then dismissed the matter from his thoughts.

This was the situation in late April, as Bevan urged the financiers to continue their efforts at marketing the debentures. At a Saunders-Bevan meeting each man learned from the other just how serious the situation had become, and of the narrowing options. Bevan was hopeful. He could buy time, and Saunders was prepared to listen to any suggestion. Preliminary reports indicated that railroad business had improved. Additional seasonal profits were possible, at least for the next few months. The corporation might limp along into early winter. Together the two men constructed a plan based upon this expectation. It was simple enough. Bevan would make the effort to sell the debentures, while Saunders went back to Washington to seek federal help. He was to inform the government that without it the Penn Central could go bankrupt, and not in months, but days or weeks. Considering the chancy situation on Wall Street, the Nixon administration scarcely would risk having the Penn Central declare insolvency, an event that could trigger a 1929-style panic. In other words, management would engage in a subtle form of blackmail.

Toward what end? Not necessarily to save the corporation, for both men seemed to know this was an unrealistic expectation. Stripped of many of its profitable holdings, with a railroad that could not be turned around and a president who knew little of the industry, the Penn Central was beyond hope. A government loan or grant could keep it alive, but without continued infusions it would soon die. Management knew this, and so did a few of the investment bankers. But the general public was unaware of the seriousness of the situation. Perhaps the insiders could salvage part of their holdings. The Pennsylvania bond issue was scheduled for May 15. Saunders would negotiate in Washington until then, while Bevan would try to keep the company afloat for several weeks beyond that date. Given a loan or grant, the corporation would be able to function; if the request was denied, Saunders and Bevan would continue on for as long as possible. Assuming the financiers played their part, the insiders would be able to liquidate their positions with time to spare.

What of the railroad—the reason for the creation of this hollow edifice? It struggled along that spring, while Gorman tried to turn a profit from operations.

The results were illuminating. Business had picked up in late March, and continued strong into April, while May shipments were the most sizable since the Transportation Company had been formed. Railroad revenues for the second quarter would come to $485 million, a record. This performance was made possible by an upturn in the economy, rate increases, and better-than-average efficiency. Yet with all of this—under the familiar "best of circumstances"—the Transportation Company reported a deficit on operations of $12 million.

As much as anything else, these figures provided the epitaph for the Penn Central, and perhaps for other railroads in similar positions as well. Major lines with important passenger traffic could no longer operate profitably. Some of the western railroads that owned mineral-rich real estate and had little competition from other means of transportation within their territories might prosper. So could the smaller freight lines, especially those that hauled raw materials such as coal and ores. Saunders had attempted to remake the Penn Central into the first kind of company, with profits from the conglomerate feeding into the railroad. Perlman and his Central staff had stressed abandonment of passenger operations and concentration upon freight. Both efforts had failed; the Penn Central had become a conglomerate too late, with insufficient capital, while the government fought the elimination of railroad passenger service in the Northeast—witness the forced merger with the New Haven.

By going to the government, Saunders and Bevan were taking the only course remaining for railroad executives in their circumstances. That they had bungled badly was obvious to insiders by then, and tales of mismanagement and manipulation would multiply in the press during the ensuing years. The sensational masked the significant. For the Penn Central was dying in 1970, partly as a result of parasitic actions by its executives and other retainers, but also because of the nature of railroading itself. Their unwillingness or inability to publicize this part of the larger picture was the final disservice Penn Central management performed for the industry.

XIII

The Fallen Colossus

Secretary of Transportation John Volpe of Massachusetts had never claimed to be a railroad or finance expert. Rather, he was a man with political credentials who had important connections with the highway lobby and related industries. While a young man in the 1920s, Volpe had worked at a variety of jobs, and in addition he became active in local GOP clubs. He formed his own construction company in 1933, a generally bleak year for the industry and nation. But Volpe Construction survived and even flourished, as its president was able to obtain contracts for local and state projects by getting along well with those in power.

After serving in the navy during World War II, Volpe returned both to politics and construction, with special interests in roads and highways. In 1956 he was named to head the Eisenhower administration's highway program, and was responsible for making certain the multibillion-dollar effort was successful. Volpe performed his tasks well, becoming a national figure in the process as well as a particular favorite in Detroit and among cement company executives. He won the Massachusetts governorship in 1960, failed to be reelected in 1962, and was returned to office in 1966. Volpe was active in the Nixon campaign, and even had been half promised the Vice-Presidential nomination in the early summer of 1968. He was disappointed when Nixon selected Spiro Agnew instead, but after a brief period of reflection decided to campaign—somewhat sedately—for the ticket. For this, and as a sop to the nation's Italian Catholics, Volpe was to receive an office in the Cabinet.

Volpe's experience and his past interests had prepared him for the Transportation portfolio, or at least this was the claim at the time the appointment was announced. More important, however, was the fact that he was not considered a key member of the incoming administration, and so was shuttled into one of the most insignificant offices in the Nixon Cabinet. The President cared little for the subject, and tended to ignore both it and his Transportation Secretary. Volpe understood this, and in early 1970 began angling for another assignment. A Washington joke of the period indicated as much: for the first time in memory a Cabinet post was being used as a stepping stone for the ambassadorship to Italy.

Volpe was the logical person for Saunders to have approached in seeking aid for the Penn Central; after all, his office was supposed to deal with railroads. There was much irony in this. The man who in large part had been responsible for the very programs that had helped wreck the eastern passenger railroads was now called upon to rescue the largest of them all. A politician in a relatively unimportant Cabinet post who had little influence, his bags already packed, was being asked to introduce the federal presence into railroading, to reverse policies of more than a century's standing, to influence a President he hardly saw and who in any case considered railroading beneath notice. To further complicate matters, Saunders and Bevan had been less than frank with Volpe during the late winter. They wanted aid, to be sure, but at no time did they reveal just how serious the Penn Central situation had become, perhaps in the hope that Wall Street financing would obviate the need for a Washington bailout. Volpe and other eastern politicians had heard much of this before—the railroads and their lobbyists for years had talked and written about how the industry was on the verge of chaos, and yet the trains continued on. So it was not surprising that Volpe's initial reaction had been to usher the Penn Central team out the door and point Saunders in the direction of the Pentagon.

The situation in early May 1970 was no more promising.

At that time Jonathan O'Herron was known as a Bevan protégé. A former vice-president at Buckeye Pipeline, he had moved to the home office to become Bevan's financial vice-president after Perlman's defeat. O'Herron quickly learned of the tight situation there, and of Bevan's accounting manipulations. He was troubled by the way subsidiary earnings had been remitted and shocked at shady deals between executives at Penn Central and Executive Jet. O'Herron had joined in when Saunders and Bevan met with Volpe in March, and he knew the Secretary hadn't been made aware of how serious the matter had become. He urged Bevan to meet again with Volpe and present him with all of the facts, but nothing came of this. When it appeared certain the debenture offering would be rejected, O'Herron persuaded Saunders and Bevan to go to Washington, open the books, reveal all, and inform the Nixon administration insiders that without federal aid the corporation would be obliged to default within a matter of weeks.

Bevan finally agreed to write a memo for presentation to Volpe, but it was far milder than the one O'Herron would have preferred. Disappointed and having decided to act on his own, O'Herron asked for and received permission to take the message to Washington. This was on Friday, May 8. Rather than wait until Monday, O'Herron set out at once. Volpe was no longer at his office, and so O'Herron went to his home. Somewhat surprised at this unusual behavior, Volpe agreed to read the memo and, as expected, found nothing in it to justify immediate action. But then O'Herron informed him that the situation was far graver than Bevan had indicated. The debenture offering could not be sold—the memo held out some hope in this area—and despite higher revenues, railroad deficits had not been reversed. Furthermore, the banks and the trust companies that had financed the Penn Central's short-term notes had become wary and were on the point of insisting upon repayment, after which they would leave the market. The news might create a panic. If and when this happened, said O'Herron, the corporation would be obliged to declare insolvency.

Only federal action could prevent this. The government had several options: lend money to the Penn Central, guarantee its notes, finance short-term demands, or sponsor legislation providing support for specific operations, passenger travel in particular. Unless something along these lines were constructed, he said, the corporation would be finished.

All of this came as a surprise to Volpe. Although rumors of new troubles had filtered down to his office, he had not taken them seriously, in large part due to the manner in which Saunders and Bevan had presented their cases. Now that he understood the implications of the situation, Volpe agreed to take action. Immediately he contacted Secretary of the Treasury David Kennedy, then attending a meeting of the Business Council in Hot Springs, Arkansas, and arranged for a conference between him and Saunders the next day. At the same time O'Herron called Saunders to inform him of what had taken place. Whether he was upset, angered, or relieved is unknown, but in any case Saunders agreed to be there. The meeting began, and, for the first time, Saunders asked for federal assistance on an emergency basis. The large commercial banks had informed him they would no longer roll over the Penn Central's short-term obligations. The corporation would be unable to raise money on the capital markets, or through private placement of long-term paper. The Penn Central was approaching a crisis, and if it collapsed, repercussions would be felt throughout the economy—which was in a shaky condition in any case.

Kennedy agreed to recommend action to the President, although not certain at that time what it might be. Could Saunders hold out for a few more weeks? The chairman said he would do his best. Meanwhile, other meetings were held, involving Undersecretary of Transportation James Beggs and Undersecretary of the Treasury Paul Volker. Randolph Guthrie was present at several of these. The former law partner of both Nixon and John Mitchell, he had been retained as an advisor by the Penn Central. His true job, of course, was to influence his former colleagues and do what he could with the bankers.

Saunders and Bevan worked with both groups during the next few days. They conferred with Kennedy on May 19, seeking assurances of federal loans but receiving nothing concrete. Two days later Bevan was in New York, where, together with the underwriters, he agreed to abandon the debenture offering. That same day he conferred with representatives of the banks, led by First National City and Chemical. He informed them of the debenture withdrawal and that the Penn Central was about to draw down its last $50 million of revolving credit. When that was gone, bankruptcy would be inevitable—unless the banks cooperated. He hoped to obtain a federal loan in one form or another. Would the banks agree to extensions until it came through? They would, but only for a short period. They took this action not out of a desire to assist the Penn Central, but rather in the knowledge that by so acting they could buy time while planning for a settlement.

Bevan was back in Washington on May 25, where he met with Kennedy, Federal Reserve Chairman Arthur Burns, and several representatives of the White House staff, including former Wall Streeter Peter Flanigan. He asked not only for a federal loan, but intervention with the commercial banks as well. Bevan was scheduled to meet with them later on in the week, and at that time would have to bring news of Nixon's intentions. A combined federal government-bank action would save the corporation from bankruptcy; nothing less would do. Perhaps the Federal Reserve Bank could be brought into the picture as well, Bevan hinted, in an attempt to stress the seriousness of the situation. It might guarantee Penn Central paper, or take some other action to help salvage the firm's liquidity. Arthur Burns didn't appear interested, and so Bevan let the matter drop.

The Penn Central was in a strong bargaining position due to developments on Wall Street. At the time the financial marketplace was on the edge of an abyss. The Dow-Jones Industrials had closed at 641.36 on May 25, down nearly twenty-one points for the day. The average had plummeted more than eighty points for the month thus far and no sign of a bottom was in sight. The index fell to 627.46 the next day, but rallied slightly to close at 631.16. Volume was heavy and the atmosphere skittish.

What might be the impact of a Penn Central collapse on such a market? Already there were rumors that one was on the way, due to a tight financial squeeze. The banks said nothing, but their portfolio managers took action soon after the meeting with Bevan and tried to empty trust accounts—Chase Manhattan alone had sold 134,300 shares on May 22.

Rumors were taking on the appearance of reality. On May 26 the *Wall Street Journal* published an item regarding the commercial paper crunch, and this had sparked the decline that day. But the story and related rumors were lost in the rush of bad news and even more catastrophic fears that washed over the district. Bevan and Kennedy knew that confirmation of rumors, additional stories, and, finally, a collapse could result in "another 1929." Even then, without a word from Nixon, they understood that federal action would be required and probably undertaken. All that remained was to decide upon the form, the scope, the timing, and the procedures.

Saunders and Bevan were in Philadelphia on May 27 to attend the regularly scheduled meetings of the board and the finance committee. That morning the *Journal* carried another story on the Penn Central's commercial paper problems. None of the directors had been informed of the seriousness of the situation; they had become aware of it through the newspaper and from rumors. Nor had they been told of the conferences with federal officials. Now they learned. Bevan spoke of the failure to market debentures, the rapidly shrinking credit line, and of a conference he would attend with the bankers the following day at which he hoped to receive additional credits in return for guarantees which still were unspecified. Then he discussed the possibility of a federal loan, and asked support for his efforts at achieving one. Clearly this was the corporation's last hope.

The board was surprised at the grimness of the recitation, especially after the optimism of the past several meetings. Mem-

Trading in Penn Central Common Stock in May 1970

Date	Penn Central Volume	Sales by Penn Central Banks*	Closing Price	Dow-Jones Industrials
May 1	28,771	6,200	18⅝	733.63
4	28,871	0	18	714.56
5	36,555	100	17½	709.74
6	56,732	19,100	18	718.39
7	37,719	6,000	18½	723.07
8	21,887	3,900	18⅝	717.73
11	25,578	0	17¾	710.07
12	182,353	15,800	15¼	704.59
13	93,649	1,500	15¾	693.84
14	138,573	36,300	15¼	684.79
15	89,720	3,717	15⅝	702.22
18	71,541	200	15¼	702.81
19	183,450	74,500	14	691.40
20	91,891	18,075	13⅝	676.55
21	154,805	16,300	13⅛	665.25
22	419,990	135,000	11¾	662.17
25	157,517	55,800	12	641.36
26	115,209	35,100	12¾	631.16
27	360,563	254,100	13⅜	663.20
28	250,507	48,100	13¼	684.15
29	212,545	47,000	12⅝	700.44
	2,758,426	776,792		

* The Penn Central banks—those which held the largest portion of the corporation's common stock—were: Chase Manhattan, Morgan Guaranty, Continental Illinois Bank and Trust, Provident National, Security Pacific, and United States Trust. In addition Investors Mutual and Allegany, both with bank and trust company connections, were included in the group.

Source: *The Penn Central Failure*, pp. 317, 325, and *Wall Street Journal*, May 1–June 1, 1970.

bers were dismayed at not having been informed earlier of the problems, and angered by the secrecy. Louis Cabot, head of Cabot Corporation, resigned the next day. Several directors hinted at an investigation. But nothing along these lines was decided upon. Instead, the board voted to give Bevan whatever authority he needed to deal with the bankers.

Thus armed, Bevan traveled to New York the following morning to bargain with the major banks. Informing their representatives of the progress in Washington, he asked for an additional line of credit contingent upon government assistance. With great reluctance the bankers decided to consider the request. After the meeting, a group of them, led by First National City, agreed to send a delegation to Washington to confer with government officials on the matter. Thus, Kennedy, Volpe, and the others would receive pressures both from the Penn Central and the major banks. Somewhat relieved, Bevan told reporters that the debenture offering had been postponed—making official what was already known—but that he was "working on alternate means of financing." Bevan did not say what it was, but given the general ignorance of most individuals interested in the company and its securities, it appeared as though a new private loan, perhaps from overseas investors, was being arranged.

That week, Chase Manhattan sold an additional 231,150 shares, and the other banks in the consortium followed suit. Even as they argued for federal aid, the banks and trust companies tried to clean their books of Penn Central paper.

Thus, there were four major forces involved in the Penn Central picture in early June 1970. First there were the banks and trust companies, without whose aid the corporation would become illiquid. Most of the Penn Central's bankers had come to doubt the possibility of a rescue effort. Even if one were mounted, with government guarantees, they might withdraw their support—after having salvaged their financial positions, of course. David Rockefeller of the Chase and Walter Wriston of First National City had lost whatever confidence they had had in Saunders, Bevan, and Gorman. They realized they had been lied to and deceived, and this was a cardinal crime in their circles. True, their institutions' relationship with the railroads had been mutually profitable, and some of the banks had been identified with either the Pennsylvania or the Central for over a century. Sentiment and tradition have places in business, but they are seldom paramount.

These views were transmitted to members of the board of directors, the second force. Clayton Gengras spoke with Wriston and learned of the banker's position. Earlier he had met with Volpe—an old friend—and so had been alerted to the difficulties. By then his firm, Security-National Insurance, owned 220,900 Penn Central shares. Naturally he was both angered and concerned about the crisis, and just as naturally he blamed management for the troubles. So did other directors—Edward Hanley, Seymour Knox, Thoms Perkins, Franklin Lunding, and even John Seabrook, who earlier had been one of Saunders's most vocal defenders. Together they decided that Saunders and Bevan had to be removed from office. This would satisfy the bankers, and perhaps provide a signal that reform was being undertaken for the third force, the government.

By early June, John Volpe understood the seriousness of the situation and most of its implications. The Penn Central was close to collapse; any doubts regarding this had been resolved by the failure of the debenture offering. At best a bankruptcy would disrupt Wall Street and undermine the slow recovery then in progress; a panic could result should the matter be mishandled. Volpe wasn't certain how bankruptcy would affect the financial community, for at the time he had no clear idea of its involvement with the corporation. Nor could he anticipate the reaction of the Federal Reserve, for Arthur Burns had been most cautious throughout, refusing to commit himself in any way. Would bankruptcy result in losses of service, freight as well as commuter? The owners of equipment bonds were bound to initiate lawsuits once bankruptcy was announced, and there was no certain way of predicting court actions. A railroad paralysis was always a dangerous situation, but at that time, with financial and industrial America dispirited and insecure, it could set off a depression.

Volpe favored federal intervention, and thought he could convince Nixon of its desirability. As a practical politician he knew there would be opposition. Antique reformers were bound to challenge aid to a major American corporation; even then, some were talking about "socialism for the rich and private enterprise for the poor," as a description of how the Nixon administration viewed the econoy. That there would be investigations and charges of corporate wrongdoing could not be seriously doubted. Volpe thought the actions and policies of Saunders and Bevan could not bear such scrutiny. With the tacit approval of the White House, he decided to sponsor an aid measure, but only after major changes had been made in the Penn Central's top management. Volpe knew the corporation's board would meet on June 8, and from friends among the directors he understood that Saunders and Bevan would be obliged to step down at that time.

On June 5 Volpe met with Senate Minority Leader Hugh Scott of Pennsylvania, and the two men discussed the Penn Central. The Secretary informed Scott of the critical situation and asked for his help. Scott agreed to do what he could; he was up for reelection that year, and the collapse of the corporation would create industrial havoc in his state and perhaps cost him his Senate seat. On June 9—four days from then, just after the board meeting—there would be a conference attended by congressional and administration leaders to discuss a Penn Central aid package. Volpe set about creating one the next day.

Thus, three of the four forces involved with the Penn Central—the banks, the board, and the government—believed the time had come to eliminate the fourth, namely, the corporation's management. Wriston, Gengras, and Volpe worked together on this, and believed that by so acting they would be able to preserve the Penn Central's solvency, for the time being at least.

This was no conspiracy. Saunders and Bevan must have known what was happening. Part of the May 5 board meeting had been devoted to a discussion of the reorganization of top management. Seabrook and others had presented a plan to accomplish this. Perlman and Bevan would be retired, Saunders would be given an honorary post, and Gorman would be the new chairman and chief executive officer, while the board would lead the search for an experienced railroader for the presidency. According to those present, Saunders and Bevan had accepted the proposal in good grace, while Perlman was silent. But there must have been a misunderstanding, perhaps due to Seabrook's desire to moderate the force of his recommendation so as not to insult his friends. Saunders and Bevan continued their work for the rest of the month and into June. In effect, they had been given a vote of no confidence, and then had gone off to negotiate with Volpe and the New York bankers.

In retrospect all of those involved conceded that it was an impossible situation, and at times most painful. Finally, on June 3, Wriston informed Saunders and Gorman that he could no longer deal with Bevan, that even with him gone and federal guarantees in place the First National City might not wish to be a party to the rescue effort. But Saunders did not comprehend fully that he too had to go. Nor did he inform Bevan of the conversation, even though he was then involved in complicated and pointless negotiations for a new loan. Saunders and Gorman did discuss with Volpe a proposed government aid package, but the Secretary gave no hint that it was contingent upon Saunders's resignation as chairman.

The matter was resolved at the June 8 meeting. After preliminaries, Gorman told the board of Volpe's recommendation. The Secretary, together with Senator Scott, would support legislation providing $750 million to help financially troubled railroads, and some $300 million of this amount might be taken by the Penn Central. In addition, Volpe hoped the government would guarantee $200 million of the Penn Central's notes for the next six months, or until the legislation passed Congress and was signed into law. The banks had agreed to go along with this plan, said Gorman, but would not do so unless three conditions were satisfied. New cash had to be used for essential programs only, and this would be done under outside supervision. The banks would receive collateral for their loans, and would be able to dispose of it in case of default. And the top management would have to be reorganized. In effect, the Penn Central would cease to be an autonomous corporation, but rather enter into a disguised receivership, with the banks in control, functioning through their appointees.

Those directors who had not been involved in the negotiations of the past month were shocked by the harshness of the terms. Saunders and Bevan had their defenders, but toward the end they capitulated, knowing that unless the terms were accepted and the changes made, the Penn Central would have to default on loans due that week, and shortly thereafter be unable to meet payrolls. Saunders agreed to step down and be replaced by Gorman. Bevan submitted his resignation, and his position as chairman of the finance committee was taken by O'Herron. Only Alfred Perlman fought the inevitable; he refused to leave his largely symbolic office and threatened a lawsuit if attempts to unseat him were made. In time he too left the Penn Central, which then eliminated the post of vice-chairman.

Now the Penn Central was a creature of the banks and the government. There is an old Wall Street saying to the effect that in times of stringency your creditors become your partners. This was what was happening at the railroad.

Word of the management shake-up had a salutary effect on Penn Central common stock, which closed at 14 the following day, up three-quarters of a point from the previous session, and at its highest point in three weeks. Clearly the news had been interpreted bullishly by many small investors and speculators. The total trading volume that day was slightly more than 7 million shares and Penn Central, with over 250,000 shares changing hands, was the most active stock by a wide margin.

Who was selling? The Penn Central's bankers accounted for one-fifth of the volume, with the Morgan Guaranty alone disposing of 96,500 shares that day. The public thought the railroad was being saved and so went in on the buy side. The politicians meeting in Washington assumed the bankers would cooperate in the recovery effort and program. And so they did—but at the same time as their public actions helped create an optimistic atmosphere which served to push Penn Central stock higher, they sold to the unwary.*

Meanwhile the government undertook the salvage job. The day after the Penn Central revamped its management Volpe and Scott met with ranking GOP congressmen and representatives of the executive branch to discuss proposed legislation. The Volpe plan was as Gorman had outlined it to the Penn Central board. The Penn Central was an exclusive supplier to many defense installations and so qualified for aid under the terms of the Defense Production Act—virtually the same portions cited by the New Haven when it applied for aid prior to the Penn Central merger. Volpe indicated that assistance would have to be granted in the national interest, for to refuse such action would be to paralyze the Northeast and force the closing of defense plants. He asked for government loan guarantees of up to $200 million, noting that this could be done under existing legislation.

The second stage would require congressional action and cooperation from the banks. Volpe recommended passage of a law giving his department the authority to guarantee $750 million in loans to troubled railroads. After passage of this measure, he said, the Defense Department would transfer its $200 million guarantee to Transportation, and then further guarantees would be made—sufficient to save the Penn Central.

Despite some opposition, Volpe's associates agreed to the plan. Democrats were brought into the discussion, and they too went along with the idea. Scott and Senator Warren Magnuson

---

*This operation was quite similar to the stock pools of the 1920s, now illegal. Groups would organize to push stock prices up or down, going in at the low and out at the high, and always at the expense of small investors, speculators, and rival pools. An investigation of the Penn Central stock transactions undertaken two years later indicated that the banks had operated as though organized as a selling pool, but no direct proof of collusion had been presented, and there were no indictments to grand juries. During the next three sessions Morgan Guaranty sold 52,500 Penn Central shares, Continental Illinois 109,450, and Chase Manhattan 90,700. The leaders of all three later swore they were not acting on inside information. *Ibid.* pp. 326 *passim.*

TRADING IN PENN CENTRAL COMMON STOCK IN JUNE 1970

Date	Penn Central Volume	Sales by Penn Central Banks*	Closing Price	Dow-Jones Industrials
June 1	117,008	45,940	$13\frac{1}{4}$	710.36
2	151,921	36,416	$13\frac{1}{4}$	709.61
3	119,478	24,400	14	713.86
4	126,771	49,600	$13\frac{3}{8}$	706.53
5	113,410	31,952	$12\frac{1}{2}$	695.03
8	48,595	4,900	$13\frac{1}{4}$	700.23
9	253,804	98,100	14	700.16
10	258,515	47,825	$12\frac{1}{2}$	694.35
11	117,413	13,700	$12\frac{1}{8}$	684.42
12	399,457	201,150	$11\frac{1}{8}$	684.21
15	151,746	57,100	$10\frac{5}{8}$	687.36
16	114,957	39,500	11	706.26
17	113,086	45,900	$11\frac{3}{4}$	704.68
18	88,783	38,800	$11\frac{1}{8}$	712.69
19	77,786	23,500	$11\frac{1}{8}$	720.43
	2,252,730	436,300		

* Chase Manhattan, Morgan Guaranty, Continental Illinois Bank and Trust, Provident National, Security Pacific, United States Trust, Investors Mutual Fund, Alleghany Corporation.

Source: *The Penn Central Failure,* pp. 317, 326, and *Wall Street Journal,* June 1-22, 1970.

of Washington were to co-sponsor the legislation and as was customary both men indicated confidence the measure would pass by a narrow margin. This resulted in a brief rally on Wall Street. Penn Central stock rose slightly on the bullish news.

Ordinarily, major sellers would have waited until the price stabilized and then tried to unload their holdings gradually. But the banks didn't hesitate. Instead, they sold into the rising market, and to such an extent as to hammer Penn Central common to 12½ on June 10, off a point and a half on the day. Market analysts interpreted this movement as a classic confrontation between bulls and bears, another example of the phenomenon of selling on good news. Only the *Wall Street Journal*—which had broken most of the Penn Central stories—understood that the institutions were heavy sellers, but for the moment didn't comprehend the situation fully. It was a sellers' panic, and one with good cause. For the banks had reason to panic, knowing as they did that the Volpe package had little chance of passing Congress, and that even if it was accepted, action could not be completed in time to save the line.

Congressman George Mahon of Texas quickly put an end to talk of a rapid salvage job. Mahon was chairman of the House Appropriations Committee, a seventy-year-old veteran who had entered the House in 1935. A staunch defender of military expenditures, he also was noted for his antibusiness, antibank, and anti-Eastern proclivities. To him, the Volpe measure involved assistance to all three. Mahon announced that his committee would conduct hearings on the Volpe plan beginning on June 11, but together with other Democrats, the chairman indicated initial opposition to the measure. Without Mahon's support the legislation could not get out of committee. Furthermore, the Defense Department would not grant the Penn Central short-term guarantees, knowing the action would anger such a key congressman.

Mahon's point was simple and easily stated. During the hearings several Treasury Department officials testified as to the willingness of the banks to provide funds contingent upon government guarantees. Undersecretary James Beggs told the committee that Gorman had assembled a consortium of seventy-seven banks committed to providing up to $200 million on that basis. As had others, Beggs sketched the dire circumstances that would accompany default. To this, Mahon replied, "Mr. Secretary, from where I sit, it looks as if we are being asked, or will be asked, to bail out the big banks and the big railroads, and the reason or the excuse for this is that the country cannot afford to let bad business procedures lead to bankruptcy because the bankruptcies might lead to the economic ruination of the country."

Others on the committee said as much, with only slight variations. Jamie Whitten of Mississippi and Robert Sikes of Florida, both of whom had come to the House in 1941, were skeptical of the plan. Whitten didn't believe the situation to be as serious as had been painted; to him it appeared the Penn Central and its bankers wanted a federal handout. Sikes feared the company was about to default, and that the banks would discover some way to oblige the government to pay the $200 million.

Veteran Congressman L. Mendel Rivers of South Carolina—also of the class of 1941—headed the Armed Services Committee. He scheduled hearings, and before they opened told reporters he would oppose Department of Defense guarantees for the Penn Central. So did John Stennis of Mississippi, chairman of the Senate Armed Services Committee. Representative Wright Patman of Texas, seventy-seven years old and in Congress more than four decades, let it be known that his Committee on Banking and Currency would investigate all aspects of the program beginning June 22. The Defense Production Act had been enacted to assist small contractors which dealt with the Defense Department, not a giant railroad which only serviced these firms.

The Volpe program was opposed by old-line southern Democrats, distrustful of eastern business interests in general, railroads and banks in particular. It had been bred into them in youth, and became an article of faith at maturity. Many of these individuals had fathers and grandfathers who had fought on the Confederate side, and who had learned to hate railroads as a symbol of northern domination of the nation. They would not support a Penn Central assistance program. A century after the end of the Civil War, the southern Democrats had a victory over the descendents of Tom Scott and J. Edgar Thomson of the Pennsylvania.

The major banks sent representatives to a meeting held on the morning of June 10. As the southern Democrats indicated their opposition to the Volpe program, the bankers conferred with Federal Reserve officials, and in the end signed a moratorium agreement in which they pledged not to call in loans made to the Penn Central for the next ten days. As far as the general public was concerned, the banks were still wedded to the idea of salvage. But the following day, when the news appeared on the Dow-Jones ticker, the banks sold over 200,000 shares of Penn Central, accounting for half the volume traded. Most of this selling originated at the Chase and Continental Illinois. Ordinarily such sales would have caused a collapse in the stock's price, and that day Penn Central did fall by a point, closing at $11\frac{1}{8}$, while the Dow Industrials was off by only a fraction. But the fact that it held up as well as it did—that there were buyers for such a large number of shares—can be traced to the campaign of optimism continued by the major financial institutions. Most of them had cleaned house by then.

Those congressmen interested in the situation were cognizant of the hectic trading, even though they did not know of its origins at the time. The Defense Department signaled its intentions of granting the loan guarantees, on June 19 at the latest. Patman moved into action a week before. He asked the Penn Central officials to provide him with detailed accounts of the corporation's relationships with its bankers, and he pored over the books with the aid of his staff. This hardly was sufficient time for the job, but from what he was able to uncover Patman concluded that the Penn Central—and before it, the Pennsylvania Railroad—had been manipulated and milked by bankers and insiders. He studied the origins and actions of Penphil, and the acquisition of non-railroad companies by Bevan and Saunders. Throughout his public life, Patman had argued that most of the nation's economic ills emanated from Wall Street, and the Penn Central situation, combined with the selling wave, offered a splendid opportunity to prove his point. He told his committee of his findings, and indicated that there was more to be discovered. Supported by the five senior Democrats, he approached the Defense Department on June 18 and asked for a delay in granting the loan guarantees until after hearings were completed.

This was the situation on the morning of June 19. Penn Central officials believed the Department of Defense was about to grant the loan guarantees. Gorman thought congressional opposition might block the rest of Volpe's program, but was reasonably certain the company was not about to collapse. The bankers had better sources of information. They knew the problem was more complicated and chancy than that, and so continued to empty their trust and other accounts of Penn Central shares. The press and the public believed corporation and government news releases. The Penn Central no longer was front-page news—the fighting in Indochina and talk of forthcoming elections were considered more important that day.

There should have been some suspicion that the situation had not been resolved. A week earlier the Dow Industrials had been below 684, and within five sessions the index rallied sharply, so that it touched 720 the morning of July 19. Yet Penn Central remained steady, at slightly above 11. Of course, the reason it did not participate in the rally was massive selling by financial institutions. The press did not take note of this, but instead tended to follow the story as it emerged from Washington and Philadelphia. And no major newspaper analyzed carefully the political implications of the guarantee and legislation.

Richard Nixon appreciated the politics of the matter even while he may have paid scant attention to the economic details. Actions and statements by southern congressional Democrats had demonstrated there would be careful scrutiny of any aid package. It could become a major consideration in the forthcoming congressional elections, and Nixon wanted a victory that autumn in order to vindicate the policies and programs of his first two years. Losses might result should his administration be branded as unswervingly pro big business.

Nixon knew, too, that implications of wrongdoing resulting from special interests could be drawn from a Penn Central bailout. Several members of his official family had connections with the corporation. Secretary of the Treasury David Kennedy, who had supported the Volpe package, had been head of the Continental Illinois Bank and Trust prior to joining the Cabinet. Secretary of Commerce Maurice Stans had been a partner at a leading brokerage which had recommended and accumulated Penn Central common. Not only had Peter Flanigan been a broker prior to 1969 but his father had served as chairman of the Manufacturers Hanover Trust Company. In fact, the Nixon administration was filled with men who had commercial and investment banking backgrounds, and although none had direct affiliations with the Penn Central, they might easily have been charged with having supported assistance to serve their own financial ends.

Secretary of Defense Melvin Laird could find no important philosophical reason to oppose the Penn Central loan guarantees, but he knew that his relations with the southern Democrats would become strained should they be granted. Laird had come to the Cabinet from Congress, and more than most Nixonians appreciated the implications of their opposition. Patman, Mahon—and especially Rivers—had consistently supported American involvement in Vietnam. Without their work Department of Defense budgets would have been slashed by antiwar senators and representatives. They were powerful friends, not to be angered unless there were overriding reasons to do so. Laird didn't think the Penn Central bailout was that important, and he informed the White House of his feelings on the subject.

Nixon agreed, and the necessary orders went down the line. Volpe was one of the last Cabinet members involved to learn of the decision, an indication of his standing within the administration. On the afternoon of June 19—after the Stock Exchange had closed down for the day—the Department of Defense released the news. It would not guarantee the Penn Central loans. "The Department of Defense considered guaranteeing the loan based on indications from Congressional leaders that legislation could be passed promptly under which the guarantee could be taken over by the Department of Transportation. In the light of growing uncertainty regarding enactment of that legislation, the Department of Defense had declined to make the guarantee." Only three days earlier the President had spoken over television of the need for railroad aid legislation. Now he had backed down. All those involved awaited the expected firestorm of reaction out of New York.

There was none. For weeks it had appeared that a Penn Central collapse would set off a major financial panic. There had been talk of banks and trust companies collapsing like so many dominoes, of economic paralysis, and a major crash in the wings. Those who had been following the Penn Central situation had come to accept all of this as articles of faith. Now that the government had withdrawn from the scene, default appeared inevitable, and, surprisingly, there was no sign of panic that afternoon. It was a Friday—the talk was that Nixon had selected that day in order to give the financial community a weekend during which to recover—and so the crash might be delayed. But the scenario seemed to be set. The market would decline sharply on Monday, with the Penn Central leading the way. Shortly thereafter the corporation would announce its bankruptcy, and that would transform the decline into a panic.

This did not occur. Gorman, O'Herron, and other Penn Central leaders traveled to Washington to confer with Patman on Saturday, and in essence ask him to reconsider his position. They explained that the corporation had current liabilities of close to three-quarters of a billion dollars while current assets stood at less than half a billion. On Monday, $2 million in loans would come due, and another $30 million would be required within the next two weeks. The Penn Central had slightly more than $7 million in cash on hand. Income from operations would not cover the deficit. Without bank aid there would be default, and there could be no assistance from the banks without a federal guarantee.

The congressman was unmovable on this point. He spoke of what he considered to be the evil history of banks and banking, unsound corporate practices, and irresponsibility in high places. Patman was not at all convinced bankruptcy was necessary, or that if it did occur would result in widespread suffering. In effect, he called the Penn Central's bluff, not really caring whether it was one or not.

The board gathered in special session the following day to decide upon its next action. A few members—those who had not been fully apprised of the situation—wanted to make one more effort at winning banker support for loans without federal guarantees; a telephone call to Wriston followed by similar ones to other bankers indicated the hopelessness of such an approach. Others wanted to contact Volpe, not realizing perhaps that the Secretary had lost considerable face in the matter and his power base with the President had been shattered. The calls were made throughout the day. Volpe would talk with the leaders, but there was nothing he could do or even suggest.

In the end, Gorman, Seabrook, and the others were obliged to recommend the filing of a petition under the terms of section 77 of the Bankruptcy Act of 1933, which had been written specifically for the railroads. The Penn Central would not be liquidated. Its assets would not be sold off to satisfy creditors, as might be the case in ordinary bankruptcies. The loan indentures on its equipment bonds would be suspended.* Rather, the line would continue to operate under the direction of the courts, which would function as a receiver and try to maintain services.

Gorman put in one more telephone call, this one to Judge C. William Kraft, Jr., of the United States District Court for Eastern Pennsylvania. The Penn Central's attorney, Carroll Wetzel of the law firm of Dechert, Price & Rhoads, spoke with the judge and informed him of the situation. The papers were being prepared and would be ready for his consideration within a few hours. Kraft understood the procedure, and indicated he would stand by. Then the board reconvened and took the necessary vote, which ratified the decision to seek relief from the courts. That evening, shortly before dinner, the petition was delivered to Judge Kraft at his home, by special messenger. It was signed soon after. With this act, the Penn Central became a ward of the court.

Kraft was familiar with the legal requirements of the situation. Early the following week he would gather the senior judges within his district, and by lot they would select a referee, who would then assume more authority and power over the Penn Central than had ever been exercised by Saunders or Perlman. That was the usual procedure in a bankruptcy case. But of course this was an extraordinary situation. The Penn Central employed over 110,000 workers. It was the tenth largest American corporation in terms of assets. Although some parts of its business had declined since the glory days, others remained strong. Without the railroad there would be industrial paralysis in the Northeast which would quickly spread to other parts of

*Had a true liquidation taken place—had the Penn Central's assets been sold off over a period of time—the shareholders would have received upward of $80 per share after all debts had been paid. To assert that the stockholders wanted a "bailout" from the federal government indicates little comprehension of how finance capitalism actually works. At the time Penn Central common stock was traded at slightly more than $11 per share.

the nation. This could not be allowed to happen. Through designated managers the federal government would have to operate and finance the railroad, and meet deficits, negotiate labor contracts, petition the ICC for rate increases, and make political and economic decisions on abandonments, contracts, and other policies. All the while, the Penn Central would remain legally private, and the shareholders would have rights which would have to be maintained. The situation was unprecedented, at least on this scale. Never before had the national government assumed such power over so huge a private corporation.*

These political, economic, and financial problems were of secondary importance for the moment. News of the Penn Central bankruptcy appeared on the evening television and radio news programs and the story was on the front pages the following morning. The key word was "liquidity." Would the collapse spread to the financial institutions? And if it did, would their stringencies result in a general collapse? What would occur later that week, when the Penn Central employees were to receive their pay checks and several loans came due? Would the government make up the difference, and if not, would this result in layoffs and disruptions? How would the shippers be serviced in the future? What of the Penn Central's relationship with other lines, now that it was a federal ward? Such were the questions asked before the NYSE opened for trading on June 22. As had been anticipated, there were many sell orders on the floor. Alerted to the problem and after a series of consultations, the Exchange decided to suspend trading in the stock until buy and sell orders could be matched, and the specialist could decide at what price the shares would open.

Penn Central common traded at $6\frac{1}{2}$, down $4\frac{5}{8}$ points from the Friday close, a tremendous drop and one that had been anticipated. It remained at that level for the rest of the day, during which 455,000 shares were exchanged. Most of these came from funds of various kinds as well as individuals. Few shares were sold by the Penn Central banks and trust companies, which had disposed of the bulk of their holdings the previous week and month.

*This is not to say that the federal government had no experience in running business operations. The post office alone was many times larger than the Penn Central, in terms of personnel and budget—and deficit. During the Civil War, World War I, and World War II, the federal government regulated many industries and even initiated new corporations, while regulating much of the rest of the economy. At no time, however, did the government actually manage the corporations in the way it would have to do in the Penn Central case. In this respect, the bankruptcy opened a new chapter in the history of American capitalism.

It was a hectic day for the Penn Central specialist, but, to the surprise and relief of others, not for the Exchange itself. Only 8.7 million shares were traded that day, below the monthly average—seven of the fifteen June sessions up to then posted over 10 million shares, and two of these saw more than 15 million shares traded. The Dow Industrials dropped sharply that morning, but recovered in the afternoon, ending the day with a loss of fewer than five points. There was a major decline on Tuesday—the Dow fell eighteen points on a volume of 10.8 million shares—but this was unrelated to the Penn Central failure; in fact, that stock jumped $1\frac{1}{2}$ points to close at $7\frac{5}{8}$. The same situation developed on Wednesday, when the Dow fell another six points while Penn Central common rose $\frac{7}{8}$ of a point to close at $8\frac{1}{2}$. For the week as a whole, the Dow fell more than thirty points to close at 687.84. The brief rally that began in late May had ended, and analysts attributed the decline to the Penn Central bankruptcy. Penn Central itself fell $3\frac{3}{5}$ for the week, closing at $7\frac{1}{2}$, on a heavy volume—1,735,500 shares on the NYSE alone.

There was no panic. Perhaps one might have developed had the news broken in mid-May. There might have been severe distress had the banks indicated they were having trouble, but this did not occur. The Federal Reserve stood guard, awaiting adverse developments, ready to offer assistance should it be required. Volpe and his allies in the Treasury Department were prepared to revive the aid package in the event of a rough transition at the railroad, but it was smooth—with hardly a difference between federal and private control, as far as the shippers and workers were concerned. Instead, Federal Judge John Fullam was selected by lot to referee the situation and help reorganize the railroad and corporation. He in turn named a four-man board of directors, which included one man with railroad experience—Jervis Langdon, Jr., the retired former chairman of the Rock Island and Pacific—and three others.*
With their selection, the Penn Central became what amounted to a federal company, the final stage in the evolution of the railroad and industry, and perhaps the next one in the metamorphosis of American capitalism.

*The other three directors were former Dean of the Harvard Business School George Baker, Richard Bond of Wanamaker's department stores, and former Secretary of Labor W. Willard Wirtz.

XIV

Metamorphosis

Judge Fullam and the four-man board proceeded cautiously, befitting a group of prudent trustees who found themselves in unprecedented circumstances. They weren't certain of the extent of their authority, the role to be played by management, the position of the federal government, the obligations of the states, the status of labor relations, or the rights of stockholders and the banks. Already there was talk of the formation of a stockholders' committee, perhaps several, which would bring suit against Saunders and other administrators, demand an inquiry into accounting practices, and safeguard equity against government actions. The banks had gone to court to prevent management from feeding any more of the Pennsylvania Company assets into the parent company, and the courts agreed with them. Penn Central would be enjoined from shifting funds from one subsidiary to another.

This was a vital point, one that casual readers of newspapers missed, but which was of paramount interest to stockholders, banks, and lawyers, and which troubled the government and the court-appointed board. For embedded in the dead structure of the Penn Central was the solvent Pennsylvania Company, which was expected to show a profit for the year, as it had in the past. All of its common stock was owned by the Pennsylvania New York Central Transportation Company, which in turn was owned by the Penn Central. Legally, these were separate entities. Some of the loans granted the Transportation Company had been collateralized by Pennsylvania Company securities, and so the banks had moved swiftly to protect their interests in that property.

In late June 1970 the bankrupt Penn Central had three major

assets which attracted speculative attention. There was the railroad itself, a decayed giant which owned valuable real estate along its rights of way, and which in time might be made profitable once again. More important, however, was the Pennsylvania Company. There was reason to believe the courts would separate the Transportation Company from the Pennsylvania Company, leaving the latter to the shareholders and placing the railroad under some form of federal receivership, perhaps even nationalizing the operations. If this occurred, the Penn Central shareholders would receive stock in a valuable conglomerate and a near-worthless railroad. But was it really without value? Whatever the government did, the shareholders could claim their interests had been abused, and they could seek recourse in law. Nationalization would prove a bonanza, for then the government would have to pay the shareholders for properties that truly were worthless while the line ran under existing franchises. After accounting and legal manipulations this could come to over $100 a share. Thus the bankrupt corporation did have assets—a potentially successful conglomerate and a series of lawsuits.

The situation was ideal for lawyers and accountants, who in a way were the major legatees of the Penn Central. In the next three years the corporation paid out more than $7 million to two dozen law and accounting firms.

In the summer of 1970 newspapers and magazines offered two explanations for the collapse, and two different sets of solutions to the problem. The first was that the Penn Central had been the victim of poor management, the second that the corporation had crashed as the result of a general decline in railroading.

The former view was simpler and more appealing, especially to those who preferred conspiracy theories to economic and financial analysis. According to it, management had bungled the job, and in such a way as to suggest the need for criminal indictments.* The two railroads never should have been merged as they were, or had been united in the wrong fashion and at the

---

*The indictments did come, for there was much validity to aspects of the conspiracy theory. In September 1974 Bevan and four of his colleagues were charged with conspiracy to misapply over $4 million in Penn Central funds, most in relation to dealings between the corporation and Penphil. The following month Goldman, Sachs & Company was found guilty of having defrauded its customers of some $3 million in the sale of Penn Central commercial paper. Other lawsuits are in the works, so that ultimately the banks and former Penn Central executives may lose parts of their holdings and some of their freedom. See Michael Jenson, *The Financiers* (New York, 1976), chapters 7 and 8.

Metamorphosis 313

wrong time, or were handled badly by men with power in the executive suites. The corporation's assets had been frittered away, manipulated and diverted to non-transportation activities. Congressional investigations exposed the activities of Penphil, unwise loans and advances to shaky subsidiaries, the manipulations by accountants, the ineptness of some managers, the conflict between the Saunders and Perlman factions, and the activities of the banks and trust companies in selling their securities. At the same time, the Securities and Exchange Commission castigated the directors. "Throughout the entire Penn Central debacle, including the loss of many hundreds of millions of dollars by shareholders, the board had done nothing," it concluded. The board failed in two ways, said the SEC. It neglected to create procedures whereby information could be obtained, and later on, members did not respond to specific warnings regarding the true condition of the company. "It is not necessary to say whether the bankruptcy of the Penn Central was caused by mismanagement and malfeasance," thought the Commission. "We can say, however, that during the decline of the Penn Central management acted improperly and engaged in conduct designed to deceive shareholders, and that the directors apparently made no effort to uncover or control this misconduct."

Some believed that with a new management—fresh, clean, efficient, and effective—the Penn Central would be able to fulfill much of its early promise, and, given government aid on a temporary basis, would become a profit maker. Others suggested scrapping the merger. The profitable Metroliner service that ran between Boston and Washington would remain a government operation. The rest of the Transportation Company would be divided between the old Pennsylvania and the New York Central railroads. It had been foolish to combine the two, so it appeared, for no railroad company that size would be expected to operate efficiently, much less at a profit.

Subsequent events indicated this approach was ill-considered. The railroad did get a new management team—in fact, several over the next five years. With government approval the company abandoned rights of way, completed the Perlman program of meshing the two lines, and upgraded additional run-down facilities. In addition, the work force was cut from 95,000 in 1970 to 76,000 in 1975. After having rejected Volpe's recommendations for loan guarantees, the government proceeded to grant the Penn Central close to $150 million over the next five years, pressured creditors to extend their notes, and guaranteed a $100 million bank loan which it knew could never be repaid from corporate profits.

The Penn Central posted a loss of $159 million for the rest of 1970. Then, in 1971, when the economy was recovering and the net income of all American railroads was more than 50 percent above that of the previous year, the corporation recorded a loss of $560 million, or over $23 per share. The line's leaders claimed they had cleaned the stables, that all the deficits hidden by Bevan and his office had been uncovered and revealed, and that this accounted for the dismal showing. But during the next three years the Penn Central lost a total of close to $600 million, and in this period the reporting was supposed to have been "clean."

The Saunders-Perlman-Bevan team might have been inept, inefficient, and, in part at least, even corrupt. But it never racked up losses of this magnitude. Inferior management may have contributed to the Penn Central's bankruptcy, but this was not a major cause for the collapse. With the best of leaders, combined with wholehearted government cooperation, the Penn Central would have been a shaky operation in even the boom years, and would have had to default during a period of economic distress. Unfortunately, the machinations of management, together with the search for scapegoats in the summer of 1970, masked this simple fact of railroading.

In the aftermath of the collapse, when many individuals were eager to find the cause of management failures, it became fashionable to compare the Penn Central's experience with those of foreign railroads. Americans who had traveled on the British Railway noted the trains were cleaner, the schedules maintained, the passengers relatively content, and the crews in good cheer— and the lines reported a profit. In fact, the British lines lost money constantly, the profits being made possible by differences in accounting procedures between the nationalized system and the Penn Central. Too, the British government had permitted the railroad to abandon underutilized trackage—almost half of total mileage of 1945 had been abandoned in the next ten years. As for efficiency, it was true that the key trains—such as those on the London to Liverpool run—ran on time, but the others were in worse shape than the most dismal American lines, with close to half running behind schedule.

Had they used American accounting practices, all of the western European nationalized railroads would have reported deficits for the past ten years; in contrast, the privately owned and operated American railroads outside of the Northeast were quite profitable, and their efficiency far beyond that of most European lines. In 1973, for example, the American railroad industry reported net profits of $319 million. The German Federal Railway, one of the best on the continent, helped maintain its reputation through large-scale expenditures on track and rolling stock, and altogether reported a deficit of close to $2.7 billion. The privately owned Canadian Pacific had a slim profit that year, while the Canadian National Railway reported a loss of $174 million. Those Americans who traveled on Japanese railroads, especially the crack Tokyo to Osaka train, spoke with admiration of its speed, efficiency, and comfort. But it was a money loser, as were the other nationalized Japanese trains, many of which were crowded, run-down, and operated at lower efficiency than their American counterparts. In 1973 the Japanese National Railway posted a $2 billion loss.

By almost all criteria, the American lines were at the top or close to it in efficiency, revenues per passenger and ton mile, and other relevant measures. In other words, there is no convincing evidence that nationalization would resolve America's real and imagined railroad ailments. Still, many individuals who traveled in Europe and Japan, and knew little of profits and losses, spoke of the possibility of learning from their experiences. While it was true that some European and Japanese technologies were in advance of those used in the United States—and that these were most likely to attract the attention of travelers—in most respects American methods were as good as or better than those in use overseas. In fact, some of the advanced switching and scheduling operations practiced by foreign railroads had been based upon the American experiences—including those of the Penn Central.

Railroaders throughout the world recognized this, but the details and even the broad overview remained unknown to political leaders, and these were the kind of people who were coming to power at the Penn Central. This, too, was a result of the belief that the collapse had occurred as a result of management failures, the end product of the decay of free-enterprise capitalism.*

The second approach to understanding the failure—that the Penn Central had been forced to the wall due to the nature of railroading in the post-World War II period—had fewer sup-

*This is not to say, of course, that the railroads were a prime example of free enterprise, or that this had been the atmosphere at any time in their history. Rather it is to say that in the public mind private ownership and free enterprise are sometimes confused and the two terms used interchangeably.

porters among the general public, but was widely held within the industry. Railroaders knew the story by heart—that of a major and vital industry which had been crippled by subsidized competitors and vilified by opponents for crimes committed decades earlier by leaders who had passed on. Still, the industry's statistics were not those of a failing enterprise. Revenues, net income, dividends—all were at post-1945 peaks in the early 1970s, while by some measures the industry was in better shape than it had been in the 1920s. To this, railroaders responded that the records were due to inflationary tendencies, that the lines hadn't been able to keep up with rising costs, and that other yardsticks were more important. Furthermore, the United States had undergone a major boom in the post-war period, one in which the railroad industry hadn't shared.

There was something to be said for this. For example, in 1947 there had been 45 million revenue carloadings in the United States, and of these, 21 million had originated in the Northeast. By 1970 the number of carloadings nationally had declined to 27 million, and in the Northeast, 10 million. But the size of the freight cars had increased in the interim, as had their distances traveled. In 1970, the nation's railroads reported 765,000 million ton miles, against 1947's 655,000, a slight advance considering the size of the economic expansion that had taken place in the period, but an advance nonetheless. In the Northeast, however, the number of ton miles actually declined, going from 295,000 to 255,000. The national figure would rise to 854,000 in 1974, an all-time record, while the statistic for the Northeast declined further, to 249,000. The Northeast did not do as badly in the category of passenger miles. For the nation as a whole, the 1947-1970 decline had been from 46,000 million to 11,000 million, while the Northeast fell from 24,000 million to less than 6,000 million. But most of the Northeast's passengers were commuters, which meant certain deficits for the lines, while the western and southern lines were able to retain at least a portion of the longer-distance travelers, whose trains could be part of a freight carrier and so might show a slight profit.

By any measure, however, the Penn Central was bound to become a deficit operation. In 1970 the line handled 5.6 million carloads of freight. The next year—the first under government supervision and court-ordered control—carloadings fell to 5.2 million, and after a slight recovery, declined to 5.1 million in the recession year of 1974. The coal business remained strong, as did the hauling of ores and other raw materials. Increasingly, however, shippers of manufactured goods turned to trucks and, in some cases, airplanes. The Penn Central's freight revenues continued to follow the business cycle, but at the same time remained in a long-term secular decline. And despite much talk after the arrival of the energy crisis of the need to return to passenger railroads, there was only a slight upturn in this segment of the business.

The western and southern railroads were viable in the 1960s, and most of them remained so in the 1970s as well. But the Northeast was depressed. The collapse of the Penn Central was only the first chapter in the railroad crisis of that part of the nation. In 1969, when the nation's railroads as a whole reported net income of $514 million, the Northeast's lines had a profit of only $21 million, the last ever recorded. During the next five years the industry had net income of $23.7 billion, while the northeastern carriers reported a total deficit of $8.3 billion. The Norfolk and Western and the Chessie remained highly profitable, but the rest of the Northeast was an unqualified financial and operational disaster area by the end of the period. By 1975, the Penn Central had been joined in bankruptcy by the Erie Lackawanna, the Reading, the Lehigh Valley, the Central of New Jersey, the Lehigh and Hudson River, and the Ann Arbor. In early 1975 these seven railroads—which had assets of over $7 billion— were losing money at the rate of $1.5 million per day.

This record was not the result of mismanagement or corruption. Rather it was signal proof that the ailments of which the industry had complained for more than five decades were not fictitious.

Ever since the end of World War II, railroad executives had claimed that most of their problems were caused by the requirement to carry passengers at a less than break-even price. Whenever called upon to defend themselves against charges of inefficiency and antiquated technology, concepts, and methods, industry leaders would cite figures to demonstrate that without the burden of having to transport people most of the companies would do quite well. Freed from passenger business, they said, the railroads would be able to compete successfully with trucks, barges, and airplanes for freight. The collapse of the Penn Central, the largest passenger carrier in the industry, heightened talk of the need to grant subsidies for passenger travel on railroads, or at the least remove this liability from the private sector.

Even while some congressional committees investigated the reasons for the bankruptcy, others studied ways to save the industry, and most of these concentrated upon the passenger business. In 1929, total passenger revenue had reached $874 million, and in 1944, at the height of World War II, the figure peaked at $1.8 billion. For a while revenues remained high; the railroads took in $963 million from passengers in 1947, for example, even while new automobiles and trucks were pouring onto the roads and turnpikes. Then the decline set in, and revenues sank steadily, as did profits. The railroads posted a loss of $9 million on passenger-related travel in 1963, when revenues were $588 million. By 1970, revenues had fallen to $420 million, and direct losses to a quarter of a billion dollars. The deficits were mounting at a geometric rate, with no sign of a slowdown. Clearly, losses of this magnitude could not continue. Congress and the administration had to make the choice of either permitting widespread abandonments and cutbacks or finding some means of helping the commuter and long-distance travelers.

The Nixon administration favored direct aid to the railroads, in the form of grants and loan guarantees, though the position was not carefully thought out. Volpe continued to back his original proposal for help by the Department of Defense and additional assistance through congressional action, but he had little encouragement from the White House, which was more interested in foreign affairs and the international monetary situation. Unwilling to accede to any significant program of direct aid, congressional Democrats spoke of the possibility of nationalizing the defunct lines, and then cooperating with those that remained. For a while there was a stalemate, caused in large part by the White House's belief that any government railroad corporation would prove a boondoggle. In the end there was a compromise that satisfied neither Congress nor the President, and made little sense to most railroaders. On October 30, 1970, Nixon signed a bill creating the National Railroad Passenger Corporation, which initially was known as Railpax but soon after took the title of Amtrak.

Amtrak, which was to go into operation on May 1, 1971, was supposed to bring the railroads together into a consortium, under which they would pool their resources to create a truly national rail service for passengers—the kind of system Robert Young had dreamed about two decades earlier. Congress voted Amtrak an initial appropriation of $40 million, knowing this to be an inadequate sum, but realizing that Nixon would veto the measure if it contained a larger figure. In addition Amtrak had

$100 million in federal loan guarantees and hoped to receive an additional $200 million from the nineteen participating railroads, in the form of cash, advances, and equipment. Penn Central, the key member of the consortium, was to pay $52.4 million over a three-year period. And with this, would no longer have to concern itself with long-distance passenger deficits.

Even while debating the measure, those legislators who understood the industry's problems knew there was little chance for the creation of a viable passenger system. Railroad executives had estimated that it would require upward of a billion dollars just to establish such a service, and most doubted it would ever become profitable. The initial appropriation was only a small fraction of what Amtrak would require—even its supporters knew the sum would enable the agency to become established, and little more. Amtrak ran through this money during its first two months. Despite federal guarantees, the banks refused to lend the corporation more than $45 million in its first year. The participating railroads happily rid themselves of their passenger operations, but proved less eager to commit funds and other resources to the venture.

The new agency was understaffed from the start, and never had the kind of strong leadership such an organization would have needed to succeed. Amtrak's first president, Roger Lewis, had no experience in railroading, but he was adept at dealing with legislators, bureaucrats, and the White House. In 1962 he had taken over at General Dynamics, after that defense-oriented corporation had posted the largest losses in American history to that time. Rather than cut back, Lewis had gambled on obtaining a huge government contract, for the TFX fighter plane. In what was widely considered a superlative lobbying effort he managed to win sufficient support for his team, and so received the contract and saved the corporation. Now he was to use the same skills for Amtrak.

Only four railroads—the Penn Central; the Burlington Northern; the Chicago, Milwaukee, St. Paul and Pacific; and the Canadian-owned Grand Trunk—had signified their intention to join Amtrak by the time the corporation initiated operations on May 1, 1971, and they hadn't sent their representatives to the board. President Nixon had failed to select the public representatives. No one at Amtrak headquarters seemed to know how to proceed or what to do about routing, relations with the private railroads, or the implementation of development programs, one of the more important aspects of which involved the elimination of unprofitable operations. Lewis initially planned to shut down nearly half the nation's passenger trains, and so bypass hundreds of cities and towns he felt no longer required passenger service. The publication of his list of abandonments caused an uproar in Congress, as legislators from cities as large as Cleveland, Ohio, to many small rural towns in the South demanded restoration of services. Even before Amtrak was scheduled to go into operation, Congress voted appropriations of $100,000 to study additional routes that might be established. Senator Vance Hartke of Indiana, who headed the surface transportation subcommittee of the Senate Commerce Committee, thought Amtrak "got off to a poor start, imagewise." Senate Majority Leader Mike Mansfield of Montana observed the abandonments were not legal, since the new board had not been constituted. Representative Harley Staggers of West Virginia, Hartke's counterpart in the House, asked for a reconsideration of the abandonments. In the end changes were made. The Cleveland stops were restored. Indianapolis was made a major Amtrak stop, pleasing Hartke's constituents. Four trains a day were routed through Montana to placate Mansfield, while a special line was set up for Staggers's district. The White House had predicted Amtrak would become a new pork barrel, and so it was, almost from the first.

Operating under these trying conditions, Lewis did manage to eliminate more than half the existing passenger trains in the first year—the number went from 547 to 243. But the corporation was and is a financial failure. In 1972 it went to Congress for an appopriation of $170 million which was supposed to take care of needs until July 1, 1973. There was no assurance that the operation would be profitable by that time. Lewis was discouraged. He was certain the nation wanted and needed passenger trains, and that given time and financial support, Amtrak would prove a profit maker as well.

Some of the statistics bore him out. Amtrak carried 16.6 million passengers in 1972, its first full year of operation, and the number rose to 18.3 million in 1974. During these years, revenue passenger miles went from 3 billion to 4.3 billion, and presently Amtrak accounts for close to half the nation's total, and functions over a 25,000-mile network. Some of the services were quite successful—the New York-to-Washington Metroliners not only showed a profit but cut deeply into the air shuttle business between the two cities.

But the financial results were far worse than had been expected, even by the most gloomy forecasters of 1971. Amtrak lost $600 million on operations during its first four and a half years, all of which had to be provided by government grants. An additional $900 million was spent for equipment, and this came from loans that never will be repaid unless the system is drastically changed. Amtrak's president, Paul Reistrup, who took over from Lewis in 1975, asked Congress for $3 billion to cover expenses for the next five years, and wanted another $1 billion for capital spending exclusive of track improvements, this being paid for by the railroads themselves.

According to its own figures, Amtrak would lose $75 million a year on operations even if all of its seats were paid for, on every one of its trips. Reistrup's ambitious and costly improvement program would add to this deficit; Amtrak estimates 1980 losses on the order of $400 million a year. There seems little doubt that whatever remains of long-distance passenger travel will have to be supported by large-scale federal subsidies. Kenneth Tuggle of the ICC spoke for many interested parties when he pronounced Amtrak "a noble experiment doomed to fail."

Lewis's hopes for a return to passenger trains were not to be realized, even after the advent of the energy crisis and higher gasoline prices. By 1976 trains carried less than 1 percent of all intercity travelers, with airplanes accounting for 10 percent and autos and buses the rest. The train passengers paid an average of 6.7 cents per mile, while costs were 15.4 cents. The difference was made up by government grants, loans, and subsidies. Nor would this change; surveys indicated that almost all the interurban railroad travelers are eldery, infirm, or those fearful of dangers on other means of transportation.

Barring a drastic alteration in the energy situation and the American way of travel, the long-distance trains of the Northeast appear doomed, with only bureaucrats, politicians, a handful of old-timers, and those interested in nostalgia and preservation for its own sake, to fight for their retention and expansion. Yet this combination did manage to achieve a few victories. In late 1975, for example, Amtrak announced the return of the New York to Chicago run, and there was talk of a revival of the glory days when the Twentieth Century and the Broadway Limited were rulers of the route. The new train was to take the Twentieth Century's water level path, through Albany and Buffalo, and then along Lake Erie and on to Chicago in about the same time the old train made the run a half century earlier. But it would not be a luxury trip; the train would consist of an engine, three coaches, a sleeper, a diner, and a baggage car. It was not an economic success, and certainly did not justify the expenses in upgrading roadbeds and equipment.

Amtrak did not solve the railroad industry's passenger-train problem; within a year of its founding it was evident that no agency or plan could accomplish this. But it did manage to shift most of the burden onto government. At the same time, state governments were assuming obligations in the commuter area. The governors, legislatures, and transportation authorities of New York, Connecticut, and Pennsylvania came under voter pressure to preserve and even improve travel to and from their large cities. These states leased Penn Central trackage, paid the corporation subsidies in various forms, and underwrote financial obligations in order to provide commuters with better cars, reliable schedules, and improved roadbeds and stations. The New York Metropolitan Transit Authority even purchased the right of way from the New York City line to Connecticut, paying the Penn Central $7.2 million for the property, which the railroad no longer could afford to maintain in decent shape.

State intervention was not carried out according to a plan, or even a strategy. Rather, discontented commuters demanded relief from elected officials, which in turn was translated into election-year promises. When Governor Nelson Rockefeller pledged to make the state-owned Long Island Railroad "the best commuter line in the country," travelers in Westchester County demanded the same for their Penn Central operation, and the governor obliged with leasebacks and credits. Less than three years after the bankruptcy, the Penn Central's eastern commuter lines were still publicly owned and managed, but they were financially dependent upon the states as well as the federal government.

The Nixon administration had no plan for the eastern railroads in 1970 or 1971. Congress discussed the industry's problems in 1972, but the President was more concerned with his reelection and foreign problems that year, and so did nothing in the transportation area. Secretary Volpe was silent too. Unhappy with his job and eager to leave Washington, he had been promised his long-desired ambassadorship to Italy after the election, and he headed overseas as soon as the ballots were counted.

Claude Brinegar, a petroleum company executive, succeeded Volpe at the Department of Transportation. He had no significant political experience, no direct knowledge of railroads, and no discernible plan to solve outstanding problems. "Brinegar came here with two basic assumptions," remarked a Department of Transportation holdover. "The first was that any institution can be managed if approached properly. The other is that any problem is susceptible to an intellectual solution if enough brainpower is applied."

The assessment proved accurate. Brinegar demonstrated a capacity for hard work, a fine intelligence, and an ability to solve problems. But he still lacked an understanding of railroading and the political ability to get things done outside of his own department. Furthermore, he had come to office on the eve of the Watergate affair. Several key Nixon appointees had been placed in the Transportation Department but worked for the White House—a further indication of the low status of that office in the Nixon years. One of them, Egil Krogh, Jr., was Under Secretary of Transportation. Krogh was under fire almost from the first, and after several months he was obliged to resign his post. This was no great loss, insofar as Krogh had little to do with policy making or implementation. His replacement, John Barnum, was experienced and able, and in most ways a better choice for the position. Still, the taint of Watergate was on the Transportation Department almost from the moment Brinegar took office, and this couldn't help but have an adverse effect upon morale.

Brinegar made it clear that he considered two problems to be paramount. He would attempt to assist urban transportation, and try to find a solution to the northeastern railroad tangle. The former was by far the less complex, and he had some success there, leading a fight to modify the Federal Aid to Highways Bill of 1973 so as to provide $1 billion a year for urban mass transit facilities. The railroad situation would require far more than that, and, realizing it, Brinegar set about educating himself on the nature of the industry.

Before he could do this, however, he had to face a crisis. On January 1, 1973, the Penn Central trustees told Judge Fullam that the line was close to insolvency, and that without massive federal aid would soon be obliged to close down operations. There was a strong implication in their message that nationalization might prove the best—perhaps only—solution to the problem.

The stockholders would have supported what they deemed to have been "the right kind of nationalization," one under which the government would have paid book value for their shares. Doubtless other bankrupted northeastern lines would have lobbied for a federal takeover of their assets too, and under similar terms to those demanded by the Penn Central. The final determination would have come after years of legislation and litigation, while the ultimate price might have run into the billions of dollars. But in the end there could have been created a nationalized system, similar in many respects to the European railroads. Political pressures would have resulted in low charges, high wages, inefficiencies in routing and operations, and promises of reform followed by regular requests for higher subsidies.

The Northeast would have had two kinds of railroads—the large nationalized system and a group of smaller lines operating much as they had in the past. In areas where they overlapped the privately owned railroads would have to compete with the subsidized lines, and of course they could not do so on the basis of price. In the end they too would face financial disaster and ask for inclusion into the federal system, which would spread so as to take over the entire nation. At least this was the fear of industry leaders when they learned of the trustees' report to Judge Fullam.

Up to that time the nation's railroad executives had been content to say little and do nothing about the Penn Central. This reaction had not been due to short-sightedness but rather an awareness of just how complex and dangerous the situation had become, and the difficulties involved in any resolution of the problem. The Association of American Railroads did not want nationalization, for example, but knew the industry leaders would not cooperate in a bailout plan of their own, and wholesale abandonment was out of the question. The Chessie and the Norfolk and Western were particularly interested in remaining on the sidelines, fearing they would be drawn into a regional grouping under private or public auspices and unwilling to take on the burdens of the Penn Central. Little was done in early 1973, despite growing talk of nationalization. Watergate and impeachment were the prime topics of conversation in Washington, not railroads. Perhaps it would blow over.

Astute railroaders sensed that nationalization was a possibility, and that the Penn Central would be without cash in a matter of months at the very most. The AAR discussed the situation, but was unable to come to an agreement. Several ideas were considered, however, in particular one presented by William McDonald, a vice-president of the Union Pacific. Working with that railroad's chairman, Frank Barnett, McDonald had developed a plan whereby the bankrupt lines would be gathered into a single entity which might sell bonds with government support and use the proceeds to rationalize and simplify operations. Such a railroad might not be profitable, but it would not compete with the healthy private lines in the matter of charges. This solution would be cheaper than nationalization, said

McDonald, for there would be less of a pork barrel in private as opposed to public railroading. Stockholders in the bankrupt lines could be offered shares in the new corporation, and indeed might be obliged to accept them. This could result in litigation, but the dangers and costs would have been far less than under nationalization. And in addition to all of these factors, President Nixon soon made it known that he would oppose any nationalization measure. Nixon's powers were under attack, but all involved knew his veto of a nationalization bill would hold.

McDonald's proposal was perhaps the best that might have been expected under the circumstances. It was sketchy, incomplete in details regarding finances, and contained contradictions. This was to have been expected, for it had been put together rapidly and was not meant to be a polished final version. It might have been refined, discussed, and then accepted or discarded later that year or the next were it not for the news from the Penn Central.

There was a short strike in early February 1973, and a month later the trustees told Judge Fullam their position had become untenable, that without further financial aid they would have to resign. Fullam responded in March. He ordered the trustees to cease all operations by October 1 and begin liquidation soon after, unless the government acted to provide aid to the line prior to that date.

This ultimatum stirred both Congress and the private railroaders. A nationalization bill had been prepared for introduction in the House of Representatives and would be placed on the floor unless blocked by the industry. Knowing this, and appreciating the seriousness of the situation and the requirements of time, the AAR moved into action. In effect, it would offer a version of the McDonald proposal as an alternative to nationalization, and would do so before having the opportunity to put it into proper shape.

Barnett was to be the industry's spokesman. In April he presented a version of the McDonald draft to an audience of transportation executives gathered in Washington. It was a complex proposal, the convolutions made necessary by the lack of time to create a harmonious whole. But it did become the industry recommendation, and was viewed as such by members of the House subcommittee on transportation and aeronautics then considering legislation pertaining to the railroad picture in the Northeast.

The subcommittee was chaired by Representative Brock Adams of Washington, a Democrat wary of both industry motives and attempts on the part of the Nixon administration to extend its grasp over railroads. Not certain of which of several drafts to support, Adams tended to be eclectic, seeking some method of reconciling differences. But he did not want nationalization. Nor did he favor an administration draft which would have created a new federal agency—as part of the executive branch—to take over the lines. McDonald and Barnett met with Adams and others on the subcommittee, but had no success in winning converts. In fact, no member was willing to sponsor the measure, which in the end was taken up somewhat reluctantly by Representative Dick Shoup of Montana, a Republican whose district was served by the Union Pacific.

The subcommittee was deadlocked, with all the Republicans except Shoup supporting the administration measure while the Democrats tended to favor nationalization and drafts somewhat similar to the McDonald-Barnett recommendation. Knowing that he had to report a bill before Judge Fullam's deadline, Adams decided to throw his support behind the McDonald-Barnett plan, which then became the Shoup-Adams bill and was reported out of committee. With this, Judge Fullam relented. Somehow the Penn Central scraped together enough money to remain in operation, and it limped through the autumn and winter sessions as Congress discussed railroad legislation in an almost absent-minded fashion, while Watergate continued to occupy center stage.

Intensive lobbying and horse trading followed. The unions were promised special job protection and layoff benefits in return for their support, which was given in late November. President Nixon opposed the measure on the grounds that it was too costly, and indicated he would veto the Shoup-Adams bill should it reach his desk. The measure passed both the House and Senate by wide margins in late December, and what came to be called the Regional Rail Reorganization Act was sent to the White House at year's end. With some reluctance, Nixon signed the measure into law on January 2, 1974. The hastily drawn and considered bill, which had no ardent support in Congress and was a stew for individual interests, now became the foundation for the northeastern railroads. It also marked the next step in the metamorphosis of the Penn Central.

The United States Railway Association—which quickly came to be known by the uncomfortable name of "Usury"—was created under the terms of the Reorganization Act. This agency, which was to be financed by the issuance of $1.5 billion in government-backed bonds, had a single task, that of creating a unified railroad network from the bankrupt lines. To accomplish this, USRA was empowered to slice some 12,000 miles of main track from the 30,000 then in operation. Saunders, Perlman, and their predecessors had spent years pleading for the right to abandon a few hundred miles of underutilized and unprofitable track. One might argue that had they been allowed to cut back where necessary, the Penn Central might have survived, and no government aid would have been required. But the Penn Central had failed, and afterward the government proposed to permit USRA to abandon more trackage than the combined Central and Pennsylvania had operated at the height of their power and reach.

After this was accomplished, the new network was to be turned over to a private railroad company, to be known as the Consolidated Rail Corporation, or "ConRail." Stockholders in the bankrupt lines were to turn their shares over to ConRail, and in return receive stock in the company plus around $1 billion in government-guaranteed bonds. In addition, ConRail was to get well over a half a billion dollars to enable it to begin operations. Another quarter of a billion dollars was to be set aside to compensate laid-off workers, the price paid for union support. The terms were most generous. Those with five or more years of service were to collect their present salaries until reaching the age of sixty-five.

This last clause led critics on the political right to label ConRail a gigantic boondoggle. Those on the left thought the entire Transportation Act to be a prime example of "special interest socialism," while economist John Kenneth Galbraith thought it to be "socialism for the rich." But was it that? Whatever happened, ConRail was certain to be criticized. Should the venture fail it would require further government aid, as much as or more than had been required to keep the Penn Central afloat, and this would lead to congressional investigations. What might occur if ConRail was successful? Then, instead of having to vote new aid packages, Congress might find itself involved in an inquiry as to why the government had spent so much money to assist a private corporation.

In any case, there was no assurance as to what ConRail would do once it was established, or for that matter, whether or not it would ever go into operation, for additional legislation would be required before this could come about. Some experts suggested that ConRail might create several lines rather than try to handle a single operation. Referring to the Penn Central debacle, they argued that the collapse had resulted from the inability of management to direct so vast an empire, and thought ConRail would do well to learn from this example.

A small minority thought ConRail too limited in its vision. The energy crisis would accelerate, they claimed, to the point where American travelers would have to reject the automobile and businessmen the trucks. Turnpikes and superhighways would be abandoned, and there would be a widespread return to waterways and railroads. ConRail should not try to cut back on main track, but under the circumstances increase the mileage in operation in preparation for a new era of transportation based upon old technology.

From the first there was little consideration given to the possibility of developing more than a single railroad, or to reconstituting the old New York Central and the Pennsylvania. Harmony, not competition, was required, thought the leaders of the Railway Association, and even the antitrusters agreed that it would be harmful to have more than one ConRail. As for the idea that the new railroad was mistaken to abandon trackage, this was discredited during the fuel shortages of 1974, when railroad travel failed to expand significantly and freight shipments moved only fractionally higher nationally and on the Penn Central.

The USRA had little trouble rejecting plans, but far more difficulty framing a program and developing a strategy that would satisfy all interested parties. As expected, stockholder suits were filed shortly after passage of the Shoup-Adams bill, as the owners of the bankrupt lines protested plans to remunerate them even before the final figure had been established. Judge Fullam agreed with the shareholders, ruling that the provisions of the Reorganization Act were "not fair and equitable to the estate." As anticipated, these lawsuits had become the major asset of the Penn Central shareholders. Their common stock was selling for around a dollar a share, and became a speculative item on Wall Street. Should the government be obliged to pay a handsome sum for the railroad's assets, the owners would do very well indeed. Major law firms appreciated the situation, and were willing to take cases on a contingency basis. Surveying the scene, one government official remarked, "Every lawyer in Philadelphia has a piece of the action, and he isn't about to let go." As might have been expected, the Penn Central management spent little money on improvements or even maintenance. Why expend shareholders' assets when ConRail can do the job when it takes over? But when would that be?

The work of the USRA proceeded slowly, as the agency picked

its way through a jungle of lawsuits, tried to deal with political complications, and fought the industry's traditional inertia. Those involved with the project justified their deliberateness by noting that they were trying to complete the largest corporate reorganization in history, one that couldn't be accomplished in a matter of a few months. They had started the work of dismantling the railroads, abandoning hundreds of miles of main track each month, and would continue to do so through 1974. Other than that, USRA had little to show for its efforts. It had to act, however, for it operated under a deadline. According to the terms of the legislation, ConRail was scheduled to come into existence on November 9, 1975, unless Congress decided otherwise. So while the legislators considered a variety of measures to implement and fund ConRail, USRA developed a master plan, together with a strategy to put it into place.

It was finally decided that ConRail would initially own all the rights of way used by Amtrak, in addition to the commuter lines in many parts of the Northeast. The new corporation would also take over most of the Penn Central, Ann Arbor, Reading, Lehigh Valley, Central of New Jersey, and Lehigh and Hudson River, as well as a sizable part of the Erie Lackawanna. Altogether the corporation would have some 21,000 miles of track. ConRail was to continue the abandonment effort begun by USRA, and even expand upon it by cutting off 6,000 miles of main track which carried only 2 percent of the railroad's freight and none of its commuters. As for the rest of the Erie Lackawanna, that would be taken up by the Chessie System, which was to become the focus for a second northeastern railroad network.

ConRail came into existence, but the plan did not take effect. In mid-November the new entity moved from Washington to Philadelphia, across the street from the Penn Central headquarters, which it took over in 1976. The advent of ConRail set off another series of lawsuits. In addition, the managers of the bankrupt lines tried to sell off parts of their operations prior to the final takeover, and were sued by the government to prevent such actions.

Meanwhile, Congress debated two plans to implement the Shoup-Adams bill. The critical parts of both measures involved the amounts of money to be paid to stockholders of the bankrupt lines, and the initial appropriation for ConRail. These were tied together, for without acceptable remuneration, the properties could not be transferred, and ConRail could not begin functioning without control of the railroads. The Railway Association suggested the payment of $621 million to the bankrupt lines, arriving at this figure by estimating scrappage value. Some of the bondholders would have received payment had this sum been accepted, but there would have been nothing left for the stockholders, who were bound to protest any but the most outlandish and lavish settlement. For their part, the railroads claimed their net worths to be in the neighborhood of $7 billion. There was no chance that Congress would accept this estimate, but even had it been paid, would there have been funds left for the stockholders? No one cared to answer, due to the contingency nature of legal fees, lawsuits, and related complications.

The resolution of price may take decades of litigation to finally settle, and the spillover could carry over into the next century. In the process law firms, accountants, and various expert witnesses would be enriched, for they would have been compensated out of current income, thus adding to the deficits. Speculation in the shares of Penn Central and the other bankrupts would continue too, and in effect they would become the new scarlet ladies of Wall Street.

Congress debated the final funding measures for ConRail in 1975. Both the House and Senate versions of the implementation legislation provided $2.1 billion for the corporation. The House draft would have added $1.4 billion for rehabilitation of the Boston to New York rail corridor, while the Senate version allocated $3 billion in low-interest loans for the project, with $5 billion in subsidies for other railroad operations. A compromise was worked out, passed both houses of Congress, and was sent to the White House for consideration. For a while it appeared that President Ford would veto it, for, like Nixon, he hadn't a clearly worked out transportation policy, and tended to reject high-cost programs in the name of economy. But on February 5 he did sign into law the Railroad Revitalization and Regulatory Reform Act of 1976, which became the foundation for a new transportation program.

Under the terms of the omnibus legislation ConRail received a new finance committee, consisting of the secretaries of the treasury and of transportation and the chief executive officer of USRA. This committee would control the flow of funds into the quasi-national corporation, and in effect have a veto over actions taken by the board. The corporation was to receive initial government aid of $2.1 billion, and the authorization for the Northeast Corridor was set at $1.75 billion.

Government officials and railroad industry leaders professed enthusiasm for the measure. Stephen Ailes of the American

Association of Railroads called it "the most comprehensive railroad legislation that has been enacted in this century," adding, "at long last [legislation] puts into place a private enterprise solution of the critically important rail transportation problems faced by the Northeast and Midwest as the result of the bankruptcy of the Penn Central and other railroads." Nils Lennartson of the Railway Progress Institute thought the bill was "a major step in one of the most important developments in the nation's transportation history."

Secretary of Transportation William Coleman was deeply involved in the debate as to whether or not the supersonic airliner, the Anglo-French Concorde, would be allowed to land in the United States. He took time out from considering the technology of the future to comment upon the new organization for that of the past. The bill was the "right idea," he thought, in that it did not provide for a "railroad dole." Yet the airlines had been on the dole—the recipient of government largess—ever since they first were organized. As for the Concorde, it could not have been constructed, and would not be able to fly, without substantial aid from both the French and British governments. In any case, Coleman conceded that he was unable to predict the next step in railroading—and he didn't seem to think it worth undo consideration.

With unconscious humor—was he referring to the pocked road beds of the Northeast?—President Ford spoke about the new agency. ConRail "certainly does not have a smooth road ahead," he said, and indicated hope that the legislation would "provide the tools to make the reorganization of the bankrupt railroads a success."

ConRail went into operation on April 1, 1976. The new entity received $2.1 billion from USRA in return for its preferred stock and convertible debentures. The bankrupt northeastern railroads turned over their transportation assets—including some 20,000 miles of track—and in return received 25 million shares of ConRail common stock, 31 million shares of junior preferred, and certificates of value issued by USRA. ConRail also inherited hundreds of lawsuits, the most important being a billion-dollar litigation instituted by the Penn Central Institutional Investors Group, which included most of the creditor banks and insurance companies.

ConRail would dominate rail transportation in the Northeast; every weekday its 100,000 workers would help move 500,000 commuters and intercity travelers and 160,000 carloads of freight. It would be a vital ingredient in the economic health of the region, as its components had been in the past. Could it also be profitable? USRA Chairman Arthur Lewis estimated that the entity would lose a million dollars a day in its first year of operations, but would break even in 1979, and by 1985 show a profit of close to $600 million. No railroad executive or Wall Street financial analyst took him seriously. They knew, as did businessmen and politicians involved in the matter, that whatever the losses, railroading would continue in the Northeast. There was no alternative, and no plans for what in 1977 seemed an inevitable financial failure.

Once more the nation's northeastern railroads lurched forward into unknown territory, without a clearly defined objective, a well-focused strategy, or carefully considered and tested tactics. As had been the case so often in the past, the American businessmen and politicians improvised, without quite comprehending what they would create.

It had been so in the beginning. There was no inspired moment of truth, stroke of genius, or grand design. Instead there was a problem—or to be more precise, a complex of interrelated problems—that demanded attention. Talk, dreams, and empty resolutions no longer satisfied. Action was demanded and, given the circumstances, those in positions to make decisions and carry them out did the best they could. As is the practice in such matters, they explored solutions to old issues for answers to apply to the new ones. In the process they were setting into motion a chain reaction they could not fully comprehend.

Coda

Monumental events—and those perceived as possessing that quality—are supposed to result from important and far-reaching causes. Misunderstandings, accidents, misapprehensions, blunders, and mindless improvisations may intrigue and titillate us, but something within our brains and hearts rejects the notion that they alter the ponderous design of history.

To be sure, we know that wars and revolutions and other major events may be sparked by some minor incident, or even a series of them. While conceding as much, historians go on to indicate that the significant development would have taken place even without the incident. Causes demand effects and preconditions cry for conditions. The catalyst does not cause the reaction, but merely moves the participants into the proper juxtaposition. In the minds of many history is drama, and events are to be fashioned in such a way as to create an elegant play. Where designs do not exist, they must be created. This is not to say that the historian creates individuals or fabricates actions, but rather that he fits both into his preconceived—and at times post-conceived—pattern.

At the time of the Penn Central collapse there was much material from which to create patterns, along with a strong demand for them. It had occurred when both the nation and its economic system were at their post-World War II nadirs. The 1960s had been a period of major economic expansion, during which significant reforms had been put into motion and old abuses were being recognized, rectified, and even ended. It also was a time of political assassinations, social unrest, and a rejection of established values and public morals. To many Americans the new causes and ideas of the time seemed mindless and destructive, while others talked of the birth of countercultures, of a new civilization which rejected the old ways—including capitalism and most forms of materialism. There was the Vietnam War as well, the most divisive and unpopular struggle in a century, and one without a clearly stated purpose or rationale. Armageddon seemed imminent.

Believed to be a major barometer of American capitalism, the stock market peaked and then began an erratic decline in 1969. Wall Streeters experienced a crisis of confidence. By 1970 both the financial and business communities had become more frightened, insecure, and apprehensive than they had been since the early 1930s.

The Penn Central failure took place in the midst of all this. To those journalists who had followed the story and to other students of the business scene, it seemed an omen of sorts, a symbol of what might prove to be a fatal malaise within the American economic system. Many explored the collapse searching for deep, portentous meanings. The suspicion of conspiracy that was in the air in 1970 added spice to the quest, and conspiracy was found at the Penn Central. Thus were confirmed the prejudices of those who were blaming American capitalism for a variety of ills, from racism to the Vietnam War. Such individuals may have been surprised by the bankruptcy, but they also derived some satisfaction from the event. It had a place in their scenario of decline.

Of course, not all Americans thought the Penn Central's collapse worthy of more than passing attention. It had taken place on a crowded national canvas. The failure of a major corporation, no matter how large, was hardly as dramatic as a confrontation in front of the White House, for example, or a war. It could not be pictorialized easily on television. The Penn Central's failure could be understood and appreciated only after study and analysis, and nowadays the railroads lack the glamour and excitement required to command such attention.

This changed somewhat during the energy crisis three years later, when a variety of reformers, usually with little knowledge of the industry, called for a revival of railroads. There was much talk of revamped operations on existing roads and the development of a different kind of railroad technology. For a time it appeared the nation truly might effect a return to the rails. Simultaneously a wave of nostalgia swept the land—perhaps this was a method of escaping what were considered the baleful realities of the 1970s—and railroads had their part in it. Individuals who never had traveled for more than an hour or so on commuter lines spoke glowingly of the good old days when one might take a thousand-mile trip on a sleeper. They mourned the passing of the luxury trains, and purchased replicas of them as well as glossy books on the "golden age" of railroading. But the hopes for a revival were based more upon enthusiasm than an understanding of the American people and economy, while nostalgia for railroads was founded upon what perhaps was an unconscious realization that the age had passed.

As is usually the case, the symbol proved more attractive and probably will be more permanent than the reality. What one team of talented journalists called "the wreck of the Penn Central" seems destined for a place in the mythology of American history. What the assassination of Franz Ferdinand was to World War I and the stock market collapse of October 1929 was to the Great Depression, the bankruptcy of the Penn Central may prove to be for the accelerating evolution of American capitalism in the last quarter of the century.

The men who originated the American railroad industry in the 1820s and 1830s were not geniuses, theoreticians of the national destiny, or even visionaries. They literally did not comprehend the meaning and implications of their actions, were unable to see "the big picture," and did not plan beyond a few years and miles. These men worked within the confines of their own times and institutions, into which they tried to place the new technology. They had been obliged to do so by failures of the old, and not by a belief in railroads as such. In today's terminology these men would be called "problem solvers," and the ability to perform that task has always bestowed a special cachet in American life. Another, more pejorative name for such people is "opportunists," and the railroad pioneers certainly were that. They lacked a basic philosophy of business, a frame of reference, and often even long-range goals and strategies. For them, tactics predominated, the end product was profit, measurable in dollars and status. They were out to serve their own interests, not those of a disembodied muse or a poetic concept of society. Those who succeeded did so by seeking the main chance, adjusting when conditions altered, and by standing prepared to abandon unworkable schemes when necessary. This was possible while the system was fluid, the industry young and pliant, and the investment in time, money, energy, and emotion minimal.

Success required the erection of a structure, however, and

over time loyalties were created and rationales developed. Young men with novel concepts took command, but thirty years later they were old men, and too often their ideas had become outworn, but still were retained. The more complex and permanent the institution, the greater the need to defend and strengthen what should have been discarded as antique and flawed. In almost all successful industries there was an ossified kernel which in time decayed. Large enterprises were not crushed from without as much as they were betrayed by outmoded ideas and principles from within, which usually were petrified versions of what originally had been opportunism.

This was the pattern with most economic ventures. It was highly visible in railroading, perhaps because this was the nation's first big business. The petrifaction could be detected first in the two major founding firms within the industry, the Pennsylvania and the New York Central.

The railroad was accepted and developed once businessmen perceived and suffered from the flaws in canal operations. These artificial waterways had been embraced by farmers and merchants as a means of shipping goods that was superior to the turnpikes. First they supplemented the roads, and then they supplanted them. In a similar fashion, trucks, automobiles, and airplanes supplemented and supplanted the railroad in the twentieth century. The creation of new technologies to replace the old is a familiar enough story, and hardly unusual in transportation. But each of these industries was organized and financed differently, the result of opportunism and problem solving, and therein lay the problem.

In the early nineteenth century transportation in America was based upon natural waterways. The nation was sparsely settled, and the economy dominated by the individual farmer who had little need for transportation and less willingness to pay for the facilities. Merchants and the southern plantation class utilized the oceans and rivers for their businesses, and so the coastal cities expanded while the tobacco, cotton, and indigo farms were located on the banks of rivers or in areas along the coastline.

The mercantile and planter interests recognized the need for better internal transportation and, realizing that small farmers would not construct anything longer than a local road, called upon government to do the job. Alexander Hamilton argued for national transportation, and later on Albert Gallatin took up the cry. Young John C. Calhoun and Henry Clay started to build political careers on the transportation issue. Out of their work and that of their allies came plans for a national turnpike as well as many state roads, some of which were financed by a combination of public funds and private investments. In New York the mercantile community, politicians, and land speculators—often united in the same people—supported plans for a canal that would make New York City the focal point for the western trade by creating a huge waterway running from the Great Lakes to the Atlantic. The state government would sponsor this Erie Canal, while private investors took shares in the enterprise.

The Erie was a huge success, benefiting the state's merchants, opening the western counties to settlement, and returning a large profit. Other eastern states and some in the Midwest rushed to imitate the New York experience. Where private investment capital was available, it was accepted, but in those states where such funds could not be obtained, governments took on the obligation of running the canals.

Thus was evolved a hybrid capitalism. Governments and the private sector cooperated to finance and direct those enterprises relating to the economic infrastructure—turnpikes, canals, and banks, for example—while local businesses were owned and operated by individuals. Did this mean that large-scale, national businesses would become the interest of the federal government? This development might well have taken place were it not for two interrelated events.

The first of these was the election of Andrew Jackson to the Presidency in 1828. Jackson adamantly rejected the intrusion of government into the economy, which he believed destructive of freedom in both sectors. Throughout his administration he opposed those who would unite the two, doing so dramatically in the area of banking and somewhat less so in transportation. He succeeded. The Jacksonian stamp was placed upon national policy. The federal government's early experiments with this form of business partnership came to a halt in the 1830s.

The second event was the financial panic of 1837, which marked the beginning of the nation's first major economic collapse. During the late 1830s and throughout the 1840s many canals went bankrupt, due in part to the overbuilt nature of the industry and also to the shady and shaky financing methods used to raise money. Now the states no longer could afford to finance large enterprises, even had they so desired. What Jacksonianism had done for the federal approach to the economy, the canal bubble accomplished for the states. They too would remain out of the business of owning and operating transportation facilities. Taken together, these two developments helped shape the railroad industry in its formative years.

Most of the early American railroads were state sponsored or owned, as local politicians tried to fit the new technology into the pattern established first by turnpikes and later on by canals. Several of the small railroads in upper New York were privately owned, however. For the most part these had been organized by businessmen and speculators after the counties and the state rejected the notion of erecting feeders into the Erie Canal. Why build a railroad when the waterway was so huge a success? The railroads troubled the politicians, who granted charters obliging the lines to remit sums to the Canal equal to the business diverted therefrom. Hemmed in by restrictions and required to compete on unequal terms with the Erie, these small operations managed to survive, though they were no bonanzas for their shareholders. But they did represent the intrusion of private enterprise into the transportation industry.

A similar situation developed in Pennsylvania, where the state government concentrated upon the creation of a canal-railroad system in the 1830s and 1840s and failed miserably. The state's businessmen knew they needed a transportation link to the West, for unless one were erected, Philadelphia would be crushed under the weight of New York and the Erie. So they organized their own railroad, which in 1846 appeared as the Pennsylvania. The new line was to have a state subsidy, and would have to take over operations of the canal-railroad complex, but for the most part it was to be a private enterprise corporation. Seven years later New York's private lines united with a few public ones to organize the New York Central, also a nongovernment operation.

Shortly after their formative years, then, the first American railroads of any consequence lacked public sponsorship. The economic infrastructure would not be owned and operated by governments after all—this was one of the last and most important legacies of Jacksonianism.

It might have been quite different with a Henry Clay in the White House and no crash or depression. Railroading could have become a public project, or at least developed from a union of the public and private sectors, as had the Erie and a majority of the canals. If this had occurred in the 1830s and 1840s, the western lines too would have been owned and operated by the government or some quasi-governmental agency.

The idea may be somewhat startling, but one should recall that private enterprise was not conceived in the Declaration of Independence or promised by the Constitution. What had begun with the postal service and evolved with the turnpikes, the Bank of the United States, and the canals could have continued with the railroads and then spread into other parts of the economy, and not been confined to the infrastructure. An America with publicly owned transportation, banks, insurance companies, telephone and electric utilities, and radio and television might easily have evolved out of the Hamiltonian vision as augmented by Gallatin and Clay. In their infancies Carnegie Steel, Standard Oil, and other giants might have had federal sponsorship—and at least partial public ownership and control as well.

There were alternate capitalisms available in Jacksonian America, when the railroads were still in their embryonic state. The nation chose one direction of several. Whether or not it was for the best cannot be judged, for there are limits to speculation of this kind. We do know, however, that the creation of privately owned and operated giant businesses resulted in problems in the area of relationships with the public, the work forces, and government. These were not evident when J. Edgar Thomson came to rule the Pennsylvania and Erastus Corning looked upon the New York Central as one of several jewels in his collection. They would dominate public political conversation and debate toward the end of the century, and the questions raised in that period have never been answered completely or satisfactorily.

Free enterprise always implied control by private interests, and private enterprise necessarily had to be free of constant political intervention. This was not a tautology, even though it appears as such, but it does indicate the two terms were and are related to one another. It was an article of faith to the American business community in the four decades following the organization of the Pennsylvania and the Central. But the beliefs were not sacrosanct nor even present at their creations. Rather, these two lines had originated out of a desire to utilize a superior technology and from the hopes of the New York and Philadelphia business communities, each of which tried to control a large portion of the midwestern trade.

Soon both became dominant forces in their regions, their industry, and the nation. The Pennsylvania and the Central were highly profitable, and considered to be pioneers in technology and management. The railroads grew faster than their regions, exploiting all opportunities that came their way and constantly seeking to create new ones. Despite much talk of the great wealth and promise of the trans-Mississippi region, the Northeast and Midwest remained the American heartland in the second half of the nineteenth century, containing most of the nation's factories and grainlands as well as the largest share of its population and almost all of its major cities. It was to be a century of iron, steel, and machines, and the facilities that produced them were in those territories served by the Pennsylvania and the Central. The railroads benefited hugely from this situation and contributed greatly to the region's development.

By the 1880s, however, almost all the virgin territory in the section had been taken and exploited, and the two lines became more involved in competition with one another. This in turn obliged business and political leaders to come to terms with the limits of free enterprise.

Theoreticians of free enterprise admired unbridled competition. It was supposed to lead to low rates and good service to customers, oblige the lines to become more efficient, and weed out uneconomical and inept units. Railroading was a capital-intensive industry, however, and one in which competition might easily prove wasteful to all and result in higher rather than lower rates. Overbuilding was a constant problem in the post-Civil War era. Should a company show profits in a territory, others might enter and charge lower rates. In the end a town that required only a single line might be served by three or four, with each of these reporting losses. True, one might survive and then raise rates again so as to recoup deficits. And then the cycle might be repeated. Who won from such a situation? Socialists and other radical elements saw this flaw in free enterprise and called for the nationalization of railroads. The railroaders and their bankers had the same diagnosis but a different remedy. They created communities of interests, divided territories, and planned consolidations and mergers. Had the Socialists, Populists, or related radical groups captured national leadership at the turn of the century, a government takeover of some kind might have occurred, in which case the American railroad industry would have had the same kinds of benefits and liabilities as those in Europe and Japan. Given their heads, the businessmen and bankers would have erected some kind of rational system, perhaps under the aegis of J.P. Morgan and Company. There would have been a relative handful of lines, each of them dominating its own territory. Rates would be set so as to maximize net income, while losing operations would have been pruned and eventually abandoned. The Socialists would have been obliged to make up deficits caused by low rates from the public purse; the bankers would have extracted this sum from users of the facilities.

Had either of these interest groups obtained power, the United States would have turned its back upon much of the

Jacksonian legacy and sought answers in the economic ideas of Hamilton, Gallatin, and Calhoun—we would have evolved some form of quasi-socialism or economic fascism. But America was not to be controlled by Socialists, Populists, or plutocrats. Rather, the nation chose the paths of reform, one branch symbolized by Theodore Roosevelt, another by Woodrow Wilson, and both dedicated to the idea of free enterprise regulated by governments.

The first reform era of the twentieth century was exciting, but finally accomplished little in the way of essential structural change within the business system. Radicals had spoken of the desirability of nationalizing various parts of the infrastructure, and reformers often agreed with them. Yet the electric utilities remained in private hands despite several experiments with public control by municipalities. Prior to World War I it appeared the telephone industry might be taken over by the federal government, but this effort was diverted, and so that business too remained in the private sector. Wall Street talked of the need for a national bank, to be directed by financiers, while radicals wanted to nationalize banking and then centralize control in Washington. Neither proposal was accepted. Instead the Wilson administration created the Federal Reserve System, itself a compromise, a government organization that was supposed to work with the private banks.

The large railroads wanted regulation, which they saw as a means of halting wasteful competition and harmonizing efforts. In the late nineteenth century the industry's leaders had approved of the idea of an Interstate Commerce Commission. But early in the next century the ICC mounted a campaign against railroads, long the symbol of unbridled plutocracy. The battle was joined, and the ICC was able to hold down rates, reject proposals for abandonments of uneconomical lines, and mergers between ailing competitors. The agency improvised, temporized, mediated, and in the end acted in such a fashion as to leave the industry starved for capital and on the defensive, at a time—the eve of the automobile and aviation ages—when massive funding was necessary for improvements.

Before World War I it seemed inevitable that the passenger auto would successfully challenge the horse and carriage. There was no hint, however, that cars would be able to replace the train. The autos were too fragile for long-distance travel, they had limited capacities, and, most important, the nation lacked the kind of roads the passenger cars and trucks would have required. In contrast, the steam locomotive was at its zenith, while diesels and electrics offered the promise of still greater efficiencies and comfort. According to some scholars, it was possible to travel from New York to Cleveland by trolley cars; the interurbans were still expanding in this period and had loyal passengers. Interurban and urban railroads, combined with major lines like the Pennsylvania and the Central, seemed invulnerable to competition from the early autos. And if the trains couldn't be defeated by them, they hardly could be troubled by airplanes— dangerous, unpredictable, and expensive as their services were bound to be.

Within a generation, however, the automobile and truck had cut deeply into the railroads' passenger and freight businesses, while civil aviation was expanding rapidly. Their growths were made possible by a variety of factors, one of the most important being massive aid from governments on all levels. Municipalities, counties, and states assisted in road and highway construction, and then the federal government joined in as well, in addition to constructing air terminals and providing services and subsidies to civil aviation. Such assistance expanded greatly after World War II, with the advent of the state-sponsored turnpikes and the Federal Highway Program. In this same period Cold War requirements dictated federal aid in various forms to the aviation industry, which in turn helped the airlines.

The railroaders protested against what they considered unfair treatment. They had to maintain roadbeds and stations and pay taxes on both, for example, while automobiles, buses, trucks, and civil aviation didn't have this burden. To this the automobile and aviation defenders responded by noting that the transcontinentals had received construction and land grants. There was some merit in this argument. But in return for the land grants the transcontinentals had to haul government freight and mail at greatly reduced rates, a situation which continued until after World War I, while civil aviation was kept afloat in the 1920s and 1930s by lucrative mail contracts. Furthermore, none of the important eastern railroads had received such assistance. The Central and the Pennsylvania had been organized at a time when government aid and partnership with the private sector was out of favor; the automobile and airplane industries had contrived to effect a subtle, barely recognized return to the philosophy of the pre-Jacksonian era.

Canals and the early turnpikes received government help prior to the advent of the railroad, the automobile and civil aviation afterward. In between there was the railroad. There was no consistency in excluding the railroad from assistance, only the accident of history and the lack of methods to overcome tradition.

From the end of World War II until the Penn Central collapse, there had been only a single federal program to help railroads, one involving loan guarantees of less than $250 million, almost half of which has been repaid. The industry received no tax rebates, grants, or additional services in lieu of grants. In the five years after the bankruptcy, Amtrak alone required $300 million in loan guarantees and a half a billion dollars in direct grants. These are huge sums, but only a small fraction of what had been expended on roads, highways, canal improvements, airport facilities and services, and other forms of assistance to privately owned transportation excluding railroads. These costs came to well over $400 billion in the period since 1952—and more than $175 billion since the appearance of Amtrak.

That the eastern railroads were destined to lose much of their passenger business and a portion of their freight to the new transportation operations was perhaps inevitable. The decline of the railroads need not have been so swift, however, or their defeat so complete. The eastern carriers were crippled without consideration being given as to how they would be replaced, or if the surviving units could perform their tasks given the rules of the game under which they had to play.

Unable to obtain government assistance and led by managers with a defensive point of view, the Pennsylvania and the Central tried to improve their services, even while sinking deeper into debt and facing declining returns on investment. As had been the case in the early part of the century, the solution was consolidation and abandonments. Had these been permitted shortly after World War II—or even as late as the first part of the 1950s—these two giants might have survived, and perhaps returned to a measure of prosperity. But having subsidized rival forms of transportation that caused a loss of business, the government refused to permit the companies to make the necessary adjustments in their operations. With such a situation, it hardly was surprising that the Pennsylvania and the Central reacted as they did—first by seeking unification, and then by diversifying into nonregulated areas of business. Given an appreciation of the complexity of the problem, the nature of the industry, the conditions of the merger, and the national mood of the period— and the benefits of hindsight—one could also understand why the Penn Central was foredoomed to failure.

The collapse was not sudden, but it appeared to be so in New York and Washington. This massive default on the part of private enterprise resulted in the unusual situation whereby one of the nation's major corporations was managed by a federal judge and his appointed board of directors. For five years these men, the Congress, and the White House struggled to create some kind of rational response and program for the Penn Central and the other bankrupt lines of the Northeast. In the end they came up with a hybrid, a unification of public and private enterprise, which none of the parents seems to believe will offer a final solution to the problem.

The process is important, for it is part of a new stage in the evolution of American capitalism. The old ideology of private enterprise was intact in the late nineteenth century. The gospel had changed little in its basic focus from the time of Andrew Jackson to that of William McKinley. Then it survived Socialism and Populism, Progressivism of various kinds, Associationalism in the Republican 1920s and the New Deal, Fair Deal, New Frontier, and Great Society thereafter. Always it had been able to bend, for the institutions and tactics remained flexible, the businessmen imaginative, and the government unwilling to press for radical change. By the late 1960s, however, cracks began to appear at the seams, and failures required new approaches.

Since the collapse of the Penn Central other large-scale American enterprises have indicated their willingness to seek and accept federal intervention. Washington gave Lockheed—the nation's largest military contractor—what it refused to give the Penn Central, a guarantee for a bank loan for a quarter of a billion dollars. At the time the government had some $56 billion in direct loans to private corporations outstanding, as well as guarantees totaling a quarter of a trillion dollars. Soon after, Pan American World Airways and Trans-World Airways ran into trouble and petitioned for similar assistance. Without it, they implied, a federal takeover or the creation of a ConRail-style agency for airlines might be required. The Federal Reserve helped prevent the insolvency of the Franklin National Bank from spreading throughout the financial system, and in the process assumed a greater role in that industry than ever before. Should any major American industrial corporation be faced with the kinds of problems that destroyed the Penn Central, there appears little doubt that aid from Washington would be forthcoming, no matter which party is in power. In the case of bankruptcy, the government would step in and make certain employment was maintained, goods produced, and liquidity assured.

In 1974, in the aftermath of the energy crisis, there was serious talk of whether or not to nationalize the petroleum companies, and the matter continues to be debated. Several of the energy programs currently being discussed envisage a government-private enterprise structure, which will formulate master plans and then implement them. There are other signs of discontent with the present state of free enterprise capitalism. Socialism may still be anathema to a broad part of the American electorate, but nationalization is not, as several polls conducted in the mid-1970s indicate.

There is no clear philosophical base for any of this. The evolution might have dismayed Adam Smith and confused Karl Marx, and the ideological successors of each man have been alarmed by the developments and at a loss to find a rationale for it all. But policy generally has been created and applied on an *ad hoc* basis throughout American history, by improvisors seeking workable solutions rather than a cosmic design. The Penn Central intervention was not the first such salvage job, but it was the most dramatic, the event which forced a major reconsideration of national policies. What the Reconstruction Finance Corporation accomplished on a relatively small scale in the 1930s, Con-Rail and its companion entities for other industries may perform on an expanded level in the 1970s and beyond.

In 1970 the Penn Central bankruptcy was perceived as the failure of a major corporation, and another indication of the decline of American railroading. This was true as far as it went. But the disaster had wider implications, which may provide the battleground for the debate on the issue of government-business relationships into the twenty-first century. Large segments of the private sector have reached dead ends—or at least points which are seen as such. The next step may be the creation or evolution of a corporate socialism, in one of several forms, which over time may become the established norm of the American business system.

Bibliographical Essay

Like most people, historians are more concerned with living and vital institutions that occupy center stage than with those which are declining and lack glamour and excitement. Railroading was in its prime in the second half of the nineteenth century, and there are many excellent volumes covering that period, as well as fine biographies of leaders. There are only a handful for the period after 1910. By then the industry had become a problem, and interest passed from historians to economists. Those historians of transportation who do their work in the twentieth-century period usually concentrate upon the automobile and airplane and ancillary industries. Similarly, textbooks in economic and business history contain sections on the origins of railroading and the great age of the transcontinentals. Most omit discussions of the industry after World War I.

The few worthwhile historical works dealing with this period are to be found in the Bibliography. The best and most useful of these are John Stover's *The Life and Decline of the American Railroad*, and *Main Line to Oblivion* by Robert Carson. The former places the problem in perspective, while Carson's work deals with the situation in New York State. For the post-World War I leaders, only Robert R. Young has been the subject of a full-scale biography, that by Joseph Borkin. As for the Penn Central, there is one book on the subject, Joseph Daughen and Peter Binzen, *The Wreck of the Penn Central*. Both are journalistic in the best sense of the term. Borkin clearly understands and empathizes with his protagonist. Daughen and Binzen are Philadelphia-based journalists who covered the story before and after the collapse. Their book was written shortly after the event, and does not contain information that came out afterward. Little of this, however, would have altered their conclusions by much. Still, the book does lack perspective and does not discuss the railroad problem as such, only that of the Penn Central itself.

The statistical information found in this book came from three sources. The Association of American Railroads' annual volume, *Railroad Facts*, is indispensable for any student of the subject, as are other publications by the Association. While clearly a special interest organization, the AAR has been most cooperative in locating information on railroading, without subjecting me to any but the most subtle propaganda. The annual reports of the Interstate Commerce Commission, beginning in 1887, contain information on other areas of transportation as well as the railroads, along with interesting discussions of the status of the field in any particular year. *Historical Statistics of the United States from Colonial Times to 1957*, together with supplements, is published by the Department of Commerce, and is a useful guide badly in need of revision and updating. Finally, there are *Moody's Manual of Investments, American and Foreign Railroads* (after 1954, *Moody's Transportation Manual*) and *Poor's Railroad Manual*, which contain statistical and historical information for all the railroads discussed here. The 1975 edition of *Moody's* contains an excellent short history of the Penn Central as well.

The newspapers consulted were *The New York Times* and *The Wall Street Journal*. In addition, the old *New York Herald* and *New York Tribune*, along with *The New York Herald-Tribune*, were consulted for the pre-Penn Central period. The *Times* lagged behind the *Journal* in railroad reportage, while the *Journal* was one of the earliest newspapers to understand how serious the situation had become in 1970. On the other hand, *The New York Times Magazine* ran several fine stories on the railroad mess soon after.

BOOKS

Abels, Jules. *The Rockefeller Billions*. New York, 1965.
Adams, Charles F. *Railroads: Their Origins and Problems*. New York, 1893.
Adler, Dorothy. *British Investments in American Railways, 1834-1898*. Charlottesville, 1970.
Albion, R.G. *The Rise of New York Port, 1815-1860*. New Haven, 1939.
Alexander, Edwin. *American Locomotives*. New York, 1950.
———. *The Pennsylvania Railroad*. New York, 1947.

Allen, Frederick Lewis. *The Great Pierpont Morgan*. New York, 1949.
Anderson, James. *The Emergence of the Modern Regulatory State*. Washington, 1962.
Andrews, Wayne. *The Vanderbilt Legend*. New York, 1941.
Athearn, Robert. *Rebel of the Rockies: A History of the Denver and Rio Grande Western*. New Haven, 1962.
Atherton, Lewis. *The Frontier Merchant in Mid-America*. Columbia, Mo., 1939.
Baltzell, E. Digby. *Philadelphia Gentlemen*. Glencoe, 1958.
Barger, Harold. *The Transportation Industries, 1889-1946*. New York, 1951.
Barnard, Daniel. *A Discourse of the Life and Character of Stephen Van Rensselaer*. Albany, 1839.
Beebe, Lucius. *20th Century: The Greatest Train in the World*. Berkeley, 1962.
Benson, Lee. *The Concept of Jacksonian Democracy*. Princeton, 1961.
———. *Merchants, Farmers and Railroads: Railroad Regulation and New York Politics, 1850-1887*. Cambridge, 1955.
Berg, Walter. *Buildings and Structures of American Railroads*. New York, 1900.
Bernstein, Marver. *Regulating Business by Independent Commission*. Princeton, 1955.
Bishop, David. *Railroad Decisions of the Interstate Commerce Commission*. Washington, 1961.
Blaisdell, Thomas. *The Federal Trade Commission*. New York, 1932.
Bogen, Jules. *The Anthracite Railroads: A Study in American Enterprise*. New York, 1927.
Bonbright, James. *Railroad Capitalization: A Study of the Principles of Regulation of Railroad Securities*. New York, 1920.
Borkin, Joseph. *Robert R. Young: The Populist of Wall Street*. New York, 1969.
Brown, Harry. *Transportation Rates and Their Regulation*. New York, 1916.
Bruce, Alfred. *The Steam Locomotive*. New York, 1952.
Brummer, Sidney. *Political History of New York State During the Period of the Civil War*. New York, 1911.
Burgess, George, and Kennedy, Miles. *Centennial History of the Pennsylvania Railroad Company, 1846-1946*. Philadelphia, 1949.
Burt, Nathaniel. *The Perennial Philadelphians*. Boston, 1963.
Caine, Stanley. *The Myth of Progressive Reform*. Madison, 1970.
Campbell, E.G. *The Reorganization of the American Railroad System, 1893-1900*. New York, 1938.
Carr, Albert. *John D. Rockefeller's Secret Weapon*. New York, 1962.
Carson, Clarence. *Throttling the Railroads*. Indianapolis, 1971.

Carson, Robert. *Main Line to Oblivion*. New York, 1971.
Chandler, Alfred D., Jr. *Henry Varnum Poor: Business Editor, Analyst, and Reformer*. Cambridge, 1956.
———, ed. *The Railroads: The Nation's First Big Business*. New York, 1965.
Chase, Franklin. *Syracuse and Its Environs: A History*. New York, 1921.
Cherington, Charles. *The Regulation of Railroad Abandonments*. Cambridge, 1948.
Clark, Victor. *History of Manufactures in the United States, 1607-1860*. 3 vols. Washington, 1929.
Cleveland, Frederick A., and Powell, Fred W. *Railroad Promotion and Capitalization in the United States*. New York, 1909.
Cochran, Thomas. *Railroad Leaders, 1845-1890*. Cambridge, 1953.
Corliss, Carlton. *Main Line of Mid-America*. New York, 1950.
Cunningham, William. *American Railroads: Government Control and Reconstruction Policies*. Chicago, 1922.
Currie, Archibald. *The Grand Trunk Railway of Canada*. Toronto, 1957.
Curtis, James. *The Fox at Bay: Martin Van Buren and the Presidency*. Lexington, Ky., 1970.
Cushman, Robert. *The Independent Regulatory Commissions*. New York, 1941.
Daggett, Stuart. *Principles of Inland Transportation*. New York, 1934.
———. *Railroad Reorganization*. New York, 1908.
Daniels, Winthrop. *American Railroads*. Princeton, 1932.
Daughen, Joseph, and Binzen, Peter. *The Wreck of the Penn Central*. New York, 1971.
Davies, Richard. *The Age of Asphalt*. Philadelphia, 1975.
Dearing, Charles. *American Highway Policies*. Washington, 1942.
Depew, Chauncey M. *My Memories of Eighty Years*. New York, 1924.
Diamond, Sigmund. *The Reputation of the American Businessman*. Cambridge, 1955.
Dixon, Frank. *Railroads and Goverment, 1910-1921*. New York, 1922.
Dunbar, Seymour. *A History of Travel in America*. New York, 1937.
Elliott, Howard. *The Truth About the Railroads*. New York, 1913.
Ellis, David. *Landlords and Farmers in the Hudson-Mohawk Region, 1790-1850*. Ithaca, 1946.
Farrington, S. Kip, Jr. *Railroading from the Rear End*. New York, 1946.
———. *Railroading: The Modern Way*. New York, 1951.
———. *Railroads of Today*. New York, 1949.
Fink, Henry. *Regulation of Railway Rates on Interstate Freight Traffic*. New York, 1905.
Fishlow, Albert. *American Railroads and the Transformation of the Ante-Bellum Economy*. Cambridge, 1965.
Flathman, Richard. *The Public Interest*. New York, 1966.

Fogel, Robert. *Railroads and American Economic Growth: Essays in Econometric History.* Baltimore, 1964.
Fox, Dixon Ryan. *The Decline of Aristocracy in the State of New York.* New York, 1919.
Goodrich, Carter, ed. *Canals and American Economic Development.* New York, 1961.
———. *Government Promotion of American Canals and Railroads, 1800-1890.* New York, 1960.
Grodinsky, Julius. *Jay Gould: His Business Career.* Philadelphia, 1955.
———. *Transcontinental Railway Strategy, 1869-1893.* Philadelphia, 1962.
Hampton, Taylor. *The Nickel Plate Road.* New York, 1947.
Haney, Lewis. *A Congressional History of the Railways of the United States to 1850.* Madison, 1908.
———. *A Congressional History of the Railways of the United States, 1850-1887.* Madison, 1910.
Hare, Jay. *History of the Reading.* Philadelphia, 1966.
Harlow, Alvin. *The Road of the Century.* New York, 1947.
Hartz, Louis. *Economic Policy and Democratic Thought: Pennsylvania, 1776-1860.* Cambridge, 1948.
Healy, Kent. *The Economics of Transportation in America.* New York, 1940.
———. *Electrification in Steam Railroads.* New York, 1929.
Hicks, Frederick, ed. *High Finance in the Sixties.* New Haven, 1929.
Hidy, Ralph, and Hidy, Muriel. *History of Standard Oil Company (New Jersey): Pioneering in Big Business, 1882-1911.* New York, 1955.
Hilton, George, and Due, John. *Electric Interurban Railways in America.* Stanford, 1960.
Hines, Walker. *War History of American Railroads.* New Haven, 1928.
Hinshaw, David. *Stop, Look and Listen: Railroad Transportation in the United States.* New York, 1932.
Holbrook, Stewart. *The Story of American Railroads.* New York, 1947.
Hultgren, Thor. *American Transportation in Prosperity and Depression.* New York, 1948.
Hungerford, Edward. *Men and Iron: The History of the New York Central.* New York, 1938.
———. *Men of Erie.* New York, 1946.
Hurlburt, Archer. *The Cumberland Road.* Cleveland, 1904.
Husband, Joseph. *The Story of the Pullman Car.* Chicago, 1917.
James, Marquis. *The Life of Andrew Jackson.* New York, 1938.
Janeway, Eliot. *The Struggle for Survival.* New Haven, 1951.
Johnson, Emory, and Van Metre, Thurman. *Principles of Railroad Transportation.* New York, 1916.
———. *The Steam Locomotive.* New York, 1942.

Josephson, Matthew. *The Money Lords*. New York, 1972.
Kass, Alvin. *Politics in New York State, 1800-1830*. Syracuse, 1965.
Kennedy, E. D. *The Automobile Industry*. New York, 1941.
Kerr, K. Austin. *American Railroad Politics, 1914-1920*. Pittsburgh, 1968.
Kirkland, Edward. *Industry Comes of Age: Business, Labor, and Public Policy, 1860-1897*. New York, 1961.
———. *Men, Cities, and Transportation: A Study in New England History, 1820-1900*. 2 vols. Cambridge, 1948.
Klein, Philip, and Hoogenboom, Ari. *A History of Pennsylvania*. New York, 1973.
Kohlmeier, Louis. *The Regulators: Watchdog Agencies and the Public Interest*. New York, 1969.
Kolko, Gabriel. *Railroads and Regulation: 1877-1916*. Princeton, 1965.
———. *The Triumph of Conservatism*. New York, 1963.
Lambert, Oscar. *Stephen Belton Elkins*. Pittsburgh, 1955.
Landis, James. *The Administrative Process*. New Haven, 1938.
Lane, Wheaton. *Commodore Vanderbilt: An Epic of the Steam Age*. New York, 1942.
Langstroth, Charles, and Stilz, Wilson. *Railway Cooperation*. Philadelphia, 1899.
Lardner, Dionysius. *Railway Economics*. London, 1850.
Larrabee, William. *The Railroad Question*. New York, 1893.
Latham, Earl. *The Politics of Railroad Coordination, 1933-1936*. Cambridge. 1959.
Laut, Agnes. *The Romance of the Rails*. New York, 1929.
Lazarus, Simon. *The Genteel Populists*. New York, 1974.
Leonard, William. *Railroad Consolidation Under the Transportation Act of 1920*. New York, 1946.
Livingood, James. *The Philadelphia-Baltimore Trade Rivalry, 1780-1860*. New York, 1947.
Lloyd, Henry Demarest. *Wealth Against Commonwealth*. New York, 1894.
Locklin, D. Philip. *Railroad Regulation Since 1920*. New York, 1928.
Lowenthal, Max. *The Investor Pays*. New York, 1933.
MacAvoy, Paul. *The Economic Effects of Regulation*. Cambridge, 1965.
MacAvoy, Paul, ed. *The Crisis of the Regulatory Commissions*. New York, 1970.
McAdoo, William G. *Crowded Years*. New York, 1931.
———. *The Economic Effects of Regulation: The Trunk-Line Railraod Cartels and the Interstate Commerce Commission Before 1900*. Cambridge. 1970.
McGrane, Reginald. *Foreign Bondholders and American State Debts*. New York, 1935.

McKay, Richard. *South Street: A Maritime History of New York.* Riverside, Conn., 1969.
Marshall, David. *Grand Central.* New York, 1946.
Martin, Albro. *Enterprise Denied: Origins of the Decline of American Railroads, 1897-1917.* New York, 1971.
Mazlish, Bruce, ed. *The Railroad and the Space Program.* Cambridge, 1965.
Meeks, Henry. *The Railroad Station: An Architectural History.* New Haven, 1956.
Mencken, August. *The Railroad Passenger Car.* Baltimore, 1957.
Meyer, Balthezar. *History of Transportation in the United States Before 1860.* Washington, 1917.
———. *Railway Legislation in the United States.* New York, 1909.
Meyer, Hugo. *Government Regulation of Railway Routes.* New York, 1905.
Meyer, John, Merton Peck, John Stenason, and Charles Zwick. *The Economics of Competition in the Transportation Industry.* Cambridge, 1959.
Miller, Nathan. *The Enterprise of a Free People.* Ithaca, 1962.
Moody, John. *The Railroad Builders.* New Haven, 1921.
Moore, Thomas. *Freight Transportation Regulation.* Washington, 1972.
Moulton, Harold. *Waterways Versus Railways.* New York, 1926.
Mowbray, A.Q. *Road to Ruin.* Philadelphia, 1969.
Mowry, George. *The Era of Theodore Roosevelt, 1900-1912.* New York, 1958.
Muhlfeld, John. *The Railroad Problem and Its Solution.* New York, 1941.
Myers, Gustavus. *History of the Great American Fortunes.* New York, 1907.
Nelson, James. *Railroad Transportation and Public Policy.* Washington, 1959.
Neu, Irene. *Erastus Corning: Merchant and Financier, 1794-1872.* Ithaca, 1960.
Nevins, Allan. *The Emergence of Modern America, 1865-1878.* New York, 1935.
Noyes, Walter. *American Railroad Rates.* Boston, 1906.
Parsons, Frank. *The Heart of the Railroad Problem.* Boston, 1906.
Pierce, Harry. *Railroads of New York: A Study of Government Aid, 1826-1875.* Cambridge, 1953.
Porter, Glenn. *The Rise of Big Business, 1860-1910.* New York, 1973.
Poor, Henry V. *History of the Railroads and Canals of the United States of America.* New York, 1860.
Pringle, Henry. *Theodore Roosevelt.* New York, 1931.
Rae, John. *The American Automobile.* Chicago, 1965.

———. *Climb to Greatness: The American Aircraft Industry, 1920-1960.* Cambridge, 1968.
———. *The Road and Car in American Life.* Cambridge, 1971.
Reck, Franklin. *On Time: The History of Electro-Motive Division of General Motors Corporation.* Detroit, 1948.
Redlich, Fritz. *History of American Business Leaders: A Series of Studies.* 2 vols. in 1. Ann Arbor, 1940-1951.
Remini, Robert. *Andrew Jackson and the Bank War.* New York, 1967.
———. *Martin Van Buren and the Making of the Democratic Party.* New York, 1959.
Ripley, William Z. *Railroads: Finance and Organization.* New York, 1915.
———, ed. *Railway Problems.* New York, 1907.
Rose, Joseph. *American Wartime Transportation.* New York, 1953.
Sakolski, A.M. *American Railroad Economics.* New York, 1913.
Sarnoff, Paul. *Russell Sage: The Money King.* New York, 1965.
Satterlee, Herbert. *J. Pierpont Morgan: An Intimate Portrait.* New York, 1940.
Schotter, H.W. *The Growth and Development of the Pennsylvania Railroad Company.* Philadelphia, 1927.
Schubert, Glendon. *The Public Interest.* Glencoe, 1960.
Sellers, Charles, ed. *Andrew Jackson: A Profile.* New York, 1971.
Sharfman, I. Leo. *The American Railroad Problem.* New York, 1921.
———. *The Interstate Commerce Commission.* 2 vols. New York, 1931.
———. *Railway Regulation.* Chicago, 1915.
Sharp, James. *The Jacksonians versus the Banks.* New York, 1970.
Shaw, Ronald. *Erie Water West.* Lexington, Ky., 1966.
Shott, John. *The Railroad Monopoly.* Washington, 1950.
Sinclair, Angus. *Development of the Locomotive Engine.* New York, 1907.
Smith, Arthur. *Commodore Vanderbilt: An Epic of American Achievement.* New York, 1927.
Snyder, Carl. *American Railways as Investments.* New York, 1907.
Sobel, Robert. *The Entrepreneurs.* New York, 1975.
Sorrell, Lewis. *Government Ownership and Operation of Railways for the United States.* New York, 1937.
Southerland, Thomas, and McCleery, William. *The Way to Go.* New York, 1973.
Sowers, Don. *The Financial History of New York State from 1789 to 1912.* New York, 1914.
Spann, Edward. *Ideals and Politics: New York Intellectuals and Liberal Democracy, 1820-1880.* Albany, 1972.
Spearman, Frank. *The Strategy of the Great Railroads.* New York, 1904.
Starr, John Jr. *One Hundred Years of American Railroading.* New York, 1928.

Stevens, Frank. *The Beginnings of the New York Central Railroad.* New York, 1926.
Stevens, Martin. *Steel Trails: The Epic of the Railroads.* New York, 1933.
Stickney, A.B. *The Railway Problem.* St. Paul, Minn., 1891.
Stover, John. *American Railroads.* Chicago, 1961.
———. *The Life and Decline of the American Railroad.* New York, 1970.
Tarbell, Ida. *A History of the Standard Oil Company.* 2 vols. New York, 1904.
Taylor, George. *The Transportation Revolution: 1815-1860.* New York, 1951.
———, and Neu, Irene. *The American Railroad Network, 1861-1890.* Cambridge, 1856.
Taylor, William. *A Productive Monopoly.* Providence, R.I., 1970.
Temin, Peter. *The Jacksonian Economy.* New York, 1969.
Thompson, Slason. *A Short History of American Railways.* New York, 1925.
Turner, Charles. *Chessie's Road.* New York, 1956.
Tyler, Poyntz, ed. *Outlook for the Railroads.* New York, 1960.
Ulmer, M.J. *Capital in Transportation, Communications, and Public Utilities.* Princeton, 1960.
Van Deusen, Glyndon. *Thurlow Weed: Wizard of the Lobby.* Boston, 1947.
Van Zandt, Roland. *Chronicles of the Hudson.* New Brunswick, 1971.
Wall, Joseph. *Andrew Carnegie.* New York, 1970.
Wall Street Journal. Riding the Pennsy to Ruin. New York, 1971.
Weed, Thurlow. *The Autobiography of Thurlow Weed.* Boston, 1883.
Whitaker, Rogers, and Hiss, Anthony. *All Aboard with E.M. Frimbo.* New York, 1974.
Wiebe, Robert. *Businessmen and Reform.* Cambridge, 1962.
Wilburn, Jean. *Biddle's Bank: The Crucial Years.* New York, 1967.
Wilson, William. *History of the Pennsylvania Railroad Company.* 2 vols. Philadelphia, 1895.

PERIODICALS

American Railroad Journal
American Railway Wage
Barron's
Business History Review
Business Week
Dun's Review
Economic History Review
Forbes
Fortune
Harvard Business Review
Harvard Law Review
Newsweek
Quarterly Review of Economics
Railroadians of America
Railway Age
Time
Trains

GOVERNMENT PUBLICATIONS

United States. Bureau of the Census. *Statistical Report of the Railroads of the United States* by Armin Shuman. Washington, 1883.

United States. Congress. Senate. 59th Cong. 1st Sess. Committee on Interstate Commerce. *Regulation of Railway Rates.* 6 vols. Washington, 1906.

United States. Interstate Commerce Commission. *Activities of the Interstate Commerce Commission, 1887-1937.* Washington, 1937.

United States. Federal Coordinator of Transportation. *Public Aids to Transportation.* 4 vols. Washington, 1938-1940.

United States. Congress. Senate. *Special Study Group on Transportation Policies in the United States.* Washington, 1961.

United States. Congress. Senate. 87th Cong. 2nd Sess. Committee on the Judiciary. *Hearings Before the Subcommittee on Antitrust and Monopoly: Rail Merger Legislation.* Washington, 1962.

United States. Congress. House of Representatives. 92nd Cong. 1st Sess. Committee on Interstate and Foreign Commerce. *The Financial Collapse of the Penn Central.* Washington, 1972.

United States. Congress. House of Representatives. 92nd Cong. 1st Sess. *Staff Report of the Committee on Banking and Currency: The Penn Central Failure and the Role of Financial Institutions.* Washington, 1972.

OTHER

Annual Reports of the Pennsylvania, New York Central, Norfolk and Western, Erie-Lackawanna, Chesapeake and Ohio, Baltimore and Ohio, and Penn Central Railroads.

Index

Adams, John Quincy, 7, 9, 10, 46, 109
Adams, Brock, 325–326
Adamson Eight-Hour Act of 1916, 107
Agnew, Spiro, 291
Ailes, Stephen, 330–331
Airline industry, growth of, 204
Airmail service, beginning of, 120
Akron, Canton and Youngstown Railroad, 239
Albany City Bank, 39
Albany Iron Works, 38, 40, 41, 42
Albany Nail Factory, 38
Albany and Schenectady Railroad, 37
Albany and Schenectady Turnpike Company, 16–17
Albany and West Stockbridge Railroad, 51
Allegheny Company, 126, 174, 175–176, 177–178, 182, 199–200, 203, 238
   Young's control of, 176–182, 183, 209–210, 220
Allied Properties Company, 261
Altona Railroad, 125
American Contract and Trust Company, 129
American Notes (Dickens), 24
American Railroad Economics (Sakolski), 103
American Railroad Politics, 1914–1920 (Kerr), 108
American Railway Association, 132
American Railways as Investment (Snyder), 99
American Telephone and Telegraph, 256, 281

Amtrak, x, 318–322, 343
   Congressional appropriations for, 320, 321
   formation of, 318–319
   New York to Chicago run, 321
Andrews, Wayne, 59
Ann Arbor Railroad, 329
   in bankruptcy, 317
Annenberg, Walter, 254
Anti-Semitism, 214
Anti-Trust Division (U.S. Department of Justice), 181–182, 185
Appropriations Committee (House of Representatives), 303
Armour and Company, 256
Arnold, Thurman, 181–182, 183–184, 185
Arnold and Wiprud (law firm), 185
Aronson, Jacob, 200
Arvida Corporation, 248, 258
Association of American Railroads, ix, 142, 147, 163–164, 271, 324, 325, 330–331
Astor, John Jacob, 17, 18
Atchison, Topeka and Santa Fe Railroad, 80, 131
Atterbury, William W., 132, 134–135, 136–137
Attica and Buffalo Railroad, 19, 20
Auburn and Rochester Railroad, 19, 20
Auburn and Syracuse Railroad, 19, 20
Aurora Railroad, 43
Automobile industry, growth of, 204, 205
Ayres, Colonel L. P., 175–176

Baker, George, 310
Ball, George, 175–176, 177, 178, 179, 182, 194
Baltimore and Ohio Railroad (B&O), 20–21, 26, 27, 45, 80, 85, 86, 87, 88, 91, 102, 109, 114, 145
  acquisition program, 85
  income and revenues (1958), 226
  merger negotiations (1950s–1960s), 225–229, 232–234, 238, 239, 240
  New York City Convention (1854), 45
  organized, 14
  Pennsylvania Railroad and, 26, 27, 28, 34
    rivalry, 63
  post-war period (World War I), 124
  rate wars, 75, 77
Baltimore and Potomac Railroad, 63
Bank of the United States, 10–11, 12, 25, 39, 338–339
Barclay Hotel (New York City), 192
Baring Brothers (banking house), 58
Barnett, Frank, 324, 326
Barnum, John, 323
Beebe, Lucius, 96
Beggs, James, 294
Beginnings of the New York Central Railroad, The (Stevens), 16
Bessemer steel process, 36
Bevan, David, 258–259, 260–270, 275–276, 279, 282–287, 289, 292–295, 297, 298, 299, 314
Biddle, Nicholas, 10, 11
Biddle, Thomas, 11
Biltmore Hotel (New York City), 192
Blachford, Richard, 54
Blackstone Canal, 11
Boles, C. E., 188, 201, 203
Bond, Richard, 310
Borkin, Joseph, 202, 209
Boston and Albany Railroad, 55, 88, 251
Boston and Maine Railroad, 125
Boston and Worcester Railroad, 44
Bowman, Robert, 200, 212
Brinegar, Claude, 322–323
Broad Street Station (Philadelphia), 245
Broadway Limited, 95, 96, 103, 119, 144, 155, 321
  running time of, 98

World War I, 117
Brown, William, 104–105
Bryant Ranch, 267
Buckeye Pipe Line Company, 247, 258, 262, 280, 292
Budd, Ralph, 156, 157, 212
Buffalo Interurban Bus Lines, 130
Buffalo and Lockport Railroad, 19, 37
Buffalo and Rochester Railroad, 19, 37
Buffalo and State Line Railroad, 43
Buffalo and Susquehanna Railroad, 125
Burgess, George H., 28, 63
Burlington Railroad, 135, 212, 319
Burns, Arthur, 278, 294, 295
Business History Review, 28
Butcher, Howard, III, 261, 263
Butcher and Sherrerd (investment firm), 261

Cabot, Louis, 284, 297
Cabot Corporation, 297
Calhoun, John C., 4, 336, 341
California gold rush of 1849, 51
Callaway, Samuel, 83
Cambreling, Churchill C., 18, 19
Camden and Amboy Railroad, 29, 53
Campbell, E.G., 82
Canada Southern Railroad, 60
Canadian National Railways, 147, 315
Canadian Pacific Railroad, 315
Canal Fund (New York), 5, 11–12
Canal system, 1–14, 165–166, 338, 342
  barge speeds, 12
  cargo hauls, 15–16, 25
  foreign investors in, 11–12
  stock issues, 12
  technologies of, 13–14
  toll revenues, 2, 6
  See also names of canals
Carnegie, Andrew, x, 61, 71–72, 76, 79, 84, 86
Carnegie, McCandless and Company, 72
Carnegie Steel Corporation, 339
Cassatt, Alexander J., 82–88, 90–92, 98–99, 102, 136, 228, 229
Cassatt, Mary, 87
Centennial History of the Pennsylvania Railroad Company (Burgess and Kennedy), 28

Central Greyhound, 192
Central Military Tract Railroad, 43
Central Railroad of New Jersey, 80, 135, 329
Chandler, Alfred D., Jr., 47
Chapin, Roy, 119
Chatham Hotel (New York City), 192
Cherington, Charles R., 150
Chesapeake Company, 174
Chesapeake and Ohio Canal Company, 6–7, 9
Chesapeake and Ohio Railroad (C&O), 77, 84–85, 86, 125, 152, 176, 177, 179, 181, 182, 187, 198, 199, 203, 207, 212
  merger negotiations (1950s–1960s), 226–229, 232–233, 234, 238, 239, 240
Chicago, Burlington and Quincy Railroad, 43, 61, 245
Chicago Columbian Exposition of 1893, 94
Chicago and Eastern Illinois Railroad, 125
Chicago, Milwaukee, St. Paul and Pacific Railroad, 319
Chicago and Northwestern Railroad, 102, 193
Civil War, 31, 32, 33, 34, 35, 44, 63, 72, 107, 109, 309
Clark, Horace, 56, 57, 58
Clay, Henry, 4, 9, 10, 109, 336, 338, 339
Clayton Anti-Trust Act, 200
Clement, Martin, 146, 159, 160, 186
Cleveland, Grover, 80
Clinton, Governor DeWitt, 4, 5, 7, 165, 166
Cochran, Thomas, 41
Coleman, William, 331
Commerce Committee (U.S. Senate), 320
Commercial and Financial Chronicle, 78, 91
Committee on Interstate and Foreign Commerce (House of Representatives), 122
Committee on Interstate and Foreign Commerce (U.S. Senate), 221
Commodore Hotel (New York City), 192
Connecticut Turnpike, 252

ConRail (Consolidated Rail Corporation), x, 327–332
Continental Mortgage Investors, 259
Cooley, Thomas, 80
Cope, Thomas, 28
Corning, Erastus, 19, 38–46, 61, 71, 167, 193, 211, 249, 339
  compared to Vanderbilt (Commodore), 49–50, 51
Corning, N.Y., 39
Corning and Company, 38–39, 40–41
Corsair (yacht), 74
Corsair Agreement of 1885, 74–75, 77, 78
Council of Economic Advisors, 250
Council of National Defense (World War II), 156
County, A.J., 146
County Plan, 146
Crawford, D.A., 185
Croffut, W.A., 53
Crowley, Patrick, 132
Cumberland Road, 7
Curtis Aeroplane Company, 131

Da Vinci, Leonardo, 14
Daniels, George, 94–95
Davis, Arthur Vining, 248
Day, William, 284
Dechert, Price & Rhoads (law firm), 308
Defense Production Act, 252, 301, 304
Delaware and Hudson Canal, 12
Delaware and Hudson Railroad, 80, 88
Delaware, Lackawanna and Western Railroad, 207, 225
Denver and Rio Grande Western Railroad, 212–214, 215, 260
  modernization program (1946), 213
Depew, Chauncey M., 62, 73–74, 76, 77, 78, 83, 88, 89, 90
Depression of 1930s, 127, 136, 141, 144, 148, 150, 152, 171, 174, 204, 216, 335
Depression of 1840, 13
Detroit, Toledo and Ironton Railroad, 125, 273
Dickens, Charles, 23–25
Disneyland, 247
Dow Jones Railroad Average, 97
Dow-Jones Railroad Index, 128

Index

Drew, Daniel, 43, 50, 51, 52, 54, 56, 62,.99
Drexel, Morgan and Company, 60
Du Pont and Company (E.I.), 176, 177, 178
Duane, James, 17
Durrenberger, Joseph, 3

Eastman, Joseph, 145–146, 147, 157
Eaton, Cyrus, 180, 194, 203, 207, 226
Economic Stabilization Act of 1970, 278
Eisenhower, Dwight D., 216, 221, 222, 277, 278
Electro-Motive Division (General Motors Corporation), 142
Elkins Act of 1903, 89
Emergency Transportation Act of 1933, 145, 149
Enterprise Denied (Martin), 105
Erastus Corning (Neu), 49
Erie Canal, 8, 9, 13, 15–16, 17, 18, 19, 21, 25, 26, 33, 38, 53, 68, 94, 128, 150, 165–166, 167, 190, 193, 221, 338
  barge speeds, 15
  construction of, 4–5
  success of, 7, 337
Erie Railroad, 21, 25, 36, 45, 52, 56, 72, 77, 78, 80, 87, 99, 109, 114
  freight operations (1958), 224
  merger negotiations (1950s–1960s), 224–225, 227, 232
  rate war (1867), 56
  reputation of (1865), 50–51
"Erie Wars," 52
Erie-Lackawanna Railroad, 225, 240, 250, 329
  in bankruptcy, 317
Esch-Cummins Act of 1920, 123
Evans, Oliver, 14, 15
Executive Jet Aviation Company, 248

Fair Deal program, 344
Fargo, William, 54, 55, 56, 57
Farm Loan Bank, 111
Featherbedding, 151–152, 191
Featherstonhaugh, George, 16–17
Federal Aid Road Act of 1916, 119
Federal Control Act, 113
Federal Highway Act of 1921, 119
Federal Highway Act of 1944, 205

Federal Highway Program, 342
Federal Possession and Control Act of 1917, 110–111
Federal Reserve System, 294, 310, 344
Financial Collapse of the Penn Central, The, 267, 284
Financiers, The (Jenson), 312
Fink, Albert, 75, 77–78, 79, 80
Firestone Company, 256
Fish, Nicholas, 17, 18
Fishlow, Albert, 164
Fisk, Jim, 50, 51, 52
Flanigan, Peter, 294, 306
Flannery, Robert, 273, 274
Fogel, Robert, 164
Ford, Henry, 120, 216
Franklin Institute, 29
Frick, Henry Clay, 102
Fullam, John, 310, 311, 324, 325, 326

Gallatin, Albert, 4, 46, 109, 336, 339, 341
Gateway Center, 246
General Motors Corporation, 142, 176, 177, 178, 180, 181, 256, 271–272
General Securities Company, 174
Gengras, E. Clayton, 283, 297–298, 299
Georgia Railroad, 29
German Federal Railways, 315
Glore, Forgan, Salomon Brothers & Hutzler (underwriters), 286
Glore, Forgan, Wm. R. Staats, Inc., 259
Goldman, Sachs & Company, 312
Gorman, Paul, 281–282, 284, 285–286, 297, 303, 305, 307, 308
Goshen *Independent Republican*, 19
Gould, George, 86, 125
Gould, Jay, 50, 51, 52, 56
Grainger, Isaac, 261
Grand Central Depot (New York City), 57–58
Grand Central Station, 86, 95–96, 161, 188, 192, 210
Grand Trunk of Canada, 21, 75, 319
Granite Railroad, 14
Great Depression, *see* Depression of 1930s
Great Society program, 344

Great Southwest Corporation, 247, 258, 259, 262, 270, 280
Great Strike of 1877, 75, 78
Great Western Railroad, 42–43
Greyhound Corporation, 130
Grodinsky, Julius, 67
Guaranty Trust Company, 101–102, 174, 175, 179, 181, 182
Guthrie, Randolph, 294
Gulf and Western Company, 246, 257

Haley, William, 26
Halsey, Stuart and Company, 180, 181
Hamilton, Alexander, 336, 341
Hanley, Edward, 298
Harlow, Alvin F., 41
Harper's Weekly, 42
Harriman, E. H., 68, 86, 101, 102, 109, 145, 211, 212
Hartke, Vance, 320
Haupt, Herman, 31
Hawley, Gideon, 19
Hayes, Rutherford B., 79–80
Heineman, Ben, 246
Hepburn Act of 1906, 90, 91, 97
Highway Transport Committee (World War I), 119
Hill, James, 68, 100, 109, 211, 212, 234
Hodge, Charles, 259, 281
Hoover, Herbert, 146, 208, 281
Housatonic Railroad, 55
Hudson and Manhattan Railroad Company, 111
Hudson River Railroad, 20, 21, 38, 49, 50, 51, 55, 56
  in bankruptcy, 317
  merger of (1869), 57
  organized, 52–53
Hudson River West Shore Railroad, 73

Illinois Central Railroad, 282
Indiana Republican (newspaper), 26
Indiana State Toll Highway, 206
International Bank for Reconstruction and Development, 268
International Business Machines Corporation (IBM), 256
International Telephone and Telegraph, 246, 257

International Utilities Corporation, 261
Interstate Commerce Act of 1877, 79–80, 83, 200
Interstate Commerce Commission (ICC), 68, 83, 87, 89–90, 97, 104, 105–106, 107–108, 109, 110, 113, 117, 169, 174, 177, 178, 182, 187–188, 199, 200, 203, 207, 213, 215, 321, 341
  decline of railroads and, 142, 143, 144, 148, 150, 159
  Penn Central operations and, 267, 268, 269, 277, 280, 284, 286, 287, 309
  post-war period (World War I), 121, 122, 123, 125–127, 129, 130
  railroad merger negotiations and, 222, 223, 225, 228, 230, 233, 235, 238, 239, 244, 251, 252, 254
  Young hearings (1948), 200–202, 203
Isthmus of Panama, 51

Jackson, Andrew, 7–11, 12, 25, 36, 39, 46, 109, 149, 337, 344
  Maysville veto, 10–11
Jacksonian Democracy, 8, 27, 166, 167, 341
Japanese National Railways, 315
Jay, Peter, 18
Jenson, Michael, 312
Johnson, Lyndon B., 254, 255, 280
Joint Executive Committee, 79
Joint Traffic Association of 1894, 83–84
Jones, Casey, 120
Journal of Economic History, 164
Joy, James, 56, 58

Kaneb Pipeline Company, 259
Keep, Henry ("Henry the Silent"), 54–55, 56, 57, 58
Kefauver, Estes, 250
Kelly Act of 1925, 120
Kenefec, John, 272–273
Kennedy, David, 293, 294, 295, 297, 306
Kennedy, John F., 238, 240, 253–254
Kennedy, Miles C., 28, 63
Kennedy, Robert F., 255
Kerr, K. Austin, 108

Keyserling, Leon, 250
King, Martin Luther, 255
Kirby, Allen, 177, 178, 179, 203, 260
Kirby, Fred, 284
Kissam, William, 56
Knox, Seymour, 261, 298
Kolbe, Frank, 176
Kolko, Gabriel, 78
Korean War, 205, 208, 277
Kraft, C. William, Jr., 308
Kreyling, Edward, Jr., 282
Krogh, Egil, Jr., 323
Kuhn, Loeb and Company, 82, 84, 145

Lackawanna Railroad, 88, 124, 134
Laird, Melvin, 306
Lake Erie and Western Railroad, 124
Lake Shore Railroad, 43, 58, 85, 88, 101
Lake Shore and Michigan Southern Railroad, 58, 61, 62
Lamont, Thomas, 174, 179, 181, 215
Lancaster Turnpike, 2
Langdon, Jervis, Jr., 310
Large, Henry, 274, 275, 276, 282
Lawrence, Governor David, 253
Lehigh and Hudson Railroad, 329
Lehigh Valley Railroad, 80, 89, 125, 126, 127, 329
  in bankruptcy, 317
  request to become an all-freight carrier, 223
Lennartson, Nils, 331
Leonard, William N., 126, 250–251
Lewis, Arthur, 332
Lewis, Roger, 319–320, 321
Lincoln, Abraham, 88
Lindbergh, Charles, 120, 131
Ling, James, 193
Ling-Temco-Vought Corporation, 246
Lockheed Aircraft Corporation, 344
Lockwood, LeGrand, 54, 58
Long Island Railroad, 86, 134, 154, 229, 237, 248, 322
Louisville and Nashville Railroad, 75
Louisville and Portland Canal, 9
Litton Industries, 246, 257
Lunding, Franklin, 298

McAdoo, William Gibbs, 111–112, 113, 122–126, 145
McCallum, Daniel, 47

McClelland, Peter, 164
Macco Realty Company, 248, 258, 262, 270, 280
McCrea, James, 85, 86, 91, 102
McDonald, Thomas, 190
McDonald, William, 324–325, 326
McKinley, William, 169, 344
Madison, James, 4
Madison Square Garden Corporation, 245, 248
Magnuson, Warren, 301–302
Mahaffie, Charles, 188
Mahon, George, 303, 306
Mahoning Coal Railroad, 191
Mann-Elkins Act of 1910, 104
Mansfield, Mike, 320
Marietta and Cincinnati Railroad, 34
Martin, Albro, 105
Martineau, Harriet, 12
Marx, Karl, 345
Marxism, 78
Meet the Press (TV show), 210
Mellon family, 102, 201
Menck, Louis, 276
Merchant's Despatch Transportation, 279
Merger Protective Agreement of 1964, 253
Merrick, Samuel Vaughan, 29–30, 33
Merrill Lynch, Pierce, Fenner and Beane, 202
Metroliner service, 275, 320
Metropolitan Commuter Transportation Authority, 248–249
Metzman, Gustav, 160–161, 186–189, 192, 193–195, 198–200, 207, 220, 231
Meyner, Governor Robert, 237
Michigan Central Railroad, 38, 39, 43, 46, 56, 58, 60, 61, 64, 101
Midamerica Company, 175–176
Missouri Pacific Railroad, 125, 175, 179, 203
Mitchell, John, 294
Mohawk and Hudson Canal, 12
Mohawk and Hudson Railroad, 16–18, 19, 20, 27, 38, 68, 166
Mohawk Valley Railroad, 37, 38
Morgan, J.P., 60, 95, 97, 100, 101, 109, 123, 125–128, 138, 145, 168, 174, 179, 180, 182, 184, 211, 228, 250, 260

Index

Morgan, J. P. (cont.)
   Corsair Agreement and, 74–75, 77, 78
   Panic of 1893 and, 80–81
   railroad interests, 74–92
Morgan and Company (J.P.), 146, 174–175, 340
Morris Canal, 12
Morris Canal and Banking Company, 11
Motor Transit Corporation, 130
Murder on the Orient Express (motion picture), 96

National Committee for Prevention of Government Ownership of Railroads, 147
National Home, 259
National Railroad Passenger Corporation, 318
National Road, 6, 13, 26, 165, 166
   western advance of, 13
Neu, Irene, 49
New Deal, 137, 144–149, 150, 156, 179–180, 181–182, 222, 344
New Frontier program, 344
New Jersey Turnpike, 190, 205–206
New York, New Haven and Hartford Railroad, 55, 80, 92, 125, 237, 251–252, 257, 258
New York, Ontario and Western Railroad, 92
New York, West Shore and Buffalo Railroad, 73
New York, West Shore and Chicago Railroad, 73
New York Central:
   Boston link, 43
   Chicago link, 43, 58, 93–95
   Civil War, 44
   decline of, 141–162
      abandonments, 150–151
      deficit of 1938, 151
      featherbedding and, 151–152
      gap between Pennsylvania and, 153–154
      passenger travel, 149–150
   employees (1934), 152
   formation of, 40
   income, earnings, and expenses (1900–1920s), 93–115
   expenses-to-revenues ratio, 106, 112
   World War I, 106–110, 112
   merger with Pennsylvania, 221–255
      opposition to, 249–253
      Supreme Court on, 254
      terms of, 240–241
   mergers and acquisitions, 51, 58, 61, 81, 221–241
   New Deal and, 144–149
   origins of, 166–167
   Panic of 1907 and, 100–101, 102
   post-war years (World War I), 117–139
      earnings, 128, 137–139
      electrification program, 133–134
   post-war years (World War II), 188–241
      commuter operations (1950s), 218
      featherbedding, 191
      freight operations, 189–190, 216, 218, 219
      income and expenditures, 197–198, 208, 217, 218–219, 231, 237
      mood to merger, 221–241
      passenger service, 188–189, 191, 197, 219–220
      realty holdings, 192–193, 218
      use of labor, 191
      working capital (1958), 232
      Young and, 173–220
   rivalry with Pennsylvania, xi, 22, 23–47
      Corsair Agreement (1885), 74–75, 77, 78
      income, earnings, and expenses (1900–1920s), 93–115
      mood for merger, 221–241
      Morgan's role in, 74–92
      origins and background of, 1–36
      in prestige, 93–96
      price competition (1880s), 61
      rate wars, 56, 75, 77
      St. Nicholas Agreement (1854), 45, 63
      struggle for the East, 49–69
      yearning for security (pre–World War I), 71–92
   St. Louis link, 60
   stock issues and dividends, 41–42, 47, 60, 81, 97, 136–137, 199, 217, 218, 231

New York Central *(cont.)*
   in street names, 202
   track mileage, 38, 81, 92, 96
   westward expansion, 36, 42–43
   World War II, 155–162
     income and revenue, 197–198
   See also names of railroad presidents; Penn Central
New York Central Building, 192, 255
New York Central and Hudson River Railroad, 57, 168
New York Central Securities Company, 126
New York Central Transport Company, 279–280, 311, 312, 313
New York City, fire of 1835, 12
New York Common Council, 51
New York General Building, 255
New York and Harlem Railroad, 51, 52, 53, 55, 56
New York Herald, 12
New York Metropolitan Transit Authority, 322
New York Stock Exchange, 12, 18, 33, 176, 309
New York Thruway, 216, 219
New York Turnpike, 190
New York-to-Washington Metroliners, 320
Newman, William, 88, 93–94
Nickel Plate (New York, Chicago and St. Louis) Railroad, 60–61, 124, 174, 175–176, 178, 182, 238–239
Nickel Plate Securities Company, 174
Nixon, Richard, 206, 277, 278, 280–281, 286, 287, 291, 292, 293, 294, 295, 298, 305–306, 318, 319, 322, 323, 325, 326, 370
Norfolk and Western Railroad, 80, 86, 88, 91, 125, 249, 263, 267, 324
   in bankruptcy, 317
   income and revenues (1958), 227
   merger negotiations (1950–1960s), 227–228, 232–233, 234, 238–239, 240, 253
North River Railroad, 73
Northern Central Railroad, 63
Northern Cross Railroad, 43
Northern Pacific Railroad, 80, 276
Northern Securities Company, 89
Northwest Industries, 193

Odell, Robert, 260–261, 283–284
Office of Defense Transportation (World War II), 157
O'Herron, Jonathan, 287, 292–293, 300, 307
Ohio Turnpike, 190, 206
Olcutt, Thomas, 53
Otis and Company, 180

Pan American World Airways, 344
Panic of 1837, 25, 337
Panic of 1857, 41
Panic of 1873, 58, 64, 72, 73, 98
Panic of 1893, 80–82, 97, 98, 99
Panic of 1907, 100, 102, 104
Parcel Post, 192
Patman, Wright, 304, 306
Patterson, George, 105
Patterson, William, 30–31, 33
Peat, Marwick, Mitchell & Company, 284, 285, 286
Penn Center, 245
Penn Central Railroad:
   banker connections, 260–262, 268–269
   beginning of, 254–265
   collapse and bankruptcy, ix–xi, 265–310
     economy and, 277–280
     events leading to, 265–310
     implications of, 333–345
     June 22 trading (NYSE), 309–310
     reasons for, 311–317
     results of, 311–332
     rumors of, 295–301
     Volpe program and, 291–293, 297–301, 304–308, 310
   dividend of 1969, 280
   earnings (1967), 256–257
   Eurodollar loan to, 268
   freight revenues, 317
   holdings, 258, 262
   ICC and, 267, 268, 269, 277, 280, 284, 286, 287, 309
   income, earnings, and expenditures, 266–267, 269–270, 279
   merger, 221–255
     opposition to, 249–253
     Supreme Court on, 254
     terms of, 240–241
   Merger Day, 254–255

Penn Central Railroad *(cont.)*
  New Haven merger, 266, 270, 288, 301
  sale of assets, 267
  stockholders meeting (1968), 265–266
  track abandonments (1969), 280
Penn Central Board, 261
Penn Central Company, 267
Penn Central Failure and the Role of Financial Institutions, The 260–261, 262
Penn Central Institutional Investors Group, 331
Penn Central Transportation Company, ix, 257–258
Pennroad, 126
Pennsylvania Canal, 5–6, 12
Pennsylvania Company, 228, 229, 247, 264, 312
Pennsylvania Greyhound Lines, 130
Pennsylvania Illinois General Transit, 129
Pennsylvania Indiana General Transit, 129
Pennsylvania Railroad:
  Bessemer steel rails, 36
  B&O and, 26, 27, 28, 34, 63
  charter, 27–28
  Chicago link, 34
  Civil War, 31, 33, 34, 35, 63
  decline of, 141–162
    gap between Central and, 153–154
    passenger service, 154–155
  expenditures and revenues (post-World War II), 229–231
  Harrisburg to Pittsburgh line, 21, 27, 33
  income, earnings, and expenses (1900–1920s), 93–115
    expenses-to-revenues ratio, 106, 112
    Panic of 1907 and, 100–101, 102
    World War I, 106–110, 112
  incorporated, 21
  leadership dispute (1852), 31
  Main Line and, 25–26, 27, 34, 131, 167
  merger with NY Central, 221–255
    opposition to, 249–253
    Supreme Court on, 254
    terms of, 240–241
  mergers and acquisitions, 63, 73, 82, 86, 221–255
  modernization program (1946), 160
  New Deal and, 144–149
  New York City Convention (1854), 45
  nonrailroad acquisitions, 245–248
  origins of, 167
  post-war years (World War I), 117–139
    electrification program, 132–133, 134
    freight service, 130
    passenger bus companies, 129–130
    trucking operations, 130
  rivalry with New York Central, 22, 23–47
    Corsair Agreement (1885), 74–75, 77, 78
    income, earnings, and expenses (1900–1920s), 93–115
    mood for merger, 221–241
    Morgan's role in, 74–92
    origins and background of, 1–36
    in prestige, 93–96
    price competition (1880s), 61
    rate wars, 56, 75, 77
    St. Nicholas Agreement (1854), 45, 63
    struggle for the East, 49–69
    yearning for security (pre-World War I), 71–92
  spending program (1899), 82
  stock issues and dividends, 27–28, 33, 64, 67–68, 82, 97, 136–137, 138, 160
    price of, 32–33
    shares outstanding (1871), 65
    stockholders' investigating committee (1874), 64–66
  tonnage tax, 35
  track mileage, 35, 65, 82, 92, 96
  westward expansion, 31–35
  World War II, 155–162
  See also names of railroad presidents; Penn Central
Pennsylvania Railroad (Burgess and Kennedy), 63

Pennsylvania Railroad Company, 27, 90
Pennsylvania Special (train), 95
Pennsylvania Station (New York City), 85, 95–96, 98, 245
Pennsylvania Turnpike, 75, 190, 205, 206
Pennsylvania Virginia General Transit, 129
Penphil Corporation, 259–260, 264, 313
People's Line, 54
People's Rapid Transit Company, 129–130
Peoria and Oquawka Railroad, 43
Père Marquette Railroad, 125, 179, 183
Perkins, Thomas, 298
Perlman, Alfred, 212–220, 314, 327
  background of, 212–214
  cost cutting strategy of, 216–217
  first meeting with Young, 214–215
  merger negotiations (1950–1960s), 222–223, 231–233, 235, 236–241, 243–244, 245, 249, 251, 252, 253, 254
  Penn Central and, 255, 257, 259–261, 264–277, 281, 282, 283, 300, 308
  renovation program of, 218–219
  ruthlessness of, 217–218
Philadelphia and Columbia Railroad, 14–15, 35
Philadelphia Gas Works, 29
Philadelphia Pennsylvanian (newspaper), 26
Philadelphia Stock Exchange, 28, 33
Philadelphia Turnpike, 2
Phillips, E.B., 58
Piggy-back trains, 25
Pittsburgh, Fort Wayne and Chicago Railroad, 34
Pittsburgh and Lake Erie Railroad, 60, 72, 191
Pittsburgh and West Virginia Railroad, 125, 239
Place, Willard, 209
Plumb, Glenn, 122, 194
Plumb Plan, 122–123, 145, 147
Plumb Plan League, 122
Populism, 110, 194, 340, 341, 344
Progressivism, 111, 344

Pruyn, John V.L., 37, 40, 46, 53
Public Ownership League of America, 122
Public Works Administration (PWA), 146
Pullman, George, 71, 73
Pullman Company, 184–188, 200, 209

Railpax, *see* Amtrak
Railroad Administration, 111, 112, 113, 114, 122, 149, 170
Railroad Age (publication), 80
Railroad Consolidation Under the Transportation Act of 1920 (Leonard), 126
Railroad Leaders, 1845–1890 (Cochran), 41
Railroads:
  automobile challenge to, 119, 120, 129
  aviation challenge to, 120, 131
  cargo transfers (1840s), 25, 53
  decline of, xi, 141–162
    freight deliveries, 143–144
    ICC and, 142, 143, 144, 148, 150, 159
    New Deal and, 144–149
    passenger business, 143, 144, 149–150, 157
    Wheeler proposals and, 146–148, 149
  electrification program, 132–136
  engines in service (1920s), 133
  federal regulation, *see* Interstate Commerce Commission (ICC)
  income, earnings, and expenses (1900–1920s), 93–115
    expenses-to-revenues ratio, 106, 112
    Panic of 1907 and, 100–101, 102
    World War I, 106–110, 112
  mergers (1950s–1960s), 221–241
  noncommutation income for (1964–1970), 271
  number of (1933), 142
  origins of, 1–22
    canal system and, 1–14
    mergers, 20, 21–22
    rivalry, 14–22
  in receivership, 103–104, 107, 148
  reputation, 76–77

Railroads (cont.)
  Ripley Plan for, 123–124, 125, 126, 127, 145
  St. Nicholas Agreement of 1854, 45, 63
  strike of 1877, 75, 78
  struggle for the East, 49–69
  World War II, 155–162
  See also names of railroads
Railroads, The: The Nation's First Big Business (ed. Chandler), 47
Railroads and American Economic Growth (Fogel), 164
Railroads and Regulation, 1877–1916 (Kolko), 78
Railroads and the Transformation of the Ante-Bellum Economy (Fishlow), 164
Railway Association, 329–330
Railway Express, 192
Railway Progress Institute, 331
Ramsdell, Homer, 47
Rea, Samuel, 107–108, 124, 125, 132, 246–247
Reading Coal and Iron Company, 85
Reading Railroad, 77, 80, 85, 86, 88–89, 125, 191, 329
  in bankruptcy, 317
Recession of 1957, 210
Reconstruction Finance Corporation (RFC), 138–139, 146, 149, 175, 179, 190, 345
Reed-Bulwinkle Act of 1948, 159
Regional Rails Reorganization Act of 1974, 326, 328
Regulation of Railroad Abandonments, The (Cherington), 150
Regulatory Reform Act of 1976, 330
Reistrup, Paul, 321
Reorganization of the American Railroad System, The 1893–1900 (Campbell), 82
Report on Roads and Canals (Gallatin), 4, 46
Richardson, Sid, 209, 210
Richardson and Murchison, 209, 220
Richmond, Dean, 40, 41, 43, 44, 46, 53, 54, 167
Ripley, William Z., 123–124, 177, 194, 212, 213, 216, 250
Ripley Plan, 123–124, 125, 126, 127, 145

Rivers, L. Mendel, 303, 306
Road of the Century, The (Harlow), 41
Robert R. Young, the Populist of Wall Street (Borkin), 202, 209
Robert R. Young Yard (Elkhart, Indiana), 219
Roberts, George, 72, 73, 74, 76, 77, 78
Robinson, H.P., 80
Rochester, Lockport and Niagara Falls Railroad, 20, 21, 37
Rochester and Syracuse Railroad, 19, 37
Rock Island Railroad, 80
Rockefeller, David, 297
Rockefeller, John D., x, 61, 72, 76, 79
Rockefeller, Nelson, 237, 322
Rockefeller, William, 101
Rockefeller family, 102
Roosevelt, Franklin D., 148, 155–156, 157, 179, 184, 198
Roosevelt, George, 175–176
Roosevelt, Theodore, 89, 90, 142, 341
Roosevelt Hotel (New York City), 192
Rutter, James, 62

Safety Fund Law of 1828, 10
Sage, Russell, 37, 42
St. Lawrence Seaway, 216, 221
St. Nicholas Agreement of 1854, 45, 63
Sakolski, A.M., 103
Saratoga, Boston and Providence Canal, 12
Saunders, Stuart, 255–294, 297, 298, 299, 308, 314, 327
  merger negotiations (1950s–1960s) and, 227–229, 233, 241, 243–244, 246, 247–249, 251, 252, 253, 254
Schenectady and Troy Railroad, 19, 37
Schiff, Jacob, 82, 100, 145, 260
Schulze, Governor John, 5
Scott, Hugh, 254, 299, 300, 301–302
Scott, Thomas, 66–68, 71, 72, 78, 87, 109, 304
Scranton, Governor William, 254
Seabrook, John, 261, 298, 308
Sears, Roebuck Company, 256
Securities Act of 1934, 182

Securities and Exchange Commission (SEC), 267–284, 313
Security Insurance Company of Hartford, 283
Shapp, Milton, 254
Shoup, Dick, 326
Shunpikes, 2, 7
Sikes, Robert, 303
Simpson, H.E., 233–234
Six Flags Over Georgia (amusement park), 247, 267
Six Flags Over Texas (amusement park), 247, 267
Smith, Adam, 77, 345
Smith, Alfred H., 111–112, 124, 132, 173
Smucker, David, 273–274, 275
Snyder, Carl, 99
Socialism, 110, 340, 341
South Pennsylvania Railroad, 72, 73, 75
Southern Pacific Railroad, 102
Southern Railroad, 80
Springfield, Mt. Vernon, and Pittsburgh Railroad, 34
Staggers, Harley, 320
Standard Oil of New Jersey, 256, 339
Stans, Maurice, 306
Statistics of Railroads of Class I in the United States, 1964–1974 (Association of American Railroads), 271
Stennis, John, 303–304
Stevens, Frank Walker, 16
Stevens, John, 14, 16
Stillman, James, 101
Stockbridge Railroad, 55
Stockton and Darlington Railroad, 16
Strick Holding Company, 248
Stuart, Harold, 180, 194
Subcommittee on Antitrust and Monopoly (U.S. Senate), 250
Sullivan, James, 274, 276
Symes, James, 234–236, 240, 243, 244–246, 247, 251, 252, 259, 273
Syndicalism, 122
Syracuse and Utica Direct Railroad, 37
Syracuse and Utica Railroad, 19, 37

Taft, William Howard, 104, 105–106, 107

Tate, Mayor James, 253, 254
Texas and Pacific Railroad, 66–67
Textron Corporation, 246
Thomson, Frank, 74
Thomson, J. Edgar, 29–36, 56, 57, 62–66, 67, 68, 83, 167, 168, 229, 235, 246, 304, 339
  death of, 66, 72, 82
  mergers and acquisitions, 63–64
  stockholders' investigating committee and (1874), 64–66
Thoreau, Henry, 119
Thorne, Clifford, 108
Tide (magazine), 210
Tishman Realty Company, 245
Toledo, St. Louis and Western Railroad, 124
Tonawanda Railroad, 19, 20
Torrance, Daniel, 57
Toynbee, Arnold, 194
Transcontinental Air Transport, 131
Transcontinental Railway Strategy, 1869–1893 (Grodinsky), 67
Transportation Act of 1920, 123, 126
Transportation Act of 1940, 155–156
Transportation Act of 1958, 223
Transportation Exhibition (Columbian Exposition of 1893), 94
Trans-World Airways, 344
Tropical Gas Company, 259
Truman, Harry, 159, 250
Tuggle, Kenneth, 321
Turnpikes, 3, 5, 7, 13, 15, 165–166, 207, 336, 338, 342
Turnpikes: A Study of the Toll Road Movement in the Middle Atlantic States and Maryland (Durrenberger), 3
Tuohy, Walter, 212, 226, 233, 238
20th Century (Beebe), 96
Twentieth Century Limited, 95, 96, 103, 119, 144, 155, 321
  first trip of, 95
  running time, 98
  World War I, 117
Tyson, Job, 6

Union Iron Mills, 71
Union Pacific Railroad, 61, 66, 67, 71, 80, 86, 102, 135, 193, 273, 324
Union Railroad and Transportation Company, 35

Index

Union Terminal (Cleveland), 191
United New Jersey Railroad, 63
United States Bureau of Public Roads, 190
United States Department of Commerce, 142–143
United States Department of Defense, 287, 303, 304, 305, 306–307, 318
United States Department of Justice, 181–182, 185, 235
United States Department of Transportation, ix, 323
United States Railway Association, 326–329, 330, 331
United States Railways, 147
United States Steel Corporation, 84, 256
United States Supreme Court, 83, 123, 187, 188, 200, 254
Urban renewal (New York City), 245
Uris Brothers, 245
Utica, Paterson, and New Jersey Canal, 12
Utica and Schenectady Railroad, 20, 37, 38

Van Buren, Martin, 7, 8, 9, 12, 18, 25, 38, 39
Van Rensselaer, Stephen, 17, 18
Van Sweringen brothers, 124–125, 126, 145, 173–176, 177, 182
  bankruptcy sale of, 173–176, 177
  liquidation proceedings, 146
Vanderbilt, Commodore Cornelius, 47, 49–59, 60, 61, 62, 68, 86, 167–168, 188, 249
  compared to Corning, 49–50, 51
  coup of 1867, 55–56
  death of, 58–59
  early railroad operations, 51–55
  "Erie Wars," 52
  meeting with Corning (1867), 49
  ruthlessness of, 50
  Wall Street speculations, 50–51
Vanderbilt, Cornelius, II, 61, 62, 88
Vanderbilt, Harold, 161, 184, 199, 203
Vanderbilt, Marie, 56
Vanderbilt, Sophia, 57
Vanderbilt, William H., 54, 56, 57–62, 64, 72, 73, 74, 75, 77, 138, 239
  death of, 62

  mergers and acquisitions program, 60–61, 68, 74
  "public be damned" statement, 59, 180
  reputation of, 59
  resignation of, 61
  retirement of, 73–74
Vanderbilt, William K., 61–62
Vanderbilt Legend, The (Andrews), 59
Vanderbilts, The (Croffut), 53
Vaness Company, 174
Vaughan, John, 29
Vietnam War, 277, 334
Virginia Railway Company, 200, 201, 202
Virginian Railroad, 228–229, 253
Volker, Paul, 294
Volpe, John, 287, 291–293, 297–301, 304–308, 310, 313, 318, 322

Wabash Railroad, 125
Wagner, Mayor Robert, 237
Waldorf Astoria Hotel (New York City), 192
Wall Street Journal, 295, 302
War of 1812, 3
War Industries Board (World War I), 119
Ward, James A., 28
Washington, George, 281
Wealth of Nations (Smith), 77
West Shore Hudson Railroad, 73
Western Inland Lock Navigation Company, 1–2
Western Maryland Railroad, 125
Wetzel, Carroll, 309
Wheeler, Burton K., 146, 147–148, 178, 180
Wheeling and Lake Erie Railroad, 125, 182
Whig Party, 27, 39
White, Roy, 226
White, William, 207–211, 218, 219, 220, 231
Whitney, George, 161, 175–176
Whitten, Jamie, 303
Williamson, Frederic, 138, 139, 146, 160
Wilson, Woodrow, 109, 155, 190, 341
  antitrust policy of, 110
Wiprud, Arne, 185

Wirtz, W. Willard, 310
Woolworth Company, 256
Works Progress Administration (WPA), 137, 149, 190
World War I, 106–110, 112, 138, 155, 157, 158, 170, 250, 309, 318, 341
World War II, 112, 163, 171, 309, 342
　railroad operating revenues, 158, 159–160, 161
Wright Aeronautical Company, 131
Wriston, Walter, 297-298, 299, 307

Young, Robert, 176–220, 226, 234, 235, 318
　Allegheny negotiations, 176–182, 183, 209–210, 220
　anti-Wall Street stance, 180–181, 194
　background of, 176
　death of, 236
　four-way merger plans, 182–183
　New York Central and, 173–220
　　first meeting with Perlman, 214–215
　　ICC hearings (1948), 200–202, 203
　　passenger train beliefs, 203–204, 205–207, 215, 234
　　profit of 1954, 211
　　proxy contest (1954), 203, 207–211
　　stock in street names, 202–203
　　struggle for control, 202–211
　Pullman Company fight, 184–188, 200, 209
　railroad crusade of, 183, 201, 220
Young, Kolbe and Company, 176–177

www.ingramcontent.com/pod-product-compliance
Lightning Source LLC
Chambersburg PA
CBHW020634230426
43665CB00008B/170